WARFARE, RELIGION, AND SOCIETY IN INDIAN HISTORY

WARFARE, RELIGION, AND SOCIETY IN INDIAN HISTORY

Edited by
RAZIUDDIN AQUIL
KAUSHIK ROY

MANOHAR
2012

First published 2012

ISBN 978-81-7304-958-3

Published by
Ajay Kumar Jain *for*
Manohar Publishers & Distributors
4753/23 Ansari Road, Daryaganj
New Delhi 110 002

Typeset at
Digigrafics
New Delhi 110 049

Printed at
Salasar Imaging Systems
Delhi 110 035

Contents

Preface

Warfare and religion are two crucial drivers of Indian history. Whether it was the Mughal Army or the Sepoy Army, the principal chunk of the revenue generated by the Mughal Empire and the British-Indian Empire went to maintain these two military institutions. Even today, service in the military remains one of the principal avenues for employment of the men from the countryside. Recruitment influenced the rise of martial communities with religious overtones like the Rajputs with Hindu ethos, the Gurkhas with a focus on *parbatiya* Hinduism, and so on.

State formation, armed *sannyasis* and the *jihadis* reflect the complex interconnections between war, religion and society. Instead of a technocratic and teleological approach to warfare, this volume focuses on the dynamic interactions between war, society and religion in India. Historians of medieval India are increasingly concerned with the crucial connections between the expanding frontier (featuring swift cavalry raids, mobile wealth, and long-distance trade) and the settled society of the agricultural plains. In particular, the Middle Ages saw the expansion of agriculture, control of revenue, extensive commercial networks, gradual technological change and development of political and religious institutions. The technologies and techniques of warfare determined the politics of the time and affected the social formations. Hence, the violent interface between pastoral nomads and agrarian civilizations needs to be explored closely. In the early modern era, the rise of the West and colonialism brought in a whole range of new weapons of governmental control. These developments brought about considerable transformations in Indian history: new technologies of warfare displaced older forms of polity and forced a reconfiguration of the life of the people in different ways. At the same time, older religious traditions either resisted change or refashioned themselves to be in tune with the time.

This collection of essays covers some of the themes outlined above. In particular, we examine aspects of Hinduism and the agrarian bureaucratic empires, the rise of Islam and the emergence of the nomadic warriors from the Eurasian steppes, and finally secularization of mind and the machine-age warfare. The essays take into account the debate whether warfare in pre-British India was a ritualized combat due to the presence of *dharma*, *fitna* and resultant weak states. Alternatively, can we speak of agrarian bureaucratic polities with standing armies and decisive battles in pre-modern India? The relevance of the just and unjust war (*dharmayuddha* and *kutayuddha*), *jihad*, the role of Sufis, Hindu militarists and Christian militarism in warfare, etc., have also been covered. Studied together, these processes can help us understand the considerable social and religious changes as well as the fall of older empires in the wake of the emergence of the West. Some of these issues have been subjects of considerable interest amongst historians in recent times.

The works of Prof. Gregory Reichberg, especially as regards medieval European Just War, inspired us to explore the dialectics between warfare and religion in the South Asian context. We would also like to thank Prof. Partha Chatterjee and Dr Tilottama Mukherjee for going through parts of the manuscript and warning us of the shortcomings which could possibly reduce the value of the work as a whole. What we have offered here is a variety of essays on a wide range of themes, marked by various distinct approaches to the study of connections between religion and warfare in Indian history from the earliest times to the present. Such a collection could possibly cause some consternations, even as we began with the basic premise that some of the critical questions be discussed as freely as possible, despite constraints of ideological barriers limiting the fields of inquiry. Hopefully, this volume will be able to provoke some debate on what all could possibly be discussed as legitimate historical questions.

RAZIUDDIN AQUIL
KAUSHIK ROY

Contributors

RAZIUDDIN AQUIL is Associate Professor in the Department of History, University of Delhi. His publications include *Sufism, Culture, and Politics: Afghans and Islam in Medieval North India* (2007) and *In the Name of Allah: Understanding Islam and Indian History* (2009).

RICHARD B. BARNETT has taught at the University of Virginia since 1974. He has published *North India Between Empires: Awadh, the Mughals, and the British, 1720-1801*; *Rethinking Early Modern India* (ed.), and articles on environmental, political, and gender history. His next monograph will be on eighteenth-century Hyderabad.

C.A. BAYLY is Vere Harmsworth Professor of Imperial and Naval History at the University of Cambridge. He has recently published, with Tim Harper, *Forgotten Wars* (2005) and *Forgotten Armies* (2007).

TORKEL BREKKE is Associate Professor at the University of Oslo. He has also worked as adviser to the Norwegian Ministry of Defence. His main interest is the interface between religious history and violent conflict. He has published ten books and a number of articles and has received several research prizes. His publications include *Makers of Modern Indian Religions* (2002) and *The Ethics of War in Asian Civilizations* (2006).

RICHARD M. EATON is Professor of History at the University of Arizona. He is currently working on a co-authored monograph on architecture, power and memory in the sixteenth-century Deccan. His most recent publications include *A Social History of the Deccan, 1300-1761: Eight Indian Lives* (2005), and *Slavery and South Asian History*, co-edited with Indrani Chatterjee (2006).

MICHAEL H. FISHER holds the Danforth Chair in History at Oberlin College, USA. He has published widely on pre-colonial and early colonial interactions between Indians and Europeans that took place in India and Britain. His most recent books include: *Across the Three Seas: Travellers' Tales from Mughal India* (2007); *A South Asian History of Britain: Four Centuries of Peoples from the Indian Subcontinent*, co-authored with Shompa Lahiri and Shinder Thandi (2007); and *India's Rootless Cosmopolitan: The Inordinately Strange Life of Dyce Sombre (1801-51), Victorian M.P. and 'Lunatic'* (2010).

PRATYAY NATH is a research scholar at the Centre for Historical Studies in the School of Social Sciences at Jawaharlal Nehru University, New Delhi. His research interests include early Mughal warfare.

KAUSHIK ROY is Reader in the Department of History, Jadavpur University, Kolkata. He is also a Senior Researcher at the Centre for the Study of Civil War (CSCW) at the Peace Research Institute, Oslo (PRIO). He has written and edited fifteen books and his most recent publication is *The Oxford Companion to Modern Warfare in India.*

ARUPJYOTI SAIKIA is Associate Professor of History in the Department of Humanities and Social Sciences, IIT, Guwahati. His research interests include the social history of colonial Assam. He has published *Jungles, Reserves, Wildlife: A History of Forests in Assam* (2005) and has also edited with an Introduction a volume of the first Assamese literary journal, *Orunodoi* (1855-68), originally published by the American Baptist Missionaries from Sibsagar, Assam (2002).

SANDHYA SHARMA teaches History at Vivekananda College, University of Delhi. Her research interests include society and culture in Mughal India. She has recently published, *Literature, Culture and History in Mughal North India, 1550-1800* (2010).

Introduction

RAZIUDDIN AQUIL
KAUSHIK ROY

The 9/11-induced anxieties have brought the issue of 'militant Islam' to the limelight. In the immediate aftermath of the 'terror attack', the Bush administration gave a clarion call for war against the so-called Islamic terrorists. In February 2006, the US Central Command, based at Tampa in Florida and responsible for covering the Middle East and South-West Asia, pointed out that the global war against terror is going to be a long one. In September of the same year, President George W Bush declared that the war against terror will be the decisive ideological struggle of the twenty-first century.[1] Bush announced: it is going to be a great struggle for the survival of civilization and democracy. In fact, Bush and the then British Prime Minister Tony Blair also used the word 'Crusade' during the invasion of Iraq.[2] Western media and policy makers projected the fight as one between civilized Christian West and militant Islamic East. They discovered certain similarities between the Crusades launched by Christian West Europe between 1196 and 1291 against the Muslim powers of Middle East for recovery of the 'holy land' and Bush's war against terror. It seems that Samuel Huntington's 'Clash of Civilizations' scenario is becoming a reality.

Back in South Asia, the end of Cold War resulted in the escalation of *jihadi* violence. In recent times, bombings in Delhi and Mumbai were carried out in the name of Islam. The end of Cold War did not result in the establishment of a unipolar world dominated by the USA. Rather, the post-Cold War era seems to be characterized by numerous insurgencies tinged with religious overtones.[3] Instead of secularism triumphing with capitalism, it seems that the world is reverting to the medieval scenario with weak states disrupted by sporadic religious wars. The older languages of violence are being deployed in newer politicization of religion, and Islam is not exceptional in this matter. Also, not all forms of Islamic assertiveness necessarily lead to Taliban or Al-Qaeda kind of extremism. Muslim responses range from an intellectual movement seeking to explore a middle ground within the broader Indian nationalism to localized resistance by communities outside the purview of modern civil societies and at the margins of the apparatus of governance.[4]

This volume is not concerned with religious violence in the post-Cold War era. Rather, the ten essays chart the linkages between organized violence and religion from a historical context in South Asia. Superficially it would seem that while seven essays in this collection concentrate on the dialectics of warfare and society, only two essays (that of Raziuddin Aquil and Sandhya Sharma) focus on the interrelationship between religion and society and only one essay (Torkel Brekke's) devotes itself to the interaction between warfare and religion. The term 'religion' is defined in the context of this volume in a broad sense. Religion is not merely the sacred or the scriptural but also includes the profane. Religion is not merely the high texts, the temples, churches and mosques and the priestly elites. Religion also shapes the culture of the ordinary people and their daily routines. Till the end of the colonial rule, a soldier's dietary habits, dress, common sense and his concept of valour and chivalry were shaped by his religious consciousness.[5] At the higher level, the very concept of war and peace, the causes behind war and how to wage it are also to a great extent a product of religious ideas.[6] However, it may be noted that the lion's share of this volume goes to warfare, hence the term warfare comes before religion.

Here, we are concerned with inter-state war and its connection with religious ideologies. Aspects of Hinduism, Islam and Christianity, the three main religious traditions in South Asia, are studied in this volume. We are not interested in doctrinal debate on whether Hinduism is inherently peaceful and Islam is inherently violent. Instead of engaging in theological discussion about various prescriptions in Hindu texts or in Muslim scriptures, we are concerned with the issue of dialectics between warfare and religion in the subcontinent from the Vedic age till the collapse of the British Raj in 1947. We are interested to see when and by whom religion came to function as a force multiplier of organized violence and when religion was not used as an element during the escalatory process towards organized violence. This Introduction attempts to locate the essays within the overall historiographical matrix and chart the trajectories of the important debates in the field.

By and large, studies of warfare and religion in South Asian history remain marginal within the discipline of history. Till recently, Marxist historians dominated history-writing in India, but social and cultural histories are now becoming important. Whatever little studies on South Asian militaries have been done mostly fall within the paradigm of war and society approach. However, the cultural approach to the study of warfare is also becoming fashionable.[7]

Purists might object to the use of the term 'religion' in the South Asian context. It is argued that the term 'dharma' and *din* are not the exact equivalents of religion. After all, dharma is not merely religion but way of life. The term 'Hinduism' became common in the nineteenth century under the British influence.[8] The term 'religion' is derived from the Latin *religare* which means to bind together. It suggests a communal orientation and common purpose.[9] In the absence of better concepts, we have to do with the term religion while describing Hinduism and Islam.

Some scholars have dealt with the theological aspects of religion in India as if it was free floating without any social and cultural moorings. Others have focused on prominent figures and have highlighted their great role as social reformers, possibly influenced by Carlyle's 'great man' theory of history. Some have also glorified the peace-loving tradition of Hinduism. The overall trend among nationalist historians, especially due to the demands of political correctness, is to emphasize amity between different religious communities in South Asian history. In the Muslim case, the focus is on the Sufis who are seen as the cultural bridge between Hinduism and Islam, a sort of forerunner of post-1947 secularists. The general picture is that the Sufis emphasized mystical love and union with God.[10] Some recent studies have not only questioned the traditional portrayal of Sufis as peace-loving ascetics, but have also shown that Sufis of medieval India were interested in political patronage and had crucial linkages with military personnel.[11]

In recent times, as a response to 9/11, many fashionable trade-books are being published in a hurry, either to denigrate Islam or to defend it. For someone defending Islam, its name has been misused by certain troublesome elements for modern political purposes. It is claimed that Islam and especially the Koran emphasizes peace and criticizes violence. It is argued that the Islamic jurists throughout history have mistakenly divided the world into *dar-ul-harb* and *dar-ul-Islam* as this division is not sanctioned by the Koran. The swing of the pendulum is complete. While Huntington (implicitly) and Mark Juergensmeyer (explicitly) categorize Islam as the religion of violence, Ayesha Jalal taking a defensive stance attempts to delink jihad from organized violence and terrorism.[12] However, it is not so important whether the division of the world into abodes of peace (Islam) and violence (infidelity) has scriptural sanction or not. Instead, it would be interesting to see at what moments of history the bipolar division of the world, between Islam and its Others, was used by Muslim monarchs and theologians (ulama) and what were the consequences for such actions. Also, most of the experts of religion operate within their own separate domains. Hence, we lack any comparative analysis of religious traditions in the South Asian context. The present volume attempts to study the interface between religion and warfare and also the interaction of various religious traditions within South Asia.

Throughout history, the influence of religion on humanity has been immense. Dress, food habits, gender relations, and the social calendar, etc., are heavily influenced by religious traditions. R. Joseph Hoffmann claims that defining exactly who is an enemy of God has been the overarching theme of monotheistic traditions since their beginning. The leviathan God of monotheism is the source and model for concepts of sovereignty and absolute monarchy as these have developed in the cultures of the Middle East and Europe.[13] Images of violence are found in all the religious traditions. The rhetoric of violence is present in both Abrahamic (Semitic) and non-Abrahamic (non-Semitic) faiths. Juergensmeyer writes that the conflict between the Arabs and the Jews is considered by religious activists on both sides as the combat between good and evil. It is considered a cosmic struggle of Manichean proportions.[14] The Bible is replete with stories and parables of violence. While some Koranic verses call for violence against unbelievers, others state that violence is permitted only when one is attacked, and yet others recommend what may be characterized as offensive-defensive tactics. On the other hand, Hindu gods are often portrayed with symbols of violence. For instance, Goddess Durga is portrayed fully equipped with sword, spear and discus. Key events are set in midst of the battlefield. The *Bhagavad Gita* unfolds just before the Kaurava and the Pandava armies were to slaughter each other.[15]

Despite oft-repeated assertions to the contrary, all religions are concerned with violence. Hector Avalos writes:

> All of the major religions share the idea of sacred space. We may define sacred space as a bounded space whose value is placed above surrounding space for religious reasons. Since not everyone has access to, or can live in, a sacred space, then it becomes a sacred resource. And since sacred space is a scarce resource, then it becomes a potential centre of conflict.[16]

Juergensmeyer notes that the term 'war' is derived from the old English word *werra* and French *guerra*, which means confusion, disorder and strife. Both in the Hebrew Bible and in the Indic *Ramayana*, the enemies were warriors from the margins of civilization. They were 'foreigners', representing chaos and uncertainty. War is also ultimately confusion. Religious cultures portray warfare as something that is acknowledged and ultimately controlled, thus representing re-establishment of order over turmoil. Since religion reaffirms order, it requires violence which represents anarchy to be ultimately tamed and conquered.[17] Interestingly, Carl von Clausewitz, the greatest thinker of modern warfare, as well as the post-modern theorists of warfare consider war as the amalgam of chance, chaos and confusion.[18]

DHARMAYUDDHA AND *KUTAYUDDHA* IN HINDUISM

The idea that Hinduism is all about spiritualism opposed to Western materialism was the product of nationalist discourse which began in all earnest in the late nineteenth century.[19] Left with no or little political power, sections of Hindu intelligentsia had no option but to oppose the colonial state by emphasizing spiritualism. However, things were different in the past. Laurie L. Patton asserts that in Hinduism, weaponry is seen as an extension and sometimes as a metaphor for sacrificial power. Weapons (and their use) are tools of destruction, but simultaneously also tools of sacrificial regeneration. Their ethical use focuses on their ability to protect against wounding and to preserve the idea of the sacred order. The power of the weapons derives metaphorically from the latter's status as sacrificial tools. In the *Mahabharata*, war is frequently thought of as a sacrifice where warriors are containers and not glorifiers of force. The motif of heavenly reward of the slain sacrificer in the Vedic texts is taken up again in the motif of the slain warrior in the *Mahabharata*.[20]

In Classical Hinduism, for understanding violence, we have the twin concepts of *dharmayuddha* and *kutayuddha*, which first appear in the two epics (*Ramayana* and *Mahabharata*), partially composed some time between 500 to 300 BCE. *Dharmayuddha* means war fought in accordance with a set of rules and regulations, that is, righteous war/just war. *Kutayuddha* signifies war fought without any principles in an anarchic context and it can be conceptualized as unjust war. *Dharmayuddha* is fought by the Kshatriyas as it is their duty to fight for the preservation of what is good.[21] The objective in *dharmayuddha* is to win glory, but the objective in *kutayuddha* is to win at all cost. The mental cosmos of the proponents of *kutayuddha* is somewhat similar to the assumptions of the realists and neo-realists. The realist school emphasizing pragmatism refuses to justify or limit warfare on legal, moral and religious grounds. The realists argue that in extreme conditions all techniques are free and fair. They assert that the inter-state system is characterized by intense competition among the states; the rule of the game being the survival of the fittest.[22]

The Pandavas fought a *dharmayuddha* because they fought against the evil Duryodhana. However, *dharmayuddha* does not depend only on the ends but also on the means. In other words, not only the reason(s) behind starting the war but also the conduct of battle is important. For instance, one who is unready for battle is not to be attacked; one who is already fighting with his opponent should not be hit; the enemy should be given an opportunity to put on his armour and prepare his weapons; one who is fleeing should not be assaulted; non-combatants should not be harmed, and so on.[23] Brekke's essay in this volume analyses the *Urubhanga* episode of the *Mahabharata* to show the tension between the necessity of resorting to *kutayuddha* for gaining military advantage and the contradictory policy of retaining the high moral ground by sticking to the rules of *dharmayuddha*.

Kautilya, the astute political analyst of ancient India, in *Arthashastra* (composed around 300 BCE) observed that power was the only security in a world characterized by *matsyanyaya* (law of the pond, where big fish gobble up smaller ones). The concept of *matsyanyaya* is equivalent to the concept of perpetual anarchy used by the neo-realist theorists. Kautilya emphasized the value of *kutayuddha*, asserting that for the weaker side *kutayuddha* was the only viable strategy for survival. Like the ancient Chinese theorist Sun Tzu, Kautilya claimed that warfare was not merely a frontal clash between the armies, but was also characterized by deceit, treachery, ambush, surprise-attack, night-attack, and so on. Kautilya, like the neo-realist theorists, noted that treaties and alliances were pieces of paper to be torn away at the right time.[24]

Another influential text, *Manusmriti* emphasized at the beginning of the Common Era, the rules and regulations of *dharmayuddha* in order to reduce the lethality of war. Between fourth and sixth centuries CE, Kamandaka in *Nitisara* attempted a balance between the idealism of *dharmayuddha* and the realism inherent in *kutayuddha*.[25] By then, the subcontinent was threatened by mounted warriors from the Central Asian steppes.

The Dutch historian Dirk Kolff notes the overwhelming importance of dharma in India's public life till the eighteenth century. He states that in Indian history dharma is a sovereign domain separated from the king's sphere of authority whereas in western Europe, the polity issued rules and regulations. The Indian king was not the law-giver and the Brahmin was not subordinated to the Kshatriya ruler. And the functioning of weak polity was characterized by continuous contextual negotiations and flexible alliance. The *rajadharma* did not involve interference in day-to-day life of people and communities with the aid of a centralized bureaucracy. Rather, *rajadharma* was geared towards establishing moral leadership and a loose suzerainty over minor principalities.[26] The result was that Hindu polities remained weak with fragile war bands rather than drilled and disciplined armies capable of manoeuvre in the battlefield. Hence, 'Hindu India' collapsed between the ninth and twelfth centuries, when the Central Asian nomads, then recently converted to Islam, burst upon the South Asian landscape.

Theoretically also, the Rajput militaries were unprepared to meet the Turks pouring across the Khyber Pass. B.N.S. Yadava notes that *kshatra-dharma* was part of the ethics of *dharmayuddha* and gave rise to the ideals of chivalry. The chivalrous attitude generated vanity of personal valour at the cost of expediency and policy. The Rajputs considered warfare as a sport. Diplomacy, intrigues, surprise-attacks, tactical retreats and pursuit of the retreating foes were considered unchivalrous. Due to personal chivalry, battles were often characterized by hand-to-hand combats. The very concept of chivalry impeded introduction of collective drill and discipline. Finally, the concept of righteous warfare geared for limiting the scope of violence also obstructed technological development of weaponry. Probably the concept of righteous warfare prevented the Rajputs from acquiring mounted archery which was introduced in India by the Sakas at the beginning of the Common Era. In addition, continuous procurement and regular maintenance of good quality war-horses were not an easy proposition for Rajput armies. The net result was that the Rajput chiefs of early medieval India, like the West European knights, were only capable of launching headlong frontal attacks against the enemy with outdated weapons. In CE 1191, the battering ram-like cavalry charge was able to defeat Muhammad Ghuri's force at the First Battle of Tarain. However, apparently in accordance with *dharmayuddha*, the defeated Ghurid forces were not pursued.[27] Next year, the Turks returned and their success in the Second Battle of Tarain, as Aquil's essay in this volume shows, led to the establishment of the Turkish Sultanate in north India.

JIHAD, POLITICAL CULTURE AND WARFARE IN MEDIEVAL SOUTH ASIA

The term idolatry comes from the Greek word *eidoolon*, meaning image. The concept of idolatry emerged in the context of monotheism of Israel, as the Second Commandment forbids the making of representations of the divinity. The prophets of Israel referred to suppression of the pagan cults, that is, idolatry. The iconoclasm passed into New Testament and early Christianity and subsequently into Islam. Thus, the three great monotheistic religions censured image worship. According to one tradition, Prophet Muhammad himself ordered all the idols in and around the Ka'ba to be destroyed.[28] However, in view of his early proximity with certain forms of Christianity in Arabia, the Prophet of Islam preserved a portrait of Mary with the child Jesus.[29]

For the classical Sunni Muslim jurists, all actions are to be justified with reference to the Koran and the *sunna* of the Prophet. In this framework, God has decreed for humanity a set of laws known as the *shariat.* Most of the Muslims of the subcontinent are Sunnis, following the Hanafi school of jurisprudence. The founder of this school or *mazhab* was Abu Hanifa (died CE 767). One of his famous pupil, Al-Shaybani (died CE 805),[30] accepted the division of the world into *dar-ul-Islam* (abode of Islam/place of security) and *dar-ul-harb* (the land of the enemy). Al-Shaybani also accepted the position that jihad should be fought for a just cause, with righteous intention and under the directive of a legitimate authority. According to John Kelsay, Al-Shaybani and the early Hanafi theologians were concerned with a variety of Islamic Just War. They discussed the issue of collateral damage and possible harm to non-combatants.[31] The classic Hanafi position was to recognize the Hindus as 'people of the book', a dependent subject population which had to pay a seemingly discriminatory tax, *jizya.* Another extreme position is that a 'just' Sultan like Mahmud of Ghazni should constantly chasten the Hindus and destroy their temples.[32] The Hanafite ulama, who came to the subcontinent after the Turkish conquest at the end of the twelfth century, advocated strict adherence to the *shariat*, or Muslim law, implying that salvation lay only in complete surrender to the divine will as expressed in the Koran and interpreted by the jurists of the Hanafite school. They were opposed to the study of rational sciences and works written by the rationalist *Mu'tazilas.*[33] Some recent studies have provided a critical appraisal of the complexities of theological disputations and multiple meanings of the *shariat* and how they impinged upon certain critical issues relating to governance in medieval India.[34]

It is important to note that the Ghaznavid and the Ghurid 'jihad' were successful against the Rajputs due to superior military power of the Central Asian Turks. Jos Gommans refers to the revolution in logistics, that is, rise of a new type of dromedaries in 1000 BCE in the arid zone, which enabled steppe nomads to dominate settled agrarian society. The dromedary revolution enabled the horse warrior revolution to unfold in the subcontinent.[35] The cavalry revolution was caused by better bows (composite bows against the simple bows of the Rajputs), stirrups and better horses.[36] These techniques resulted in 'battlespace domination' by the Turks.

To an extent, the Delhi Sultanate, which replaced the Rajput-Hindu polities, was weaker from the ideological perspective. The Turkish warlords-turned Sultans, unlike the Rajput rulers, could no more depend on the legitimizing principle of dharma and often defied the dictates of the *shariat* as well. The anxieties of the ruling elite of the newly established Sultanate were reflected in Khwaja Ziya-ud-Din Barani's provocative writings.[37] This point is made clear in Aquil's essay in this volume. Aquil questions modern historians' attempt to categorize Barani (who functioned during the late thirteenth and first half of the fourteenth century) as a lonely 'fanatic' in contrast to most of the contemporary writers who exhibited 'secular' tendencies. Also, the sharp distinction between moderate peace-loving Sufis and radical Sunni ulama is more a product of modern imagination than was actually the case. The modern 'secular' historians almost worship the Sufis as peacemakers and bridge-builders between Hindu and Muslim communities.[38] Barani, who moved in the influential Chishti Sufi circle of Delhi through his association with Nizam-ud-Din Auliya, comments that the most important thing for a just Islamic ruler is to conduct jihad against the *kafirs* (infidels). Barani's recommended programme is interesting. He wrote that Sultan Mahmud commanded adequate military power to kill 200,000 to 300,000 Brahmins. After this mass execution, the rest of the idol worshippers should be given the choice of either conversion to Islam or death.[39]

As far as the practice of warfare was concerned, the concept of jihad to an extent was present in the Ghaznavid campaigns into the Indian subcontinent. Many volunteers for the holy-war, known as *ghazis*, were attracted during the Ghaznavid raids into India, as were the warrior Sufis subsequently.[40] After joining as cavalrymen or the infantry, at times they were given a sum of money for equipment and provisions, otherwise they subsisted on plunder only. When an attractive ideology and incentives for economic gains appear simultaneously, then ideology comes to play a very important role. The Ghaznavid objectives in India besides breaking idols was to capture the wealth hoarded in temples. Naturally, in such a context, the concept of jihad came to occupy an important part.[41] Demands for Hindu-Muslim amity in present-day India should not cloud our vision about the medieval past. The study of history should have autonomy as a modern professional discipline.

The vocal assertions of the ulama notwithstanding, a judicious combination of realism and religion were the hallmark of the activities of medieval Indian rulers; this could be as true of Akbar as of Aurangzeb.[42] Nevertheless, several fault-lines started appearing in Hindu-Muslim elite interaction during the second half of the seventeenth century. The Sisodiya Rana Jagat Singh (ruled 1638-52) commissioned an illustrated *Ramayana* and in this work, Ravana and his entourage are depicted in Mughal-style tents. An aggressive Rama cult reflecting Rama as an ideal monarch, a heroic king and saviour of dharma against the *mlechhas*, became popular among the Hindu chieftains possibly as a reaction to the Muslim domination of medieval India's political landscape.[43] The Kachhwaha ruler Mirza Raja Jai Singh's (ruled 1622-67) dealings with the various groups at the Mughal *darbar* were based on the politics of survival rather than religion. By 1660, the Kachhwaha ruler, though a *mansabdar* of Aurangzeb, tried to protect the Hindu warlord Shivaji (who coronated himself as king in 1674) against the wrath of the Mughal emperor. However, not all Rajput rulers were following anti-Muslim policy even if Aurangzeb was pandering to Sunni Islamic orthodoxy, especially during the latter half of his reign. Sawai Jai Singh viewed himself as a *dharmic* king, but did not discriminate against his Muslim subjects.[44]

Further, as Arupjyoti Saikia's essay in this collection shows, the origins of the Mughal-Ahom conflict was due to strategic and economic reasons rather than religious or even ethnic factors. Also, the Mughals under Aurangzeb did not wage an all-out war against the Ahoms. The Mughal *mansabdar* Ram Singh followed the policy of what could be categorized as war-truce-war. Conducting peaceful negotiations even while the armies were marching and gearing up for combat was typical of Mughal grand strategy. Whether this was due to the considerations of dharma or *fitna* is still debated. One thing stands clear: complete destruction of the enemy's combat force in the battlefield and then diplomatic parleys, in other words, complete separation of war and peace into two watertight divisions, are characteristics of the West European war-making from the early modern era and this trend seemed to be absent in this particular South Asian scenario.[45] In the Mughal-Ahom confrontations, the culture of warfare was partly shaped by religious sympathy of Ram Singh towards the Ahom ruler. A letter was sent by Ram Singh's mother to his son saying that Assam was the last kingdom left within the subcontinent where the cow was protected.[46]

Moreover, the categories Hindu and Muslim, were fluid. Even the so-called 'Hindu' Vijayanagara Empire's ruling elite was to a great extent Persianized. Many Vijayanagara monarchs appropriated the title of Sultan. So, the scenario was anything but a case of 'clash of civilizations'. Also, the rulers due to the Darwinian principle of survival of the fittest followed policies which threw religion to the wind. Not only did the Vijayanagara monarchs hire Turkish cavaliers but they also depended on the Arab merchants for importing war horses from the Middle East.[47] We have Marco Polo's testimony that 10,000 horses were annually imported in the Pandyan realm and the cost of a horse amounted to 220 gold coins.[48] Further, Richard B. Barnett's case study of the Bahawalpur state shows that from late medieval period to the early colonial era, the Muslim rulers paid only lip service to religion when it suited them. The Bahawalpur nawabs deployed financial and military resources in conjunction with environmental constraints for their survival.

THE RISE OF THE WEST *VERSUS* THE REST: RELIGIOUS IDEOLOGIES AND TECHNOLOGY RECONSIDERED

Some historians have claimed that the West was in a superior military position *vis-à-vis* Afro-Asia right from the dawn of civilization; accordingly, armies and warfare were first invented by the West. Victor Davis Hanson argues that classical Greece developed the concept of decisive battle for settling the issue in a single afternoon. The unique ethos of the small Greek farmers with their sense of citizenship gave birth to Western professional military culture of engaging in close quarter combat. In contrast, witness Sun Tzu and Kautilya—the Asiatic forces were unwilling to engage the Westerners in decisive battles but indulged in deceptions and treacheries. Geoffrey Parker has emphasized that continuous upgradation of Western military technologies occurred throughout history and it made the Western Way of Warfare more lethal, possibly because religious ethics did not obstruct the innovations. In this view, warfare which means planned inter-state violence, and armies which means organization with soldiers drilled, disciplined and capable of manoeuvre in the heat of battle, were largely absent in Asia. The gargantuan Asiatic empires had at their disposal militias capable of dispersed and sporadic violence but unable to stand up to a Western army in a confrontation. The Hindu political theoreticians and the war-lords, assert Jos Gommans and Brekke (in one of his articles), failed to establish a clear-cut division between inter-state conflicts and dispersed sporadic violence (counter-insurgency operation or intra-state conflict). The Indian states until the establishment of the British-Indian Empire were not polities with fixed external borders but open-ended entities with numerous inner frontiers. Moreover, the presence of a large number of horses and armed men prevented a monopoly over the armed forces. Hence, all the wars in India were actually civil wars. Rather than destruction of the enemy armed forces, warfare in India involved a show of force and then incorporation of the enemy within the folds of imperial power.[49]

However, as Peter Lorge has illustrated, pre-modern China developed mass infantry armies drilled, disciplined and equipped with deadly weapons. Further, a bureaucratic hierarchical officer corps as well as an attitude of tinkering with latest weapons developed in the Chinese military system.[50] Kaushik Roy has also shown that decisive battles conducted by disciplined armies occurred in pre-British India.[51] In this volume, Richard M Eaton and Pratyay Nath's essays draw attention to the armies, equipped with lethal weaponry, conducting sieges and battles in medieval India. So, standing armies and battle-centric decisive warfare were not exclusively a Eurocentric phenomenon.

When exactly the rise of the West began is an issue which is the subject of Roy's article in this collection. Historians disagree on the date of decline of Islamic civilizations compared to the rise of West European powers. David Ayalon asserts that the superiority of the Frankish naval power against the Muslim naval power in the Mediterranean Sea is evident from the eleventh century. In the land, inferiority of Muslim powers was due to the latter's failure to integrate gunpowder technology in their armies. Since the core of most Muslim armies consisted of horse warriors, they were uncomfortable with gunpowder weapons which required one to dismount from the horse and fight on foot. The Ottomans, in Ayalon's view, were an exception among the Muslims. However, Ottoman industrial backwardness prevented them from manufacturing state-of-the-art gunpowder weapons. As a result, the Ottomans lagged behind the West European gunpowder technology.[52] In addition to the social origin of the ruling class, use of firearms among the *mamluks* was also hampered due to Islamic ideology. The *mamluks* believed that using guns which were devised by the crafty Christians was equivalent to rejecting the *sunna* of the Prophet.[53]

Ayalon's argument that the military decline of Islamic civilization started from the Early Middle Age due to Islam's over-dependence on cavalry is not fully substantiated. In fact, there were good reasons for depending on horses rather than on firearms till the Late Middle Age. A skilled mounted archer was able to shoot six aimed arrows a minute.[54] The rate of firing was definitely higher than hand-held firearms. With reference to the Battle of Raichur (1520), Eaton shows that though the arrogant Sultan Ismail Adil Shah of Bijapur also used artillery and firearms, his opponent Krishnadeva Raya, the ruler of Vijayanagara, won the battle with the traditional engines of war (cavalry, elephants and foot-soldiers equipped with spears and bows). Yet, it would appear that the European intervention with better guns eventually made the difference.[55] However, Muslim rulers were not blind to the importance of gunpowder technology, which was to be the trend for the future. Eaton's essay in this volume shows that both the Bahmanis and the Vijayanagara Empire were eager to absorb gunpowder technology, either the older stuff from the Middle East or the newer improvizations by the Portuguese, or an assortment of both.

The Mughals were influenced by their Central Asian neighbours. The Uzbeg military machine was influenced by Timur's military organization. Timur cultivated the Sufi sheikhs in order to justify invasions of non-Islamic regions and invoked theological proposition that political and military success proves God's favour in order to consolidate his position in the conquered territories.[56] However, he never allowed religion and religious leaders to come in his way while organizing his army of conquest. In general, Timur divided his army into five divisions centre, right and left wings, rearguard and vanguard. At times, a special contingent was kept for ambush or launching a surprise attack.[57] This battle order could be traced back to Chingiz Khan's organization of the Mongol Army.[58] Thus, it was mainly steppe nomadic ethos than Islamic theology that shaped military culture of the most powerful Islamic power. By 1365, Timur not only put the best soldiers in the wings but also had reserves behind the right and left wings. Later, Babur maintained reserves for both the right and left wings and also deployed his 'braves' at the extreme position of both the wings. In addition, Timur resorted to mining, sapping and blasting techniques for taking forts.[59] Timur also used firearms, which he procured from the Mongols as well as from the Genoese. Turkish gunsmiths were deployed for manufacturing arquebuses. By mid-sixteenth century, the Safavids were also acquiring firearms from the Portuguese and the Russians.[60] The Uzbegs under Shaibani Khan had a department for casting guns. However, Shaibani Khan declared the saddle of his horse as his capital. The reason was not any atavistic feudal attachment to equines. Even in the sixteenth century in terms of mobility and fire power, mounted archers on Central Asian Steppe nomadic horses were more effective than Western infantry equipped with matchlocks and supported by pikemen plus slow firing cannons. Yet, the Uzbegs were not averse to experimenting with guns. After 1510, they introduced arquebuses and wheeled artillery in their force structure. Stationing of foot musketeers behind carts joined with chains, a technique used by Babur, as Nath shows, was common among the Uzbegs.[61]

As the Mughals spread towards north-east India, they confronted the Ahom kingdom in present-day Assam. Saikia in his essay emphasizes the guerrilla strategy of the Ahoms especially in combination with the difficult terrain of the Brahmaputra Valley. However, the Ahoms also brought to the field gunpowder weapons which they had acquired from Burma, which, in turn, had received this technology from the Mongols in south China.[62]

The military balance shifted in favour of the West against the premier Islamic powers during the late seventeenth century, when the Western militaries underwent a revolution during the sixteenth and seventeenth centuries. Here, we are not interested in going into the debate on whether West Europe experienced several Military Revolutions or not.[63] What is important from our perspective is that the Military Revolution identified by Geoffrey Parker, which unfolded between 1530 and 1710, had decisive significance for the world.[64] In the absence of good quality steppe nomadic horses, the West Europeans had to upgrade gunpowder technology. Slow and continuous technological development gave West Europe a decisive break in the late seventeenth century. It was not evident to anybody in the preceding centuries that gunpowder technology could culminate to such a point and lead to the making of a whole new world order.

Some Islamic polities did make an attempt to Westernize their militaries and administrative apparatus, at least, partially. However, full-scale integration meant total jettisoning of the older nobility, that is, horse warrior aristocracy. Moreover, in accordance with the social and cultural mores of the subcontinent, the horse warriors were given lucrative taxation rights in the countryside which in turn gave them a status higher than the peasants. Hence, rather than Mughal Empire, the Mughal successor states were more successful in integrating, at least, imperfectly the boons of Military Revolution within their polities.[65]

Roy's essay in this volume points out that one of the principal factors behind the supremacy of the Western militaries was their superior theory of warfare, which, in turn, was related with the mass production of military treatises. This was possible due to the emergence and large-scale use of the printing press in West Europe. Ayalon notes that the printing press came into existence in West Europe during the Late Middle Age. However, the Ottoman Empire forbade printing anything for the Muslims. In fact, printing in Arabic characters started in Europe long before than in any Muslim country. This is attributed to the different attitude of Christianity and Islam towards printing at the time of its introduction.[66] A few military treatises did generate in the

Islamic lands, but in the absence of printing press the knowledge could not be propagated and disseminated; this is not to mean that a discursive network did not exist at all in medieval Islamic civilization. The widespread styles of calligraphy and manuscript traditions were eventually marginalized with the large-scale adoption of the printing press for churning out propaganda materials for various Islamic groups from the nineteenth century onwards.

The attempts to revive the chequered past of Islam, especially the period of the Prophet and the early caliphs, have often led to violent political struggles. For Ibn Khaldun (1332-1406), a North African Muslim historian of considerable reputation, history unfolds in a cyclic way; it reproduces the same pattern with time. Though Ibn Khaldun implies change and transformation in the different patterns of historical events, the notion of 'progress' is absent.[67] In his model, the energetic nomads come from outside to conquer the stagnating sedentary population, only to be overtaken by another set of nomadic population rising to build a political dominion with greater zeal. The rise and decline of the Arabs, Turks and Mongols are thus explained from this perspective.

Rationality, for Muslim writers, hardly played an important role in explaining causation in history. Sixteenth-century Afghan historian Abbas Sarwani's *Tarikh-i Sher Shah* explains Mughal Emperor Humayun's defeat in the hands of the Afghan empire-builder Sher Shah as God's will.[68] This same trend, as Roy's essay shows, continued even in the works connected with warfare produced by Muslim writers of the subcontinent during the eighteenth and first half of the nineteenth centuries.

RACE, RELIGION, CHRISTIANITY AND COLONIAL WARFARE

Like *dharmayuddha*, the classical Christian doctrine of Just War comprises *jus ad bellum* (justifications for waging war) and *jus in bello* (rules that govern warfare once fighting has started). Hugo Grotius, the Dutch legal philosopher of late sixteenth century and an advocate of Just War, argued for defensive warfare and criticized pre-emptive strike.[69] However, the Just War theory became marginal in the West European milieu due to Renaissance and Enlightenment, marked by separation of the Church from the State, a development of considerable significance.[70] The separation of *din* (religion) and *daulat* (state) in Islam[71] and between *kshatra* (sovereignty) and *rajadharma*/dharma in Hinduism did not occur in the early modern era. For Enlightenment thinkers, bipolar division of humanity did not involve division of the world into believers and non-believers as the Islamic theorists did, but into inferior and superior races.[72]

The absence of religion in Western military theory of the early modern era is exemplified in Carl Clausewitz's *Vom Kriege* which was first published in three volumes in Berlin between 1832 and 1834. Clausewitz's grandfather was a professor of theology, and a Lutheran pastor. Yet, Clausewitz made little reference to religion in his own writings. He did not cite faith as a motivation for war, nor did he view Christianity as an impulse for moderation while fighting fellow Christians.[73]

However, Western or British colonialism was not entirely secular in nature. Religion did play a crucial role in the formation of national identity in Britain. Victorian Britain witnessed the rise of 'race science' and it was tenuously connected with religion. The separation of the church and the state did not automatically result in the decline of social and political significance of religion. The crucial point is that in Britain a modern sense of Christian self was created which connected theological notions with progress and a sense of a mission in the world, giving rise to the concept of 'white man's burden' in the nineteenth century. Further, the Evangelicals who emphasized Christian morality somehow gave rise to the notion of national honour, especially among the middle class. Both the Evangelicals and the Catholics underlined their nationalism and believed that the duty of the British nation was to civilize the inferior race of 'savages' or 'heathens'. During the late nineteenth century, aggressive imperialism was sustained by muscular Christianity.[74]

The shift from religion to race in British India occurred as a reaction to the 1857 Uprising.[75] Race shaped the construction of the British-Indian armies in South Asia. The British considered themselves a superior race compared to the inhabitants of the subcontinent who were treated as racially inferior. This notion justified and shaped the British policy of preventing the entry of Anglo-Indians and the Indians into the officer corps. This point is highlighted by Michael Fisher in this volume, where he charts the military career of an Armenian and a north Indian Muslim in the Bengal Army of the late eighteenth century. However, the requirements of acquiring military manpower forced the British to use South Asians as soldiers and to an extent as non-commissioned officers. The British constructed the theory of martial races in order to induct selected communities of South Asia in the Raj's war machine.[76] The martial race theory collapsed due to the demands for massive manpower mobilization during Second World War. Increasing white officer casualties and requirements for manning the expanding British-Indian Army forced the Raj to commission Indians as officers in increasing numbers from late 1942. The number of Indian commissioned officers between 1939 and 1945 rose from 577 to more than 8,000.[77]

C.A. Bayly's essay, the last chapter of the volume, analyses the nature of the colonial state and mobilization of manpower and resources during Second World War. Bayly argues that colonialism was a blend of British and Indian collaboration and in this set up the British officers were the senior partners and the Indians were junior partners. Bayly shows that besides collaboration, the colonial state, especially in wartime, became a military regime. Wartime mobilization influenced the Partition of 1947 and partly the evolution of the post-colonial state. Religion and race took back seats in the face of pragmatism. Nevertheless, the role of these two factors cannot be totally discounted. Both the British and the American soldiers were racists and they viewed the Second World War (especially against Japan) as a sort of 'race war'. Rather than nationalism, the Indian soldiers were motivated by ethnic pride and racial hatred while fighting the Japanese. Occasionally, religious propaganda was carried out among the Hindu troops emphasizing that the Japanese indulged in cow slaughter.[78] After the publication of the Cripps Report, the Sikhs formed the Sikh Volunteer Corps in anticipation of perceived trouble from Muslims.[79] The 1947 Partition witnessed polarization of religious identities of three communities (Hindus, Muslims, and Sikhs) in the subcontinent, culminating in large-scale violence.

RELIGION AS PEACEMAKER

It would, indeed, be erroneous to always associate religion with violence. Western commentators link *fidayeens* (suicide bombers) with the concept of becoming a *shahid* (martyr) as proclaimed in Islam, forgetting that the LTTE (the Tamil Tigers, a secular militant organization somewhat influenced by Marxism and which fought for Tamil Ealam in Sri Lanka) first introduced suicide bombers. In fact, more often in history secular states and secular issues have caused the death of millions. Anti-semitism apart, the two world wars are examples of non-religious factors resulting in mass slaughter in the battlefields and mass murder at the initiatives of the state. Adolf Hitler's genocide and Josef Stalin's *gulags* along with the carpet bombing during the Second World War (both in scope and intensity) are worse than anything that the Al-Qaeda has done till date. Again, violence carried out by the extremists from Middle East is intertwined with the history of violence inflicted on the colonized by the white colonizers during the early modern era. This is not to condone violence carried out by any terror-outfit in religion's name but to notice that non-religious factors have been important in the history of warfare. Richard King writes that in contemporary USA, nationalism rather than Christianity has been a greater incitement to violence. Again, certain secular ideologies like Marxism which trace their origin to Enlightenment also display intolerance of the religious kind. Secular ideologies contain elements like claiming totalizing, universal and transcendental authority, and these elements are also present in religious fundamentalisms.[80]

At times, religion dampened the zeal for violence. Sandhya Sharma, by turning her focus on *Riti-kal* poetry in Braja-bhasa (which emerged in the north and central parts of India), argues that this literary medium functioned as a bridge rather than a gulf as far as Hindu-Muslim interaction in medieval India was concerned. Instead of awareness of the concept of a Hindu 'other', Sharma notes, *Riti-kal* poetry reveals intermingling of Hindu and Muslim elements even at the local levels and thus the border between Hindu-Muslim tended to be nebulous. This is closer to the picture of Hindu-Muslim amity advanced by generations of secular historians, as noted above. Nevertheless, Sharma has a point when she emphasizes the fuzziness of the boundary-markers of different communities in early modern India.

Romila Thapar in a powerful essay elsewhere asserts that the concept of a Hindu community is an invention of the nineteenth century. The Dharmashastras do not speak of any Hindu community. Ancient India witnessed continuous tussle between Brahmanism and Sramanism (Buddhists, Jains, Ajivikas and other sects which challenged the Vedic rituals and texts). *Ahimsa* was more a characteristic of Sramanism rather than Brahmanism. However, by the end of the first millennium CE, Brahmanism was able to marginalize Sramanism, partly by absorbing numerous local cults and sects and partly through vigorous and violent campaigns against those which resisted. With the arrival of the Turks in the eleventh century, the brahmin elites did not conceptualize them as Muslims but equated them with *yavanas* and *mlechhas*. Interestingly, even the lower castes were categorized as *mlechhas* and the Greeks and Sakas were described as *Yavanas*.[81] The Rama cult became popular from the post-Gupta era onwards. Rather than a reaction to Islamic invasion, claims Brajadulal Chattopadhyaya, this was partly due to the rise of the Bhakti cult and to legitimize large-scale monarchical forms of government.[82] So there might not have been a monolithic Hindu community in pre-modern India.

Similarly, Islam, being supposedly organized more tightly around a single book and a single prophet with the concept of *umma*, could be more homogeneous than Hinduism, but sectarian divisions within Islam and the resultant violence through the centuries have shown that there is no one authority whose writ ran large for Muslims all over the world. Certain mechanisms of British rule (that is census data, reservation, etc.) and social reform movements within Hinduism and Islam from the late nineteenth century onwards hardened community consciousness and the boundaries of both the Hindu and Muslim communities. And this to a great extent explains the Hindu-Muslim-Sikh violence during the 1947 Partition. Some controversial medieval legacies also contributed to this process of drifting and rupture.[83]

CRITICAL SUMMARIES OF THE ESSAYS IN THIS VOLUME

By making a case study of a particular episode from the *Mahabharata*, the first essay in this volume by Brekke shows how Hindu religious ethics shaped the theory of warfare. Brekke brings up the question whether Hinduism justifies pre-emptive strike and night attacks under certain contexts. In the *Mahabharata*, several heroes occasionally broke the rules of war and they are thoroughly condemned. Brekke's essay shows how both Bhima and, in retaliation, Aswatthama resorted to *kutayuddha* resulting in a gradual escalating spiral towards unregulated violence.

The second essay of this volume by Aquil depicts the languages of warfare and aggressive politics as enunciated by the ideologues of the Delhi Sultanate. Aquil focuses on Barani who was not merely an *alim* or a theologian but a close disciple of the influential Chishti Sufi of Delhi, Nizam-ud-Din Auliya. It is clear that Barani's concept of jihad is totally different from that of some modern historians for whom the literal meaning of the Arabic word jihad is merely striving for a worthy cause such as self-discipline. For Barani, humiliating the *kafirs* was a more worthy cause in the name of Allah.

Eaton (third essay) and Nath (fourth essay), taking a 'realist' perspective, assert that medieval warfare and politics were influenced by calculations for aggrandizement and survival rather than religion. Eaton makes a case study of the Vijayanagara-Bahmani/Bijapur conflict during the first half of the sixteenth century. Rama Raya's diplomacy *vis-à-vis* the neighbouring sultanates located to the north of his kingdom, writes Eaton, was motivated by the desire to gain Kalyana rather than any fascination for Hindu dharma. Territory and forts were the objectives for which the rulers (both Hindu and Muslim) fought. Nath's piece reflects the importance attached to hand-held firearms and artillery by Zahir-ud-Din Muhammad Babur. In fact, Babur's warfare reflected an amalgam of *taulqama* (flanking attacks by mounted archers) tactics of the Uzbegs and handguns-field artillery combination of the West Europeans, which the Ottomans used with great effect against Safavid Persia.

Both the Mughals and the Ahoms in Assam deployed substantial number of gunpowder arms because of terrain and ecology. In the jungle-clad river valleys and marshy regions, neither the *taulqama* charge of the mounted archers nor the frontal charge of heavily armoured Rajput cavalry in Mughal service were effective. Hence, the Mughals had to depend on elephants. And the vulnerability of the cavalry-oriented Mughal military machine allowed the Ahoms to practice guerrilla warfare with great effect, causing considerable embarrassment to the largest political power in the subcontinent and later celebrations of the strength of a regional polity backed by local militia. The chroniclers of the Mughal-Ahom conflict, as Saikia shows, depicted the identity of Ahom regional polity containing elements of Hinduism that emerged in response to military aggressiveness of the partly Islamic Mughal Empire.

Richard Barnett's piece in this volume shows that the Bahawalpur state during the first half of the nineteenth century followed a secular Westernization policy as far as statecraft was concerned. Being aware of the political, economic and military might of the East India Company, the rulers of Bahawalpur tried to avoid direct confrontation with the Company Raj and gradually became a client state.

One aspect of the dialectics between warfare and religion is the process through which the military organization accommodates the personnel coming from diverse religious and ethnic backgrounds. The East India Company's armies were multi-lingual and multi-religious military organizations. The Company's Bengal Army was able to accommodate the Muslim sowars, Hindu (Purbiya) infantry and Christian (British) officers into a composite whole. Fisher's essay portrays the perspectives and lives of two Asian subaltern officers who joined the Bengal Army in the eighteenth century. Through their own representations of their lives, claims Fisher, we can better understand the attraction of the Bengal Army to men like them and, thus, how that army emerged from asymmetrical interactions among Europeans, Asians, and their distinct cultures.

One of the factors which propelled the West European states to the stage of world history was their superior way of making warfare, both in the land and sea. Land warfare included battles, sieges and pacification campaigns. How to explain British superiority in conducting siege warfare in South Asia? The theory and practice of British siege warfare was in turn drawn from the West European method of conducting sieges. Roy's essay (Chapter 9) analyses siege warfare practised by the British in particular and the Europeans in general. This in turn requires tackling the dynamic and often contradictory relationships between warfare and the collective mentality of the societies that spawned different types of military establishments. In addition to military technology, strategy and tactics, it is necessary to tackle cultural generalities in order to understand the dyadic interaction between warfare, religion and science.

In the last essay of this volume, C.A. Bayly explores India's response to the Second World War from 1942 to 1945. A deeply unpopular alien government managed to mobilize more than three million men for active warfare and at least another ten million men and women for war-related service and labour which many of them viewed with ambivalence. The colonial state considerably extended, even if it did not systematically 'develop' the infrastructure of a poor country which had been battered by years of depression and official neglect. In a way, Roy and Bayly's pieces show the process of secularization of warfare. Roy's case study of siege warfare shows that for the professionals, religion was becoming marginal, and Bayly's essay depicts how religion functioned as a component of race and strengthened the morale of the soldiers in the service of the 'secular' polities.

The only seemingly 'odd' piece in this collection is the essay by Sharma, which focuses on peaceful Hindu-Muslim interaction through the medium of poetry generated in Braja-bhasa during the medieval period. However, a closer reading of the poems show certain undercurrents of tension which have the potential to spiral into violent conflicts in certain historical contexts. The implications are that war and peace are not two watertight, polar opposite concepts. In fact, the transition from peace to war in medieval India was indeed a grey area and in this respect religion functioned as an open-ended entity.

Indeed, major texts of the principal religious traditions are complex and ambivalent, with multiple meanings embedded in them, a characteristic known as polysemy.[84] Thus, *Bhagavad Gita* could appear as a moral struggle between good and evil for some, but for Brekke it reveals an existential expression of warfare in Hinduism. Hence, religious traditions could both heighten the passion for killing as well as check the brutal destruction of fellow human beings. Which element in a religion will be used in what manner depends on human beings, who, in turn, are conditioned by the historical context. Thus, the necessity to historicize the evolution of religions and to study the dialectical relationship (or lack of it) between different religious traditions and warfare. This is what the ten essays in this volume attempt to do.

NOTES

1. Hew Strachan, 'War and Strategy', in John Andreas Olsen (ed.), *On New Wars*, Oslo Files (Oslo: Norwegian Institute for Defence Studies, 2007), p. 13.
2. John R. Hinnells and Richard King, 'Introduction', in Hinnells and King (eds.), *Religion and Violence in South Asia* (London/New York Routledge, 2007), p. 1.
3. For an influential analysis blaming the American foreign policy in the Cold War era, especially the role of the CIA, for the current *hara-kiri* in international politics, see Mahmood Mamdani, *Good Muslim, Bad Muslim: Islam, the USA, and the Global War Against Terror* (New Delhi: Permanent Black, 2004).
4. For an intellectual movement, see Raziuddin Aquil, 'The Study of Islam and Indian History at the Darul Musannefin, Azamgarh', in Raziuddin Aquil and Partha Chatterjee (eds.), *History in the Vernacular* (Delhi/ Ranikhet: Permanent Black, 2008), pp. 322-56. For the difficulties involving a 'political society' of Muslims and others at the margins of modern civil society, see Partha Chatterjee, *The Politics of the Governed: Considerations on Political Society in Most of the World* (New York: Columbia University Press, 2004).
5. Nile Green in his *Islam and the Army in Colonial India: Sepoy Religion in the Service of Empire* (Cambridge: Cambridge University Press, 2009), p. 4, writes that Islam shaped the intellectual, emotional and spiritual world of the sepoys and sowars of the Hyderabad Contingent during the late nineteenth and early twentieth centuries. One could argue that Hinduism also shaped the common sense of the Hindu soldiers of pre-colonial and colonial eras.
6. For the impact of Hindu 'fatalism' on the strategic managers of post-1947 India, see Kanti P. Bajpai and Amitabh Mattoo (eds.), *Securing India: Strategic Thought and Practice: Essays by George K. Tanham with Commentaries* (New Delhi: Manohar, 1996).
7. For an analysis of the historiography of South Asian warfare, see Kaushik Roy, 'The Historiography of the Colonial Indian Army', *Studies in History*, NS, vol. 12, no. 2 (1996), pp. 255-73; Roy, 'Mars in Indian History', *Studies in History*, NS, vol. 16, no. 2 (2000), pp. 261-75; Roy, 'Introduction: Armies, Warfare, and Society in Colonial India', in Roy (ed.), *War and Society in Colonial India* (New Delhi: Oxford University Press, 2006), pp. 1-52.
8. Peter Gottschalk, 'A Categorical Difference: Communal Identity in British Epistemologies', in Hinnells and King (eds.), *Religion and Violence in South Asia*, pp. 202, 207.
9. R. Scott Appleby, *The Ambivalence of the Sacred: Religion, Violence, and Reconciliation* (Lanham, Boulder: Rowman & Littlefield Publishers, 2000), p. 9.

10. For a recent example, see Madhu Trivedi, 'Images of Women from the Fourteenth to the Sixteenth Century: A Study of Sufi *Premakhyans*', in Rajat Datta (ed.), *Rethinking a Millennium: Perspectives on Indian History from the Eighth to the Eighteenth Century: Essays for Harbans Mukhia* (Delhi: Aakar, 2008), p. 204.
11. *Sufis and Soldiers in Awrangzeb's Deccan: Malfuzat-i Naqshbandiyya*, tr. from the Persian and with an Introduction by Simon Digby (New Delhi: Oxford University Press, 2001); Raziuddin Aquil, *Sufism, Culture and Politics: Afghans and Islam in Medieval North India* (New Delhi: Oxford University Press, 2007).
12. Ayesha Jalal, *Partisans of Allah: Jihad in South Asia* (New Delhi: Permanent Black, 2008), see especially, p. 305.
13. R. Joseph Hoffmann, 'Introduction: The God of Hosts', in Hoffmann (ed.), *The Just War and Jihad: Violence in Judaism, Christianity, & Islam* (New York: Prometheus Books, 2006), pp. 10-11.
14. Mark Juergensmeyer, *Terror in the Mind of God: The Global Rise of Religious Violence* (Berkeley/Los Angeles: University of California Press, 2000), pp. 148, 153.
15. Hinnells and King, 'Introduction', in Hinnells and King (eds.), *Religion and Violence in South Asia*, p. 2.
16. Hector Avalos, 'Rethinking Religious Violence: Fighting over Nothing', in Hoffmann (ed.), *Just War and Jihad*, p. 106.
17. Juergensmeyer, *Terror in the Mind of God*, pp. 158-9.
18. Alan Beyerchen, 'Clausewitz and the Non-Linear Nature of Warfare: Systems of Organized Complexity', in Hew Strachan and Andreas Herberg-Rothe (eds.), *Clausewitz in the Twenty-First Century* (Oxford: Oxford University Press, 2007), pp. 45-56.
19. Peter van der Veer, *Imperial Encounters: Religion and Modernity in India and Britain* (2001, rpt., New Delhi: Permanent Black, 2006), p. 46.
20. Laurie L. Patton, 'Telling Stories about Harm: An Overview of Early Indian Narratives', in Hinnells and King (eds.), *Religion and Violence in South Asia*, pp. 13, 16, 19.
21. M.A. Mehendale, *Reflections on the Mahabharata War* (Shimla: IIAS, 1995), p. 1.
22. Alastair Murray, 'Reconstructing the Cold War: The Evolution of a Consuming Paradigm', and Charley Reynolds, 'Explaining the Cold War', in Alan P. Dobson (General Editor), Shahin P. Malik and Graham Evans (Assistant Editors), *Deconstructing and Reconstructing the Cold War* (Aldershot, Brookfield: Ashgate, 1999), pp. 31, 49-51; David R. Mapel, 'Realism and the Ethics of War and Peace', in Terry Nardin (ed.), *The Ethics of War and Peace: Religious and Secular Perspectives* (Princeton/ New Jersey: Princeton University Press, 1996), pp. 55, 60.
23. Mehendale, *Reflections on the Mahabharata War*, pp. 2-12.

24. *The Kautilya Arthasastra*, Part II, An English Translation with Critical and Explanatory Notes, by R.P. Kangle (1972, rpt., Delhi: Motilal Banarsidass, 1992), p. 10.
25. Kaushik Roy, 'Just and Unjust War in Hindu Philosophy', *Journal of Military Ethics* (henceforth *JME*), vol. 6, issue 3 (2007), pp. 232-44; Roy, 'The Theories of War', in Jyoti Bhusan Dasgupta (ed.), *Science, Technology, Imperialism and War*, vol. 15, part 1, in D.P. Chattopadhyaya (General Editor), *History of Science, Philosophy and Culture in Indian Civilization* (New Delhi: Longman Pearson, 2007), pp. 586-95.
26. Dirk H.A. Kolff, 'A Millennium of Stateless Indian History?', in Datta (ed.), *Rethinking a Millennium*, pp. 51-67.
27. B.N.S. Yadava, 'Chivalry and Warfare', in Jos J.L. Gommans and Dirk H.A. Kolff (eds.), *Warfare and Weaponry in South Asia: 1000-1800*, Themes in Indian History (New Delhi: Oxford University Press, 2001), pp. 66-98; Kaushik Roy, *From Hydaspes to Kargil: A History of Warfare in India from 326 BC to AD 1999* (New Delhi: Manohar, 2004), pp. 59-84.
28. Andre Wink, *Al-Hind: The Making of the Indo-Islamic World*, vol. 2: *The Slave Kings and the Islamic Conquest 11th-13th Centuries* (1997, rpt., New Delhi: Oxford University Press, 2001), pp. 305, 317.
29. For the continued veneration of an 'Islamized' Jesus in Muslim traditions, see Tarif Khalidi (ed. and tr.), *The Muslim Jesus: Sayings and Stories in Islamic Literature*, Convergences: Inventories of the Present Series (Cambridge and London: Harvard University Press, 2001).
30. Robert Gleave, 'Crimes against God and Violent Punishment in *al-Fatawa al-Alamgiriyya*', in Hinnells and King (eds.), *Religion and Violence in South Asia*, pp. 83, 85, 90.
31. John Kelsay, 'Al-Shaybani and the Islamic Law of War', *JME*, vol. 2, no. 1 (2003), pp. 66, 69, 71-2.
32. Sunil Kumar, 'Politics, the Muslim Community and Hindu-Muslim Relations Reconsidered: North India in the Early Thirteenth Century', in Datta (ed.), *Rethinking a Millennium*, pp. 139-60.
33. Iqtidar Husain Siddiqui, 'Learning and Intellectual Thought in the Sultanate of Delhi During the Lodi Period', in Siddiqui (ed.), *Medieval India: Essays in Intellectual Thought and Culture*, vol. 1 (New Delhi: Manohar, 2003), p. 105.
34. See, for instance, Muzaffar Alam's important intervention, *The Languages of Political Islam in India: c. 1200-1800* (Chicago: University of Chicago Press, 2004).
35. Jos Gommans, 'The Silent Frontier of South Asia, *c.* AD 1100-1800', *Journal of World History*, vol. 9, no. 1 (1998), pp. 1-23.
36. Simon Digby, 'The Problem of Military Ascendancy of the Delhi Sultanate', in Gommans and Kolff (eds.), *Warfare and Weaponry in South Asia*, pp. 311-20.

37. Rajat Datta, 'Introduction: Indian History from Eighth to Eighteenth Centuries: Problems, Perspectives, and Possibilities', in Datta (ed.), *Rethinking a Millennium*, p. 4.
38. For a recent and rare 'internal' critique of the limitations of 'secular' history, see Neeladri Bhattacharya, 'Predicament of Secular Histories', *Public Culture*, vol. 20, no. 1 (2008), pp. 57-73.
39. Raziuddin Aquil, 'On Islam and Kufr in the Delhi Sultanate: Towards a Re-interpretation of Ziya' al-Din Barani's *Fatawa-i Jahandari*', in Datta (ed.), *Rethinking a Millennium*, pp. 168-79.
40. See for the latter, Richard M. Eaton's important early work, *Sufis of Bijapur, 1300-1700: Social Roles of Sufis in Medieval India* (Princeton: Princeton University Press, 1978).
41. Wink, *Al-Hind*, vol. 2, pp. 91, 327-8.
42. For a dispassionate new work on Aurangzeb, see Katherine Butler Brown, 'Did Aurangzeb Ban Music? Questions for the Historiography of His Reign', *Modern Asian Studies* (*MAS*), vol. 41, no. 1 (2007), pp. 77–120.
43. Sheldon Pollock, '*Ramayana* and Political Imagination in India', in David N. Lorenzen (ed.), *Religious Movements in South Asia: 600-1800*, Debates in Indian History and Society (2004, rpt., New Delhi: Oxford University Press, 2006), pp. 153-208.
44. Catherine B. Asher, 'Excavating Communalism: Kachhwaha *Rajadharma* and Mughal Sovereignty', in Datta (ed.), *Rethinking a Millennium*, pp. 222-39.
45. For the argument that Mughal warfare comprised coercing the enemy by a show of force and then politically co-opting him instead of destroying him through decisive set-piece battles and sieges see Jos Gommans, *Mughal Warfare: Indian Frontiers and High Roads to Empire, 1500-1700* (London/New York: Routledge, 2002).
46. J.N. Sarkar, 'A Phase in Mughal-Assam Relations: Raja Ram Singh's Futile Expedition (1668-71)', *Journal of the Asiatic Society of Bengal*, vol. 29, no. 1 (1987), p. 48.
47. Richard M. Eaton, 'From Kalyana to Talikota: Culture, Politics, and War in the Deccan, 1542-1565', in Datta (ed.), *Rethinking a Millennium*, pp. 95-105.
48. Ranabir Chakravarti, 'Visiting Faraway Ports: India's Trade in the Western Indian Ocean, *ca.* 800-1500 CE', in Datta (ed.), *Rethinking a Millennium*, p. 260.
49. Victor Davis Hanson, *Carnage and Culture: Landmark Battles in the Rise of Western Power* (New York/London: Doubleday, 2001); Torkel Brekke, 'The Ethics of War and the Concept of War in India and Europe', *Numen*, vol. 52 (2005), pp. 59-86; Jos Gommans, 'Warhorse and Gunpowder in India, *c.* 1000-1850', in Jeremy Black (ed.), *War in the Early Modern World: 1450-1815* (1999, rpt., London/New York:

Routledge, 2004), pp. 105-27; Geoffrey Parker, 'Introduction', in Parker (ed.), *The Cambridge Illustrated History of Warfare: The Triumph of the West* (Cambridge: Cambridge University Press, 1995), pp. 2-9.

50. Peter A. Lorge, *The Asian Military Revolution: From Gunpowder to the Bomb* (Cambridge: Cambridge University Press, 2008), pp. 24-44, 66-87.
51. Kaushik Roy, *India's Historic Battles: From Alexander the Great to Kargil* (New Delhi: Permanent Black, 2004).
52. David Ayalon, 'Islam versus Christian Europe: The Case of the Holy Land', in Ayalon, *Islam and the Abode of War: Military Slaves and Islamic Adversaries* (Aldershot, Hampshire: Variorum, Ashgate, 1994), pp. 251, 254. For an opposite view see Gabor Agoston, *Guns for the Sultan: Military Power and the Weapons Industry in the Ottoman Empire* (Cambridge: Cambridge University Press, 2005).
53. David Ayalon, 'The Impact of Firearms on the Muslim World' in Ayalon, *Islam and the Abode of War*, p. 38.
54. Wink, *Al-Hind*, vol. 2, p. 76.
55. Richard M. Eaton, '"Kiss my Foot", Said the King: Firearms, Diplomacy, and the Battle for Raichur, 1520', *MAS*, vol. 43, no. 1 (2009), pp. 289-313.
56. Beatrice Forbes Manz, *The Rise and Rule of Tamerlane* (1989, rpt., Cambridge: Cambridge University Press, 1999), pp. 1-20.
57. Mansura Haidar, 'Military Organization under Timur and His Successors', in Haidar, *Medieval Central Asia: Polity, Economy and Military Organization (Fourteenth to Sixteenth Century)* (New Delhi: Manohar, 2004), p. 279.
58. Mansura Haidar, 'Military Organization under the Uzbegs', in Haidar, *Medieval Central Asia*, p. 311.
59. Haidar, 'Military Organization under Timur and His Successors', in Haidar, *Medieval Central Asia*, pp. 284, 292, 294.
60. Mansura Haidar, 'Incendiary Warfare and the Use of Firearms in Central Asia', in Haidar, *Medieval Central Asia*, pp. 325, 330, 336, 342.
61. Haidar, 'Military Organization under the Uzbegs', in Haidar, *Medieval Central Asia*, pp. 303-4, 312-13, 315.
62. Haidar, 'Incendiary Warfare and the Use of Firearms in Central Asia', in Haidar, *Medieval Central Asia*, p. 343.
63. For the concept of several Military Revolutions in West Europe, see Clifford J. Rogers, 'The Military Revolutions of the Hundred Years War', in Rogers (ed.), *The Military Revolution Debate: Readings on the Military Transformation of Early Modern Europe* (Colorado, Boulder: Westview Press, 1995), pp. 55-93.
64. Geoffrey Parker, 'The "Military Revolution, 1560-1610"—A Myth?', in Rogers (ed.), *Military Revolution Debate*, p. 48.
65. Stewart N. Gordon, 'Symbolic and Structural Constraints on the Adoption

of European-Style Military Technologies in the Eighteenth Century', in Richard B. Barnett (ed.), *Rethinking Early Modern India* (New Delhi: Manohar, 2002), pp. 155-78; Kaushik Roy, 'Military Synthesis in South Asia: Armies, Warfare, and Indian Society, *c.* 1740-1849', *Journal of Military History*, vol. 69, no. 3 (2005), pp. 651-90.

66. Ayalon, 'Islam versus Christian Europe: The Case of the Holy Land', in Ayalon, *Islam and the Abode of War*, p. 256.
67. Abdelmajid Hannoum, 'Translation and the Colonial Imaginary: Ibn Khaldun the Orientalist', *History and Theory*, vol. 42 (February 2003), p. 81.
68. Peter Hardy, 'Pre-Modern Concepts of Time in Indo-Muslim Historical Writing', in Siddiqui (ed.), *Medieval India*, vol. 1, pp. 62, 65; Aquil, *Sufism, Culture, and Politics*, especially chapters 1-2.
69. J. Harold Ellens, 'The Obscenity of War and the Imperative of Lesser Evil', in Hoffmann (ed.), *Just War and Jihad*, p. 35.
70. Appleby, *The Ambivalence of the Sacred*, p. 4.
71. L. Carl Brown, *Religion and State: The Muslim Approach to Politics* (New York: Columbia University Press, 2000), p. 1.
72. Hannoum, 'Translation and the Colonial Imaginary: Ibn Khaldun the Orientalist', pp. 71-4, 76.
73. Hew Strachan, *Clausewitz's On War* (New York: Atlantic Monthly Press, 2007), pp. ix, 32.
74. Veer, *Imperial Encounters*, pp. 20, 28-9, 34-5, 39-40, 58-9.
75. Ibid., p. 54.
76. Kaushik Roy, *Brown Warriors of the Raj: Recruitment and the Mechanics of Command in the Sepoy Army, 1859-1913* (New Delhi: Manohar, 2008).
77. Tarak Barkawi, 'Culture and Combat in the Colonies: The Indian Army in the Second World War', *Journal of Contemporary History*, vol. 41, no. 2 (2006), p. 331.
78. Tarak Barkawi, 'Peoples, Homelands, and Wars? Ethnicity, the Military, and Battle Among British Imperial Forces in the War against Japan', *Comparative Studies in Society and History*, vol. 46, no. 1 (2004), pp. 150-1, 158.
79. Tan Tai Yong, 'Mobilisation, Militarisation and "Mal-Contenment": Punjab and the Second World War', *South Asia: Journal of South Asian Studies*, NS, vol. 25, no. 2 (August 2002), p. 143.
80. Richard King, 'The Association of "Religion" with Violence: Reflections on a Modern Trope', in Hinnells and King (eds.), *Religion and Violence in South Asia*, pp. 231, 233, 237, 239, 242.
81. Romila Thapar, 'Imagined Religious Communities? Ancient History and the Modern Search for a Hindu Identity', in Lorenzen (ed.), *Religious Movements in South Asia*, pp. 333-59.

82. Brajadulal Chattopadhyaya, 'Anachronism of Political Imagination', in Lorenzen (ed.), *Religious Movements in South Asia*, pp. 209-26.
83. Satish Saberwal, *Spirals of Contention: Why India was Partitioned in 1947* (London/New York/New Delhi: Routledge, 2008).
84. Laurie L. Patton applies this concept only for the classical Hindu texts, which may as well be valid for all the classical religious texts. Patton, 'Telling Stories About Harm: An Overview of Early Indian Narratives', in Hinnells and King (eds.), *Religion and Violence in South Asia*, p. 14.

CHAPTER 1

Breaking the Thigh and the Warrior Code*

TORKEL BREKKE

The *Mahabharata* stands out in world literature as a timeless classic. In terms of longevity as well as cultural and religious importance, only works like the *Iliad* or the Bible may be placed alongside it. The *Mahabharata* is an epic poem of around 100,000 verses in classical Sanskrit that was composed, edited and re-edited over many centuries between 500 BCE and 400 CE or even longer.[1] The verses are divided into eighteen books, or *parvans* in Sanskrit. Although the *Mahabharata* is the most important mythological and religious work in Indian literature, it is not a sacred book. The Vedas are technically revelation (*shruti*, what has been heard by the seers, or *rishis*) while the *Mahabharata* belongs to the class of *smriti*, i.e. what has been remembered and handed down, as opposed to the revealed. Moreover, the *Mahabharata* is, in classical Indian terms, a work of (legendary) history, or *itihasa* in Sanskrit.

Thus, the *Mahabharata* is a vast storehouse of myths and stories where the main narrative theme is the conflict and great war between two groups of cousins, the sons of Dhritarashtra (called the Kauravas) and the sons of Pandu (called the Pandavas), all of whom are descendants of the mythic ancestor Bharata.[2] Important academic expositions of the epic discuss the war as an eschatological conflict at the end of time, or as a universal

*This chapter was written as part of a research project about the ethics of war at the Peace Research Institute of Oslo (PRIO). I would like to thank PRIO for the funding and Kaushik Roy for comments on earlier drafts of this chapter.

sacrifice. My point of departure is rather that the *Mahabharata* is fundamentally about the ethics of war. Of course, this does not exclude other readings of the epic. My aim is to discuss norms relating to warfare in classical Hindu India by looking at an exceptionally important episode in the *Mahabharata* called the Urubhanga, or the breaking of the thigh. The Urubhanga episode is part of the Shalyaparvan, which is Book 9 of the epic. My broader idea is to bring the *Mahabharata* into a dialogue about the ethics of war in human civilizations, and, one might add, in world religions, in general. In order to do this, we need to explore points of convergence between great ethical traditions on some key points on the issue of war and morality. As a point of departure it often proves useful to have in mind the distinction found in the Christian Just War tradition between rules for starting a war (*jus ad bellum*) and rules pertaining to the conduct of war (*jus in bello*). This distinction has been used by the few works that have engaged with comparative issues in the ethics of war found in the *Mahabharata*.[3] However, very little attention has been paid to the Urubhanga episode in spite of its obvious importance both in the *Mahabharata* story itself and to later Indian writers.

There is a tension throughout the *Mahabharata* between heroism and prudence, between the tradition that sees war as a duty according to dharma and the tradition that sees war as a means to the ends of security and prosperity, according to the *Arthashastra*, or the science of politics. In the Shalyaparvan, the fierce warrior Bhima breaks the thigh of Duryodhana in a mace-duel. At the same time, he breaks the warrior code (*kshatradharma*) and sets the stage for the complete breakdown of all restraint on the field of battle. The *jus in bello*, the rules of fighting, have been challenged throughout the war, but when the thigh of Duryodhana is broken, there is no turning back to heroic ideals and norms. From this point in the war, consequentialist reasoning takes complete precedence. The descent into anarchic and total war is defended and explained by the great god Krishna.

Throughout the *Mahabharata*, the heroes often refer to the *kshatradharma*, the warrior code. There is no complete and systematic presentation of this system in the epic but the references are so numerous that readers (or listeners) get a fair idea of an extensive set of specific rules. For instance, a soldier whose armour is broken, one who folds his hands or one who has thrown down his weapons may be taken prisoner but may not be killed. The aged, the children, women, one who shows he surrenders by having a straw in his mouth, and again one who says 'I am yours' must not be killed. One must not kill those that are sleeping, those that are thirsty, those that are wearied, one who is disordered or confused, one who has started out for liberation (*moksha*), one who is on the move, one who is walking, one who is drinking or eating, or one who is scattered in the mind, or one who has been struck or has been weakened. The most important moral discussions in the *Mahabharata* concern these types of rules. Should they ever be broken? Under what circumstances can they be broken? What justifies the breaking of the *kshatradharma*?

BACKGROUND TO THE URUBHANGA EPISODE

The Urubhanga episode is part of the Shalyaparvan (Book 9), but in order to understand the background we should take a brief look at the events from Dronaparvan (Book 7) and Karnaparvan (Book 8). In Dronaparvan, we see the beginnings of a chain of events that leads up to the Urubhanga. Urged by the righteous Yudhishthira, Arjuna's son Abhimanyu attacks the Kaurava army, but he is isolated on the battlefield and is forced to fight alone. His horses are killed, and his weapons are destroyed and in the end he holds his ground by taking one of the wheels of the broken chariot, fighting like Vishnu with his discus. In the end, he loses even his wheel and grabs a mace and continues his desperate fight. Then, he is attacked by Dauhshasani, who 'brought down his mace on Saubhadra's head as the boy tottered to his feet. He reeled beneath the force of the blow, and then at last the deadly son of Saubhadra toppled to the ground. He breathed no more.'[4]

In the Dronaparvan, then, Arjuna's son Abhimanyu is killed in an unfair fight and it is obvious to all good warriors that the warrior code has been broken by the Kauravas. There is no doubt that killing someone whose armour and weapons have been destroyed is a clear violation of the rules of war—the *jus in bello* of epic Hinduism. Yuyutsu, the son of Dhritarashtra, is outraged at the transgression done by his own side and warns of a great danger arising from the unrighteous killing of Abhimanyu and it is quite likely that the author(s) here indicates this as a starting point of a descent into ever more unrestrained warfare.

Thus, the cowardly slaying of Abhimanyu in the Dronaparavan starts a chain-reaction that may be seen as the start of a long series of breaches of the epic warrior code. This finally leads to the Urubhanga and subsequently to the terrible slaying of the Pandava army at night by Ashvatthama. For when Arjuna hears of the slaying of his son he is struck with grief and he vows to kill the Kaurava warrior Jayadratha, who was responsible for closing the breach in the Kaurava ranks in order to isolate Abhimanyu from his comrades. In the end, Arjuna is only able to fulfil his vow with the help of Krishna. After a day of fighting, the sun is sinking and a sudden darkness sets in. It seems as though the day has passed and the sun has set. Jayadratha turns around and looks at the horizon and thinks with relief that he is saved because the time-limit set by Arjuna has passed. However, Krishna approaches Arjuna and urges him on. The darkness is caused by the god. The sun is in fact still up. An arrow flies from Arjuna's great Gandiva bow and takes Jayadratha's head off. More arrows carry the severed head of the Kaurava hero to the hermitage where Jayadratha's father Vriddhakshatra is meditating. Again, the warrior code has been broken by deceit. The war continues and the passions rise from day-to-day. One by one the rules and restraints are broken.

The rule of ceasefire at sunset is broken. From now the battle continues into the night in the light of thousands of torches. The great Kaurava warrior Drona now shows his might and it becomes clear to the Pandavas that he is unstoppable by just means. Krishna tells Arjuna that no one can defeat Drona if they fight according to the rules of war. Dharma must be broken if Drona is to be stopped. According to Krishna, there is only one thing that will distract Drona enough to stop him. If Drona is told that his son Ashvatthama is dead, he will be so grieved that he will lose all interest in the war. But Arjuna and the other Pandavas are shocked by this proposal. In the end, it is Yudhishthira who agrees to bear the burden of sin. Bhima, the mighty warrior, kills an elephant by the name of Ashvatthama, and shouts to Drona that his son Ashvatthama is dead. But Bhima is ashamed in spite of his fearsome nature, and, of course, the lie is more unbearable for the noble and righteous Yudhishthira. When Drona asks Yudhishthira to confirm the claim that Ashvatthama is dead he is certain that he can expect a truthful answer from Yudhishthira; he is known to never utter a lie. Yudhishthira's dilemma is impossible. Drona is about to discharge his *brahmastra*, a weapon of incredible power that is certain to turn the war in favour of the Kauravas. Drona must be stopped. Yudhishthira trembles in horror at the lie he is about to tell but decides that victory is worth it. 'Yes', he says, 'it is true that Ashvatthama is dead'. In a low voice he added, 'Ashvatthama, the elephant' but nobody hears this and this does not make his lie any smaller.

HEROES: NOBLE AND TERRIBLE

This is an important turning point in the character of Yudhishthira. To this moment, his greatest concern had been to guard dharma and truth. He had stood apart from the world with its untruth. As a sign of this elevated status the wheels of his chariot never touched the earth but hovered inches above its surface. In the moment he utters the lie, Yudhishthira's chariot falls to the ground. The noblest of the Pandavas has slipped into the way of untruth because of his desire for victory. This is important for an understanding of the message of the *Mahabharata* concerning the ethics of war.

Georges Dumézil wrote extensively on the different functions of the representatives of the three classes in the tripartite ideology of the Indo-Europeans.[5] Dumézil believed that the warriors were of two different kinds. In the Indo-European ideology '*la fonction guerrière s'est réalisée en deux types de héros que les noms d'Héraclès et d'Achille caractérisent suffisamment*'.[6] In the *Mahabharata*, the two different warriors are represented by Bhima and Arjuna and in Scandinavian mythology by Thor and Odin. In the Vedic mythology the two types of warriors have at some stage been represented by Indra and Vayu, according to Dumézil, although Indra is a lonesome character; the relationship between the mythological structures contained in the *Mahabharata* and the Vedic texts are discussed in some detail by Dumézil taking the studies of Stig Wikander as the starting point.[7] The two types of warriors represent fundamentally different ideals, values, and physical abilities. The warrior type represented by gods and heroes like Vayu, Hercules, Thor or Bhima is almost like an animal in physical appearance—he is ugly, he is incredibly strong and his weapon of choice is the rather uncivilized mace. He operates on his own; he is a solitary character, uncivilized and not very intelligent. The other type of warrior, represented by Odin, Achilles or Arjuna is noble and beautiful. He is highly civilized and his weapon of choice and his techniques of fighting are more advanced. Furthermore, the civilized warrior is far superior in the region of ethics. '*Il est brilliant, intelligent, moral même, et surtout sociable*, . . .'[8] For our concern, it is most important to note that in the Indo-European mythology and ideology, the ethical aspects of war resided in one distinct type of warrior, represented by Arjuna and Yudhishthira, and was almost absent in the other type, represented by Bhima.

The Pandava's immoral lie about Drona's son saves the day. Drona reacts by losing all interest in the war and in life. He throws his weapons away and sits down in his chariot to meditate. While in trance, Drona has his head cut-off from behind by Dhrishtadyumna. Karna now becomes the commander-in-chief of the Kaurava forces and the Karnaparvan (Book 8) begins. Karna is an exceptionally interesting hero. The eldest son of Kunti and the Sun-god Surya, he is not only the half-brother of the Pandavas but a potential rightful claimant to the throne. However, this fact is not known to Karna until conversations with his biological mother and with Krishna just prior to the outbreak of war. At this time, however, Karna has pledged loyalty to Duryodhana and he is destined to fight his half-brothers, the Pandavas. His hidden identity, the fact that he is proud and a braggart, and all the troubles it causes, makes Karna the most tragic figure of the story; it has even been argued that he is the most important of all the heroes of the great epic.[9]

The Karnaparvan contains one of the most violent scenes of the epic as Bhima slays Duhshasana with his bare hands and drinks his blood and performs a mad dance on the bloody battlefield. This is the fulfilment of the vow Bhima made in the assembly hall when Duhshasana dragged Draupadi (the five Pandava brothers' common wife) by the hair and tried to undress her in public. As this horrible insult is one of the key reference points for the rest of the conflict, we may briefly recall the episode here. In the Sabhaparvan (Book 2) of the epic,

Yudhishthira engages in a dice-game against the cunning Shakuni, the uncle of the arch-villain Duryodhana. Yudhishthira loses everything in the game. Then, Shakuni, enjoying his victory with the dice, urges his opponent on; 'One throw remains, O king—stake your dear wife Draupadi of Panchala, and win yourself back!'[10] Of course, Yudhishthira loses again. When Draupadi hears that she has been gambled away, she is shocked. 'What prince wagers his wife in a game?' she asks.[11] Everyone is so ashamed of what has happened that they do not dare to approach Draupadi and ask her to enter the hall and give herself up to the Kauravas. Then, Duhshasana goes to her apartment and asks her to come with him. She tries to escape, but Duhshasana runs after her and grabs her hair. 'He dragged Draupadi, of jet-black hair, into the hall as if there were no one to protect her, tossing her around like the wind a banana tree.'[12] Begging for mercy, Draupadi complains that she is menstruating and wearing only one piece of clothing but Duhshasana mocks her. Nobody cares what she is wearing; she is now a slave. Karna, Shakuni and Duryodhana laugh as the Pandava queen is dragged before her husbands by Duhshasana. A discussion ensues among the Kauravas as to whether Draupadi was fairly won but Karna mocks the debate calling to Duhshasana to strip Draupadi. 'Duhshasana, however, took violent hold of Draupadi's robe and began undressing her right in the middle of the assembly hall.'[13] Draupadi hides her face and prays to God for protection against the humiliation by the Kauravas. Bhima cannot contain his anger. He makes his promise: 'Kshatriyas of the world, take to your hearts these words of mine—words no man has ever uttered, words no man will ever utter again! If I do not act upon this oath, may I forget my journey to my ancestors! If I do not tear open in battle this wretched scoundrel's chest and drink the blood of this Bharata outcaste!'[14]

After this brief detour back to the original insults of the conflict, we return to Book 8 and note the other great episode of the Karnaparvan, namely the inevitable clash between Karna and Arjuna in battle. Karna's chariot gets stuck in the mud and Karna requests Arjuna to wait. According to the rules of war repeated throughout the *Mahabharata*, Arjuna is required to wait and let his opponent get ready. Again, Krishna intervenes. He mocks Karna's appeal to dharma. Karna has himself caused so many breaches of dharma in the past and Krishna reminds him of all the occasions. Arjuna kills Karna with an arrow from his bow.

One of the key elements of the warrior code is firmness and fearlessness. For instance, at the height of the battle in Shalyaparvan, Bhima cries out his lion-roar and makes the Kauravas flee. King Duryodhana calls his army back to the battlefield by reminding them of the rights and wrongs of the life of the warrior. 'Come back! You know what is wrong, so fight!'[15] What is wrong (*adharma*) for the warrior in this situation is turning one's back and running away and Duryodhana expects his people to be people who know what is wrong in the context of battle even though the rights and wrongs of the larger war is irrelevant at this particular moment. In other words, it is quite possible to follow the *jus in bello* even though one is engaged in a war whose morality is doubtful. In the next moment, the same warrior code is referred to by Sahadeva in order to make Shakuni, his opponent in battle, stay and fight in the face of imminent death. At this point the battle goes in favour of the Pandavas and, evidently, Sahadeva is worried that Shakuni will run away: 'Be firm in the warrior code (*kshatradharma*) and fight! Be a man!'[16]

THE URUBHANGA OF THE *MAHABHARATA*

The story about the mace-battle is extraordinarily interesting for a study of the ethics of war in the Hindu tradition because it is so ambiguous. Indeed, from an ethical point of view, the episode is fundamentally unresolved in spite of all the weighty arguments made by the heroes for and against the action of the Pandavas. In my opinion, the mace-battle stands out as a long and difficult argument about one of the core issues concerning the ethics of war in any civilization. It is an argument between a consequentialist reasoning saying that the war must be won at all cost and a deontological argument saying that the warrior code must be followed regardless of the consequences.

In order to engage the great warrior Duryodhana in the mace-duel, the Pandavas must first make him stand up to their challenge. Strangely, Duryodhana has entered a frozen lake to rest and heal his wounds and the Pandavas approach him and taunt him to make him fight. At the same time, Krishna insists that Duryodhana himself is so prone to divine magic (*maya*) that the Pandavas must use magic and trickery to defeat him. Krishna tells Yudhishthira 'It is through a *maya* (trick) that you must destroy this magician's magic, O Bharata! A trickster must be killed by a trick!' Krishna goes on to describe how many great and righteous victories have been achieved through ploys (*kriya*) and devices (*abhyupaya*).[17] Expedience (*kriya*) is powerful, Krishna says. The Pandavas taunt Duryodhana about his supposed heroism (*shaurya*) and manliness (*paurusha*) to get him out of the water. Duryodhana assures his enemies that it was not out of fear (*bhaya*) that he retreated to the lake but simply out of weariness.[18] Duryodhana adds that he really has no desire to rule over the earth now that all his friends and kinsmen are dead; he prefers to enter the life of a hermit in the forest. However, Yudhishthira is shocked by this stupid suggestion; the earth is not Duryodhana's to give away and the world is simply not big enough for both potentates. One must die and the other must rule. Duryodhana replies that it would be against the warrior code if he were to fight alone, without arms and chariot, against an entire army.

Thus, at this point Duryodhana refers to one of the standard phrases of the warrior code about the immorality of fighting one who is armour-less, exhausted, wounded and whose troops and animals are fatigued—words that are repeated more or less in the same order and manner in many places in the epic.[19] In response, Yudhishthira makes one of his too noble vows and reveals his tendency for gambling, which brought disaster upon the Pandavas during the game of dice in the assembly hall. Yudhishthira promises that if Duryodhana kills only one of the Pandavas in duel, the kingdom is his. However, just to show his own generosity, Yudhishthira turns Duryodhana's pleas for rightful combat against himself. If Duryodhana really wants to follow the warrior code (*kshatradharma*) how come he broke it so easily when it was expedient to do so? If it is unfair to fight one against many, how could all those Kauravas, who knew the dharma, slaughter poor Abhimanyu the way they did? No, in a difficult situation, everyone turns to morality (dharma), Yudhishthira says.[20] His observation implies that true loyalty to dharma presupposes steadfastness even when circumstances are difficult and it underscores how righteous the Pandavas are, and how badly the Kauravas have behaved during the war.

Krishna is shocked by Yudhishthira's suggestion. How could Yudhishthira act so recklessly? Krishna's voice is that of reasoned consequentialism. He has helped the Pandavas along the way to regain their kingdom. Now that goal is within reach and Yudhishthira puts everything in jeopardy by engaging in a new gambling match. Yudhishthira lost the kingdom in gambling in the past and he is about to lose it again through recklessness and misguided compassion for the villain Duryodhana. How can anyone gamble away his kingdom in this manner? No one will conquer Duryodhana in a duel if he fights by fair means (*nyaya*), Krishna laments.[21] By this stupid promise Yudhishthira has given away the kingdom and the Pandavas are destined once more for life in the forest. It is decided that Bhima will fight the duel and Bhima assures his friends that he is capable of killing Duryodhana in a mace-fight. Bhima and Duryodhana then face each other on the battlefield and ready themselves for a crucial duel.

As the duel proceeds, the Pandavas are rightly worried because they know that everything now depends on the outcome of this fight. Arjuna asks his friend Krishna about his opinion. Who is the strongest and the most skilful of the two powerful warriors? Krishna is not optimistic. Through Yudhishthira's folly (*abuddhi*) victory has again been jeopardized, Krishna points out.[22] The only thing that matters now is that Bhima conquers Duryodhana. However, Bhima will not win if he fights justly (dharma) but only if he fights by unlawful means (*anyaya*). Krishna again points out that even the gods use deceit (*maya*) to destroy their powerful enemies. Arjuna understands that Krishna is right. In order to convey the message to Bhima on the battlefield, Arjuna slaps his own left thigh as a sign. Bhima understands the sign and prepares for the last strike. Sanjaya, who is narrating the battle scenes to blind Dhritarashtra exclaims:

> Charging at him and roaring like a lion, the Pandava violently hurled his mace at Duryodhana's thigh as his opponent leaped in the air once more in order to deceive his enemy, Your Majesty. With the crash of a thunderbolt, the mace hurled by that warrior of terrifying deeds broke Duryodhana's handsome thigh. His thigh smashed, your son, that tiger among men, fell to the ground, making the earth resound, Your Majesty.[23]

With this unlawful move, Duryodhana, the most important of the Kaurava heroes, is destroyed and this is an important turning point in the story of the war. Of course, the Pandavas are relieved when they see that Bhima has conquered the arch-villain but nature around them displays ominous signs, like earthquakes, a great meteor, and strange behaviour among beasts, men and other beings. The Pandavas rejoice but Bhima is not satisfied with conquering Duryodhana: instead of retreating to let his opponent die alone he approaches him and rubs his head with his left foot. He abuses him and scorns his opponent with foul language reminding him of how the Kauravas used dishonesty, fire, dice-games and the like to fool the Pandavas. When Bhima has finished abusing Duryodhana, Yudhishthira is not happy with Bhima's treatment of Duryodhana. He asks him to stop the disgraceful treatment of a mortally wounded hero; this is a glaring violation of the warrior code. Then, Yudhishthira himself approaches Duryodhana as if to appease him. He asks Duryodhana not to be angry and explains how this outcome is the fruit of terrible deeds committed in the past. And besides, it is better to die now than to go on living after so many relatives have been killed. On top of everything the Pandavas will have to answer to the grieving, widowed wives of the fallen heroes of the Kauravas.

GOD'S CROOKED PATH OF WAR

At this point, the god Balarama leaps on the stage. He has watched the mace-duel and he is now raging with anger.

> Shame on you, Bhima! Shame on you! It is shameful to strike an opponent below the navel in honourable combat (*dharmavigraha*). I have never seen an action like Vrikodara's before in a mace contest. The Teachings (*shastra*) state that one should never strike below the navel. This fool does not know the Teachings and acts according to his own will![24]

Balarama charges at Bhima in anger but is restrained by Krishna. Krishna explains that there is no fault (*dosha*) in Bhima's act because he once made a vow to break Duryodhana's thigh; a warrior must keep his vows. Besides, says Krishna, we have blood connection with the Pandavas and our prosperity comes from their prosperity. Krishna's explanation is a bit far-fetched and Balarama does not buy it. He refrains from attacking Bhima but he makes it clear that he is extremely displeased. Indeed, Bhima will be known as a crooked fighter (*jihmayodhi*), Balarama says, whereas Duryodhana will reach the heavens as he was killed as a fair fighter (*rijuyodhi*).[25] This moral verdict is taken up by the poet Bhasa, to whom I shall return shortly.

Thus, in the aftermath of the mace-duel there develops an angry debate about the moral implications of the means used by Bhima and in this debate many of the most serious grievances of both sides are brought to the fore. Soon, Duryodhana himself enters the debate by hurling terrible accusations at Krishna. He saw the discussion between Krishna and Arjuna when it was decided that they should give the sign to Bhima to make him strike at the thigh. Duryodhana is terribly angry that Krishna feels no shame that he was felled unjustly (*adharma*) or in using every crooked means (*jihma upaya*) to kill kings who fought according to the rules. 'Who has acted more wickedly (*papa*) than you?', Duryodhana asks.[26] He goes on to point out all the evil things Krishna has done during the war; indeed, Krishna has been following an ignoble (*anarya*) and crooked (*jihma*) path (*marga*).[27] Krishna replies that it was not his fault at all. It was because Duryodhana himself followed an evil path (*papamarga*) that all these things had to happen.

Now, the debate takes an interesting turn as the Pandavas themselves feel ashamed when they are reminded by Duryodhana of all the wrongs committed by them in their war against the Kauravas. Krishna must turn to his own side and explain why it was necessary to break the rules again and again. If the Pandavas had fought by fair means they would have lost the war. 'For your sake, I have killed these great warriors in battle by using numerous crooked means', says Krishna. Krishna urges the Pandavas not to feel sorry that unjust means have been used throughout the war by their own side. The end justified the means:

> When enemies are numerous and too many, they should be killed through deception and ploys. Gods in the past followed this path when they slew demons. If the path has been followed by the good, then it can be followed by everyone. Our purposes have been achieved and it is evening time. Let us retire. Let us rest, lords of men, along with our horses, elephants, and chariots.[28]

I started this section of my chapter by pointing to the ethical relevance of the Urubhanga episode and it seems that Krishna's conclusion is less ambiguous than many other dialogues and debates in this part of the *Mahabharata*. He states bluntly that the ends justified the crooked means. It is victory for the consequentialist reasoning; the deontological ethics of the warrior code that the heroes know so well is relativized by God himself. However, there is another, and somewhat related, way to see the final statements of Krishna regarding the relationship between means and ends. In fact, the great war between the Pandavas and Kauravas is not strictly a just war at all, according to the reasoning of Krishna. It is a holy war in the sense that the Pandavas can be absolutely certain they are fighting on the side of righteousness as God is taking part in the war; this makes the means of fighting irrelevant for the righteousness of the war.

We could add here that the Urubhanga episode is the cause of Ashvatthama's motivation to leave all the traditional rules of the warrior code behind and embrace an amoral position close to the consequentialist ethics of the *Arthashastra*. The Shalyaparvan ends with Ashvatthama being consecrated as the new commander of the Kaurava army. Ashvatthama shows signs of grief when he speaks to the mortally wounded Duryodhana. He claims that not even the slaying of his father, Drona, pained him so much as the killing of Duryodhana and he makes vow that he will use any means (*upaya*) to slay the Pandavas. Ashvatthama is a Brahmin but even a Brahmin can follow the law of the Kshatriya on the field of battle, says Duryodhana, as he gives Ashvatthama his permission to continue the war.[29]

In the beginning of next book, the Sauptikaparvan, Ashvatthama sees an owl killing sleeping crows in a tree and he reflects upon the meaning of this episode, concluding that the owl has indeed taught him a lesson in statecraft. This reminds the reader of stories contained in the *Panchatantra*, where one can detect early traces of the *Arthashastra* tradition. Reflecting on the tensions between the moral laws of dharma and the realist maxims of *artha*, Ashvatthama makes his final decision to massacre the Pandavas and Panchalas at night when they would be sleeping. This crucial line of reasoning is a turning point in the story of the *Mahabharata*. The Pandavas are enjoying their victory at the end of the Shalyaparvan, but in the Sauptikaparvan, everything is turned around by Ashvatthama's renewed war, which is unrestrained by rules and conventions.

MEANS AND ENDS

Krishna is busy on the side of the Pandavas throughout the great war and there is no time to rest when Duryodhana has been killed. Yudhishthira's first thought after the mace battle is that Duryodhana's mother, Gandhari, would be extremely angry when the news reaches her. This would be dangerous to the Pandavas because Gandhari had gained enormous power through austerities and would be able to incinerate them when she hears of the outcome of the war. Thus, Krishna hurries off to Hastinapura to talk to Gandhari and convince her not to do anything rash.

Krishna approaches old Dhritarashtra and insists that the terrible results of the war are really the fault of the old king himself. In fact, the whole of the Kshatriya race has been destroyed because of Dhritarashtra's wrongdoing, Krishna insists: 'The heroic Pandavas have not committed even a slight transgression, enemy-scorcher—whether in morality, propriety or affection.'[30] Then, he approaches Gandhari with his petition. He asks Gandhari not to think of revenge on the Pandavas. Instead, she should recall how she herself had scolded her son when he sought victory through battle: 'Where there is *dharma*, there is victory (*yato dharma tato jayah*)!'[31] Gandhari weeps but realizes that Krishna is right. Her son has brought about his own destruction by refusing to make peace.

Later, in the Book of the Women (Striparvan, i.e. Book 11), the Pandavas approach Gandhari, who is grieving with the other women after taking account of the terrible consequences of the war. When Gandhari recognizes Yudhishthira, she plans to curse him as a revenge for the death of her son, but Vyasa sees her evil intentions. The seer convinces her to let go of such evil thoughts by reminding her of her own words at the beginning of the war. At that time, when Gandhari's son approached her to get her blessing before the battle, she had told him that 'Where there is Law there is victory'. Gandhari realizes that Vyasa is right, that she does not really want the Pandavas to perish but that she was about to lose her mind from the grief for her sons. In fact, she says, the destruction came about as the result of wrong committed by Duryodhana and other Kauravas. This verdict seems to carry weight because of Gandhari's status as a most righteous woman. As Vyasa has just told her, he knows of no case where she ever said anything inaccurate or false and she had admitted herself that the righteous would win the war. In other words, it would be completely inconsistent of Gandhari to claim that the Pandavas won by *adharmic* means. An *adharmic* victory seems to be logically impossible in this short discussion between Gandhari and Vyasa.

However, there are aspects of the war that Gandhari does not understand and she now demands explanations from the Pandavas. She is not angry that the five brothers had to beat the Kauravas but she cannot understand how Bhima could break the rules of dharma by hitting Duryodhana below the navel in the fight with clubs. 'How can heroes forsake the *dharma* that has been taught by great men, simply in order to save their own lives?' In other words, Gandhari demands an explanation of the Urubhanga episode. Bhima answers in a conciliatory tone. He says that what he did—whether right or wrong—was out of terror, and he begs for pardon from Gandhari. Then, Bhima explains that there was not much else he could do. He would never beat his opponent in a fair fight with clubs and he simply could not let Duryodhana win to take over the kingdom In other words, Bhima is saying that what seemed to go against dharma in the situation was actually not against the law if seen in the larger context of the struggle between right and wrong.

Again, Bhima is applying a consequentialist moral reasoning to his own actions. Nothing he did was really against dharma if held up against the likely consequences of a different course of action. In short, the function of the discussion between Gandhari and the Pandavas is not to debate the moral status of different actions; it is rather to illuminate actions that seemed to be *adharmic* from a larger perspective. It is a discussion of *the jus in bello* from the point of view of *jus ad bellum*. Indeed, it is a fundamental relativization of *jus in bello* from the point of view of the necessity of war. The Pandavas broke rules because the larger cause was too important. But the meeting is also a chance to ask for forgiveness. Bhima is forgiven and then Gandhari turns to Yudhishthira. Yudhishthira approaches her, bending down and folding his hands. He is very afraid of this great woman who knew dharma so well. He admits that he has killed all her sons and that he is an evil man who deserves neither life nor kingdom nor wealth. But, why does he say this if the war was so necessary?

A NOTE ON BHASA'S URUBHANGA

The great Indian dramatist Bhasa, dated to the third or fourth century CE by Maurice Winternitz,[32] wrote six plays based on the Mahabharata war. If we look at the plays by Bhasa based on the *Ramayana*, we see that the author has tried to capture the whole of Rama's story within his plays and his ambition with the *Mahabharata* plays seems to be rather similar. Through his six plays, Bhasa wants to present the most important acts of the *Mahabharata*. In this context, it is significant that he chooses the Urubhanga episode as the matter for one of his plays. Among Bhasa's *Mahabharata* plays, Urubhanga is clearly the most tragic. The concept of tragedy, however, is really ill-suited to capture the idea behind Bhasa's play, which is better analysed according to Indian dramatic theory, where the theory of *rasas* is of fundamental importance. The *rasa* of Bhasa's Urubhanga seems to be *virya*, the heroic *rasa*. However, it seems reasonable to say that the play about Duryodhana is meant to convey the idea of a particular form of heroism, i.e. the *dayavira*, the hero in compassion. Indeed, the point of Bhasa's play is to treat one absolutely crucial turning point in the great *Mahabharata* story—the fall of Duryodhana, from the point of view of the Kauravas rather than the main protagonists of the epic, the Pandavas.[33]

Clearly, Bhasa makes serious changes to the character of Duryodhana. In the epic itself, Duryodhana is the perfect villain but in Bhasa's play he becomes a noble character.[34] After a ferocious duel, Bhima strikes Duryodhana's thigh and wins the fight. Lying broken on the battlefield, Duryodhana is approached by his son, his wives, and his parents. They all lament. Then, Ashvatthama approaches Duryodhana and promises that he will wage war on the Pandavas in the cover of the night. Duryodhana exclaims that he must not attempt to continue the war. Kings must be embodiments of honour (*manasharira*), says Duryodhana, insisting that he has already resigned himself to his injury because of honour. But Ashvatthama does not listen to the dying man, believing that his pride (*darpa*) has been shattered along with his thigh. Ashvatthama has made up his mind to carry out the night-attack. He says, 'Now for the massacre at night, weapons ready in hand'.[35]

Of course, this is Bhasa's invention for it is clear from the Sauptikaparvan that the motivation of Ashvatthama to attack at night comes during the time of night when he watches the owl attacking the birds in the tree reflecting on the usefulness of the *arthashastra* tradition. In other words, Bhasa connects the Urubhanga episode completely with the motivation of Ashvatthama. The problem with Bhasa's version is that it becomes rather uninteresting as an example of moral reasoning in war. Ashvatthama is not granted any serious thoughts on the moral status of his emerging plan to slaughter his opponents at night; the plan simply pops into his head without the real psychological motivation that we get in the Sauptikaparvan. Bhasa chooses to change the moral status of his main protagonist Duryodhana, not unlike the makeover that Julius Caesar gets from Shakespeare. All other characters are on stage to make the tragedy of Duryodhana complete and his family members and his guru are clearly enough for this purpose. In this respect, Ashvatthama seems unnecessary in the play and his appearance seems to be inserted simply to point forward to the later episode of the night attack.

CONCLUSION

The Urubhanga episode of the *Mahabharata* is a key story in the great epic and it has been used by Indian authors such as Bhasa to explore the moral meanings of the great war and the roles of some of its main protagonists. From the discussion of the morality of the Urubhanga in the Shalyaparvan, continued in the Sauptikaparvan, it is clear that there is a deep tension between two visions of the ethics of war in the story. On the one hand, there is a great sense of honour surrounding the knowledge of and internalization of the rules contained in the warrior code. This tension is one of several deep contradictions in the political and social vision of the *Mahabharata*. The tension between the consequentialist and the deontological morality within the world of the *kshatradharma* may have some connections to the tensions within the crucial notion of dharma. In his introduction to the Book of Peace, James L. Fitzgerald discusses two contradictory notions of dharma present in the great epic. On the one hand, there is the old sense of dharma, which refers to actions performed to gain some important good, such as wealth or victory in war. On the other hand, there is a newer sense of dharma connected to the rise of yoga, referring to the overcoming of desires and the individual's connectedness with all other beings.[36] This is clearly relevant to our ethical analysis. In Fitzgerald's words, 'the duties of kingship that cause pain and death run counter to the prevailing intellectual trend in ethics in the latter half of the first millennium BC.'[37] Thus, we need to understand the character of Yudhishthira, the son of Dharma, as a representation of a basic 'bipolarity' of dharma. It is clear by all accounts that the breaking of Duryodhana's thigh is also a breaking of the heroic norms, the *kshatradharma*, regulating the kind of warfare that the *Mahabharata* describes. After this unlawful killing of the arch-villain of the Kauravas, there is no turning back and the conflict descends further into irrational and revengeful atrocities, first of all the massacre at night in the Sauptikaparvan.

NOTES

1. For a short and concise discussion, see the 'Introduction', in *The Sauptikaparvan of the Mahabharata* (Oxford: Oxford University Press, 1998), tr. W.J. Johnson.
2. The sons of Pandu are not really his but have different gods for fathers.
3. See in particular Nick Allen, 'Just War in the *Mahabharata*', in Richard Sorabji and David Rodin (eds.), *The Ethics of War: Shared Problems in Different Traditions* (London: Ashgate, 2006), pp. 138-49.
4. *Mahabharata* Book Seven, Dronaparvan, vol. I, ed. and tr. Vaughan Pilikian (New York: NYU Press, 2006), p. 375. Saubhadra is a metronymic for Abhimanyu.
5. See Georges Dumézil, *L' idéologie tripartie des Indo-Européens* (Bruxelles: Latomus, 1958).
6. Georges Dumézil, *Aspects de la fonction guerrière chez les Indo-Européens* (Paris: Presses Universitaires de France, 1956), p. 9.

7. Dumézil, *L' idéologie tripartite*, p. 77.
8. Ibid.
9. Kevin McGrath, *The Sanskrit Hero: Karna in Epic Mahabharata* (Leiden: Brill, 2006).
10. *Mahabharata* Book Two, The Great Hall, tr. Paul Wilmot (New York: NYU Press, 2006), p. 419.
11. Ibid., p. 427.
12. Ibid., p. 435.
13. Ibid., p. 449.
14. Ibid., p. 451.
15. The *Mahabharata*, Book Nine, Shalya, vol. 1, tr. Justin Meiland (New York: NYU Press, 2005), p. 312.
16. Ibid., p. 316.
17. Ibid., vol. 2, p. 44.
18. Ibid., pp. 48-50
19. Ibid., pp. 58-60
20. Ibid., p. 68.
21. Ibid., p. 72.
22. Ibid., p. 312.
23. Ibid., p. 319.
24. Ibid., p. 332.
25. Ibid., p. 336.
26. Ibid., p. 346.
27. Ibid., p. 348.
28. Ibid., p. 352.
29. Ibid., p. 396.
30. Ibid., p. 372.
31. Ibid., p. 374.
32. Maurice Winternitz, *History of Indian Literature*, vol. III, tr. Subhadra Jha (1922, rpt., Delhi: Motilal Banarsidass, 1985), p. 205.
33. Edwin Gerow, 'Bhasa's Urubhanga and Indian Poetics', *Journal of the American Oriental Society*, vol. 105, no. 3 (1985), pp. 405-12.
34. V. Venkatachalam, *Bhasa* (Delhi: Sahitya Publishing, 1986), p. 83.
35. I have used the version of the play contained in *Complete Plays of Bhasa*, text with English tr. and notes by K.P.A. Menon, vol. 1 (Delhi: Nag Publishers, 2003). Another translation of Asvatthama's statement is: 'I go, arrow in hand, on a night attack'. Edwin Gerow, '*Urubhanga*: The Breaking of the Thighs', in Arvind Sharma (ed.), *Essays on the Mahabharata* (1991, rpt., Delhi: Motilal Banarsidass, 2007), p. 82.
36. James L. Fitzgerald, *The Mahabharata. 11. The Book of the Women. 12. The Book of Peace* (Chicago: University of Chicago Press, 2004), p. 101.
37. Ibid., p. 99.

CHAPTER 2

Dispatching *Kafirs* to Hell?

The Languages of Warfare, Politics and Religion in the Delhi Sultanate

RAZIUDDIN AQUIL

> When the imperial army reached the city of that land, the sword of the righteous monarch completely conquered the province.... Much blood was shed. A general invitation was issued to all the beasts and birds of the forest to a continuous feast of meat and drink. In the marriage banquet, at which the Hindus were sacrificed, animals of all kinds ate them to their satisfaction.
>
> AMIR KHUSRAU in his *Khaza'in-ul-Futuh* on the Khalji conquest of Anhilwara, the then capital of Gujarat[1]

> The Muslim Sultan cannot establish the supremacy of Islam in Hindustan unless he makes concerted efforts to overthrow infidelity and destroy its leaders, called Brahmins. He should make a firm resolve to overpower, capture, enslave and degrade the infidels. The full strength of the Sultan and the warriors of Islam should be devoted to religious campaigns and *jihad*.
>
> ZIYA-UD-DIN BARANI'S counsel to the Delhi Sultans in his *Fatawa-i-Jahandari*[2]

Scholars of medieval Indian history are increasingly viewing the eleventh and twelfth centuries as the period of adaptation between expanding the frontier—featuring swift raids, mobile wealth, and long-distance trade—and settled society of the agricultural plains. Large swathes of territories, roughly covering the whole of the subcontinent, witnessed considerable churning. The agricultural plains of north India were gradually brought under a Muslim Sultanate with its base in Delhi, and facilitated by professional armies, built around Turkish slave-soldiers and

Afghan mercenaries on horseback, with loot constituting the foundational basis of economy in the early period of political flux. As things settled down, several other dimensions of economy needed attention. A steady stream of migrants from Central Asia and Iran further consolidated the formation of a new ruling elite. These centuries saw the expansion of agricultural frontier, the establishment of extensive commercial networks, gradual technological change and development of political and religious institutions, even as technologies of warfare and outcomes of military campaigns determined the politics of the time and affected social processes as well.

This essay illustrates the entanglement of the languages of warfare and religion in the making of the political structure of the Delhi Sultanate and argues how much of it could be properly understood if one looks at the processes dispassionately. In doing so, it offers a critical overview of some key themes in Sultanate history and indicates the need to rethink some of the older propositions. Thus, the aim here is twofold: present a synthesis of existing literature and chart fresh vistas for understanding the complexities of religion and politics in the Delhi Sultanate. In a measure, this will be an intervention in the current contestations over the controversial legacies of Muslim rule in India. However, it is important to make it clear at the outset that, unlike the two broad trends, divisive questions will neither be swept away as unimportant nor recommended for abuse by contemporary political propagandists. The intention here is to write a dispassionate history of warfare and religion in the Delhi Sultanate, warfare and religion being two of the most contested terrains in Indian history. There is already a considerable literature on the theme, my debt to which will be evident throughout the pages of this essay, though many of the older interpretations are reconsidered and substantially revised.[3]

EMERGENCE OF ISLAM

A new chapter in the history of the subcontinent begins with the eastward expansion of Islam in the last decade of the twelfth century and the establishment of a series of Islamicate Sultanates. The Ghurid forces of Mu'iz-ud-Din bin Sam, referred to as the *lashkar-i-islam* (literally, army of Islam) in the early sources, overran Ghaznavid Punjab. The Rajput resistance was smothered in the Second Battle of Tarain in 1192. The Muslim army went on to occupy large parts of upper north India. It eliminated the symbols of Rajput power and prestige in the region. Remarkably, there was no general massacre and no major demographic dislocation. Much as the chroniclers celebrated the conquest of new territories, the conquerors themselves preferred minimum use of force and violence. Though iconoclasm may have been a motivating factor for some soldiers, the places of worship were generally plundered for their wealth. Alternatively, their despoliation was aimed at hammering home the point that the old regime was overthrown; it could no longer protect the people and their religious places. The general public was thus made aware that the Turks and their Sultan had established a new, Islamic order. Indeed, the minaret attached to Delhi's congregational mosque, later known as the Qutb Minar, was subsequently perceived as a victory tower. Among the prime targets of Ghurid campaigns were Muslim Ghaznavids as well, but the Muslims of the Sultanate period particularly liked to remember the crushing of the infidels (*kafirs*), especially the army of the Rajput ruler Prithviraj Chauhan, who was referred to as Rai Pithaura.[4]

In their misplaced understanding of the Sultanate as an Islamic state, the ulama (Muslim religious scholars) wanted the Sultans to confront the Hindus of the dominion with the alternative of death or Islam. In a measure, which speaks of the rulers' attempts for rapprochement with non-Muslims, they ignored the pressure tactics of the ulama. The Turks had realized that it was difficult to rule a vast majority of non-Muslim population through a strict adherence to a narrow interpretation of the *shari'at* (Islamic law). Instead, they evolved a broad, secular state law (*zawabit-i-mulki*) with public protestation of respect to the Muslim divines and their institutions.

Significantly enough, the enthronement of Qutb-ud-Din Aybak (ruled CE 1206-10) at Lahore coincided with the election of Chengiz Khan as the great leader of the Mongol hordes. The raids of the Mongols witnessed large-scale devastation in Central and West Asia in the next fifty years. Major centres of Islam like Bukhara and Baghdad were sacked. The subcontinent was yet protected, though Punjab and Sindh were exposed to the threat of a possible onslaught. Escaping the wrath of the Tartars, Islam prospered in the Delhi Sultanate with the name of the caliph still being mentioned in the *khutba* (Friday sermons) and the *sikka* (coins). The period witnessed large-scale immigration of Muslims. A number of Sufi saints had also come to settle here.

The arrival of the Sufis, especially of the Chishti order, ensured that force and violence were not used for converting the general population to Islam. Much as Islamic orthodoxy strove for total annihilation of the *kafirs*, the seemingly liberal approach of the Sufis proved to be more appealing to the early Sultans. The rulers themselves detested the arrogance of the ulama, and felt that the Sufis' position on such questions as the treatment to be meted out to the Hindus, and generally on matters related to the *shari'at*, was more correct. The Sultanate was thus going to have a secular and broad-based polity, though religious ideas and institutions did play important roles. Controversial religious issues which had the potential to break the pluralistic fabric of medieval India did come to the public arena, but in the end sanity prevailed.

In a way it augured well for the history of Islam in India that the earliest Muslim to have been born in the capital city of Delhi after the Turkish conquest went on to become a Chishti Sufi of considerable reputation for syncretistic proclivities. Sheikh Hamid-ud-Din (died 1274) was a disciple and *khalifa*, spiritual successor, of none other than the great Khwaja Mu'in-ud-Din Chishti Ajmeri (died 1236). Mu'in-ud-Din, in turn, was said to have been directed by Prophet Muhammad in a dream in Medina to go to Hindustan. The Khwaja's arrival coincided with the conquest of the Turks. Sufi tradition claims that Mu'in-ud-Din had prophesied Shahab-ud-Din Ghuri's victory in the Second Battle of Tarain in 1192. The Chauhan ruler Rai Pithaura or Prithviraj was said to be harassing the sheikh and his disciples at Ajmer. Later traditions also suggest that the Sufi sheikh had to display his miraculous power to subdue the opponent. The sheikh's charisma won him a large following, and his *khalifas* spread in different directions. Hamid-ud-Din, referred to above, went to live in a village near Nagaur. He cultivated a small plot of land, became a vegetarian, and seemingly led a life conforming to the Hindu environment.

Mu'in-ud-Din Chishti chose a more sophisticated Qutb-ud-Din Bakhtiyar Kaki (died 1235), preceptor (*pir*) of Sheikh Farid-ud-

Din Ganj-i-Shakar (d. 1265), for the cosmopolitan *wilayat*, or spiritual territory, of Delhi. Bakhtiyar Kaki was born in Ush in the province of the Jaxarates, Transoxania, Central Asia. He met Mu'in-ud-Din for the first time in Baghdad, and became his disciple. Amongst the noted Sufis in the Abbasid capital at that time were Sheikh Abdul Qadir Jilani and Sheikh Abun Najib Suhrawardi. Bakhtiyar Kaki, however, followed his *pir* Mu'in-ud-Din, also referred to as the Sultan of Hind, and reached Delhi during the reign of Shams-ud-Din Iltutmish (ruled CE 1211-36). The Sultan welcomed the sheikh and invited him to live in the city. Though he was hesitant initially, he agreed to the ruler's request. Bakhtiyar Kaki had to compete for a space in the spiritual geography of the city. Besides the ulama, quite a few eminent Sufi sheikhs of various orders had come to settle there. Many of them had just arrived following the Mongol invasions in Central Asia and Iran. Bakhtiyar Kaki found the most powerful antagonist in Sheikh-ul-Islam Najm-ud-Din Sughra, a Sufi of his own order. Najm-ud-Din and Kaki's *pir* Mu'in-ud-Din were disciples of the same sheikh, Khwaja Usman Harwani. Najm-ud-Din did not take the growing popularity of Kaki and his influence in political circle kindly.

To prevent the tension between Najm-ud-Din and Bakhtiyar Kaki from escalating further, Mu'in-ud-Din, who was on a visit to Delhi, asked his disciple to leave the place and accompany him to Ajmer.[5] The news of the departure of the saints was perceived as a sign of calamity by the Sultan and the people. They followed the two for miles, crying and wailing. Touched by the grief of the ruler and the ruled alike, Mu'in-ud-Din allowed Kaki to remain in Delhi.[6] As a patron saint of the city, Bakhtiyar Kaki enjoyed prestige and authority, and in a measure influenced Iltutmish's style of governance. We shall return to the question of the significant social and political activities of the Sufis in the concluding part of this essay.

RAZIYA SULTAN

The weakness of the rulers and the supremacy of the nobles were two important features of the period following the death of Iltutmish. Within a decade of his death, the nobles put four of his descendants on the throne and removed them at will. The next twenty years saw the slaves of Iltutmish exterminating his dynasty by executing all the male members of his family. Iltutmish had nominated Raziya as his heir-apparent.[7] Disregarding her claim, the Turkish slave-officers had enthroned Rukn-ud-Din Firuz Shah as the Sultan of Delhi. However, Rukn-ud-Din did not display much interest in matters of governance. Instead of the court, the reins of power got transferred to the harem from where his mother Shah Turkan controlled the affairs of the dominion. According to reports, unleashing a reign of terror, the queen mother started persecuting her detractors. The nobles began to distrust the government, leading to rebellion and disorder.[8] Raziya took advantage of the situation to stake her own claim to the throne. Putting on red garments, usually worn by aggrieved persons seeking justice, she went to the Jama Masjid (the Qubbat-ul-Islam Mosque of Delhi) at the time of the congregational prayer and complained to the people that Shah Turkan had planned to kill her. Invoking the name of her father, she appealed for protection. In a rare example of sensitivity shown by the people of Delhi, the palace was attacked, Shah Turkan was seized and Raziya was placed on the throne. The nobles and the soldiers pledged their allegiance to her. Soon Rukn-ud-Din was imprisoned and put to death.[9]

Several important features marked Raziya's enthronement. The people of Delhi had played a key role in her accession, and their continued support was crucial for her survival. She is reported to have given her tenure as the Sultan the form of a contract, with the people having the right to remove her if she failed in her duties. Further, her enthronement not only vindicated Iltutmish's choice, but also exposed the limits of the power of Islamic orthodoxy. The elevation of a woman to royal authority was seemingly contradictory to Islamic practice. The contemporary chronicler, Minhaj-us-Siraj, himself a distinguished theologian, maintained an ambiguous position on this issue.[10] Later, Sheikh Abdul Haqq Muhaddis Dehlavi expressed surprise at the attitude of the ulama and explained that probably they were scared of the wrath of the Sultan. Indeed, the legends (*sultan-i-azam jalal-ud-duniya wa ud-din*) inscribed on her coins highlighted the wrathful aspects of Muslim sovereignty. Raziya also sought to gain legitimacy by reminding people, through her coins, that she was the daughter of Sultan Iltutmish. Further, she may have placated the ulama through patronage and endowments to mosques and *madrasas* (Islamic schools) in the capital.

Minhaj-us-Siraj thus recorded in his *Tabaqat-i-Nasiri* that Raziya was a great sovereign, sagacious, just, beneficent, the patron of the learned, a dispenser of justice, and the cherisher of her subjects. He added that Raziya was endowed with all the attributes and qualifications necessary for a Muslim Sultan. He, however, put a question mark on her abilities by pointing out that she was not, by virtue of her gender, destined to rule, despite all her excellent qualities.[11] However, even if her gender may have been a great disadvantage in that context, that was not the main cause of her fall. With a view to assuming direct control of affairs, Raziya had thrown off the veil. She used to wear the cloak (*qaba*) and the *kulah* (cap), and ride out in public.[12] The Turks disliked her assertive role in administration. The opposition against her was organized mainly on racial grounds. She had attempted to curb the power of the Turks by appointing non-Turks to important positions. In particular, the favour shown to the Abyssinian Jamal-ud-Din Yaqut proved to be her undoing. Condemnation of the manner in which the black slave Yaqut used to help Raziya in riding the horse or elephant can be found in near-contemporary sources. The alleged romance did not last for long, as the rebels killed Yaqut in a clash.

Though Raziya had suppressed her opponents early in her reign, the powerful provincial governors remained at large. They were, however, not in a position to march to Delhi and capture it. An uprising of the Carmathians, or Ismailis, who had attacked the Jama Masjid of Delhi, was crushed soon after Raziya's enthronement.[13] Thus, even as Raziya's dominion was shrinking, with Rajputs also reasserting themselves, Delhi was secure. However, the rebellion of her own loyal officers proved to be her nemesis. Her tactical marriage (*nikah*) with one of the rebels did not help either. Defeated by an army of the rebels who had enthroned Mu'iz-ud-Din Bahram Shah as the new Sultan, Raziya was captured by the Hindus near Kaithal. She died an ignominious death at their hands.

SULTAN GHIYAS-UD-DIN BALBAN

Rising from the ranks of Iltutmish's slaves, Ghiyas-ud-Din Balban ruled for over forty years from about the middle of the thirteenth century, acting first as *naib* (deputy) of the puppet Shamsi Sultan Nasir-ud-Din Mahmud (ruled 1246-66) and subsequently ascending the throne of Delhi as Sultan (ruled 1266-87) in his own right. Balban had come to the throne at a time when the Mongols had ravaged a major part of the Muslim world. Having sacked Punjab, they were threatening to take Delhi by storm. Balban's aggressive-defensive Mongol policy protected Delhi from the depredation of the Mongol hordes.[14]

Originally dwellers of the steppe region north of China and east of Lake Baikal, the Mongols created an empire which by the close of the thirteenth century covered vast parts of the known world. The subcontinent escaped horrendous massacres of the type that occurred in China, Central Asia, Iran and Russia. Yet, between 1221, when Chengiz Khan first appeared on the bank of the river Indus, and 1398, when Delhi was sacked by Timur, there were numerous incursions. The threat posed by the Mongols, principally in the North-West Frontier and Punjab, but also in Kashmir, was at times considerable. However, most Mongol invasions into India were relatively small, led by second-rate commanders and often ill-timed.[15]

Celebrating the destruction of the Abbasid seat of power at Baghdad, the Mongol leader Halaku Khan had sent his envoys to Delhi in 1259-60. The *naib*, Balban, who was himself a captive of the Tartars not long back, welcomed the guests in typical Mongol fashion. The route that the visitors' cavalcade took was ornamented with severed heads of the rebels from the neighbourhood of Delhi. Their hide was stuffed with straw and was displayed. Besides, 200,000 footmen and 50,000 horsemen were posted along the way. The chronicler Minhaj-us-Siraj records in his *Tabaqat-i-Nasiri* that nothing in particular occurred on the occasion, but exposed to the spectacle of violence, both visual and suggestive, the envoys must have returned with a sufficient idea of Delhi's power and its aggressive intentions.[16]

Further, Balban not only rebuilt and fortified the cities in Punjab and Sindh which had suffered at the hands of the Tartars, but also constructed large forts on the route to the north-west in order to block the Mongol advance into the Sultanate's territories. The Mongols, perceived as the 'fire from hell', were to be checked on the frontier itself. Huge forces were also garrisoned in the forts en route to Punjab, which prevented the penetration of the invaders into Hindustan.[17] Balban, thus, ensured that Delhi did not go the way of Baghdad, even as the Sultan lost his favourite son, Muhammad, who was killed by the Mongols in an engagement at the western frontier. Immigration from Central Asia, Iran and the Middle East continued in his reign; and even erstwhile rulers and princes of those regions, including two Abbasid princes, came to Delhi as refugees. Balban included them in his nobility and established separate localities (*muhallas*) for their residence. In the early seventeenth century, Farishta listed as many as fifteen *muhallas* set up by Balban for his august immigrants.[18]

Significantly, as an all-powerful noble under Nasir-ud-Din Mahmud, Balban, then known as Ulugh Khan, was a devotee of the Chishti Sufi Farid-ud-Din Ganj-i-Shakar.[19] Ali Asghar, himself a descendant of the sheikh, recorded in his early-seventeenth-century text that the saint had married Ulugh Khan's daughter Bibi Huzaira and had six sons and three daughters from her.[20] Amir Khwurd also noted in his more reliable fourteenth-century account that the sheikh had several wives and had five sons and three daughters.[21] The saint's favourite son, Nizam-ud-Din (not to be confused with his spiritual successor Nizam-ud-Din Auliya) had joined Ghiyas-ud-Din Balban's army. He is said to have died fighting the Mongol invaders in Punjab.[22]

Delhi was protected from the Mongol menace, but nearer home the Mewatis or Meos were a constant source of headache. They were accused of indulging in all kinds of crime in the city, including theft, robbery, and molestation, after which they disappeared in the neighbouring forests. Ziya-ud-Din Barani records in his mid-fourteenth-century text *Tarikh-i-Firuzshahi* that the Meos had plundered all the inns in the vicinity, and frequently attack the city at night. Unable to check the problem, a weak Delhi administration ordered the gates of the city to be closed before sunset. No one had the courage to go out of the walled city (identified as the Qila Rai Pithaura) after that time. Those wishing to visit the tombs of the saints or to enjoy the pleasant environs of Hauz-i-Shamsi went at their own risk. The *Tarikh-i-Firuzshahi* notes that the Meos robbed the water-carriers and molested slave girls, who went to fetch water from the tank, even during the day. Balban took a whole year to suppress the miscreants. The forests around Delhi were cut and an estimated 100,000 Meos were put to death. Many military posts (*thanas*) were established and assigned to the Afghan warlords and soldiers. The land allotted for the maintenance of the *thanas* was made tax-free. The city was thus secured from the Meo onslaught. This account of the Meo problem reflects of course the viewpoint of the 'ruling party' or the Delhi administration of the time; Meo narrative will, indeed, have a different story to tell.

The destruction of the rebels in the Ganga-Yamuna Doab and Katehar (Rohilkhand) and the protection of trade routes, especially the road to Awadh, were other achievements of Balban which brought great prestige to the throne of Delhi.[23] He also checked the political upheavals in the capital by providing a veneer of divinity to his rule. He called himself the 'Shadow of God on Earth' (*zillullah*), and proclaimed that kingship was the vice-regency of God (*niyabat-i-khudai*). Tracing his genealogy to the mythical Afrasiyab, the Sultan emulated the customs and ways of life of the pre-Islamic Sassanid rulers of Persia. Elaborate court rituals, including prostration (*sijda*) and kissing of feet (*paibos*) were introduced. The nobles meekly submitted to his wishes. Those who refused to toe the line were eliminated, either silently or with a ruthless display of his power in public. Seen against the backdrop of the anarchy in the aftermath of the death of Iltutmish, Balban's measures restored the authority of the crown and provided peace and tranquillity to the common people.[24]

COMPOSITION OF NOBILITY AND TERRITORIAL EXPANSION

The Turkish rulers brought with them two institutions. One was the *iqta*, or assignment of land or its revenue, in some cases in return for military service. The other was the military slave, variously referred to as *mamluk*, *ghulam* or *banda*. However, the slave status bore none of the degrading connotations associated with other types of slavery: Turkish slaves were highly prized by their masters. They were converted to Islam, imparted a rigorous training in contemporary technologies of warfare and were not employed in any menial capacity.[25] The first century of the Delhi Sultanate was previously designated as a Mamluk Sultanate or slave dynasty, as an elite corps of Turkish slaves provided military leadership, provincial governors and great officers. However, apart from Iltutmish and Balban, no other prominent member of the emerging Sultanate was technically a slave.[26] Hence, the nomenclatures 'slave kings' and 'slave dynasty' are not entirely accurate.

The rise of the Khaljis broke the hold on Sultanate politics previously enjoyed by Turkish slaves and their progeny.[27] The Khaljis were also ethnic Turks, but they had entered the Sultanate as free men; yet the emergence of the Khalji dynasty did not spell the end for Turkish slaves. Though Turkish nobility of varying antecedents still dominated, new elements were increasingly applying pressure.[28] This is reflected in the advocacy for restricting offices to persons of the so-called 'high-birth' by historian and political theorist Ziya-ud-Din Barani.

For various reasons, including Mongol invasions, the first century of the Delhi Sultanate did not see any large-scale expansion after the initial territorial gains. It was only after the consolidation of the Sultanate's early conquests that attention was paid to the extension of its boundaries, especially under Sultan Ala-ud-Din Khalji (ruled 1296-1316). His successor, Sultan Qutb-ud-Din Mubarak Shah Khalji (ruled 1316-20), continued the campaign for the conquest of Devagiri in the Deccan and annexed it to the Sultanate. Soon, the Tughluqs captured power in Delhi with Ghiyas-ud-Din Tughluq (ruled 1320-5) ascending the throne after a violent struggle with the usurper Khusrau Khan. Subsequently, Muhammad bin Tughluq (ruled 1325-51) led a vigorous campaign of conquest and consolidation in large parts of the subcontinent.[29]

Apart from the continued Mongol threat to the Sultanate,[30] the rise of the Khaljis and the Tughluqs created upheavals in the ruling elite more generally. Soon after his accession, Ala-ud-Din Khalji brought in new elements in the aristocracy. Reflecting the concerns of the older group, Barani later trivialized the change that was taking place. He charged that musicians, barbers and cooks were recruited to positions of power. He was equally hostile to non-Muslims, condemned as *kafirs*, occupying key posts in the Sultanate government.[31]

POLITICAL THEORIES

Recent researches on the question of norms of governance under Muslims rulers of medieval India have called for a clear-cut distinction between the meanings of *shari'at* for Muslim jurists, who were bound by law books, and for philosophers and intellectuals, who wanted to break free from the clutches of Sunni Muslim orthodoxy. The *shari'at* in early *adab* writings, or treatises on principles and practices of government, generally referred to as 'mirrors for princes', was informed by the jurists making its scope narrow and theological. Though the authors of early texts on norms of governance within Islam wrote from different vantage points and drew on the ancient Greek and Iranian texts as well, for them defence of the *shari'at* and keeping alive of religion were among the most important duties of a ruler. In other words, Muslim law as interpreted by the *ulama* was to be the guiding principle for governance.[32]

Early Indo-Muslim works on political ideals such as Fakhr-i-Mudabbir's *Adab-ul-Harb* (early thirteenth century) and Ziya-ud-Din Barani's *Fatawa-i-Jahandari* (mid-fourteenth century) extended this genre of 'mirrors for princes'. However, it may be noted that despite Barani's invocation of the hereditary principles and the appropriation of non-Islamic Iranian or Indian political traditions, he is often accused of serving the narrow sectarian interests of the early Islamic regime. Yet it is suggested with some satisfaction that Barani's exclusionist ideas hardly influenced the policies of even the most powerful of the Delhi Sultans. Unlike *adab*, another set of texts on political theory, called *akhlaq*, advised the ideal ruler to ensure the well-being of people of varied social and religious backgrounds and not of Muslims alone. The influence of these much more inclusive texts could be later seen in Mughal India. Further, despite cases of intolerance, considerable appropriations were taking place in the realm of popular culture, religious traditions and institutions of governance. Many Persianate-Muslim institutions were adapted by the 'Hindu' states which emerged in the medieval period, as could be seen in the case of Vijayanagara.

DEVOTIONAL MOVEMENTS: ISLAMIC MYSTICISM

Aspiring for a direct communion between God and man, Islamic mysticism or Sufism reached the subcontinent when it had entered an important phase of its history—the organization of *silsilas* or orders. Among the Sufi orders, only two—Chishti and

Suhrawardi—were the really important ones in the Delhi Sultanate. They came almost simultaneously with the founding of the Sultanate. Soon, the spiritual geography of the subcontinent was dotted with large *khanqahs* (spacious buildings with living apartments), smaller *jama'atkhanas* (hospices with dormitories for disciples), and crowded *dargahs* (tombs) of the Sufis of different lineages.

Historians have claimed that the institutions of the Sufis have contributed a great deal to the making of the harmonious culture of the subcontinent. However, Sufi activities were not about secularism in the modern sense. The larger issues included (a) miracle or *karamat* as a source of authority, (b) relations with the Sultans and nobles, (c) Sufi music, cultural appropriations and possibilities of defying the writ of orthodoxy even while remaining within the fold of Islam, and (d) attitude towards non-Muslims and issues of conversion and Islamization.[33]

A recurring theme in the Sufi literature, both biographies (*tazkiras*) and compilations of discourses (*malfuzat*), is the authoritative position of the Sufi sheikhs in the society and politics of the Delhi Sultanate. An important source of the sheikh's authority was his perceived ability to perform miracles. The Sufi sources are also replete with stories of incredible feats of the saints. This is as true of Nizam-ud-Din's authoritative discourses as of many other 'popular' Sufi writings from the fourteenth century. Indeed, the two main Chishti texts, *Fawa'id-ul-Fu'ad* and *Khayr-ul-Majalis*,[34] are full of fantastic anecdotes of miracles attributed to the Sufis of the past. Nizam-ud-Din himself believed in miracle as an integral part of Sufi discipline, but he was against those who advertised their own ability to perform them. For him, it was obligatory for Muslim saints to hide their supernatural exploits and binding on prophets to display them. The sheikh classified miracles into four categories: *mu'ajiza* (miracles of the prophet), *karamat* (marvels of the saints), *ma'unat* (paranormal feats of saintly people) and *istidraj* (occasional tricks performed by an obstinate sinner or magician). He also believed in the power of the evil eye (*nazr*) and black-magic (*jadu/sehr*). He criticized the rationalist sect, *mu'tazila*, for treating them merely as fancy ideas and not a reality. A liberal, tolerant approach towards other religious traditions did not make the Chishtis rational. Chishti Sufism was a part of Sunni Islam and, in a measure, it followed Imam Ghazali in attempting to wed theology with mysticism and in condemning the rationalists or philosophers. For this purpose, the use of political power was not abhorred.[35]

Some scholars have suggested that Sufis, particularly the early Chishtis, kept themselves away from politics and government of their times, for they believed that involvement in politics led to materialism and worldliness which they wished to avoid. A careful perusal of the sources, however, reveals that the above formulation is not sustainable. In theory, the Chishtis may have felt the need to keep their distance from the king and his nobles, but in practice this was not always the case. We have examples from the careers of leading Chishti saints of their proximity to political power in Delhi, as in the case of Qutb-ud-Din Bakhtiyar Kaki and his companions, even as they resisted becoming veritable courtiers. Differences over the question of power and patronage in the *wilayat*, spiritual or political territory, led in some cases to severe conflict between the Sufis and the monarchs in the Sultanate capital. Sheikh Nizam-ud-Din's troubles with Qutb-ud-Din Mubarak Shah Khalji and Ghiyas-ud-Din Tughluq have been much discussed in Sufi narratives. Alternatively, examples of their collaboration abound. Sufi literature particularly highlights the cordial relations between Nizam-ud-Din and Ala-ud-Din Khalji, after the initial suspicions of each other's intentions were set to rest. Thus, the relationship between Sufis and rulers was complex, and reveals that the mystics were not indifferent to the context in which they flourished.

The Sufi sheikhs were not ascetics. They were supposed to live amongst the people and help mitigate their sufferings. For Nizam-ud-Din Auliya, *tark-i-duniya*, or renunciation of the world, did not mean that one should wear a *langota* or loincloth and set-off to live in the forest. Shunning all the anxieties of attachment to this world, whether private and public, the Sufis called for soul searching, remembrance of God beyond the ritual prayers of the mosques, meditation in solitude and wandering around as dervishes to Muslim cities and non-Muslim or semi-Islamized hinterlands. At the end of it, they reappeared with claims of personally experiencing the truth of Islam, of the loving God and the righteousness of the path of the Prophet (strengthening here the ulama's position). As religious exemplars, then, the Sufis were supposed to guide Muslims, ignoring or tolerating human weaknesses, and also bringing non-Muslims to the fold of Islam. Their claims for religious and, at times, political authority could run them into trouble with the ulama who interrogated their religious practices and resorted to violence to keep them in check. Music was one such contested practice.

In the opinion of some scholars, interest in music, among the authorized forms of remembrance (*zikr*) in the Chishti tradition, distinguished it from other *silsilas* such as the Suhrawardis, their major mystical rivals in the Sultanate period. It is suggested that the Chishti practice of *sama* or *qawwali* served a valuable practical function: it separated the Chishtis from the Suhrawardis, and also opposed them to the official ulama. Thus, music became, if not the monopoly of the Chishtis, the pre-eminent symbol crystallizing their position. Though the difference between the Chishti and Suhrawardi approaches to music is generally known, the Suhrawardi attitude towards the musical assemblies has not been explored properly. Several leading Suhrawardis of the Sultanate period were fond of devotional music. Also, within the Chishti order there were differences over the use of instruments and performance by female singers. While Fakhr-ud-Din Zarradi permitted the use of the drum and tambourine in music assemblies, his preceptor Nizam-ud-Din Auliya did not recommend the instruments. Nizam-ud-Din was also against the participation of female *qawwals*, but his disciples did employ both instruments and female singers in their music assemblies. The ambivalence is also reflected in later reports, which attributed the invention of several musical instruments to Nizam-ud-Din's closest disciple and courtier, Amir Khusrau.

Music then as a neat marker of Chishti practice as against Suhrawardis and other Sufi orders will not hold. Similarly, the Shattaris, a branch of the Suhrawardis, were close to the Chishtis in their preference for music as a spiritual exercise. Nor is the use of Hindi verses typical of the Chishtis. The Rishi Sufis of Kashmir, too, used non-Arabic vocal *zikr* formulae. Like the Chishtis, the Shattaris were also open to the idea of adopting spiritual practices belonging to non-Muslim mystical traditions. It has traditionally been argued that the Chishti attitude towards the doctrine of *wahdat-ul-wujud* (monism as a reality) propounded by Ibn Arabi was an important marker of difference between the Chishtis and Suhrawardis in the Sultanate period and between Chishtis and Naqshbandis in the Mughal era. It is also suggested that the Chishti belief in the *wujudi* doctrine brought it very close to various streams of non-Muslim mystical traditions, and, therefore, tolerant and accommodative.

This brings us to questions concerning Chishti attitude towards non-Muslims, conversion, Islamization, claims of local Muslim communities converting to Islam, and the long-term cultural accretion around the shrines. There is a vast body of literature on these issues, both in early Sufi writings and later secondary sources, which historians have tended to ignore. Sufi literature clearly reveals how the Chishtis were not averse to the idea of conversion of non-Muslims to Islam, either directly at the hands of a leading *pir*, or through a long process of Islamic acculturation in localities made sacred by the shrines of medieval saints. The sources also record a large number of anecdotes of miraculous encounters between Sufis and non-Muslim miracle-workers or spiritual power-holders such as yogis, *sannyasis*, gurus, and Brahmins. Provoked by the competing claims to territorial authority, these stories narrated by Nizam-ud-Din Auliya and his disciples are significant for a more informed understanding of the religious complex and the processes of diffusion of Islam. Even if reports of miracles cannot be proved rationally, in recounting them Sufi writers and biographers were celebrating the image of the saints as propagators of Islam wherever they settled down. Such reports appear in both the 'authoritative' texts and the so-called 'spurious' literature and are important for understanding Sufi tradition on its own terms. Contrary to the modern political ideals advanced by the secularists and imposed on the past, Chishtis have long celebrated the Islamizing role of their preceptors led by Khwaja Mu'in-ud-Din Chishti. A critical, dispassionate appreciation requires that even as exaggerated accounts of conversion are questioned, Sufis' interest in conversion and the spread of Islam be recognized. This is not the case with much of modern historical writings.[36]

In this context, mention may also be made of the court-poet and closest disciple of Nizam-ud-Din Auliya, Amir Khusrau, who is much admired in modern secularist scholarship for his 'patriotism' and other such virtues expected from a good Muslim. However, his court-chronicles are full of hostile references to the

Hindus, condemning them as *kafirs* or infidels. Khusrau celebrated the Sultan washing the earth clean with the blood of the impure idol-worshipping Hindus whom he also referred to as the 'pharaohs of infidelity'. Ignoring Khusrau's reports on the countless infidels being sent to hell for the satisfaction of the Sultans, historians highlight his patriotism by quoting all the nice sentiments expressed by him about the goodness of the land of Hindustan (often confused with the whole of India) and achievements of its people in various fields. However, Khusrau's glorification of Hindustan might have been related to the Muslim supremacy and splendour of Islam. The poet appreciated the reports that the strong men of Hind were trodden under the foot and were ready to pay tribute, and that Islam was triumphant and idolatry subdued. Khusrau was convinced that religious truth was to be found in Islam alone, reflecting the consensus prevailing in the contemporary Muslim society. Many Chishtis, indeed, believed in the superiority of Islam over other religious traditions and took considerable pain to establish that.

Nizam-ud-Din Auliya's another disciple and courtier, Ziya-ud-Din Barani certainly did not differ with Khusrau on this question. It is important to note, however, that Khusrau's approach towards Brahmins worshipping the sun, stones and some animals was different from that of Barani. For the latter, all these smacked of polytheism, while Khusrau explained that these are not considered as similar to God, but only a part of His creation. Khusrau would go to the extent of saying that as a religious group Hindus were better than many others, including Christians. Evidently, there is a need to de-sanitize modern histories of Sufi traditions by taking into account all the evidence and not one set of them only.

However, as several historians have highlighted, Sufi activities in the Indian environment were not always marked by conflict. Interactions between diverse religio-intellectual traditions at various levels were distinguished by the concern to learn about/from each other. This is reflected in music, painting, architecture, growth and development of vernacular literature, and evolution of 'syncretistic' communities that incorporated beliefs and practices common to Islam and other religious currents. A particularly remarkable development in Sufi circles was the popularity of Hindu themes in Hindi (Hindavi) poetry written by Sufis. Sufism also developed several offshoots, absorbing some local Hindu features, notably in cults such as Qalandars, Madaris, and Haidaris. These locally influenced Sufi orders cared little for recommended Islamic practices. The violation of Islamic norms and the absorption of the evidently anti-Islamic features were blatant. It was the Sufic belief in unity in multiplicity, *wahdat-ul-wujud*, which provided the doctrinal basis for these developments in the process of religious synthesis and cultural amalgamation. The Bhakti saints asserted the fundamental unity of Hindus and Turks, despite political differences and religious tensions. The influence of the ideology of *wahdat-ul-wujud* was particularly strong in the late fifteenth and early sixteenth centuries, when figures like saint-poet Kabir and the founder of Sikhism, Guru Nanak, could attract wide following even as they transcended conventional boundaries.[37]

In areas undergoing agrarian settlement, Sufis played a key role as agents of conversion and Islamicization, serving as mediators of both worldly and divine powers and contributing to the emergence of large Muslim populations over the centuries in regions such as western Punjab and eastern Bengal.[38] In this context it is important to note that whereas Nizam-ud-Din Auliya denied the value of the use of force to convert the *qaum* or community of the Hindus to Islam and, instead, recommended ways to win their heart,[39] his closest disciple Amir Khusrau wrote in the violent language of Islam for the satisfaction of his political patron, Ala-ud-Din Khalji: 'He (the Sultan) made the killing of all Hindus, who were out of the pale of Islam, such an obligation on the infidel-smiting sword (*zulfiqar*) that should Muslim heretics (*rafizis*, or Shias) in these days even nominally demand their rights, the pure Sunnis would swear in the name of this rightful Caliph of God.'[40] As is indicated above, Khusrau's colleague Ziya-ud-Din Barani also spoke in a language which might be termed in modern times as communal or anti-Hindu.[41]

Clearly many forms of Islam, including violent and peaceful, were already taking shape in the Delhi Sultanate. The Sultans struggled to keep the contradictory impulses and agendas in check, even as they themselves needed the support of Muslim men of religion to justify their conquests and rule. So, in one instance *kafirs* could be ordered to be sent to hell, in another they could be treated as *zimmis* or *ahl-i-kitab* (People of the

Book) who were to be protected on payment of a discriminatory tax, *jizya*, and in yet another case they could be invited to share power as ministers and governors in the Muslim Sultanate, beginning with the incorporation of revenue officials at the local level. Context-specific inquiries of respective cases of hatred, tolerance and sharing can lead to a more informed understanding of the divergent tendencies.

NOTES

1. 'The Campaigns of 'Alauddin Khalji, Being the English Translation of "The Khaza'inul Futuh" of Amir Khusrau', in K.A. Nizami (ed.), *Politics and Society during the Early Medieval Period: Collected Works of Mohammad Habib*, vol. 2 (New Delhi: People's Publishing House, 1981), pp. 181-2.
2. Mohammad Habib and Afsar Umar Salim Khan, *The Political Theory of the Delhi Sultanate, Including the Translation of Ziyauddin Barani's Fatawa-i-Jahandari, circa 1358-59 AD* (Allahabad: Kitab Mahal, n.d.), p. 46.
3. The exercise here is similar to Shahid Amin's call for a non-sectarian study of contested historical legacies and traditions in his ongoing work on the legend of Salar Ma'sud Ghazi, see Shahid Amin, 'On Retelling the Muslim Conquest of North India', in Partha Chatterjee and Anjan Ghosh (eds.), *History and the Present* (New Delhi: Permanent Black, 2002), pp. 24-43. For an older account of the rise of the Delhi Sultanate, see A.B.M. Habibullah, *The Foundation of the Muslim Rule in India* (Lahore: Sh. Muhammad Ashraf, 1945) and more generally, Mohammad Habib and K.A. Nizami (eds.), *A Comprehensive History of India*, vol. V, Part One, *The Delhi Sultanate* (1970, rpt., New Delhi: People's Publishing House, 1992). Important recent works include, Andre Wink, *Al-Hind, The Making of the Indo-Islamic World*, vol. 2: *The Slave Kings and the Islamic Conquest, 11th-13th Centuries* (Leiden: E.J. Brill, 1997); Peter Jackson, *The Delhi Sultanate: A Political and Military History* (Cambridge: Cambridge University Press, 1999); and Sunil Kumar, *The Emergence of the Delhi Sultanate, 1192-1286* (New Delhi: Permanent Black, 2007). Catherine B. Asher and Cynthia Talbot, *India Before Europe* (Cambridge: Cambridge University Press, 2006) offers a fine synthesis of the political and cultural history of medieval India before European intervention.
4. The above paragraph is largely derived from an earlier discussion of the material in Raziuddin Aquil, 'From *Dar-ul-Harb* to *Dar-ul-Islam*? Chishti Sufi Accounts and the Emergence of Islam in the Delhi Sultanate', in Satish Saberwal and Mushirul Hasan (eds.), *Assertive Religious Identities: India and Europe* (New Delhi: Manohar, 2006), pp. 59-84.

5. Amir Khwurd, *Siyar-ul-Auliya* (Islamabad: Markaz Tahqiqat-i-Farsi Iran wa Pakistan, 1978), p. 64.
6. Ibid., 65.
7. Maulana Minhaj-ud-din Abu-'Umar-i-'Usman [Minhaj-us-Siraj], *Tabaqat-i-Nasiri: A General History of the Muhammadan Dynasties of Asia, Including Hindustan*, translated from original Persian manuscripts by Major H.G. Raverty, 2 vols., rpt. (New Delhi: Oriental Books Reprint Corporation, 1970), vol. 1, p. 638.
8. Ibid., vol. 1, pp. 630-2.
9. Ibid., pp. 635-6.
10. Ibid., pp. 638-9.
11. Ibid., pp. 637-8.
12. Ibid., p. 643.
13. Ibid., p. 646.
14. Ziya-ud-Din Barani, *Tarikh-i-Firuzshahi*, British Museum Ms. 6376, OIOC, British Library, London, fols. 23b-24a.
15. For the details of the Mongol threat, see Jackson, *The Delhi Sultanate*, chapter 6.
16. For a detailed account, see *Tabaqat-i-Nasiri*, vol. 2, pp. 854-9.
17. *Tarikh-i-Firuzshahi*, fol. 28b.
18. Muhammad Qasim Farishta, *Tarikh-i-Farishta*, Urdu translation by Abdul Hai Khwaja, vol. 1 (Deoband: Maktaba Millat, 1983), p. 280.
19. *Siyar-ul-Auliya*, pp. 89-90. See also Shaikh Jamali, *Siyar-ul-Arifin*, Ms., IO Islamic 1313, OIOC, British Library, London, fols. 56b-57a; Ali Asghar, *Jawahir-i-Faridi* (Lahore: Victoria Press, 1884), pp. 204, 214-15. For Balban's religiosity and his veneration of Sufi saints generally, see *Tarikh-i-Firuzshahi*, fols. 21b-22a.
20. See *Jawahir-i-Faridi*, pp. 215-18; also Maulwi Ghulam Sarwar, *Khazinat-ul-Asfiya*, vol. I (Kanpur: Newal Kishore, n.d.), p. 301.
21. *Siyar-ul-Auliya*, pp. 76, 195.
22. Ibid., pp. 100, 200.
23. *Tarikh-i-Firuzshahi*, fols. 26a-28a, 38a-45a.
24. Ibid., fols. 13b-17b.
25. Sunil Kumar, 'When Slaves were Nobles: The Shamsi *Bandagan* in the Early Delhi Sultanate', *Studies in History*, vol. 10 (1994), pp. 23–52. Also see Indrani Chatterjee and Richard M. Eaton (eds.), *Slavery and South Asian History* (Bloomington: Indiana University Press, 2006).
26. The older propositions have reappeared in Wink, *Al-Hind: The Making of the Indo-Islamic World*, vol. 2, *The Slave Kings and the Islamic Conquest*.
27. For an earlier account of the rule of the Khalji Sultans, see K.S. Lal, *History of the Khaljis* (Delhi, 1967).
28. For a study of the origins and early history of the Sultanate ruling elite, see, Irfan Habib, 'Formation of the Sultanate Ruling Class of the

Thirteenth Century', in idem, ed., *Medieval India I, Researches in the History of India, 1200-1750* (rpt., New Delhi: Oxford University Press, 2002), pp. 1-21. For a review of political and institutional factors leading to social change, see Iqtidar Husain Siddiqui, 'Social Mobility in the Delhi Sultanate', in Habib (ed.), *Medieval India* I, pp. 22-48.

29. For a traditional account of the rule of the Tughluq Sultans, see Agha Mahdi Husain, *Tughluq Dynasty* (Delhi: S. Chand, 1976).
30. For a detailed account of the continued invasions of the Mongol hordes in the fourteenth century, see Jackson, *The Delhi Sultanate*, chapter 11.
31. For more on Barani's observations regarding the position of non-Muslims in the Delhi Sultanate and his suggestions regarding the treatment to be meted out to them, see his *Fatawa-i-Jahandari*, ed. Afsar Salim Khan (Lahore: Research Society of Pakistan, 1972). Also see Raziuddin Aquil, *In the Name of Allah* (Delhi: Penguin-Viking, 2009), chapter 3.
32. This paragraph and discussion of related themes in the next are based on my reading of Muzaffar Alam's important work, *The Languages of Political Islam in India, circa 1200-1800* (New Delhi: Permanent Black, 2004).
33. Aquil, 'From *Dar-ul-Harb* to *Dar-ul-Islam?*'. For an up to date and analytically-oriented synthesis on the growth and development of Islamic mystical tradition in the Abbasid Caliphate and its spread to many parts of the Muslim world during the period between the ninth and the twelfth centuries, see Ahmet T. Karamustafa, *Sufism: The Formative Period*, The New Edinburgh Islamic Surveys (Edinburgh: Edinburgh University Press, 2007). For a synthesis of material on the history of Chishti Sufism, see Carl W. Ernst and Bruce B. Lawrence, *Sufi Martyrs of Love: The Chishti Order in South Asia and Beyond* (New York: Palgrave Macmillan, 2002).
34. *Fawa'id-ul-Fu'ad*, Conversations of Sheikh Nizam-ud-Din Auliya, compiled by Amir Hasan Sijzi. Persian text with an Urdu translation by Khwaja Hasan Sani Nizami (New Delhi: Urdu Academy, 1990); *Khayr-ul-Majalis*, Conversations of Sheikh Nasir-ud-Din Chiragh-i-Dilli, compiled by Hamid Qalandar, ed. K.A. Nizami (Aligarh: Muslim University, 1959).
35. For a fuller discussion of relevant issues, see Raziuddin Aquil (ed.), *Sufism and Society in Medieval India*, Debates in Indian History and Society Series (New Delhi: Oxford University Press, 2010).
36. Also see, Raziuddin Aquil, 'Conversion in Chishti Sufi Literature (13th-14th Centuries)', *Indian Historical Review*, vol. 24, nos. 1-2 (1997-98), pp. 70-94.
37. For related discussions, see Raziuddin Aquil, *Sufism, Culture and Politics: Afghans and Islam in Medieval North India* (New Delhi: Oxford University Press, 2007), especially chapters 5 and 6.

38. See Richard Eaton's valuable explorations in the area, *Essays on Islam and Indian History* (New Delhi: Oxford University Press, 2002) and *The Rise of Islam and the Bengal Frontier* (New Delhi: Oxford University Press, 1994). For an older Muslim assessment of difficulties involving Islam in India, see Aziz Ahmad, *Studies in Islamic Culture in Indian Environment* (Oxford: Clarendon Press, 1964).
39. *Fawa'id-ul-Fu'ad*, vol. 4, 40th Meeting.
40. Amir Khusrau, *Khaza'in-ul-Futuh (The Campaigns of 'Alauddin Khalji)*, pp. 189-90.
41. Also see, Aquil, *In the Name of Allah*, chapter 3.

CHAPTER 3

India's Military Revolution

The View from Early Sixteenth-century Deccan*

RICHARD M. EATON

In recent decades, historians have written of a worldwide 'Military Revolution' that took place in the centuries following the fourteenth.[1] Such a notion has in turn prompted several lines of inquiry. Some have tried to locate the moment in time when this revolution occurred in particular regions.[2] Others have sought to identify and compare the various effects that the advent, spread and use of gunpowder had in different socio-political environments across the planet.[3] The present essay explores the little-studied Battle of Raichur (1520), with a view to evaluating the nature and timing of the Military Revolution in South Asia. Raichur occupies the heart of an exceptionally fertile tract in India's Deccan Plateau—the so-called 'Raichur Doab'—which lies between the Tungabhadra and Krishna rivers (see Figure 3.1). For several centuries prior to 1520, the Bahmani sultans to the north of the Doab and the kings of Vijayanagara to the south repeatedly fought over access to the Doab's economic resources.[4] Control of the fortified city of Raichur figured in all of these struggles. The battle in question was also a prelude to

*This essay stems from an ongoing collaboration between the author and Phillip B. Wagoner, focussing on the architecture of the contested sites in the sixteenth-century Deccan. It draws on my earlier essay, '"Kiss my Foot" Said the King: Firearms, Diplomacy, and the Battle for Raichur, 1520', *Modern Asian Studies*, vol. 43, no. 1 (2009). I wish to thank Lois Kain for preparing the map of the Deccan Plateau that accompanies this essay.

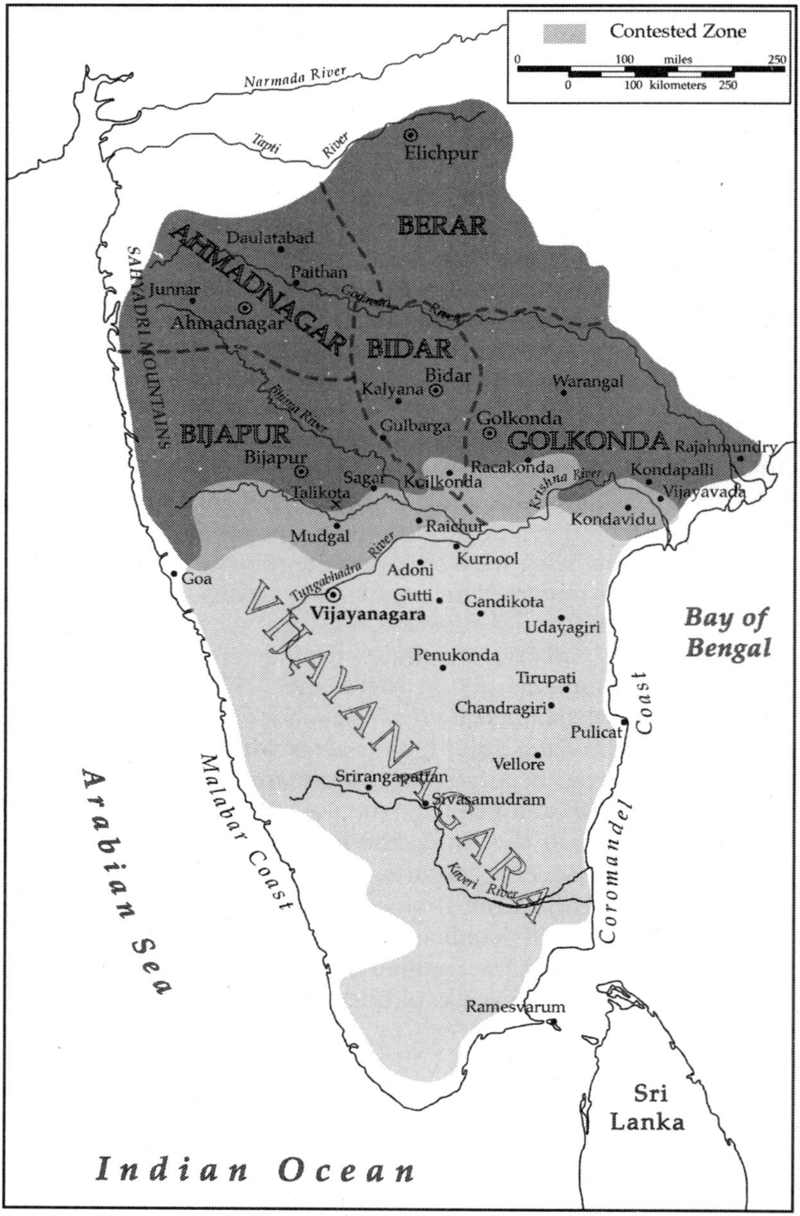

Figure 3.1: Map of Deccan

the more famous Battle of Talikota (1565), a conflict that permanently reconfigured the geopolitics of the Deccan Plateau.

BACKGROUND

The Raichur Doab had been a contested region even before the Bahmani and Vijayanagara states came into being. In the twelfth and thirteenth centuries, the tract lay at the conjuncture of three regional powers—the Hoysala kings of Dwarasamudra, the Yadava kings of Devagiri, and the Kakatiya kings of Warangal. In 1294, a subordinate of the last monarch of the Kakatiya dynasty seized the Raichur Doab from Yadava control and built the imposing complex of walls and gates that encircle Raichur's present core. With their massive slabs of finely dressed granite, these walls were in their own day considered an engineering marvel; even today some local residents regard them as the work of gods, not men. They are certainly the most impressive of any Kakatiya fortifications still standing, apart from those in Warangal, the dynasty's capital.

Notwithstanding its strength, Raichur's fort got swept into the general chaos that engulfed the Deccan in the early fourteenth century following invasions by armies of the Delhi Sultanate. After the collapse of the Kakatiya state in 1323, Sultan Muhammad bin Tughluq (ruled 1325-51) systematically colonized much of the northern Deccan with settlers transplanted from north India. At the same time, he sub-contracted governance of much of the central and southern Deccan to local client-chiefs. Administration of the Raichur Doab appears to have been assigned to a chief who, appointed *amir* (commander) by the Delhi Sultan in 1327, led an anti-Tughluq uprising nine years later. This rebel *amir* was likely Harihara Sangama, a Kannada chieftain known to have been in Tughluq imperial service in the 1330s.[5] By 1347, when Delhi lost control of all its Deccan possessions to anti-Tughluq rebels, Harihara and his brothers had carved out a new state centred on the city of Vijayanagara, located directly south of the Raichur Doab on the southern banks of the Tungabhadra River.

Raichur, however, did not long remain in southerners' hands. In the confusion surrounding the expulsion of imperial forces in 1347, the Doab apparently fell to the other power that simultaneously arose on the ashes of Tughluq imperialism in the Deccan, the Bahmani Sultanate (1347-1538). Ruling from a series of capitals located to the north of the Raichur Doab—Daulatabad, Gulbarga, and Bidar—the Bahmani Sultans claimed the territory clear down to the Tungabhadra River, which included the Raichur Doab. Yet, the fact that Vijayanagara's founders seem to have held the Doab *before* Vijayanagara's creation formed an important basis for the southern state's repeated claim to the region. For the next century and a half, rulers of Vijayanagara and the Bahmani sultanate fought bitterly for control of this agriculturally rich tract. For most of this period, however, the greater part of the Doab remained under Bahmani control, despite major invasions launched by Vijayanagara's kings in 1362, 1378, 1398, and 1443.[6] From 1444, and possibly from as early as 1398, those kings were even forced to make annual tributary payments to the Bahmani treasury.[7]

In 1468-9, capitalizing on new engineering technology imported from north India and the Middle East, the Bahmani authorities built an entirely new wall around Raichur's old Kakatiya fortifications, complete with an outer moat, numerous bastions, and imposing gates on the city's eastern and western ends.[8] By this time, however, the dynasty had begun experiencing crippling factional struggles within its ruling elite. On one side were the 'Deccanis', or nobles descended from the original north Indian migrants who had settled the upper Deccan in the 1320s. And on the other were the so-called 'Westerners' (*gharbian*), or immigrants freshly recruited from the Middle East, especially the Persian-speaking world of Iran and Central Asia.[9] Sectarian rivalries reinforced ethnic and linguistic differences between the two factions, as most Westerners were Shi'i Muslims, and most Deccanis were Sunnis.

By the 1480s and 1490s, the Deccani-Westerner tensions had so intensified that the Bahmani sovereign, Sultan Mahmud (ruled 1482-1518) could no longer command absolute loyalty among his most powerful nobles, some of whom began establishing *de facto* independent states within his domain. One of these was Yusuf 'Adil Khan, an immigrant from Iran who in 1490 carved out a new state of Bijapur from the Bahmani Sultanate's western and southern districts, which included the Raichur Doab. Although

Yusuf continued to pay formal homage to Sultan Mahmud, his audacious actions alarmed other independent nobles one of whom sought to weaken Bijapur's position by inviting Vijayanagara's forces to invade Raichur. Accordingly, in 1492 the southern state invaded the Doab and momentarily seized Raichur city, although Yusuf 'Adil Khan managed to retrieve the fort later that same year. Until as late as 1515 Sultan Mahmud's name continued to appear on Raichur's inscriptions as the region's legitimate sovereign, maintaining the fiction that Yusuf 'Adil Khan and his successors in Bijapur were merely Bahmani 'governors'. Nonetheless, Bijapur's rulers from Yusuf onwards behaved as though they were independent sultans, as indeed later chroniclers styled them.[10]

Despite prolonged northern hegemony over the Raichur Doab, by the first decade of the sixteenth century the balance of power began to tilt toward the south for the first time since 1347. By 1500, the integrity of the Bahmani state had already become seriously compromised, and by the second decade of the sixteenth century the kingdom had disintegrated into five *de facto* successor-states. This meant that any invasion of Raichur from the south would now be met not by the full might of the old Bahmani sultanate, but by the 'Adil Shahi rulers of Bijapur, who could field armies only a fraction the size of those of its parent state. What is more, Bijapur inherited the same Westerner-Deccani factionalism that had plagued the Bahmani sultanate, which compromised its socio-political cohesiveness.

To the south of Raichur, meanwhile, a vigorous new dynasty of kings, the Tuluva, had arisen in the sprawling metropolis of Vijayanagara. In 1509, Vijayanagara's throne was occupied by the famous Krishna Raya (or 'Krishna Deva Raya', ruled 1509-29), whose twenty years of rule are widely acclaimed as having seen the acme of Vijayanagara's power and glory. Between 1509 and 1520, while the Deccan north of the Raichur Doab fragmented into five mutually quarrelling states, Krishna Raya conquered and annexed the entire peninsula from the southern edge of the Raichur Doab nearly to Cape Comorin, thereby amassing immense manpower and capital resources, which, in turn, enabled him to make serious effort to regain Doab from the control of Bijapur.

Another factor tipping the balance of power in Vijayanagara's favour at this time was the advent of the Portuguese *Estado da*

India. A formidable coastal power since 1498, these European newcomers not only sought to monopolize control over Arabian Sea commerce, but arriving on the heels of Iberia's anti-Muslim *reconquista,* the Portuguese in India also sought to roll back Muslim states everywhere, and especially the newly emerged sultanate of Bijapur, which had inherited from the Bahmanid control over a good deal of India's western seacoast in addition to the Raichur Doab. Such objectives naturally inclined the Portuguese to seek allies in Vijayanagara, that being the Deccan's principal non-Muslim power, and to exploit that kingdom's hostility toward Muslim states to its north. A dramatic step in this direction was taken in 1510, when the Portuguese viceroy and master-strategist Afonso de Albuquerque (1509-15), assisted by a coastal warlord loyal to Vijayanagara, seized the port of Goa (today's 'Old Goa') from Bijapur's Yusuf 'Adil Khan. 'With this action in Goa,' the viceroy wrote triumphantly to Portugal's King Manuel,

> we can diminish the credit that is enjoyed by the Turks [i.e., Bijapur], and the fear in which they are held, and persuade them [Vijayanagara] that we are men who can do deeds as great on the land as on the sea.... [Let us] thus see if I can have them move their armies against the Turks in the Deccan, and desire our true friendship.[11]

The key to Albuquerque's newly-acquired leverage over the states of the Deccan interior, both to the north and to the south of the Raichur Doab, lay in those states' dependency on war-horses imported by sea from the Middle East. Prior to 1510, Bijapur had imported most of its war-horses through its port of Goa, while Vijayanagara imported its horses through ports further down the coast, in particular Bhatkal. But after 1510, by negotiating separately with Yusuf 'Adil Khan and Krishna Raya, by seizing the port of Hormuz in the Persian Gulf (1515), and by deploying his sea power to pressure the merchants of Bhatkal, Albuquerque hoped to drive the entire traffic in war-horses to Goa, and thus through the hands of the *Estado.*[12]

The Portuguese also introduced new forms of gunpowder technology to the Deccan. The extent of their influence in this regard, however, has been a topic of considerable scholarly dispute, largely because it depends on how one evaluates the state of Indian firearms prior to the Europeans' arrival. Gunpowder had certainly been in use in India before the advent of the *Estado*. We know, for example, that in 1472 Bahmani engineers deployed explosive mines while besieging the fort of Belgaum, an ally of Vijayanagara.[13] But the move from exploding mines to firing cannons or matchlocks represents a major advance in military technology. Iqtidar Alam Khan has argued that Indians were using cannons cast in brass or bronze and handguns in the second half of the fifteenth century.[14] But the matter is complicated. The nomenclature of weapons changed over time; few Indian sources are contemporary with the battles they describe; and later sources often used terms anachronistically, projecting terms of their own day backwards to earlier periods. In view of such considerations, Jos Gommans has questioned Iqtidar Alam Khan's assertions respecting a fifteenth-century horizon for the earliest appearance of firearms in India.[15]

Notwithstanding Gommans' reservations, there is evidence that firearms were being used in western India before the establishment of Portuguese power in the region. Gaspar Correia, Albuquerque's secretary and a chronicler of the *Estado*, records that in 1502 Portuguese naval squadrons were bombarded from the hill-top overlooking the port of Bhatkal.[16] According to the historian Firishta (fl. 1611), gunners and rocketeers were among the 5,000 foot-soldiers that Sultan Ahmad Nizam Shah of Ahmadnagar used in a 1504 military expedition into Khandesh.[17] About the same time the Italian traveller Ludovico di Varthema recorded seeing artillery at the port of Chaul, then controlled by the same ruler.[18] In Bijapur following the death of Yusuf 'Adil Khan in 1510, a palace struggle broke out between royalists supporting the king's youthful son Isma'il and the latter's regent. Both sides in the conflict reportedly used firearms. Firishta speaks of 'matchlock-men' (*tufangi*), and of 'the fort's large cannon being brought up' in order to batter down the citadel's walls.[19] Albuquerque's son noted that when his father took Goa, also in 1510, Bijapuri defenders greeted the invaders with artillery fire.[20] Later that same year, after first losing and then recapturing the city, Albuquerque seized from Bijapur's defenders a hundred large guns (*bombardas*) and a 'large quantity' of smaller artillery.[21]

Significantly, many if not most of these weapons were locally manufactured, for when they seized Goa, the Portuguese found that the Bijapuris had already established their own munitions plant in that city. How did this indigenous tradition evolve? According to a document published by Gaspar Correia, at the time of the Portuguese conquest there already were in Goa:

> large houses with storage space which the Turks [*os rumes*] had filled with all the materials necessary for shipbuilding, and lots of iron and mortar artillery, large and small, and also two of our camel cannons and eight cradles and mortars which the Turks had brought from the defeat of Dom Lourenco at Chaul [in 1508], and other metal pieces in their fashion and a great number of metal guns, and a large quantity of gunpowder, saltpetre and utensils used in the making of these, and an enormous quantity of all kinds of weapons.[22]

Further information on the identity of these Turks is furnished by the Portuguese historian Duarte Barbosa, who was in India from about 1500 to about 1516. He writes that Bijapuri authorities in Goa had received Turkish escapees following the Battle of Diu (1509), in which the Portuguese defeated an Egyptian fleet that was allied with the Sultan of Gujarat and manned mainly by Turks. These men, writes Barbosa, were resettled in Goa with the help of Muslim merchants who financed the building of shipyards and plants for the manufacture of iron and copper ordnance.[23]

It thus appears that Mamluk and Gujarati naval engagements with the Portuguese off the Konkan and Gujarat coasts had led to the settlement of Turkish gunners and gunsmiths in Bijapuri territory after the Battle of Chaul in March 1508, and that these Turks had brought the latest Ottoman gun technology to the Goa arsenal. We cannot doubt the very high quality of work that was done there. Albuquerque was so impressed with Goa's gun-making tradition that he sent to the King of Portugal samples of the heavy cannon used by the Muslims of that city, together with the moulds from which the guns had been cast.[24] On 1 December 1513, the Portuguese viceroy reported that matchlocks manufactured by Goa's master gunsmiths were as good as those made in Bohemia; he even sent one of those gunsmiths to Lisbon to work for the Portuguese crown.[25] Several days later Albuquerque reported to the king that Muslim gunsmiths, who had formerly served Bijapur but were induced to return to Goa after the Portuguese conquest of that city, were capable of turning out iron cannons and matchlocks of a higher quality than anything produced in Germany, then considered the source of Europe's finest guns.[26] From this point on, a tradition of German and Bohemian gun-making that had been brought to India by the Portuguese seems to have merged with Turkish gun-making traditions already present in 'Adil Shahi Goa, producing what has been called an 'Indo-Portuguese' tradition of matchlocks. These weapons, considered at the time to be superior to anything produced elsewhere in India or Europe, would soon spread not only into the Deccan interior but, by the mid-sixteenth century, throughout Portuguese Asia as far as Japan.[27] These important developments notwithstanding, before 1520 we hear of no major battles in which firearms were used in the Deccan, or indeed, anywhere else in the Indian interior. All this would change with the Battle of Raichur.

THE BATTLE

Krishna Raya of Vijayanagara soundly defeated Isma'il 'Adil Khan in the 1520 contest for control of Raichur fort and the Doab.[28] Two original authorities can guide us in reconstructing the contours of the struggle. One is the above-mentioned Firishta, who lived in Bijapur and in 1611 dedicated his monumental *Tarikh-i Firishta* to Isma'il's great grandson, Sultan Ibrahim 'Adil Shah II (ruled 1580-1627). The other is Fernão Nunes, who around 1531 wrote a chronicle of Vijayanagara's kings based on local traditions and his own interactions with Portuguese and Indians.[29] There is evidence that Nunes, a Portuguese horse-trader who resided in metropolitan Vijayanagara for three years, had been living in coastal India since 1512, in which case he would have heard first-hand reports of the battle shortly after its conclusion.[30] Or, he might have recorded remembered traditions some eight years later, most likely from participants. It is even possible that he witnessed the battle himself.[31] Firishta is the less trustworthy of the two sources, not only because he was writing about 90 years after the event, but because he had the unenviable task of accounting for the crushing defeat of his patron's own forebear. In his version, Isma'il 'Adil Khan in 1520 took an army of 7,000 cavalry, all Westerners, down to the northern shore of the Krishna River in order to recover Raichur and Mudgal from Krishna Raya.[32] On learning of these manoeuvres, the Vijayanagara king brought up a much larger cavalry of 50,000 to the southern shores of the same river, seizing control of its ferries. Firishta here introduces the factor that doomed Isma'il's enterprise to failure. While the sultan was reposing in his tent soon after pitching camp, a Bijapuri courtier proposed a drinking bout. Isma'il responded enthusiastically and got so thoroughly inebriated that he decided to cross the river and attack Krishna Raya at once. Although his officers pleaded for more time to build sufficient boats and rafts for the operation, Isma'il ignored the advice and, mounting his elephant, rode straight to the river and plunged into the water, ordering his officers and soldiers to follow. On reaching the opposite side, however, the Bijapuris confronted a huge body of cavalry and also, so Firishta writes, cannon, matchlocks, and rockets.[33] Isma'il now found himself trapped between two Krishnas: before him the king of Vijayanagara, and to his rear the swirling currents of the Krishna River. In panic and disorder, the Bijapuris retreated and tried to recross the river, in the process losing many men both to drowning and to the arrows and shots of Vijayanagara's pursuing forces. Isma'il, who himself barely survived the debacle, sank into deep remorse for his rashness and swore off wine for good.

Firishta thus framed his story as a morality play, the essential point being that the debacle had been the fault of the wine, or rather, Isma'il's weakness in succumbing to wine at a wholly inappropriate time. Only as an aside does he mention perhaps the most arresting feature of his account, namely, that while Isma'il's retreating men were attempting to recross the river, Vijayanagara's forces killed nearly half of Bijapur army with cannon shot, matchlocks, and rockets. We shall bear this in mind as we explore the contemporary, or near-contemporary account of Fernão Nunes.

Nunes's account is far more detailed, less tendentious, and above all more contemporary with the battle than is that of Firishta. When he assumed the Vijayanagara throne in 1509, writes the Portuguese chronicler, Krishna Raya knew that his royal predecessor Narasimha Tuluva had regretted never having reduced three forts—Raichur, Mudgal, and Udayagiri. His opportunity to invade the first two came about ten years into his reign, when he entrusted a Muslim merchant with the sum of 40,000 *pardaos* to purchase war-horses from Goa. Instead of proceeding to the Portuguese-held seaport, however, the merchant absconded with the money to Bijapur. When the king wrote to Isma'il 'Adil Khan demanding the return of the merchant and the money, the sultan refused to oblige. He even gave the port of Dabhol to the merchant, which so enraged Krishna Raya that he resolved to invade that town. The king's advisors tried to dissuade him, noting that the sum given to the merchant—which would have purchased approximately 120 horses—was too trifling an amount over which to wage a war. But on seeing that the king could not be deterred from invading Bijapuri territory, his advisors counselled invading Raichur rather than Dabhol, since the former city had once belonged to Vijayanagara. Accepting this advice, Krishna Raya in early 1520 moved north with an immense force of 27,600 cavalry and 553,000 infantry. In all, writes Nunes, the army included archers, cavalry using a variety of weapons, matchlockmen (*espimgardeiros*), swordsmen with shields, war-elephants, and 'several cannons' (*allgũs tiros de fogo*).[34]

After crossing the Tungabhadra River, the Vijayanagara army camped in the town of Maliabad, an ancient Kakatiya fort situated some 10 miles south of Raichur city, and from there it moved on to Raichur itself. The city, writes Nunes, was defended with three lines of strong walls of heavy masonry made without lime-mortar and packed with earth inside. Built into the outer walls were bastions positioned so close to one another that men posted on them could hear the words spoken by those on neighbouring bastions. The defenders used matchlocks (*espimgardas*) and heavy cannons (*tiros de fogo grossos*), as well as bows and arrows. Along the walls were mounted 30 stone-hurling catapults (*trabucos*), 200 heavy cannons, and many smaller cannons, all the artillery being positioned along the curtain walls between the bastions. Garrisoned inside were 8,000 Bijapuri foot-soldiers, 400 cavalry, and 20 elephants.[35]

Although his forces encircled the entire fort, Krishna Raya concentrated his main attack on the city's eastern side, probably near the present Kati Gate. The fort's defenders, writes Nunes, fired on Vijayanagara's forces with heavy cannon and matchlocks, together with arrows. But the besiegers used no artillery against Raichur's walls. Instead, Vijayanagara's commanders offered their men monetary inducements to go directly to the walls and dismantle them with pick-axes, paying them in sums proportionate to the size of the stones dismantled. They were also paid for dragging off the bodies of comrades killed at the base of the walls. In this slow, dreary manner the siege dragged on for three months.[36]

In early May, while the siege was still in progress, Krishna Raya learned that Isma'il 'Adil Khan had marched down from Bijapur to relieve the embattled fort and was camped on the northern side of the Krishna River. With him were 18,000 cavalry, 120,000 infantry, 150 war-elephants, and considerable artillery. Suspending the siege of Raichur, the king moved his entire army up to the Krishna River to prevent Bijapur's forces from entering the Doab. The battle between the two armies began several hours after dawn on 19 May 1520 when the sultan, having moved his forces to the southern side of the river, fired all his artillery at once into Vijayanagara's massed front lines. When those lines broke and Bijapur's cavalry advanced, Krishna Raya became so desperate that he entrusted his ring to one of his pages, instructing him to show it to his queens as a sign of his death. The king then mounted his horse and moved forward with all of his remaining divisions, driving the Bijapuris back toward, and finally into, the Krishna River. Like Firishta, Nunes reports the horrific slaughter that then occurred by the river, in the midst of which Isma'il 'Adil Khan jumped on an elephant and barely escaped with his life.[37]

It is clear that Isma'il 'Adil Khan had brought a great deal of ordnance to the battlefield for, as Nunes reports, his retreating army was forced to abandon 400 heavy cannons and 900 gun-carriages—implying that he also had 500 small cannons—in addition to 4,000 war-horses and 100 elephants.[38] In fact, writes Nunes, Isma'il boldly crossed the Krishna River not because he was drunk, as Firishta would later write, but because he was confident that the great strength of his artillery (*a gramde artelharya*) would give him a quick victory. Indeed, the sultan's opening barrage did give him temporary advantage. But Nunes does not report that Krishna Raya used artillery in that battle, although Firishta, as we have seen, did make such a claim. Since Nunes wrote much closer in time to the event than did Firishta, it seems reasonable to conclude that if Krishna Raya used fire-arms at all on this occasion, they did not play a decisive, or even noticeable, role in his victory.

This inference is supported by Nunes' account of the siege of Raichur fort, an engagement that Firishta does not even mention, in which the Portuguese chronicler describes Krishna Raya's men clawing at the fort's walls with crowbars, rather than bombarding it with cannon. And in his description of Krishna Raya's immense army during its initial march to Raichur, the king is said to have brought along only 'several' cannons. All of this suggests that by 1520 cannons were being used in the field—extensively by Bijapur, at best minimally by Vijayanagara—but, with only limited effect. Defensively, whereas cannons were mounted on Raichur's ramparts, they had not yet displaced stone-hurling catapults, which were also still present, fixed atop the fort's projecting bastions. In short, the cannon appears to have made a noticeable appearance at Raichur, but it was not yet sufficiently effective as to play a decisive role in the outcomes of military engagements. After all, in Nunes' account Isma'il possessed and used significant firepower in the battle by the Krishna River, yet he still lost that battle.

Having soundly defeated the Bijapuris on the battlefield, Vijayanagara army returned to Raichur to resume its siege of the fort. At this point a new factor enters Nunes' narrative—the arrival of twenty Portuguese mercenaries who, led by one Cristovão de Figueiredo, had just joined Krishna Raya's forces at Raichur as matchlockmen (*espimgardeyros*).[39] Noticing how fearlessly Bijapuri defenders roamed about the fort's walls, fully exposed to the view of the besiegers, de Figueiredo and his men began picking them off with their guns. Nunes remarks, very significantly, that the defenders 'up to then had never seen men killed with fire-arms nor with other such weapons'.[40] What is more, it seems that the fort's cannon proved ineffective against the besiegers, who continued to assault the fort's walls with crow-bars and pick-axes as they had been doing before the battle by the Krishna River. The reason the fort's cannon were ineffective, Nunes explains, had to do with how they were mounted. Being placed high on the curtain walls, they could not fire down on those dismantling the walls at their base. And the defenders who tried to fire on them with arrows, matchlocks, or stones were themselves picked off by de Figueiredo's sharp-shooters, allowing Krishna Raya's men to continue dismantling the walls relatively unhindered. This operation was so successful that the defenders were forced to abandon their first line of fortification and place their women and children in the city's hill-top citadel.

Several inferences may be drawn from this part of Nunes' narration. First, although the Bijapuri defenders were using matchlocks to fend off the besiegers, their weapons must have been inferior to those used by de Figueiredo and his men if, as Nunes reports, the defenders at Raichur had never before been killed by firearms. This is quite possible, given that de Figueiredo would have had access to the superior firearms that were then being produced in the Goa arsenal, recently described as 'without doubt one of the largest arsenals of the world at that time'.[41] It was here that, during the early decades of the sixteenth century, Portuguese and Muslim gunsmiths had been exchanging designs and developing the latest hybrid matchlocks.[42] Second, the inability of Raichur's cannon shots to reach besiegers at the base of the fort's walls indicates that while the defensive use of cannons on forts had certainly reached the Deccan interior by 1520, engineers had not yet learned how to manoeuvre them so as to screen the walls with flanking fire. Being fixed between the battlement's merlons and not mounted on swivels, the cannon would have been immobile and hence quite useless against besiegers beneath them.

A turning point in the siege was reached on 14 June when the governor of the city, seeking a better view of exactly where the Portuguese snipers were positioned, leaned out in front of one of the embrasures and was instantly killed by a matchlock shot that struck his forehead. This snapped the morale of Raichur's defenders, who promptly abandoned the wall. The next day the Bijapuris opened the city gate and filed out, begging for mercy. All that remained now was a formal ceremony of capitulation and a transfer of authority. That came the following day, when Krishna Raya, after performing his customary prayers, rode into the city accompanied by his highest-ranking officers. Along the way the townspeople stood awaiting him—although, as Nunes remarks, they bore 'more cheerful countenances than their real feelings warranted'.[43] Speaking to a gathered crowd, the king generously assured the city's leaders that their property rights would be respected; he even gave them the option of leaving the city and taking their movable property with them.

Before returning to his capital, Krishna Raya lingered in

Raichur for some days making arrangements for the city's new administration. Nunes reports that he also repaired the walls that had been damaged during the siege, surely a reference to the new regime's programme of rebuilding the fort's northern sector.[44] Here, they added a new gate, the Naurangi Darwaza, together with three bastions to the west of it, two of them round with projecting bracketed balconies, and one of them square with brackets only on the outer face. In the Naurangi Darwaza they also built a large inner courtyard whose upper walls contain narrative sculptural panels depicting scenes from the *Mahabharata,* the *Ramayana,* the Krishna cycle, and Vaishnava *avataras,* as well as court scenes from metropolitan Vijayanagara. In all, this gateway complex and the new bastions to its west register a clear and deliberate attempt to stamp a distinctively Vijayanagara aesthetic onto this frontier site, which had for so long been a Bahmani and Bijapuri possession.

CONCLUSION

At first glance, the outcome of the Battle of Raichur might seem a paradox, inasmuch as the side that relied more extensively on cannon not only lost, but lost decisively. Just six years later, in April 1526, one of the most famous battles of Indian history was fought at Panipat, more than 1,000 miles north of the Raichur Doab. In that battle, the Central Asian Turkish prince Babur deployed field cannons and matchlocks, in addition to mounted archers, in defeating the last ruler of the Delhi Sultanate, which led directly to the establishment of the Mughal Empire. Given the great significance of the battle's outcome, and the fact that the winning side used firearms, Panipat is sometimes seen as having inaugurated India's 'Gunpowder Age'. The Battle of Raichur, by contrast, has been largely ignored in the literature, even though cannons were used more extensively there than at Panipat. This neglect likely owes to the battle's counter-intuitive outcome—that the side that had more firepower lost.

Yet, the battle's outcome points to an important lesson. States normally assimilate new technologies by a gradual process of trial-and-error, in respect to which failures can be as important as successes. It seems certain that a principal cause of Isma'il's crushing defeat by the banks of the Krishna River lay in his gunners' inability to quickly reload and fire successive rounds of shot before being overwhelmed by Vijayanagara's swift and powerful cavalry. Much had to be learned about the manufacture and deployment of the field cannon, and considerable practice would be necessary before this new technology could become truly lethal to opponents who had mastered the tactics and techniques of cavalry warfare. Similarly, Isma'il was probably the first to mount cannons on the battlements of forts in the Indian interior. But, here too, the technology's very novelty proved its users' undoing. Several hundred heavy and light cannons were positioned on Raichur's battlements alongside 30 stone-hurling catapults. However, owing to the arrangement of the fort's defenses—with catapults placed on the bastions and cannons fixed along the curtain walls in immobile positions between the merlons—Krishna Raya's men were able to dismantle a portion of the city's walls without suffering prohibitively high casualty rates. In short, Bijapur's forces at Raichur fort deployed the new gunpowder technology in a manner that proved just as disastrous there as did their deployment of the cannon in the pitched battle by the Krishna River.

Notably, the two sides drew very different lessons from the battle's outcome. Krishna Raya, while clearly impressed with the effectiveness of the matchlocks used by his Portuguese mercenaries, failed to see cannon warfare as the wave of the future. Prevailing over Bijapur's artillery both in pitched battle and at the fort seems to have reconfirmed the king's confidence in the efficacy of the day's conventional warfare. There is no evidence that he followed up his victories by establishing an arsenal or matchlock foundry in his kingdom. Nor did he or his successors ever mount cannon on the walls of any of their forts. For the next forty-five years, until the state was virtually extinguished following its catastrophic defeat at Talikota (1565), Vijayanagara's use of offensive firearms was modest at best. Indeed, the Battle of Talikota was itself decided by the effective deployment of the field cannon. In that fateful engagement, in which the combined forces of Bijapur, Ahmadnagar, and Golkonda faced Vijayanagara's immense army, three lines of the allies' artillery, linked together with chains, were placed at the front of the centre. The first line of artillery consisted of heavy cannons, the second of light cannons, and the third of swivel cannons—all commanded by Chalabi Rumi Khan, an Ottoman artillery officer who had served with distinction in Europe. Several thousand archers were also used, but only to mask the artillery and to lure Vijayanagara's advancing forces toward the cannons. When those forces reached close range, Rumi Khan ordered his gunners to load bags of copper coins in the cannon, which when fired, devastated the advancing army, killing 5,000 close to the guns' muzzles. 'The repulse of this charge', wrote Firishta within living memory of the battle, 'seems to have decided the fate of the day'.[45] Clearly, Vijayanagara since the Battle of Raichur had fallen far behind its northern neighbours in terms of artillery development.

The rulers of Bijapur, by contrast, responded very differently to the outcome of the Battle of Raichur. Throughout the rest of the sixteenth century, they not only continued to recruit to their arsenals master gunsmiths from Ottoman domains, as they had begun doing in Goa even before the arrival of the Portuguese. They also experimented aggressively with European artillery design, pioneering techniques of gun manufacture and cannon-mounting that had no precedent elsewhere in the world. As Phillip Wagoner has shown, cannons dating to the 1550s now lying atop forts at Yadgir, Kalyana, and Ausa reveal how Bijapur's engineers took European features such as the trunnion and the swivel fork—both found on small, one-metre long Portuguese breech-loaders called *berços*—and ingeniously incorporated them into the making of huge swivel guns up to 7 meters in length, which were mounted on corner bastions or on free-standing gun platforms equipped with elaborate recoil walls.[46] It is as though Bijapur's failure to defend Raichur's fort with mounted cannon in 1520 spurred their engineers to embark on a frenzied drive to improve both their guns and the designs of their forts.

How, then, can we evaluate the Battle of Raichur in the larger context of South Asian military history? Recently, Geoffrey Parker and Sanjay Subrahmanyam have quite reasonably argued against monolithic categories like 'Asia' and 'Europe' when assessing the worldwide Military Revolution. Instead, they point to the many different ways *within* Asia that firearms were (or were not) incorporated into military systems, citing the complex mix of variables that led to the various military paths taken during the sixteenth century in, say, Mamluk Egypt, Tokugawa Japan, or the Ottoman, Safavid, Mughal, or Ming empires.[47] But Bijapur in the early sixteenth century presents a case quite unlike the others. First, firearms were introduced to their realm not by one but by two vectors. The Turkish gun makers under Bijapur's auspices had already been employed in Goa's gun foundry prior to the advent of Portuguese power in India. This meant that Albuquerque, upon seizing Goa in 1510, could combine German with Turkish gun-making traditions, resulting in the production at Goa's gun foundry of the technically sophisticated, hybridized 'Indo-Portuguese' matchlock. Since new weapons developed at the Goa arsenal inevitably diffused into the hands of 'Adil Shahi authorities, Bijapur's engineers had not only Turkish and European models to draw upon, but also the hybridized weapons made in Portuguese Goa.[48] Second, the peculiar topography of the Deccan—with its many steep hills rising above the plateau—had for centuries encouraged the building of hill forts as a means of controlling the surrounding countryside. Over time, inhabitants came to conceive of power itself in terms of the ability to seize, hold and defend forts.

Such factors help explain why, in the decades after 1520, Bijapur's rulers entirely rebuilt former Bahmani forts such as Ausa, Yadgir, Kalyana, Naldrug and Kandhar. Such measures were taken mainly to accommodate their much improved cannons whose designs combined, and built upon, Turkish and European models of the day. What is remarkable is how this impulse for military modernization took root and flourished in Bijapur, but not in Vijayanagara. The difference appears to lie in the very different lessons that participants of the Battle of Raichur drew from the outcome of that conflict. Whereas victory lulled Vijayanagara into a state of relative complacency, defeat catalysed Bijapur to embark on a remarkable drive for military modernization.

NOTES

1. See Michael Roberts, 'The Military Revolution, 1560-1660', in his *Essays in Swedish History* (London: University of Minnesota Press, 1966), pp. 195-225; Geoffrey Parker, *The Military Revolution: Military Innovations*

and the Rise of the West, 1500-1800 (Cambridge: Cambridge University Press, 1988); William H. McNeill, *The Age of Gunpowder Empires* (Washington DC: American Historical Association, 1989), pp. 27-40; Richard Hellie, 'Warfare, Changing Military Technology, and the Evolution of Muscovite Society', in John A. Lynn (ed.), *Tools of War: Instruments, Ideas, and Institutions of Warfare, 1445-1871* (Urbana/Chicago: University of Illinois Press, 1990), pp. 74-99; David Eltis, *The Military Revolution in Sixteenth-century Europe* (London: Taurus Academic Studies, 1995); Bert S. Hall, *Weapons and Warfare in Renaissance Europe: Gunpowder, Technology, and Tactics* (Baltimore: Johns Hopkins Press, 1997), pp. 201-35; Jeremy Black, *War and the World: Military Power and the Fate of Continents, 1450-2000* (New Haven: Yale University Press, 1998).

2. For India, see Iqtidar Alam Khan, *Gunpowder and Firearms: Warfare in Medieval India* (New Delhi: Oxford University Press, 2004), and Jos Gommans, *Mughal Warfare: Indian Frontiers and High Roads to Empire, 1500-1700* (New York: Routledge, 2002).
3. See David Ayalon, *Gunpowder and Firearms in the Mamluk Kingdom: A Challenge to a Medieval Society* (London: F. Cass, 1956); Noel Perrin, *Giving up the Gun: Japan's Reversion to the Sword, 1453-1879* (Boston: D.R. Godine, 1979), William H. McNeill, *The Pursuit of Power: Technology, Armed Force, and Society since AD 1000* (Chicago: University of Chicago Press, 1982); Brian M. Downing, *The Military Revolution and Political Change: Origins of Democracy and Autocracy in Early Modern Europe* (Princeton: Princeton University Press, 1992); Kenneth Chase, *Firearms: A Global History to 1700* (Cambridge: Cambridge University Press, 2003); Michael C. Paul, 'The Military Revolution in Russia, 1550-1682', *Journal of Military History*, vol. 68, no. 1 (2004), pp. 9-45; Gabor Agoston, *Guns for the Sultan: Military Power and the Weapons Industry in the Ottoman Empire* (Cambridge: Cambridge University Press, 2005). For a discussion of the theme as it relates to South Asia, see Sanjay Subrahmanyam, 'The *Kagemusha* Effect: The Portuguese, Firearms and the State in Early Modern South India', in *Moyen Orient & Ocean Indien*, vol. 4 (1987), pp. 97-123; Geoffrey Parker and Sanjay Subrahmanyam, 'Arms and the Asians: Revisiting European Firearms and Their Place in Early Modern Asia', *Revista de Cultura* (Macau) (2008).
4. P.M. Joshi, 'The Raichur Doab in Deccan History: Re-interpretation of a Struggle', *Journal of Indian History*, vol. 36 (1958), pp. 379-96.
5. Ibn Battuta, *The Rehla of Ibn Battuta*, tr. Mahdi Husain (Baroda: Oriental Institute, 1953), p. 96; Zia al-Din Barani, *Tarikh-i Firuz Shahi*, in *The History of India as Told by its Own Historians*, ed. and tr. H.M. Elliot and John Dowson (Allahabad: Kitab Mahal, 1964), vol. 3, p. 245. 'Abd al-Malik 'Isami, *Futuhu's Salatin*, ed. and tr. Agha Mahdi Husain (New York: Asia Publishing House, 1977), vol. 3, p. 902.

6. Vijayanagara's kings did achieve a few successes in the disputed region. In 1362, 1436 and 1443 their forces briefly seized Mudgal, which is located in the Doab some sixty miles west of Raichur city. On each occasion, however, the fort was soon recovered by Bahmani authorities. A.A. Kadiri, 'Bahmani Inscriptions from Raichur District', *Epigraphia Indica, Arabic and Persian Supplement* (1962), pp. 54-5.
7. Literary evidence suggests that during the second of his three campaigns against Vijayanagara, Sultan Firuz had forced Harihara II to make annual tributes to the Bahmanis. A 1444 Sanskrit inscription at Bidar confirms that Harihara's successor, Deva Raya II, was paying tribute to the Bahmani sultan, Ahmad Shah I. Ibid., pp. 54-5.
8. In the course of their Deccan campaigns, 'Ala al-Din Khalji and Muhammad bin Tughluq had brought with them new siege technology, including extensive groundworks, earthen battlements (*pashib*), mines, wooden siege towers, mangonels, and counterweight trebuchets. The Tughluqs, especially, were great fort builders. At sites like Tughlaqabad, in Delhi, one sees their distinctive architectural features: massive projecting buttresses, merlons, turrets, and crenellations. Such features quickly diffused to the Deccan, as at Daulatabad, where ramparts were replaced with a double line in lime-mortar masonry, round bastions, and turrets. The Bahmani rulers continued these traditions in such major forts as Gulbarga, Firuzabad, and Bidar. Gommans, *Mughal Warfare,* pp. 141-4.
9. Some modern historians have referred to this group as *afaqi* or *'ajami.* Contemporary sources, however, call them *gharbian* (Westerners), or sometimes *ghariban* (foreigners).
10. Two inscriptions of Raichur dated 1515, one on an unidentified mosque and the other on a bastion of the outer wall, record the names of both Sultan Mahmud Bahmani and Isma'il 'Adil Khan, Bijapur's effective sultan. K.M. Ahmad, 'Inscriptions of Raichur in the Hyderabad Museum', *Epigraphia Indo-Moslemica* (1939-40), pp. 14, 16. But it was not until 1538, after the last nominal Bahmani sovereign had sailed off on a pilgrimage to Mecca from which he never returned, that the fourth of Bijapur's rulers, Ibrahim, styled himself 'Sultan'.
11. R.A. de Bulhão Pato and H. Lopes de Mendonca (eds.), *Cartas de Affonso de Albuquerque eguidas e documentos que as elucidam* (Lisbon: Typographia da Academia real das sciencias de Lisboa, 1884), vol. 1, p. 28. Cited in Maria Augusta Lima Cruz, 'Notes on Portuguese Relations with Vijayanagara, 1500-1565', *Santa Barbara Portuguese Studies*, vol. 2 (1995), p. 21.
12. As the viceroy cynically wrote to Yusuf 'Adil Khan's successor, Isma'il Khan of Bijapur, 'I shall be ever your friend, and I will assist you against the King of Decan [Isma'il's nominal overlord, Sultan Mahmud Bahmani], and against your enemies; and I will cause all the horses that arrive

here to be carried to your stations and your marts, in order that you may have possession of them.' Walter de Gray Birch (tr.), *Commentaries of the Great Afonso Dalboquerque* (1884; rpt., New York: B. Franklin, 1970), vol. 3, pp. 20-1. For further discussion, see Sanjay Subrahmanyam, *The Political Economy of Commerce: Southern India, 1500-1650* (Cambridge: Cambridge University Press, 1990), pp. 116-35. See also Jean Aubin, 'Un Voyage de Goa à Ormuz en 1520', *Modern Asian Studies*, vol. 22, no. 3 (1988), pp. 417-32.

13. John Briggs (tr.), *History of the Rise of the Mahomedan Power in India* (1829, rpt., Calcutta: Editions Indian, 1966), vol. 2, p. 303. Firishta not only mentions the 'fire-workers' (*atish-bazan*) employed for the job, but states that until that time, people of the Deccan had never seen such battering devices or mines ('*bi sakhtan-i sarkub va naqb ki ta an zaman dar Dakan sha'i 'nabud*'). Muhammad Qasim Firishta, *Tarikh-i Firishta* (Lucknow: Newal Kishore, 1864-65), vol. 1, p. 352.
14. Iqtidar Alam Khan, *Gunpowder*, pp. 42-4.
15. Gommans, *Mughal Warfare*, p. 146, and fn. 52.
16. Gaspar Correia, *Lendas da India*, vol. 1, pp. 289-90. Cited in Subrahmanyam, *Political Economy*, p. 124.
17. 'Five thousand foot-soldiers who were gunners, bowmen, and rocketeers, and five thousand mounted archers' ('*Panj hizar piada tup-chi va kamandar va ban-dar, va panj hizar sawar ki hama tir-andaz budand*'). Firishta, *Tarikh-i Firishta,* vol. 2, p. 98. Briggs translates *tup-chi* as 'matchlock-men'. Briggs, *History*, vol. 3, p. 124. The historian of Ahmadnagar's Nizam Shahi dynasty, 'Ali Tabataba, notes that on this occasion Sultan Ahmad Nizam Shah had with him a detachment of rocketeers and musketeers (*ban-kari va tufang-andazi*). 'Ali Tabataba, *Burhan-i ma'athir* (Delhi: Matba' Jam'a Dihli, 1936), p. 223. T.W. Haig, 'The History of the Nizam Shahi Kings of Ahmadnagar', *Indian Antiquary*, vol. 49 (1920), p. 126.
18. John Winter Jones (tr.), *The Travels of Ludovico di Varthema* (1863, rpt. New York: Hakluyt Society, n.d.), p. 114.
19. '*Avardan-i tup-hayi kalan ki ham dar an qil'a budand* . Firishta, *Tarikh-i Firishta*, vol. 2, p. 17. Briggs, *History*, vol. 3, p. 24.
20. Birch, *Commentaries*, vol. 2, p. 89.
21. Ibid., vol. 3, p. 16.
22. Gaspar Correia, *Lendas da India* (Lisbon: Typographia da Academia Real das Ciencias de Lisboa, 1860), vol. 2, p. 60. Tr. in Rainer Daehnhardt, *The Bewitched Gun: The Introduction of the Firearm in the Far East by the Portuguese* (Lisbon: Texto Editora, 1994), p. 37.
23. Mansel L. Dames (tr.), *The Book of Duarte Barbosa* (1918, rpt , Nendeln/ Liechtenstein: Kraus Reprint, 1967), vol. 1, pp. 175-7.
24. de Bulhão Pato and Mendonca (eds.), *Cartas*, vol. 1, p. 28. Cited in Daehnhardt, *Bewitched Gun*, p. 38.

25. Ibid., p. 174. Cited in Daehnhardt, *Bewitched Gun*, p. 39.
26. '. . . e asy se tornaram todolos oficiaees d artelharia, de bombardas e espimgardas, as quaees se fazem de ferro em goa milhores que has d alemanha.' de Bulhão Pato and Mendonca (eds.), *Cartas*, vol. 1, p. 203. Cited in Daehnhardt, *Bewitched Gun*, pp. 38-9.
27. Ibid., p. 41.
28. It is sometimes claimed, based on Firishta's account, that Krishna Raya had invaded and occupied Raichur in 1512, and that Isma'il therefore moved an army there in 1520 to *reconquer* the city from Krishna Raya. See H.K. Sherwani and P.M. Joshi (eds.), *History of Medieval Deccan (1295-1724)* (Hyderabad: Government of Andhra Pradesh, 1973), vol. 1, p. 308. But such a possibility is refuted by epigraphic evidence confirming Isma'il's continued occupation of Raichur from his accession down to 1520. An inscription dated 1511-12 records the construction of the Hazara Baig mosque in the time of Isma'il 'Adil Khan and Sultan Mahmud Bahmani. An inscription dated 1513-14 records the construction of the Yak Minar mosque, mentioning the same two figures. In 1515-16, a third mosque was built in the city, with its inscription again mentioning Isma'il 'Adil Khan. And in the same year, a bastion was built onto the fort's outer wall, which mentions Isma'il 'Adil Khan. See Kadiri, 'Bahmani Inscriptions', 66 and 65; K.M. Ahmad, 'Inscriptions', 14 and 16.
29. Joan-Pau Rubiés, *Travel and Ethnology in the Renaissance: South India through European Eyes, 1250-1625* (Cambridge: Cambridge University Press, 2000), p. 270, fn. 49. For thoughtful discussions of Nunes as a chronicler of Vijayanagara, see ibid., pp. 257-79, and Sanjay Subrahmanyam, *Penumbral Visions: Making Polities in Early Modern South India* (New Delhi: Oxford University Press, 2001), pp. 188-92.
30. Rubiés writes that the Portuguese chronicler can 'perhaps be identified with the Fernão Nunes who in 1512 was *escrivão de feitor* of Calicut, and who in 1526 appears as *escrivão de fazenda* in Cochin'. Rubiés, *Travel and Ethnology*, p. 204.
31. Robert Sewell, who translated Nunes's account and also wrote the first modern history of Vijayanagara, notes that throughout Nunes's account of the battle, 'there is much that impels the belief that either himself or his informant was present at the Hindu camp while these events were taking place. The narrative of the campaign, in complete contrast to that of the remainder of the history, reads like the account of an eye-witness; especially in the passages describing the fortress of Raichur and the camp—where the supplies were so great that "you could find everything that you wanted", where "you saw" the goldsmiths and artisans at work as if in a city, where "you will find" all kinds of precious stones offered for sale. . . .' Robert Sewell, *A Forgotten Empire*

(Vijayanagara): A Contribution to the History of India (1900, rpt., New Delhi: Asian Educational Services, 1984), p. 153.

32. Firishta gives the date as AH 927, which is not possible since that year began on 12 December 1520, and Sewell demonstrates that the battle took place earlier that year, in May and June. See Briggs, *History*, vol. 3, p. 29; Sewell, *Forgotten Empire*, pp. 140-7.
33. The text reads '*zarb zadan-i tup va tufang va digar atish-bazi*'. *Tarikh-i Firishta*, vol. 2, pp. 19-20. Briggs, *History*, vol. 3, pp. 29-30.
34. 'Chronicle of Fernão Nuniz', in Sewell (tr.), *Forgotten Empire*, pp. 316-28; David Lopes (ed.), *Chronica dos Reis de Bisnaga* (Lisbon: Imprensa nacional, 1897) p. 28.
35. 'Chronicle of Fernão Nuniz', p. 331.
36. Ibid., pp. 330, 332.
37. In Nunes's vivid account, 'The troops advanced thus, pursuing the foe, till the King reached the river, where, seeing the death of so many—for here you would see women and boys who had left the camp, there horses and men who through clinging one to another could not escape as there was so much water in the river—and the King's troops stood on the bank, so that whenever a man appeared he was killed, and the horses that tried to clamber up the bank of the river, unable to do so, fell back on the men, so that neither one nor the other escaped, and the elephants went into the stream, and those that they could seize were cruelly killed by them'. Sewell, *Forgotten Empire*, p. 339.
38. '*quoatro centos tiros grossos d artelharia, afora meuda, forão o numero das carretas d ellas nove-centas. . . .*' Lopes (ed.), *Chronica*, p. 39. Sewell (tr.), *Forgotten Empire*, p. 342.
39. Although European mercenaries and renegades had begun appearing in the service of Indian coastal powers as early as 1502, this was the first major conflict in the Indian interior in which Europeans are known to have participated. But, as Maria Augusta Lima Cruz notes, in European accounts only those who served armies under Muslim control were understood as renegades. Thus Cristovão de Figueiredo, otherwise a horse-merchant, is depicted by Nunes not as a renegade but as a courageous *fidalgo* who boasted to Krishna Raya that 'the whole business of the Portuguese was war' and that the greatest favour the king could grant would be to allow him to accompany the Vijayanagara Army to Raichur. On the other hand, the fifty other Portuguese mercenaries who fought and died for Isma'il 'Adil Khan at the battle by the Krishna River were called renegades (*arrenegados*), even though Nunes could not refrain from admiring their 'great deeds' in killing 'so many men that they left a broad road behind them which no one dared enter'. Maria Augusta Lima Cruz, 'Exiles and Renegades in Early Sixteenth Century Portuguese India', *Indian Economic and Social History Review*,

vol. 23, no. 3 (1986), pp. 258, 260. Sewell, *Forgotten Empire,* pp. 342, 343 (Sewell mistakenly gives the number of Portuguese mercenaries fighting for Bijapur as 500, instead of 50. Cf. Lopes (ed.), *Chronica,* p. 39).

40. 'Chronicle of Fernão Nuniz', p. 344. '. . . *pellos mouros estarem tão descuydados e sem temor, como aquelles que atee ly numca lhe matarão homẽs com espimgardas, nem com outros tiros que lhe tirarão. . . .*' Lopes, ed., *Chronica,* p. 40.
41. Daehnhardt, *Bewitched Gun,* p. 42.
42. 'From the 16th century until the 19th century', writes Daehnhardt, 'Portuguese and Goan gunsmiths worked side by side, harmoniously mixing technical influences and decorative capacities'. Daehnhardt, *Bewitched Gun,* p. 71.
43. 'Chronicle of Fernão Nuniz', p. 347.
44. Ibid., p. 349. The radical renovations and additions made to the fort's northern side suggest that this was where the walls had been breached, and not the eastern side, where Nunes reports that Vijayanagara's forces had concentrated their attack.
45. Briggs, *History of the Rise,* vol. 3, pp. 78, 151-2.
46. Phillip B. Wagoner, 'Firearms, Fortifications, and a "Military Revolution" in the 16th Century Deccan', a paper read at Philadelphia, University of Pennsylvania, 17 March 2007.
47. Parker and Subrahmanyam, 'Arms and the Asian'.
48. Portuguese anxieties that their gun-making techniques might migrate to their adversaries on the plateau is seen in an incident, cited by Sanjay Subrahmanyam, in which Goan authorities in the 1620s sent an assassin to Bijapur to eliminate a Portuguese cannon founder who had taken up service at the 'Adil Shahi court. The assassin first ingratiated himself with his victim and then, 'having eaten and drunk well, murdered him and buried him under the floor of his own house'. The killer was subsequently rewarded with a clerical position to the magistrate in Diu. Subrahmanyam, '*Kagemusha* Effect', p. 111.

CHAPTER 4

Rethinking Early Mughal Warfare

Babur's Pitched Battles, 1499-1529

PRATYAY NATH

Mughal historiography has traditionally focused on the Mughal state as a distinct, if not isolated, Indian phenomenon. This has led, on the one hand, to the lack of analysis of the Mughal state in a broad comparative framework over time and space,[1] and, on the other, minimum effort towards investigating the multilayered nature of the Central Asian and West Asian legacies of the Mughals. In the later field, the few works that exist focus more on the politico-ideological, cultural and religious inheritance of the Mughals from Central Asia.[2] The literature specifically on Babur numbers quite a few. These range from biographical romances to more analytical works. While these have shed much light on various aspects of Babur's career, the military dimension of the warrior-prince's achievements have rarely been explored thoroughly.[3]

This is indeed quite strange, keeping in mind that the state that Babur founded on the north Indian plains between 1526 and 1530 was first and foremost a conquest-state based on decisive military superiority demonstrating itself in three major battles. Babur's force was partly a Central Asian cavalry army that descended on the north Indian plains from Kabul and swooped over the vast plains passing eastwards. The Battle of Panipat gave Babur direct access to the north Indian plains and possession of the politically as well as logistically important cities of Delhi and Agra. As a result, Babur acquired the Lodi imperial treasures of these two cities, which helped him to finance his later wars and in fact, double his manpower resources before the next battle against the Rajput-Afghan alliance.[4] The victory at Khanua secured the south-western frontier of the state based around Delhi-Agra and neutralized for the time being an ascendant Rajput power-centre, while the Mughals' exclusive control over the resources of the plains of the Ganga basin up to the western limits of the Afghan Sultanate of Bengal was confirmed by the victory in the riverine battle of Ghaghra. Thus, Mughal hegemony was confirmed over the larger part of the most fertile zone of the subcontinent—the north Indian plains stretching from Punjab to the fringes of Bihar. Without occupying these tracts, it would not have been financially or logistically possible for Babur to build up a conquest-state and sponsor the post-Panipat campaigns so far away from his original base in Kabul. Although existing works on Babur often do offer detailed description of these battles and indicate their political significance for the nascent Mughal state, their military nuances and their position in the broader fabric of medieval Eurasian warfare are yet to be charted out.

The methodology of studying battles in order to comprehend the nature of warfare has not been in much favour in India's historical landscape.[5] Jadunath Sarkar's pioneering work on the topic had to wait for another forty-five years for another such venture.[6] The study of military institutions, technology and weapons has in general found more favour than that of tactics, strategy and logistics.[7] Several recent publications of Jos Gommans have broken new ground by bringing ecological and geographical factors under historical analysis in the context of medieval Indian warfare, but the lack of empirical study of the actual battles and sieges has made his analysis somewhat abstract.[8]

The objective of the present paper is to fill the above-mentioned historiographical gap. In the first two sections, this paper traces the development of cavalry tactics and fire-power centric warfare in Eurasian battles until the sixteenth century and locates Babur's battles prior to Panipat in light of the two above-mentioned trends. Next, the two battles of Panipat and Khanua are analysed in order to identify the basic techniques and technologies involved in these clashes and their relation to the larger world of Eurasian warfare in general. After this, two riverine battles, one on the Ganga and the other on the Ghaghra, quite different in engagements from Babur's earlier battles, will be taken up and the structural dissimilarity accounted for. Lastly, the much debated question of jihad in the context of Babur's military campaigns against Hindus will be reviewed.

It should be pertinent to mention here that in spite of being aware that the term 'Mughal' is in fact 'the misspelling of a misnomer',[9] I go for the term in preference to other terms like 'Indo-Timurids'[10] or 'Timurid-Mughuls'[11] used by some others because of its wide consensual acceptance among successive generation of historians which has bred into the term a significance of its own and made the representation of the dynasty somewhat inseparable from the use of its misnomer.

DEVELOPMENT OF CAVALRY TACTICS IN EURASIA TILL THE SIXTEENTH CENTURY

The Scythians were the first to make effective use of the cavalry around the ninth century BCE. Cavalry played a major role in their victory against the Assyrian Empire two centuries later.[12] From that period onwards, the development of cavalry tactics took place on two different lines—heavy cavalry and light cavalry. Light cavalry warfare, involving fast campaigns by horsemen using minimal armours, was the specialty of nomadic tribes of the Central Asian steppes. While the Scythians mastered mounted archery in the western sector of the Central Asian plains, so much so that Scythian mounted archers were used as auxiliaries in the Indian campaigns of Alexander,[13] in the eastern sector of the steppes, the Hsiung-nu were its champions in their battles against their sedentary neighbours of China. The tradition of mounted archery was to remain a dominant feature in warfare in Central Asia for a long time, even after the arrival of firearms right into the eighteenth century. In the grasslands of the steppes, the nomads' habitual familiarity with the horse, with which their socio-economic life was closely integrated, made them excellent horse-riders. This combined with the use of the composite bow, a weapon that flourished in the dry climate of Central Asia, made the Central Asian light cavalry of highly mobile mounted archers one of the deadliest and feared offensive agencies in world history.

The development of heavy cavalry was on the contrary mostly the work of sedentary states to the west, south and east of the Central Asian arid zone. It was probably first developed by the settled people of Chorasmo-Massagetae people in modern Uzbekistan to counter the light cavalry of the steppe. These cavalry men and their horses wore bronze scale-armour and carried lances and other weapons for close combat. The Achaemenids borrowed this technique and brought it to western Asia. From them, heavy cavalry was adopted later by the Parthians. But it was under the Sassanians that we first see large-scale and effective use of heavy cavalry tactics.[14] The enemy of the Sassanids, the Byzantines, learnt the use of heavy cavalry from the Avars during the sixth and early seventh centuries. This was also the time of the discovery and rapid dissemination of the stirrup, which made cavalry forces deadlier by increasing the mobile horse-rider's control over his horse and thereby his efficiency in shooting arrows.[15] In the eighth and ninth centuries, the Islamic armies, led by the Arabs, fielded large numbers of heavy cavalrymen. With their emphasis on the use of sword and spear, shooting from stationary, even though mounted, position and fighting at close quarters, the Fatimid culture of cavalry warfare was nearer to that of the Romans than to that of their nomadic brethren of Central Asia.[16] However, with the gradual rise of Turkish dominance in West Asia, the Islamic armies bent more towards light mounted archery. The Mamluks of Egypt at the time of the Crusades also formed a heavily armed and highly trained corps. Nearly all these heavy cavalrymen of West Asian states were trained to fight with the sword and other close-range weapons as well as bows and arrows.[17]

The development of battle tactics on such different lines cannot be adequately appreciated without taking into account their ecological and geographical underpinnings. Kenneth Chase locates at the heart of the Eurasian continent, an approximately Z-shaped arid zone including all the drier zones of Eurasia, stretching from east of the Ukranian plains to Mongolian deserts, and again from the Atlantic in the west, across the northern part of Africa up to Indian peninsular plateau in the west. This arid zone has been home to many great nomadic empires over time. The arid zone is surrounded by fertile, populous, sedentary lands of China in the east, Indian subcontinent in the south and eastern European plains in the west. These have traditionally been the regions that have been victims of repeated waves of invasion from their nomadic/semi-nomadic neighbours of the arid zone. Beyond these regions lie temperate areas of Western Europe in the west and Japan in the far east, and the wet rain-forested sub-tropical and equatorial regions of South-East Asia, which never faced any threat from pastoral nomads due to the cushioning effect by the middle zone.[18] Warfare here developed without any direct correlation with arid zone warfare. In terms of battle tactics, light cavalry warfare was invented in and flourished in the arid zone. Central Asia, with its temperate climate and high proportion of rich feather grasses provided men of the arid zone the ideal conditions for horse-breeding. The composite bow, made of bone and sinew, also retained its shape best in the temperate climate of the Central Asian arid zone. Large plains to practice mounted manoeuvres, lack of resources to procure armour, relatively smaller size of horses which grazed on the open fields, etc., precipitated a particular nature of mounted warfare that the arid zone allowed to evolve. On the other hand, greater resources for investing in and easy availability of metal armour, possibility of maintaining larger horses fed on corn and the fact that they had to deal with other sedentary powers fielding large infantry armies[19] prompted the sedentary states to develop heavy cavalry.

However, exclusive monopoly by any power of either heavy or light cavalry over its opponents did not last and as a direct corollary of interaction and confrontation between nomadic/semi-nomadic and sedentary modes of warfare, the armies gradually came to reflect both the types of cavalry, although their proportions varied widely over time and space. The Saljuq Turks, who fought the Crusading armies, mastered this combination of heavy and light cavalry. The Mongol Army also used this combination of heavy and light cavalry. The light mounted archers were put in the vanguard and in the flanks in the battle formation, and the heavy cavalry in the centre. The skirmishers of the van would shower arrows on the enemy and draw away quickly, in a bid to lure him to attack. This would be followed by encircling manoeuvres towards the flanks and rear of the enemy by the light cavalry of the wings. Finally, the enemy, demoralized by a failed pursuit of the elusive light mounted archers and their formation, jeopardized or often converted into a confused mass by the ceaseless volleys of arrows from all sides, was smashed through by the heavy cavalry which fell on them with swords and other weapons of close combat.[20]

The Turks who battled with northern Indian states at the turn of the first millennium CE also mastered this tactic of combined use of heavy and light cavalry. In the tenth century, Subuktagin applied such tactics against Jaipal, the Hindu ruler of Kabul. The Turkish mounted archers rained arrows from a distance without coming in direct contact with Jaipal's forces. This lured the Rajputs out of their battle formation to pursue the nimble Islamic horse-archers. Finally, a heavy cavalry charge by Subuktagin's reserve corps destroyed the frustrated and confused Jaipal's army.[21]

In 1192, in the Second Battle of Tarain, Shahab-ud-Din Muhammad Ghuri deployed similar tactics against the Rajputs under Prithviraj Chauhan. His light cavalry rained arrows on the enemy from the flanks and rear and when pursued by the enemy, they resorted to the the tactic of feigned retreat. Finally, the confused, demoralized and frustrated Rajput force was smashed by a cavalry charge by Shahab-ud-Din's 12,000 steel-clad heavy cavaliers posted in the centre.[22]

At this juncture, a look at three battles that Babur fought in Central Asia in the early stage of his career would help us understand how they fit into this structure of arid zone warfare.

BABUR'S BATTLES

Battle of Khuban (ce 1499-1500)

In 1499-1500, Babur faced Ahmad Tambal Mughul in what would be Babur's first, although a minor, pitched battle near the village of Khuban. Deciding to face Tambal in a set-piece battle, Babur 'moved out against him, formed up with right and left, centre and van, our horses in their mail, our men in theirs, and with foot-soldiers, bearing mantelets, flung to the front'.[23] The main engagement took place mainly between Babur's left wing and Tambal's right wing. The foot-soldiers could not keep pace with the swiftly moving cavalry, fell behind and could not take any part in the battle. Babur's left wing beat back Tambal's right, prompting the enemy to flee.[24]

Battle of Sar-i Pul (ce 1501)

Babur's second pitched battle occurred some time between April and May 1501, against the Uzbeg chief Shaibani Khan, when the latter attacked Samarqand, which was then held by Babur. Before the actual battle, both the parties engaged each other in skirmishes and the Uzbegs delivered at least one night attack on Babur's camp. The nocturnal attack had no impact on Babur's camp as it was protected by ditches and fortified with close-set branches. The strength of Babur's army was around 5,000.[25] On the day of the battle, they marched out with most of the men and horses in mail and arranged by Babur into left, right, van and centre. Shaibani Khan's men were arrayed into left, right and centre. The Uzbeg army was numerically superior to Babur's force.

When the two armies marched against each other to offer battle, Shaibani Khan's right wing wheeled round Babur's left to attack from the rear. Babur immediately directed his centre to his left to reinforce his left wing. But by doing this, he let his centre come out from behind the van. Finding the front of Babur's centre exposed, Shaibani led a heavy cavalry charge on it. Babur's centre initially beat back this frontal charge but soon started retreating. Meanwhile, the Uzbeg left wing had beaten Babur's right and wheeled again to Babur's rear and rained arrows on them. This combined Uzbeg assault of heavy cavalry from the front and wheeling mounted archers from the rear carried the day for the Uzbegs. Babur's army melted away and the Mughals lost the battle. Here, Babur's observation regarding Uzbeg warfare is worth noting: 'This same turning-movement is one of the great merits of Auzbeg fighting; no battle of theirs is without it. Another merit of theirs is that they all, begs and retainers, from their front to their rear, ride, loose-rein at the gallop, shouting as they come and, in retiring, do not scatter, but ride off, at the gallop, in a body.'[26] This turning movement which resulted in the defeat of Babur was the famous *taulqama* tactic of the highly mobile mounted archers of the arid zone. Like the Parthian shot, this was another expertise that the nomadic horse-warriors picked up and developed with ease, into a dreaded battle weapon.

Battle of Kandahar (ce 1507-1508)

In 1507-8, Babur occupied Kandahar after defeating the Arghuns under Shah Beg and his younger brother, Muhammad Muqim. Before the battle, Babur deployed his men, around 1,000 in number, into left, right, van and centre.[27] The total force of his enemy, estimated by him at 6,000-7,000, consisted of two sections—Shah Beg's force with 4,000-5,000 heavy cavalry under his personal command facing Babur's right and a smaller force under Muqim facing Babur's left.[28] The battle began with Muqim leading a charge on Babur's left. Shah Beg also fell on Babur's van and pushed it towards his centre. After a discharge of arrows, Babur's centre also advanced, only to be faced by a determined opposition. But soon, Babur's right turned the tables on their enemy and put them to flight. The left wing of Babur also made a detour and blocked the way of Muqim's defeated troopers. The Arghun force melted away leaving Babur victorious.[29]

In this period of his career, particularly before his occupation of Kabul, Babur had a small army. His was mainly heavy cavalry, whom he mentions to have been clad in mail armour in the Battle of Khuban and who specialized in fighting at close quarters as well as in archery from a distance. The *Baburnama* is replete with instances of Babur and his associates performing various feats of archery as an integral part of their routine military activities. The defeat in the hands of the Uzbegs taught him the value of the *taulqama* tactic performed by lightly armed mounted archers and this he was to use to perfection in his later battles on the plains of north India. It was to this cavalry army that Babur accommodated the new technology of firearms that he received from Ottoman professionals. But before tackling the question of how this combination was achieved, a glance at the development of fire-power centric warfare until Babur's days would be instructive.

DEVELOPMENT OF FIREPOWER-CENTRIC WARFARE IN EURASIA TILL THE SIXTEENTH CENTURY

Gunpowder was discovered in China in the ninth century CE and firearms in the twelfth century CE. From China, gunpowder and firearms spread throughout Central Asia, Arabia and Europe in the fourteenth century, most probably via the agency of the Mongols. The Turks, Persians and Indians received the firearms technology in the fifteenth century, directly or indirectly from European agency.[30] In Europe, the arrival of gunpowder meant a resurgence of the infantry in the European battlefield. By the first half of the sixteenth century, handgun-equipped infantry, supported by pikemen, made the heavy feudal cavalry an anachronism, thus resulting in the much debated 'Military Revolution' by the mid-seventeenth century.[31] In the arid zone, however, nothing of this sort happened, at least in the sixteenth century. In this region, the use of artillery was integrated into the current mode of warfare involving the coordinated deployment of heavy and light cavalry, without any fundamental change in the theory of warfare. This was done by the borrowing of an old battle tactic of East Europe—the wagon *laager*, or a defensive tactic involving artificial and temporary fortification in the battlefield using chiefly wagons mainly to shelter the infantry. The wagon *laager* was repeatedly used by the Goths against the Roman armies, especially in the famous Battle of Adrianople in CE 378.[32] The Goths moved around with their wagon forts, or *laager*. These were the basic units of their domestic life. Their usefulness lay in the fact that they could be used as defensive arrangements, yet it did not take much effort to transport them. Instead, these wagons carried their logistical requirements. During battles, these were arranged in a circle and this 'fortified' place functioned as a base for the whole army and a rallying point at different junctures of the engagement.[33] The *laager* culture lived through the feudal-age combat. In the High Middle Ages, the Flemings dug ditches and arranged the wagons in the form of a fortress behind their lines, on which they could fall back upon when hard pressed.[34] The *laager* was put into great use by the Hussites, who stationed crossbowmen and handgun-bearing infantry behind them. They, like the Goths, arranged the wagons, tied them with iron chains to form an impregnable *laager*. Heavier guns were mounted on these wagons. In 1421, it was the wagon-centric artillery fire that kept the Catholic army of King Sigismund at bay.[35]

The Ottomans from the fourteenth century onwards had been in close proximity with Europe due to their sustained conflict over the Near East and the Levant region. This physical proximity, and deriving from it, technological and military exchange increased when the area of contact shifted to the Balkan region during the fifteenth century. By late fourteenth century, the Ottomans introduced the institution of the Janissary, which meant a specially trained infantryman equipped with bows and arrows, and gradually replaced by arquebuses after their introduction in the Ottoman Empire. In the 1420s, the method of graining of gunpowder was perfected in Western Europe, and by the 1440s, this spread in Europe and Ottoman territories. It was possibly at this time that the Ottomans took up the idea of using a defensive *laager* in battlefield from their western neighbours—the Hussites, who were using it successfully in the 1420s.[36]

However, the wagon *laager* assumed a different shape in the Ottoman battlefield. Unlike the European scene, where the *laager* would be built in the rear of the army, the wagons were arranged by the Ottomans along the front of their battle formation. The wagons, placed at regular intervals, were chained with each other to prevent the storming of the *laager* by the enemy cavalry. The defensive function of protecting the firearms-equipped infantry was done with great efficiency by the Swiss pikemen in Europe. This defensive function during the fifteenth and sixteenth centuries for the Janissaries was performed by the wagon *laager* behind which the Janissaries were posted.[37] The select royal corps of heavy cavalry was stationed behind this *laager* in the centre and the two wings, while light cavalry was arrayed in the extremities of the flanks and in the van. Some irregular infantry, recruited from the landless peasants, was used in front of the centre as skirmishers or for protecting the rear. Thus, a new lethal technology—artillery—and a new defensive mechanism—the wagon *laager*, were adopted by the Ottomans without fundamentally changing the war-making practice of the arid zone. The infantry from behind the *laager* in front held the enemy centre at bay while the mobile light cavalry attacked the flanks and rear of the enemy. The final decisive blow was delivered by the heavy cavalry of the centre, who were released at the right moment. Thus, artillery warfare buttressed rather than marginalized the centrality of cavalry in arid zone warfare, unlike the developments in West and Central Europe, where the rise of the handgun-bearing infantry sounded the death-knell for the feudal cavalry in the sixteenth century.

A classic demonstration of the Ottoman tactics can be seen in the Battle of Chaldiran. In the summer of 1514, Sultan Selim led an army of around 70,000, including 12,000 Janissaries, eastwards to deal with the rising power of the Safavids of Persia. The

Safavid leader Shah Ismail confronted him with around 20,000 cavalrymen near Chaldiran in Azerbaijan. The advice of the senior Qizilbash commander of the left wing to attack the Ottomans before they could set up their *laager* was ignored by the Shah at the contrary suggestion by the commander of the right wing. Consequently, the Ottomans got ample time to array their wagons along their front line and shelter their well-trained Janissaries behind them. The battle was decided in favour of the Ottomans mainly due to their use of firepower. The Safavid cavalry charge almost carried the day, but the impact of Ottoman fire by cannons and Janissaries was too much for them. The battle was closely contested, but the *laager* won the day for the Ottomans.[38]

The combined impact of cavalry and artillery also proved difficult for the European powers. In 1526, the Ottomans invaded Hungary after capturing the fort of Belgrade. The Hungarian army met the invaders at Mohacs, between Belgrade and Buda. The Hungarians initially routed the Ottoman left as it was pitching its tents. But the Ottoman centre had enough time to set up its wagons along the front face of its centre and align its guns behind them. After the musketry of the Janissaries decimated the Hungarians, the Ottoman heavy cavalry charge made Hungarian defeat decisive. The Hungarian army was destroyed, the king and several of his nobles were killed and Buda surrendered without a fight.[39]

The technique of the combined use of artillery fire, cavalry tactics and the wagon *laager* was transmitted to the Safavids of Persia at about this time and this technique was used against the Uzbegs at the Battle of Jam. The Khurasan-Transoxania region was a battleground for the Safavids and the Uzbegs in the first half of the sixteenth century. In 1528, the Uzbegs besieged the city of Herat. The Safavid Shah Tahmasp led a relief army to Herat. A day-long battle resulted between the two armies near Jam and Khirgird. The Uzbeg cavalry numbered around 3,00,000, although they used only 1,00,000 in the actual battle. The Safavids on the other hand had between 50,000 to 1,00,000 men. Tahmasp, son of the defeated Shah Ismail from Chaldiran, organized his front in the *Rumi* style of wagon *laager*, placing his guns behind the line of wagons chained to each other and placed himself along with 20,000 choice heavy cavalry behind the carts.[40] The Uzbeg cavalry broke the two Safavid wings. They even wheeled to the Safavid rear and started looting the Safavid baggage and animals. But Safavid artillery fire checked the Uzbeg centre. After the initial setback, the Qizilbashes rallied around Tahmasp's standard. At the opportune moment, the chains between the wagons were lowered and the heavy cavalry, charged out from behind the centre. They were driven back thrice, but subsequently they saved the day for the Qizilbashes.[41]

The Uzbegs on the other hand seem to have learnt the above-mentioned technique from their experience against the Safavids and also from Ottoman professionals in their service. During the Herat campaign, the Uzbegs used the wagon *laager* tactics. Under the supervision of the Ottoman professional gunner Ustad Rumi, wagons were collected from all over Bukhara, chained with each other and placed along the front of the army to shelter the arquebusiers.[42]

From a study of the above-mentioned battles, we see that by the first half of the sixteenth century, the powers of the Eurasian arid zone had struck a perfect balance between cavalry warfare and gunpowder technology, without fundamentally altering the combination of heavy and light cavalry warfare that had been worked out in the later half of the first millennium CE. Babur's pitched battles in the Indian subcontinent attain a different significance altogether when viewed in this light. Such warfare was entirely novel in the Indian subcontinent. But again, the achievement was not Babur's alone. His early battles, prior to Panipat, show how he was already using in his army the combination of heavy and light cavalry, trademark of arid zone armies of the time. So his war-machine was structurally ready to accept firearms and the wagon *laager* when they were brought to him by the Ottoman gunners, Ustad Ali Quli and Mustafa Rumi.

BABUR'S BATTLES IN THE NORTH INDIAN PLAINS

First Battle of Panipat (CE 1526)

On 12 April 1526, Babur reached the plains of Panipat with his army. He kept the town of Panipat and its suburbs on his right flank, while the otherwise unguarded left flank was secured by digging ditches and gathering branches of trees. This meant that the army now became relatively secure from the enemy's possible charges on the flanks and the rear. Along the front of the army, around 700 carts, procured beforehand, were arranged under the direction of the Ottoman gunner Ustad Ali Quli in *Rumi* fashion.[43] These carts were joined together by ropes of raw hide with five or six mantelets fixed between every two carts, behind which the matchlockmen were to stand and fire. Such sheltering of the gunners was essential so as to give the primitive and slow firing matchlocks the time to be reloaded after every shot.[44] For the next seven-eight days, Babur deployed several skirmishers against the Afghan troops of Delhi, whose duty was to 'go, a few together, close up to Ibrahim's camp, rain arrows down on his massed troops, cut off and bring in heads'[45] and lure the enemy out of its camp. A body of skirmishers of around 4,000-5,000 men were also deployed, especially during the night to inflict losses and provoke the enemy to battle. But these provocations bore little fruit. Frustrated, Babur commented about Ibrahim, '. . . he made no move; nor did his troops sally out'.[46] This shows that the wagon *laager* tactic that Babur was using at Panipat was essentially defensive technique, dependant on the enemy making the first offensive move.

At last on 20 April, the Afghan army, numbering around 1,00,000 cavalry and 5,000-10,000 elephants along with a large number of infantry, advanced in battle array.[47] Seeing this, Babur's army, the strength of which has debatably been put around 10,000 cavalry,[48] also deployed in its formation—heavy cavalry in the centre, right wing, left wing, advance guard, reserve and the two flanking light cavalry units ('turning party') at the two extremities of the right and left flanks respectively. At the outset of the battle, the Afghans seemed to bear down more towards the right of Babur's army. The reserve was immediately directed to support that wing. The frontal charge of the Afghans was slowed down partially by cramping caused by charge by a longer frontal line on an enemy with a smaller frontal face and partially by hesitation generated by the sight of such a well-fortified enemy battle array. Consequently the Afghans failed to deliver the shock impact. Combat began along the left, right and centre of Babur's force. The Afghan elephants raging along the front were countered and several, like a particular one countered by Mahdi Khwaja, were driven back by intense arrow shots. The turning parties meanwhile encircled the Afghan Army and poured arrows on its flanks and rear. The combined action of heavy cavalry from the front and light mounted archers from the flanks and rear rolled up Ibrahim Lodi's army into a confused huddled mass, on which artillery and handgun fire from the left and right of Babur's centre, under the direction of Ustad Ali Quli and Mustafa Rumi, wreaked havoc. The Afghans lost the battle by the afternoon.[49]

Battle of Khanua (ce 1527)

On his way to meet Rana Sangram Singh in a battle, Babur first camped near Sikri. Like Panipat, skirmishers were dispatched against the enemy at this stage. But several of these groups suffered reverses at the hands of the Rajputs. It was at this stage that the incident of Babur's renunciation of wine as un-Islamic and the recognition of the impending battle against Rana Sangram Singh as a Holy War against *kufr* took place.[50] After completing all the arrangements, Babur marched with his army towards the plains of Khanua on 13 March 1527. His men were sent there beforehand, so that the defensive arrangements were ready by the time the army reached the site. Babur probably had around 20,000 men with him.[51] Along the front of the army were aligned carts, 7 or 8 yards apart, bound with one another by iron chains, instead of raw hides used at Panipat. At places where the carts were not present, Khurasani and Hindustani spadesmen dug ditches. In some places, strong wooden wheeled tripods were positioned at intervals of 7 or 8 yards and between them ropes of raw hides were stretched. These, besides the wagons, could act as shelter for matchlockmen and also as a platform for firing the heavy matchlocks. All these arrangements took 20 to 25 days to be completed.[52] The army camped near the village of Khanua, around 10 miles away from Sikri, facing west and south, with its left resting on, or partially flanked by the Khanua hill.[53] Rana Sangram Singh's Rajput-Afghan force with its cavalry, infantry and elephants, had the typical huge size of Indian subcontinental armies. Babur estimated its strength to be around 2,01,000.[54]

With the onset of the battle, the Rajputs charged on the two wings of the Mughals. The Rajput left wing bore down heavily on Babur's right wing. But reinforced by the contingent placed at the right of centre, the right wing fought back successfully, and beat back the Rajput attack, driving them almost to the rear of their centre. The repeated and desperate attacks of the Rajput right wing on Babur's left were also successfully repulsed. While the wings were engaged in desperate face-to-face close quarter combat, the artillery of the Mughals was put to great use by the Ottoman gunners, Ustad Ali Quli and Mustafa Rumi. Babur's infantry with their matchlocks and the canons made a heavy impact on the 'iron-clad fortress of the pagan ranks'.[55] The Mughal heavy cavalry was assisted on the wings by the fast-moving light cavalry of mounted archers who rained arrows constantly on the flanks and rear of the enemy forces by conducting an encircling manoeuvre. Finally, when the Rajputs and the Afghans had been rolled up into a confused and huddled mass by combined attack by heavy cavalry on the wings, artillery fire on the centre and continuous discharge of arrows from the flanks and the rear, Babur released from behind the artillery park in the centre, his *tabinan-i khasa-i padshahi*, or the royal corps of armour-clad heavy cavalry. Leaving the artillery park in between, they came out from its two sides and smashed through the enemy ranks. This shock charge, combined with a general advance of the whole army towards the now demoralized Rajput force carried the day decisively in favour of the Mughals. Babur notes in his memoir: 'Mounds were made of the bodies of the slain, pillars of their heads'.[56]

Having gone through brief descriptions of these battles, it would be useful to note the kind of battle formations, tactics, weapons and logistics Babur used in these battles. His army was always arrayed according to the traditional Central Asian battle formation—centre, left and right wings and advance and rear guards, with the leader of the force commanding the centre. Prior to the Battle of Kandahar, Babur explains this layout of his army in great detail. Babur also grouped his troops into tens and fifties, each under a leader who would lead his group in the battle array, thus making a separate *tawachi* (a sort of adjutant) unnecessary.[57] This was the traditional battle array of Central Asia. The armies of Chengiz Khan and Timur were also arrayed in a similar fashion.[58] Usually, in their big armies, different positions were hereditarily assigned to different clans. As far as Babur's battles are concerned, his Central Asian army was comparatively small. It is also interesting to note that at least at Panipat, the flanking parties were manned by Mongol auxiliaries, who probably specialized in mounted archery and swift manoeuvres.

The overwhelming majority of the army was cavalry of two main types—heavy and light. Heavy cavalry was stationed in the centre and the two wings. A special contingent of heavy cavalry, often acting as the personal troopers of Babur, was stationed at the centre (in these two battles, behind the wagon *laager*) along with the *Padshah*. Heavy cavalry led the frontal charge and engaged in combat with the enemy at a relatively close range. Armours of the heavy cavalrymen were fairly elaborate. Both mail as well as plate armour were used. Mail armour was usually worn over a quilted coat (*kubcha*) or *jama*. Mail was also used to protect the head and neck of a soldier. Plate armour was worn on the chest, on the back and on the limbs, while the head was protected by a hemispherical helmet. A shield was the principal defensive weapon. The importance of armour in the battles of Babur is well-evidenced by the important post of armourer in Babur's military establishment. Even the horses were covered with armour in battles.[59] For close combat, the cavaliers were equipped with spears, maces, battle-axes, bows, arrows and swords of various kinds.[60]

On the contrary, light cavalry, provided with light armour, was stationed at the extreme end of the two flanks. They had a completely different role in battles. Babur calls them 'the turning party (*tulghuma*)' and they were supposed to envelope the enemy from three sides, attack its flanks first and then its rear and rain down arrows constantly on them from a distance. The light armours of these archers and their horses made such fast tactical mobility possible. Such light mounted archers had another function, especially prior to the beginning of the battle proper-skirmishing. Groups of archers went near the enemy camp, shot arrows in quick succession, and then galloped back. The aim was to inflict quick losses of man and horse, and to enrage the enemy enough so that it was forced to get out of its formation and lead a charge towards Babur's well-fortified *laager*. As the wagon *laager* was essentially a tactically defensive formation, only such a charge by the enemy could get Babur's battle plan unfolding successfully. Hence, provoking the enemy to initiate the fighting was essential. This key function was assigned to the skirmishers. They could be seen in action against the Afghans, where they were credited with rapid successes. They, however, did not fare so well against Rana Sangram Singh, and successive advance parties were defeated by the Rajput forces.

As one notes these cavalry tactics of Babur's army operating in the Indian subcontinent, one is struck by its striking resemblance with Saljuq cavalry warfare, demonstrated at Manzikert in West Asia in the eleventh century. R.C. Smail sums up Saljuq light cavalry tactics under four points: (1) keeping convenient distance from their enemy and waiting for the ripe moment at which they would be near enough for being attacked; (2) performing feigned retreat to lure the enemy to chase them and thereby break their formation; (3) attacking the flanks and rear of the enemy; and (4) attacking an enemy and to force him to fight on the march. Smail goes on to say that the mobility and archery of the Turks alone were usually insufficient to give them victory. By such means they weakened the enemy, but final defeat on the battlefield was only achieved by close quarter combat with lance, sword and club.[61] The uncanny similarity this bears with Babur's battle tactics is due to the fact that the armies of both Babur and Saljuqs belonged to the same arid zone culture of warfare, preconditioned, above all, by ecology and geography of the region.

From the technological point of view, Babur's strength lay in two principal weapons—the composite bow and the firearm. Manufactured out of wood, horn and sinew by a complex process and arguably the most deadly weapon prior to the coming of modern firearms, the composite bow was an ancient weapon discovered first in Siberia and Central Asia in the third millennium BCE. It arrived in the Mediterranean civilizations in fifteenth-sixteenth centuries BCE.[62] Modifications were brought in the design of the bow in the ninth century BCE by Cimmerians to the north of Caucasus. Such bows were used against the Assyrian Empire in the seventh century BCE by the Scythians, who subsequently introduced it to the ancient Greeks. This latest variety was less angular than the earlier one and was more suited for mounted archery than the previous one. The Central Asian composite bow continued in this basic form ever since, in two main varieties—the Scythian and the Turkish composite bows—although undergoing minor alterations to suit purposes like penetrating tougher armours that often were built to counter the arrows shot from composite bows.[63] It was this technology of the arid zone that Babur had inherited. The *Baburnama* mentions Babur using different types of the composite bow—the slur bow, easy bow, etc.[64] Both his light and heavy cavalrymen used the composite bow from horseback efficiently and thus had a clear edge over his Indian adversaries, who mainly preferred to fight at close quarters.[65]

While Babur was a natural inheritor of the composite bow of the arid zone, the know-how of the other decisive weapon—firearms came to him from West Asia. The incident of Babur's first acquaintance with them is not recorded in the *Baburnama.*[66] The technology was brought to him by two Ottoman professionals, Mustafa Rumi and Ustad Ali Quli. The *Baburnama* mentions several types of firearms, *tufang* (matchlock), *firingi* (swivel gun), *qazan* (mortar), *zarb zan* (field cannon), culverin, etc. All these guns threw stones, and the use of metal projectiles was not yet known. Babur's *tufangs* or matchlocks were long arquebuses whose gunpowder had to be ignited with lighted matches, and hence the name. These were very much like the earliest matchlocks developed in Europe in the middle of the fifteenth century. It had a long barrel mounted on wooden butt and was fired with the butt resting on the right shoulder.[67] The loading of such guns was time-consuming and required precise repetitive skill, acquired through training.[68] This also made the rate of firing extremely slow, compared to archers.[69] The matchlockmen under Babur were all foot-soldiers. This, combined with slow firing rate of the matchlocks necessitated their sheltering behind the wagons. The *firingi* was also probably a matchlock, but one of European design[70] while a culverin was probably a larger and heavier matchlock, requiring the assistance of an attendant to work it.[71]

Zarb zan was light field cannon made of brass or bronze, with a long barrel and a funnel-shaped mouth.[72] During the battles, these were mounted on baggage carts (*araba*).[73] *Qazans* (mortars) were heavier guns with longer barrels designed for high-angle fire. While the *zarb zans* shot stones in a straight path up to a distance of 1,600 paces to strike a charging opponent from the front, the *qazans* fired stone balls in a parabolic path, so that the projectiles fired by it fell on the rear ranks of the enemy lines.[74]

Both these two types of guns were extremely heavy and required enormous manpower to haul them. Once inside the Indian subcontinent, however, these were conveniently drawn by elephants.[75]

FROM THE PLAINS TO THE RIVERS AND TRANSITION IN WARFARE

After the Battle of Khanua when the Rajput danger was suppressed, the major problem for Babur was caused by the Afghans, who were particularly strong in the Ganga basin and in the Bengal-Bihar region. Hence, in the aftermath of the Battle of Khanua, Babur had to devote much time to deal with the Afghans in eastern India. Hearing that Afghan forces had ousted his men from Lucknow and were besieging Kanauj, Babur, immediately after his occupation of Chanderi, had to rush with his forces to meet this threat. On hearing this, the Afghans, led by Malik Biban Afghan, Shaikh Bayazid Farmuli Afghan and Maruf Yaqub-khail Dilazak Afghan, fled from Kanauj. They crossed the Ganga and camped on its eastern bank so as to prevent Babur from crossing the river.[76] The military engagement that followed in the next few days between Babur's men and the Afghans cannot be called a battle keeping in view the relatively small scale of the engagements. However, a description of the engagement can bring out how the nature of it was starkly different from the two battles fought on the vast plains of north India.

BATTLE OF GANGA (CE 1528)

Babur with his troops bypassed Kanauj and encamped on the western bank of the river on 27 February 1528. Arrangements for crossing the river were started straightaway. Several *amirs* got engaged in assembling boats while Mir Muhammad *Jalaban* (raftsman) was sent to locate a convenient spot where a bridge of boats could be set up for the crossing. Thirty to forty boats of different sizes were soon collected. A place 1 *kos* downstream was selected for the crossing. Immediately work was begun there and supervisors were appointed to direct the work. Ustad Ali Quli found a place near that spot and started firing his mortar from that position, while Mustafa Rumi, along with his carts and matchlockmen, crossed over to an island below that spot and engaged the Afghans by matchlock-fire. Besides these two positions, yet another station was created a little upstream from the spot for the proposed bridge, from where the matchlockmen started firing at the Afghans. Several of Babur's *amirs* crossed the river in boats on skirmishing expeditions, but without much impact. In the end, when a group under Malik Qasim crossed over and provoked the Afghans, the latter charged with an elephant. Malik Qasim and his men got into the boat, but could not pull it off and the boat was sunk by the elephant, killing Qasim.[77]

It seems that the most commendable and useful job was done by Babur's artillery which kept the Afghans at bay while the bridge was being built. Ustad Ali Quli, from his mortar that had been named Ghazi after the Battle of Khanua, fired eight shots on the first day, sixteen on the second day and continued like-wise for another three to four days. Another large mortar that he managed to set up, however, burst after a single shot. The matchlockmen also worked efficiently, bringing down several of the Afghan men and horses.[78]

On 11 March, with the bridge nearing completion, Babur marched with his army to the crossing site. Babur noted that the slow pace of the bridge-making process was ridiculed by the Afghans. The next day the bridge was finished. Eventually, a body of infantrymen and Lahoris crossed over to the other side and was involved in a minor skirmish with the Afghans. On 13 March, the right and the left wings along with the centre of Babur's army crossed the bridge on foot. At once the whole Afghan force, fully armoured, charged on them with a contingent of elephants. Although they drove Babur's left wing back, the centre and right did well to hold in the face of the charge and pushed the Afghans back. The combat went on till late in the day. After this, all those who had crossed were again brought back to the camp. Babur noted in his autobiography that he did not order the whole of his army to cross over on that night be-cause he intended to attain victory on Sunday due to emotional reasons.[79] Consequently, on Sunday, the entire army was ordered to cross over. But, soon men from the advance guard reported that when the Afghans had realized that the whole of Babur's army was crossing, they fled leaving the field to the Mughals.[80]

BATTLE OF GHAGHRA (CE 1529)

In order to consolidate the existence of the nascent Mughal state, it was imperative for Babur to move east and destroy the Afghan threat. On 28 April 1529, Babur decided to cross the river Ganga near its confluence with the Ghaghra. The battle plan was made in a meeting involving all the Turkish and Hindustani *amirs*. According to the plan, the artillery was arrayed carefully to have maximum impact. Ustad Ali Quli, with his mortar, *firingi* and culverin would be stationed on a high ground between the Ganga and Ghaghra and would engage in battle from there with a large number of matchlockmen. Mustafa Rumi, along with several matchlockmen, would fire from the Bihar side of the Ganga, opposite to an island where the Afghans had stationed an elephant and tied up many boats. These artillerymen would be provided with shelters in the ground, which were to be built by men equipped with shovels and coolies. Muhammad Zaman Mirza, who was also provided with matchlockmen, was to dismount with his troops behind Mustafa Rumi as his reinforcement. Meanwhile, Askari and other *amirs* were to move north, cross the Ghaghra over to the enemy's side at the Haldi passage and be ready to charge the Afghans from that side.[81] Knowing that there might be a place for crossing the river further upstream, some other men were sent with a few raftsmen to inspect the ford, and cross the river from there. Mahmud Khan's *shiqdar* reported from Sikandarpur that he had collected 50 boats there and had paid the boatmen as well. Meanwhile, it was rumoured that the Afghans from Bengal were approaching.[82]

Hard pressed for time, Babur decided to assign a large contingent to cross the Ghaghra by boat at the Haldi ford and attack the enemy. They were to be guarded by the firing of the gunners. If Askari's force succeeded in drawing near, Babur's group would engage in battle from there and try to cross over. Muhammad Zaman Mirza, along with Mustafa Rumi, would also fight from the Bihar side. Thereby, a large army under Askari was dispatched towards the Haldi ford.

On 1 May, Babur's army began to cross the Ganga at dawn. Babur crossed over by boat around 6 a.m. Two days later, Babur's army marched for a *kos* from the place they had crossed the river and dismounted at the confluence near Ali Quli's position.[83] From their respective positions, Ali Quli and Mustafa were striking and sinking the boats of the Afghans at regular intervals. Babur brought in the big mortar to the fighting ground and assigned Mulla Ghulam, assisted by some *yasawals* (guards) and soldiers, to superintend its installation. That night, while Babur was sleeping in a boat near his camp, there was a night attack, which was checked by the Mughals.[84]

Next morning, Babur boarded his boat *Gunjaish*, went near the position of the artillerymen, and supervised operations there. A detachment of 1,000 men was sent to cross the Saru further upstream. Meanwhile, a large number of Bengali foot-soldiers crossed over in 20 to 30 boats to attack Askari's camp, but were routed by a timely charge from the Mughal detachment. Seven or eight boats of the Bengalis were captured and brought upstream under the cover of the night to facilitate their crossing. On the same day, some Bengalis also crossed over and offered to fight Muhammad Zaman Mirza. They fled when attacked, and three boats full of Afghans were drowned and one was captured and brought to Babur. Meanwhile, Askari succeeded in crossing the Ghaghra. Hence, all the parties which had been ordered to cross were instructed to rally around Askari's camp and advance to confront the Afghans. Ustad Ali Quli continued to fire stone balls from his mortar and *firingis*, while the Mughals got a taste of fire-works of the Bengali Afghan army, although, which, Babur says, was not particularly effective, as they did not fire counting to hit a particular spot, but fired at random.[85]

That afternoon, Babur ordered several boats to be hauled upstream opposite where the Afghans were stationed, and several *amirs* were ordered to provide them some protection. But, the protecting detachment proceeded somewhat ahead of the boats, and the Afghans spotted the boats being taken up-stream, and launched an attack. A boatman was shot in his leg and the mission failed.[86] Next morning, the artillerymen informed Babur that all the boats were coming downstream. The Afghan cavalry now started advancing towards the Mughal army. At this juncture, Babur ordered several of his *amirs* to cross the river at the ford with their men immediately and join forces with Askari, who was awaiting the Afghan attack. The Afghans did send a group of foot-soldiers, who could not sustain the charge of the Mughal horsemen and soon fled. Several Lahori and Hindustani nobles also crossed swimming or holding bundles of reeds or rafts made out of them. Seeing this, a mass of Bengalis opposite the artillery station turned their boats downstream and fled.[87] As per Babur's directions, the army that assembled on the other side under Askari was divided into three or four groups. As the Bengal Afghan army approached, they deployed their infantry forward to meet the Mughal cavalry charge. The Bengal Afghan army was attacked on one side by a detachment from Askari's army led by Kuki and on the other by a group led by the Mughal princes. The Mughal *amirs* fought well and won the day.[88]

Visibly, these two battles were quite different from the previous battles that Babur had fought. The military world of the arid zone, of which Babur was a part, did not necessarily demand great skill in crossing large rivers. Babur's army did not possess any boats before fighting the amphibious battles of Ganga and Ghaghra, neither did they have adequate knowledge of the geography of the region. Hence, much time and energy was spent in searching for suitable places to cross the river. In contrast, the Bengal Afghans evidently had the advantage of fighting on familiar terrain. They seem to have possessed many boats without which they could not have held their sultanate in the riverine and marshy region of Bengal and also a large infantry which often made up for the difficulty in deploying cavalry in the jungle and swampy tracts of eastern India. Nevertheless, the fact that even with such drawbacks, the Mughals did assemble a large number of boats without much difficulty, by applying force or by paying the boatmen beforehand proves their logistical expertise. The mention of raftsmen in the Battle of Ganga, who were never mentioned before this encounter, proves that new geographical necessities had prompted creation of new units with specialized skills. The employment of a mass of spadesmen and workers in building shelters for the artillerymen proves that the availability of cash aided Babur to gather cheap labour.

Unlike the first two major battles at Panipat and Khanua, the battles of Ganga and Ghaghra were not totally pitched battles. In the initial phase, the Mughals had to face attacks on a different ground that they had never faced before—water. The Mughals and their Mongol auxiliaries were adept at manoeuvring cavalry and mounted archery over flat plains. But countering an offensive while crossing a river on boats, where their horse-power was neutralized, was completely new. Once the army landed, the tougher part of the job would be done.

The wagon *laager* had proved to be a real Mughal strength in Panipat and Khanua. But in the battles of Ganga and Ghaghra, the artillery had to be deployed for some other purpose—assisting the crossing of the river by Babur's army by engaging the enemy with constant firing over several days and thus keeping him at bay. In both these battles, the artillery units did their jobs well, and Babur narrates how he succeeded in drowning several of the Afghan vessels. But precisely owing to this success at this altered role, the artillery was absent in the climactic field battle on the banks of Ghaghra and the cavalry had to fight in the pre-Panipat fashion without their *laager*. The cavalry probably engaged in close-quarter combat, with neither the deadly flank attack by the mounted archers, nor coordinated and joint mounted archery-artillery firepower being used. Fortunately for Babur, this did not affect the outcome of the engagement.

That these two riverine engagements do not fit into the structure of arid zone warfare that has been discussed above does not require much effort to understand. However, the significance of this misfit and its implications for the Mughal state might demand a bit more attention. The battles of Panipat and Khanua were fought in north-western plains of the Indian subcontinent. Geographically, this region belongs to the eastern fringes of the arid zone. It has vast plain lands and temperate grasslands and is much drier than other parts of the subcontinent. Between this region and the extension of the South-East Asian humid sub-tropical forested zone, extending into north-eastern India which receives above 200 cm of annual rainfall and houses moist tropical evergreen forests, there lies the vast river basin of Ganga and its tributaries. Covering the mainly modern Indian states of West Bengal, Bihar and Orissa (although the Ganga does not flow through the last), this has moist tropical deciduous vegetation and a moderate annual rainfall. This is climatically a unique zone in Eurasia. The Ganga basin has built here one of the most fertile and hence populous plains of the world. Several perennial, snow-fed large tributaries, like the Gomati, Ghaghra, Gandak, Kosi, and Tista flow into the Ganga while it flows through the modern Uttar Pradesh and Bihar region. Once it enters Bengal, the river breaks into several big and small distributaries. The Ganga plain hence is not continuous but broken repeatedly by the tributaries and distributaries of the Ganga, which poses a geographical peculiarity in itself. It was owing to such geography that the rulers of Bengal always had to have a large number of *paiks* and boats (riverine flotillas) in their army. Such geography and its military demands would be completely new to anyone coming from the Eurasian arid zone, and this was exactly the case with Babur. Since other than the recurrent big rivers, the terrain is almost entirely flat over this expanse and hence ideally suited for cavalry warfare otherwise, the major challenge for cavalry forces coming from the arid zone was tackling these rivers. This Babur did successfully, as in the battles of Ganga and Ghaghra.

Nevertheless, these battles signify that unlike the other major powers of contemporary Eurasian arid zone (i.e. the Ottomans, the Safavids and the Uzbegs), the Mughals under Babur were venturing into a completely new ecological and geographical zone, where their arid zone war machine could not be always deployed in its original form. About the weather of Hindustan (meaning largely the northern Indo-Gangetic plains), Babur comments,

> Sometimes it rains 10, 15 or 20 times a day; torrents pour down all at once and rivers flow where no water had been. . . . The fault is that the air becomes very soft and damp. A bow of those (Transoxanian) countries after going through the rains in Hindustan, may not be drawn even; it is ruined;[89] not only the bow, everything is affected, armour book, cloth, and utensils all; a house even does not last long.[90]

At another place he says, '. . . there are no good horses [in Hindustan]'.[91]

The two battles were not isolated events, but were representatives of the kind of warfare that the Mughals would have to adapt to in this ecological and geographical environment that changes progressively eastwards. In 1659-60, when the Mughal imperial army under Mir Jumla chased the army of the rebel prince Shah Shuja across the Bihar-Bengal region, possession of boats and flotillas would again prove to be the single most important factor in deciding the fate of the contest.[92] When Mir Jumla started from Dacca in 1661 for the conquest of the Kamrup-Assam region, his cavalry numbered 12,000 and his infantry

30,000. But the backbone of this expedition was a huge flotilla with at least 323 boats, which were used for transportation of troops and artillery.[93] Ultimately, the inhospitable eco-geographical conditions led to the disastrous defeat of the Mughals in this region.[94]

In the heyday of the Mughal Empire under Akbar, Jahangir, Shah Jahan and Aurangzeb, the Mughals had to campaign in four different eco-geographical zones—the drier arid zone in the north-west and west, the moist tropical river basin across the north, the rain-forests of eastern Indian subcontinent and the broken jungle-tracts of the peninsular plateau—a feat unparalleled by any other power of contemporary Eurasia. The success rate would vary considerably from one zone to another, owing primarily to the ecological and geographical factors. The Battle of Ghaghra represents the first such challenge that the Mughals had to face in the Indian subcontinent. The fact that they handled the crossing of the river well, showing much logistical expertise by procuring a large number of boats in a short time, won the day for them. Once they had crossed the river safely and been able to engage the Afghans in a pitched battle, the Mughals, with their superior cavalry, had a much better chance of overpowering the enemy from a wet tropical zone, possessing a large number of infantry but inferior war horses.

JUSTIFICATION OF WAR AND THE QUESTION OF JIHAD

Besides ecology and geography, ideology to an extent shaped the dynamics of Babur's battles in India. Two kinds of historiography press the issue that the war that Babur fought against Rana Sangram Singh on the plains of Khanua was a jihad. The first of this comes from pro-Hindu nationalist authors who often equate the scenario of Rajputs fighting against Mughals under Babur with the modern Indian hero fighting a foreign force. In such a world-view, from the later part of the first millennium CE, the Rajputs, who are seen as Indian-ness personified and vanguards of the land, are seen fighting against alien Muslim invaders but ultimately losing, only by chance, mistake or intrigue and thus failing to protect their motherland. In this spirit one biographer of Rana Sangram Singh writes that the Mughals won the battle because in spite of the greatness of their leader, the different Rajput clans had no sense of duty to their state or nation, no national feeling and no spirit of resistance to foreigners.[95] Another historian writes

> The Mughals came with new weapons and new strategy of war, but their religious ideology of *Jihad* and zeal remained as of old. This is borne out by the difference in Babur's attitude and actions in his two wars, one against the Muslim Ibrahim Lodi and the other against the Hindu Rana Sanga. Babur's war against Ibrahim Lodi was only a war, against Rana Sangram Singh it was *Jihad*. . . . Such language is used, such towers of heads of the slain are piled up, only in the case of Hindus. Similar ideas and actions are not found in Babur's description of wars against Muslims in India. The language betrays the psychology developed by the ideology of *Jihad* contained in Islamic scriptures. The ideology is not universal brotherhood. Its brotherhood is confined to Muslims only.[96]

And yet another describes the implication of the result of the battle thus: 'The Rajput ambition of banishing the foreign rule was completely shattered. Hereafter the rulers of Rajasthan never made any combined attempt to re-establish Hindu rule in northern India.'[97]

The second kind of understanding sees Babur's war against the Rajputs as a small chapter of a long history of Islamic Holy War against other religions that has continued from the birth of Islam and stretched up to the present day all over the world. I take as a representative of such a historical understanding a recent American publication. It locates Babur's jihad against Hindus in Khanua (and in also Chanderi) in a *longue duree* history of jihad in the Indian subcontinent on the one hand[98] and the Afro-Asian landmass, over a long time span stretching from the seventh century CE to the twentieth century. In doing so, this publication has brought a very large number of military expeditions by Muslim states across such a broad frame of space and time under the ideological umbrella of jihad. The confessional identity of these aggressors has been selectively, if not purposefully, highlighted at the cost of political, ethnic, ideological, cultural and other identities to create a monolithic world history of jihad.[99]

The issue of Babur's jihad at Khanua needs to be viewed as a part of Babur's search for legitimacy of his military expeditions, on the one hand, and as a matter of practical political expediency, on the other. Conquest and warfare were the social production of the class of military elite to which Babur belonged to. It was purely imperialist intentions that made him search in the Indian subcontinent a scope of carving out a kingdom for himself. The pretext he used for his expeditions here was that the territories of Punjab had once been a part of the empire of his paternal ancestor Timur, and hence regaining them for his house was his moral duty. Had he ventured towards China, as he had once planned to do,[100] surely he would have had to invent some other novel excuse. In this light, jihad was just another additional legitimizing factor that Babur found convenient to use to justify his battle against the Rajputs in particular and other non-Muslim powers of the subcontinent in general.

Prior to the battle, the atmosphere in the Mughal camp was tense, owing to the reputation of Rana Sangram Singh as a valiant warrior, who supposedly had never tasted defeat. Besides, several of Babur's skirmishing parties, that had been effective in causing considerable damage to the encamped Afghans prior to the Battle of Panipat, had suffered defeat at the hands of the Rajput forces. Babur knew that the battle would be crucial in terms of opening up or shutting down his politico-military prospects in the subcontinent. To top it all, just before the battle, an astrologer predicted that Babur would be defeated in the battle due to unfavourable position of stars.[101] In such a context, Babur used the declaration of jihad and the accompanying dramatic actions of oath-taking, renouncing of wine and smashing of his wine-vessels as a way to lift up the morale of his army and motivate them against a strong enemy.

That Babur placed many other things ahead of religious idiosyncrasy is clear from his memoirs. Religious sectarianism did not come in his way while accepting military aid from Shah Ismail of Persia, a Shia. In lieu of this, Babur accepted Shia creed, struck coins and read *khutba* in the name of the Shah, and even donned the red cap of the Qizilbash, much to the anger and irritation of his devout Sunni subjects of Samarkand.[102] While in Gwalior in September 1528, Babur visited some Hindu temples of the city. Babur describes the trip in a matter-of-fact way without the iconoclastic zeal expected of a religious fanatic. He says, 'We rode from the flower-garden to visit the idol-houses of Gualiar. Some are two, and some are three storeys high, each storey rather low, in the ancient fashion. On their stone plinths (*izara*) are sculpted images. Some idol-houses, college-fashion, have a portico, large high copulas and *madrasa*-like cells, each topped by a slender stone copula. In the lower cells are idols carved in the rock'.[103] Unlike at Khanua, where Babur had to pose as a *jihadi*, here he did not have to pretend to be an iconoclast, simply because there was no political expediency.

CONCLUSION

The soldiers of Babur had inherited the Central Asian culture of warfare by virtue of their origin from the specific ecological and geographical set up of the arid zone. Their military victories inside the subcontinent, however, were not always founded on systematic demonstrations of the same. The victories at Panipat and Khanua were due to the structural superiority of the arid zone war-machine based on the centrality of the warhorse and the composite bow, lately buttressed by the use of firearms. However, in the battles of Ganga and Ghaghra, the Mughals had to adjust to a terrain that was completely alien to the Central Asian scenario in terms of ecology and geography, and hence to the mode of warfare that the latter had generated. This adaptation signified the temporary sidelining of the Central Asian warhorse and composite bow in favour of boats and artillery. Thus, Jos Gommans' statement that '. . . as late as the eighteenth century the warhorse played a central role in the organisation of frontier empires bordering on the Central Eurasian heartlands of nomadic power'[104] does not hold good for these battles. In taking off from Gommans' depiction of the Mughal Empire as post-nomadic, this essay is part of an attempt to understand, from a military angle, the evolutionary, varied and multi-layered nature of the Mughal post-nomadic experience.

NOTES

1. For one of the major historiographical protests against this traditional isolationist treatment of the Mughals, see the introduction to M. Alam and S. Subrahmanyam (eds.), *The Mughal State, 1526-1750* (New Delhi: Oxford University Press, 2001), pp. 1-71.
2. See for example Iqtidar Alam Khan, 'Turko-Mongol Theory of Kingship', *Medieval India: A Miscellany*, vol. 2 (Aligarh, 1972); R.P. Tripathi, 'The Turko-Mongol Theory of Kingship', Alam and Subrahmanyam (eds.),

Mughal State, pp. 115-25; Richard C. Foltz, *Mughal India and Central Asia* (Oxford/Karachi: Oxford University Press, 1998); Lisa Balabanlilar, 'Lords of the Auspicious Conjunction: Turko-Mongol Imperial Identity on the Subcontinent', *Journal of World History*, vol. 18, no. 1 (2007), pp. 1-39. The otherwise wonderful contribution by Douglas Streusand, doing little justice to the title of the book, focuses majorly on Akbar's reign and imperial expansion under him, treating the reigns of Babur and Humayun as mere preludes to the Akbari period. Douglas Streusand, *The Formation of the Mughal Empire* (New Delhi: Oxford University Press, 1989).

3. William Erskine, Esq., *A History of India Under the Two First Sovereigns of the House of Taimur: Baber and Humayun*, vol. I (London: Longman, Brown, Green and Longmans, 1854); L.F. Rushbrook Williams, *An Empire Builder of the Sixteenth Century* (New Delhi: S. Chand & Co., n.d.); Stanley Lane-Poole, *Babar* (rpt., Delhi: Low Price Publications, 1990); Yusuf Husain, *Two Studies in Early Mughal History* (Simla: IIAS, 1976); Mohibbul Hasan, *Babur: Founder of the Mughal Empire in India* (New Delhi: Manohar, 1985); Yog Raj Malhotra, *Babur's Nobility and Administration in Hindustan* (Jalandhar: ABS Publications, 1996); Stephen F. Dale, 'Steppe Humanism: Autobiographical Writings of Zahir al-Din Muhammad Babur, 1483-1530', *International Journal of Middle East Studies*, vol. 22 (1990), pp. 37-58; Stephen F. Dale, 'The Poetry and Autobiography of the Babur-nama', *Journal of Asian Studies*, vol. 55, no. 2 (August 1996), pp. 635-64.
4. For a wonderful insight into the role of treasures in warfare and state-formation, see Dirk H.A. Kolff, 'A Warlord's Fresh Attempt at Empire', in Alam and Subrahmanyam (eds.), *The Mughal State*, pp. 75-114.
5. For a larger historiographical debate over this methodology, see Yuval Noah Harari, 'The Concept of "Decisive Battles" in World History', *Journal of World History*, vol. 18, no. 3 (2007), pp. 251-66.
6. Jadunath Sarkar, *Military History of India* (1960, rpt., New Delhi: Orient Longmans, 1970); Kaushik Roy, *From Hydaspes to Kargil: A History of Warfare in India from 326 BC to AD 1999* (New Delhi: Manohar, 2004); Kaushik Roy, *India's Historic Battles: From Alexander the Great to Kargil* (New Delhi: Permanent Black, 2004).
7. Works on technology include among others A.J. Qaisar, *Indian Response to European Technology and Culture (AD 1497-1707)* (New Delhi: Oxford University Press, 1982) and Iqtidar Alam Khan, *Gunpowder and Firearms: Warfare in Medieval India* (New Delhi: Oxford University Press, 2004).
8. Jos L. Gommans, 'The Silent Frontier of South Asia, *c.* 1200-1800', *Journal of World History*, vol. 9 (1998), pp. 1-23; Jos L. Gommans, *Mughal Warfare: Indian Frontiers and High Roads to Empire, 1500-1700*

(London: Routledge, 2002); Jos L. Gommans, 'Warhorse and Post-Nomadic Empire in Asia, *c.* 1000-1800', *Journal of Global History*, vol. 2 (2007), pp. 1-21.

9. Dale, 'The Poetry and Autobiography', pp. 636-7.
10. Balabanlilar, 'Lords of the Auspicious Conjunction', p. 3.
11. Dale, 'The Poetry and Autobiography', p. 637.
12. J. Russell Smith, 'Grassland and Farmland in the Cyclical Development of Eurasian History', *Annals of the Association of American Geographers*, vol. 33, no. 3 (September 1943), pp. 16, 18.
13. Around 1,000 Scythian horse-archers were deployed by Alexander against Paurava in the battle of Hydaspes in 326 BC. This was the first recorded instance when the Indian subcontinent saw the tactical application of mounted archery in battles. Roy, *India's Historic Battles,* pp. 19-20.
14. The ratio of heavy cavalryman to a light mounted archer was 1:10 during the Parthian period. This tilted radically in favour of the former under the Sassanians. Kaveh Farrokh and Angus McBride, *Sassanian Elite Cavalry,* AD *224-642* (Oxford: Osprey Publishing, 2005), p. 7.
15. Roy, *India's Historic Battles,* p. 38.
16. Helen Nicholson and David Nicolle, *God's Warriors: Knights Templar, Saracens and the Battle of Jerusalem* (Oxford: Osprey Publishing, 2006), pp. 99-102.
17. For proficiency of the Mamluks in horse-archery, see J.D. Latham, 'The Mamluk Horse-Archers', *Bulletin of the School of Oriental and African Studies,* vol. 32, no. 2 (1969), pp. 257-67.
18. Kenneth Chase, *Firearms: A Global History to 1700* (Cambridge: Cambridge University Press, 2003), pp. 6-15.
19. Fertile plain land implied the presence of a large sedentary population. Farmers of these quarters often acted as part-time soldiers as well, mostly as infantry. Hence the proportion of infantry in armies of sedentary lands was always much more than in case of nomadic/semi-nomadic armies, whose socio-economy had a surplus population of horses.
20. Rene Grousset, *The Empire of the Steppes: A History of Central Asia,* tr. N. Walford (New Jersey: Rutgers University Press, 1988), pp. 223-6; David Morgan, *The Mongols* (Oxford/New York: Blackwell Publishing, 1990), pp. 90-1; Mansura Haidar, *Medieval Central Asia: Polity, Economy and Military Organisation, Fourteenth to Sixteenth Centuries* (New Delhi: Manohar, 2004), p. 245.
21. Roy, *From Hydaspes to Kargil,* p. 65; Roy, *India's Historic Battles,* pp. 42-3.
22. Minhaj-us-Siraj, *Tabakat-i Nasiri,* in H.M. Elliot and J. Dowson, *The History of India as Told by its Own Historians* (rpt., Delhi: Low Price Publications, 2001), pp. 296-7; Roy, *India's Historic Battles,* pp. 40-5.

23. Zahiruddin Muhammad Babur, *Baburnama*, tr. A.S. Beveridge (New Delhi: Munshiram Manoharlal, 1998), p. 113. Although Babur does mention the use of foot-soldiers here, he also indicates that they were provided with mantelets, which were essentially defensive weapons, unlike the subcontinental infantry who were mainly equipped with swords and spears.
24. *Baburnama*, tr. Beveridge, p. 113.
25. Babur says that he had captured Samarkand with 240 men. To this was added a contingent of 4,000-5,000 men under Ayub Begchik and Qashka Mahmud, coming from Sultan Mahmud Khan and 100-200 men under Khalil from Jahangir Mirza. Taking a mean of these figures, an estimate of 5,000 men seems reasonable. *Baburnama*, tr. Beveridge, pp. 137-8.
26. *Baburnama*, tr. Beveridge, pp. 139-40.
27. Babur says that his forces numbered around 2,000; but half of them being busy in plundering the area, could not join him for the battle. Ibid., pp. 333-4.
28. Ibid., p. 335.
29. Ibid., pp. 333-6.
30. Chase, *Firearms*, p. 1.
31. Ibid., pp. 56-82; Geoffrey Parker, 'The "Military Revolution", 1560-1660—A Myth?', *Journal of Modern History*, vol. 48, no. 2 (June 1976), pp. 195-214; David Eltis, *The Military Revolution in Sixteenth-Century Europe* (London/New York: I.B. Tauris, 1995).
32. For the details on the battle of Adrianople and the role played by the *laager* in it, see Simon Macdowall and Howard Gerrard, *Adrianople AD 378: The Goths Crush Rome's Legions* (Oxford: Osprey Publishing, 2001).
33. Richard A. Gabriel, *The Great Armies of Antiquity* (Greenwood Publishing Group, 2002), p. 275.
34. Helen Nicholson, *Medieval Warfare: Theory and Practice of War in Europe, 300-150* (Hampshire/New York: Palgrave Macmillan, 2004), p. 136.
35. Ibid., pp. 89-90.
36. Rhodes Murphy, *Ottoman Warfare: 1500-1700* (New York: Routledge, 1999), pp. 107-8.
37. For reloading fifteenth-sixteenth-century matchlocks, a considerably long time and a complex repetitive action was required. It was hence essential to give the matchlockmen some kind of shelter at this phase of development of firearms to protect them from cavalry charge of the enemy while they were reloading their guns. Eltis, *The Military Revolution*, pp. 45-53.
38. Chase, *Firearms*, pp. 119-20.
39. Ibid., p. 90.

40. Ibid., p. 123.
41. Ibid.
42. Haidar, *Central Asia*, p. 315.
43. This refers to the wagon *laager* tactics that the Ottomans used in the famous Battle of Chaldiran against the Persians in CE 1514, which I have already described in detail. Beveridge comments that Ustad Ali Quli might have been present in this battle. *Baburnama*, tr. Beveridge, p. 469.
44. Ibid., pp. 468-9.
45. Ibid., p. 471.
46. Ibid.
47. Babur put Ibrahim's army at 1,00,000 cavalry and 1,000 elephants. Mohibbul Hasan cites Abul Fazl, Firishta and Nizamuddin agreeing with him, but Nimatullah putting the number of elephants at 500. Mohibbul Hasan, *Babur*, p. 69. Gulbadan Begum puts it at 1,80,000 cavalry and 1,500 elephants, which is clearly an exaggeration. Gulbadan Begum, *History of Humayun: Humayun-nama*, tr. A.S Beveridge (New Delhi: Oriental Reprint, 1983), p. 94.
48. Mirza Muhammad Haidar Dughlat, *A History of the Moghuls of Central Asia being the Tarikh-i Rashidi of Mirza Muhammad Haidar, Dughlat*, tr. N. Elias and E. Denison Ross (London/New York: Curzon Press, 1895), p. 358. Gulbadan Begum says that Babur had 12,000 men including the camp-followers and his fighting personnel numbered 6,000-7,000. Gulbadan, *Humayun-nama*, p. 94.
49. *Baburnama*, tr. Beveridge, pp. 472-4.
50. Ibid., pp. 551-6. The significance of this event has been infinitely debated by historians, and the present writer will return to its discussion shortly.
51. Hasan, *Babur*, p. 91. Although Rushbrook Williams differs with him, Hasan's analysis is more acceptable. Williams, *Empire Builder*, p. 152.
52. *Baburnama*, tr. Beveridge, p. 550.
53. Williams, *Empire Builder*, p. 149.
54. *Baburnama*, tr. Beveridge, pp. 561-3. Babur summarizes the battle order of the joint Rajput-Afghan force in the following manner: Rana Sangram Singh's own troops—1,00,000; Salah al-Diny—30,000; Rawal Uday Singh of Bagar—12,000; Medini Rai—12,000; Hasan Khan of Mewat—12,000; Bar Mal of Idr—4,000; Narpat Hara—7,000; Satrvi of Kutch—6,000, Dharam Deo—4,000; Bir Singh Deo—4,000; and Mahmud Khan—10,000. Gulbadan also puts the Rana's cavalry at 200,000. Gulbadan, *Humayun-nama*, p. 98. Mohibbul Hasan cites *Vir Vinod* as putting the numbers at 2,00,000 horses and a large body of foot. Hasan, *Babur*, p. 100.
55. This could signify, as A.S. Beveridge suggests, cataphract elephants. It could also indicate cavalrymen in heavy armour. But perhaps in the

context of a sixteenth-century Rajput army, the phrase was more likely to mean both.

56. *Baburnama*, tr. Beveridge, pp. 568-73.
57. Ibid., p. 334.
58. Haidar, *Central Asia*, pp. 233, 279.
59. G.N. Pant, *Mughal Weapons in the Baburnama* (Delhi: Agam Kala Prakashan, 1989), pp. 102-38.
60. Ibid., pp. 51-101.
61. R.C. Smail, *Crusading Warfare: 1097-1193* (Cambridge: Cambridge University Press, 1972), pp. 77-82.
62. Murray B. Emaneau, 'The Composite Bow in India', in *Proceedings of the American Philosophical Society*, vol. 97, no. 1 (February 1953), p. 78.
63. For Central and West Asian archery and bows, also see Charles R. Bowlus, *The Battle of Lechfeld and its Aftermath* (Aldershot, Hampshire: Ashgate, 2006), pp. 27-36; Denis Sinor, 'The Inner Asian Warriors', *Journal of the American Oriental Society*, vol. 101, no. 2 (April-June 1981), pp. 133-44; J.D. Latham, 'Notes on Mamluk Horse-Archers', *Bulletin of the School of Oriental and African Studies*, vol. 32, no. 2 (1969), pp. 257-67; Walter Emil Kaegi Jr., 'The Contribution of Archery to the Turkish Conquest of Anatolia', *Speculum*, vol. 39, no. 1 (January 1964), pp. 96-108; W.F. Patterson, 'The Archers of Islam', *Journal of the Economic and Social History of the Orient*, vol. 9, nos. 1/2 (November 1966), pp. 69-87.
64. Pant, *Mughal Weapons*, pp. 21-31.
65. Both the Afghans and Rajputs usually charged with spears, swords and maces and preferred to fight in close quarters. Roy, *India's Historic Battles*, pp. 33-8, 53, 59-60.
66. There is a gap of eleven years between 2 May 1508 and 3 January 1519 in the text of *Baburnama*. Babur's introduction with firearms seems to have taken place some time during this period. It should be noted that Babur did actually have knowledge of gunpowder from beforehand, although he might not have come across them personally. While describing Sultan Husain Mirza's siege of Hisar in CE 1496, he mentions both the use of gunpowder in mines for blasting the walls of the town and discharge of stones from mortars against the walls and towers. However, it is necessary to point out simultaneously that these were siege appliances. No mention of field artillery is found at this stage. *Baburnama*, tr. Beveridge, p. 59.
67. Pant, *Mughal Weapons*, p. 162.
68. Ibid., pp. 168-71.
69. In Europe, at the close of the seventeenth century, a musket that shot once in a minute was considered good, while an unskilled musketeer could even take ten minutes between two shots. Eltis, *The Military Revolution*, p. 15.

70. William Erskine, in his translation, equates a *firingi* with a swivel gun. He says, 'The word is now used in the Dekkan for a swivel. In common usage, *zarb-zin*, at the present day, is a small species of swivel. Both words, in the time of Baber, appear to have been used for field cannon.' *Memoirs of Zehir-ed-din Muhammed Baber, Emperor of Hindustan*, tr. John Leyden and William Erskine (London: Longman, Rees, Orme, Brown and Green, 1826), p. 306. Beveridge and G.N. Pant also hold the same opinion. *Baburnama*, tr. Beveridge, pp. 473-74; Pant, *Mughal Weapons*, pp. 160-2. However, it should be noted that the swivel gun was invented in Asia, not in Europe as the name *firingi* would suggest, and that too in the eighteenth century. These were used for the first time in the Indian subcontinent by Ahmad Shah Abdali in the Third Battle of Panipat in 1761. He mounted these on the back of camels and hence these came to be known as *shaturnals* (*shatur* meaning camel). Roy, *India's Historic Battles*, p. 89. So it was not possible for Babur to possess anything like a mobile swivel gun in the 1520s. Iqtidar Alam opines that a *firingi* was a variety of small field cannon from which the *shaturnal* was developed later on. Khan, *Gunpowder*, pp. 69-71.
71. *Baburnama*, tr. Beveridge, p. 667.
72. Khan, *Gunpowder*, pp. 71-2.
73. Erskine omitted the part of the text bearing number of these carts and due to this decontextualization, he mistook *arabas* to be gun-carriages. *Memoirs of Zehir-ed-din Muhammed Baber, Emperor of Hindustan*, tr. John Leyden and William Erskine, p. 304. Misguided by this translation, Staneley Lane-Poole equated the number of carts present with the number of field cannons and put the number of field cannons at 700. Lane-Poole, *Babar*, pp. 161-2. However, it was not possible for Babur to possess such an enormous arsenal, simply for logistical difficulties, if not for anything else. Beveridge corrected this in her translation. *Baburnama*, tr. Beveridge, pp. 468-9.
74. Khan, *Gunpowder*, pp. 64-9.
75. Among the usefulness of an elephant, Babur mentions that it can carry 'without trouble the cart of the mortar (*qazan*) it takes four or five hundred men to haul'. *Baburnama*, tr. Beveridge, p. 489.
76. Ibid., p. 598.
77. Ibid., p. 599.
78. Ibid., pp. 599-600.
79. Babur says that he had beaten Rana Sangram Singh on the fourth day after *Nauroz* the previous year. Sunday, 15 March, would also be the fourth day after *Nauroz* that year. So, if he would beat another foe on that day, it would be a remarkable coincidence. Ibid., tr., p 600.
80. Ibid., p. 601.
81. Ibid., pp. 667-8.
82. Ibid., p. 668.
83. Here the English translations differ with respect to Babur's position.

While Erskine and Thakcston have Babur dismount a *kos* away from the battlefield, Beveridge has Babur march for a *kos* and then dismount at the battleground 'near Ali Quli's emplacement'. Since Babur then mentions of having gone himself to see Ali Quli's firing, the place where his troops dismounted is more likely to have been at the battlefield, rather than one *kos* away from it. *Baburnama*, tr. Beveridge, p. 670; *The Baburnama: Memoirs of Babur, Prince and Emperor*, tr., ed. and annotated by Wheeler M. Thackston (New York/Oxford: Oxford University Press, 1996), p. 436; *Memoirs of Zehir-ed-din Muhammed Baber, Emperor of Hindustan*, tr. Leyden and Erskine, p. 414.

84. *Baburnama*, tr. Beveridge, pp. 669-70.
85. Ibid., pp. 671-2. Iqtidar Alam opines that the only type of firearms the Bengalis could have had at this time were rockets, or *bans*. Iqtidar Alam Khan, 'Early Use of Cannon and Musket in India: AD 1442-1526', *Journal of the Economic and Social History of the Orient*, vol. 24, no. 2 (May 1981), p. 154. The knowledge of gunpowder was probably brought to Bengal by the Portuguese and the Chinese. Jadunath Sarkar, *Military History of India*, p. 53. For a general discussion on rocketry in pre-colonial India, see Kaushik Roy, 'Rockets under Haidar Ali and Tipu Sultan', *Indian Journal of History of Science*, vol. 40, no. 4 (2005), pp. 635-55.
86. *Baburnama*, tr. Beveridge, p. 672.
87. Ibid., pp. 672-3.
88. Ibid., pp. 673-4.
89. The same malfunction of the composite bow, a weapon of the dry arid zone, also happened in the moist maritime regions of Europe, especially north of the Alps, and even in the Mediterranean climate. Charles R. Bowlus, *The Battle of Lechfeld*, p. 29. Bowlus also mentions how in CE 624, an unexpected shower jeopardized eastern Turkish firepower by damaging their composite bows and led to their defeat against the military forces of the Chinese Tang dynasty.
90. *Baburnama*, tr. Beveridge, pp. 519-20.
91. Ibid., p. 518.
92. Jagadish Narayan Sarkar, *The Life of Mir Jumla: The General of Aurangzeb* (Calcutta: Thacker, Spink and Co., 1951), pp. 160-201.
93. Ibid., p. 226.
94. Ibid., pp. 252-78.
95. Har Bilas Sarda, *Maharana Sanga, The Hindupat: The Last Great Leader of the Rajput Race* (rpt., New Delhi: Kumar Brothers, 1970), pp. 149-52. The narrative is otherwise replete with the stories of greatness of the Rana and how his exploits made the Mughals frightened before the battle. Among other causes of Rajput defeat, Sarda mentions treachery of the Rajput Silhadi who commanded the van of the allied forces and defected to Babur with a force of 35,000 cavalry just before the battle

and the chance factor by which the substitution of an injured Maharana by Raj Rana Ajjaji led to chaos and confusion within ill-knit Rajput-Afghan allied forces.

96. K.S. Lal, 'Jihad under the Turks' and 'Jihad under the Mughals', in K.S. Lal, *Theory and Practice of Muslim State in India* (New Delhi: Aditya Prakashan, 1999), pp. 62-8. Reprinted in Andrew G. Bostom (ed.), *The Legacy of Jihad: Islamic Holy War and the Fate of Non-Muslims* (New York: Prometheus Books, 2005), pp. 456-61.
97. Ashirbadi Lal Srivastava, *The Mughul Empire: 1526-1803* AD (Agra: Shiva Lal Agarwal & Co., 1969), pp. 28-9.
98. Thus, Babur's *jihad* has been said to have had earlier precedents inside the Indian subcontinent in the those by Muhammad bin Qasim in Sind, Yaqub bin Layth against Kabul, Subuktigin of Ghazni, Mahmud of Ghazni in Thanesar, Kanauj, Sirsawa and Somnath, Muhammad Ghuri, Alauddin Khalji, Timur, Adil Shah of Bijapur against Vijayanagara continued later by Ahmad Shah Abdali and the Moplahs. Bostom (ed.), *The Legacy of Jihad.*
99. Bostom (ed.), *The Legacy of Jihad.*
100. *Baburnama*, tr. Beveridge, pp. 157-8.
101. Ibid., p. 551.
102. Ibid., pp. 354-6; Riazul Islam, *Indo-Persian Relations: A Study of the Political and Diplomatic Relations between the Mughal Empire and Iran* (Teheran: Iranian Culture Foundation, 1970), pp. 8, 192-5.
103. *Baburnama*, tr. Beveridge, p. 613.
104. Gommans, 'Warhorse and Post-Nomadic Empire', p. 21.

CHAPTER 5

Territories, Wars, Nation

Chronicling Ahom-Mughal Confrontation

ARUPJYOTI SAIKIA

INTRODUCTION

Narratives of Ahom-Mughal confrontation (1615-82) have been carefully documented by the Ahom chronicles, *buranjis*, as well as Persian chronicles.[1] A few amongst these wars have continued to attract the attention of later scholars. These wars have also, primarily in the twentieth century, served significantly to strengthen the cause of Assamese nationalism.[2] The latter severely diminished the ways in which one could study the larger aspects of the Ahom-Mughal military engagement. What we also lost in this process was the larger and complex diplomacy that a frontier polity and the Mughals were engaged in.

The Ahom narratives are of several types. While some of them are eye-witness accounts reported by spies or ambassadors, several others are later remembrances. A few are accounts compiled through arrangement of letters of exchange between the Ahom-Mughal kings. These *buranjis* became easily accessible only in the twentieth century after their edited and printed publications became available. More importantly, these *buranjis* and their account of the Ahom-Mughal conflict have come to play a significant role in the historical consciousness of Assamese society since the early twentieth century.

The present essay aims to renew an engagement with the Ahom-Mughal military rivalry in the light of the above discussions and to emphasize how the narratives of these wars were sensitive to complexities of wars. The arguments of this essay are broadly distributed in six sections: the first section compares the Ahom military system with that of the Mughal system and the second gives a brief overview of the Ahom-Mughal military rivalry. While the third section addresses the complexities of Ahom chronicles, the two subsequent sections address key elements which occupied central position in these narratives. The concluding section sums up how later description became an integral part of the Assamese nationalistic historical imagination.

THE AHOM MILITARY SYSTEM: PEASANTS IN GUERRILLA WARFARE

> . . . the Ahom army was synonymous with the people, the *paik-peasants*, hierarchically organised and trained, ready for short notice mobilisation, and backed by the entire resources and the strategic advantages of land and the psychological sense of unity.[3]

Most historians agree that the Mughal Empire had a well-organized military system.[4] The Mughal military system made sure that the empire could defend its territory and secure more resources as and when required. Also well-known is the fact that the Mughal army which participated in wars in this region was different in composition from the one in Bengal.[5] Petty local zamindars irrespective of whether Hindu or Muslim became part of the Mughal expeditions to Assam.[6] The Ahom military system was based on *paiks* and their training as infantry soldiers.[7] The army chiefly consisted of infantry and to a lesser extent of cavalry. A hierarchy of officials brought stability to the system and their presence made sure a large force could be mobilized during the time of war. These officials were designated with various titles, and remained responsible for specific strategic operations; they underwent regular training which was physical in nature and based on tactical understanding. Primarily, the system of organization of ordinary soldiers was based on compulsory recruitment of 'able-bodied adults', between the age group of sixteen to sixty, known as *kanri paik*. A unit of four such persons—*paik*—formed a *got* that used to render services on rotation. The services they performed were manifold. There are no accurate figures to indicate the strength of such recruits during the time of crisis. Non-serving *paiks* formed the standing militia; they had to perform their duty as and when required. Various officers, forming a hierarchy in decimal system, regulated the *paiks*. During peace-time, the task of providing safety and security was entrusted to some of them but it relied more on the efficiency of superior officials rendering the Ahom system into a more bureaucratic apparatus. Since the seventeenth century newer administrative-military offices were created and the man-power pool was organized into several units known as *khel*.[8] Amalendu Guha argues that such remodelling was an attempt on the part of Ahom monarchy to strengthen itself by transforming the nobility into a military-administrative service. With their emergence as a superior political force in the region, the Ahoms began to gather the support of a number of tributary, feudatory or hill-chiefs apart from those who were conscripted.[9]

The army consisted of infantry, cavalry, elephantry, artillery as well as navy. Localized wars and supply of logistical support helped to keep the non-combatant members in the Ahom Army minimal.[10] The forces were led by two designated officials—*barbarua* in eastern Assam and *barphukan* in western Assam. Strategic preferences made one of them the commander-in-chief. These officials were also joined by the principal ministers in the Ahom court during the time of war. In the absence of a regular standing army how were soldiers trained for wars? Regular training in the *akharas* took place for the recruited *paiks*.[11] Strict discipline was enforced on them. Since 1530s the Ahoms began to acquire better technology of firearms and 130 years later 'excellent gunpowder, matchlocks, and cannon'[12] were produced locally but that hardly surpassed the Mughal achievement in gunpowder.[13] Artillery, however, was only used by the skilled soldiers. The mastery of the Ahom kingdom in matters of elephant is exemplified by a well-known text on elephant management.[14] Elephants were captured, trained, and they became the main support for wars. Elephant came as a major support for transportation of infantry in various difficult terrains as changing weather. Skilled *mahout*, elephant keepers, and officers supervised the elephants of the Ahom kingdom. Specialized guilds took care of the great stock of elephants. Tribute in the form of elephants was also collected from defeated tribes and feudatory chiefs. Linked to this heavy dependence of Ahom war strategy on elephants was the kingdom's careful utilization of local ecology and a brief outline of the ecology of the war fields would not be out of place here. The general ecology of the Ahom kingdom, the Brahmaputra Valley in particular, was characterized by flat topography regularly crisscrossed by a river system. Lines of low and jungle-covered hills would wait for the enemies and would also act as a strong shield against their weapons and people. The terrain was often muddy and sticky during the rains. This also restricted the access of everyday needs for the enemies. Linked to this was Mughal Army's great reliance on cavalry which could not withstand the difficult terrain in the plains of the Brahmaputra Valley.[15]

The wars were fought mostly through guerrilla tactics. Later works, like the *Comprehensive History of Assam*, emphasize various guerrilla tactics like deception, blockade, espionage, or mountain warfare as crucial elements to the Ahom military strategy.[16] Along with guerrilla strategy, war-diplomacy also played an important part is evident from the presence of elaborate staff holding the rank of ambassadors. Years of diplomatic experiences helped them to get to higher ranks. Since the early seventeenth century the Ahom kings began to employ Brahmin ambassadors exclusively though other ambassadorial families also existed.[17] Ramparts and forts, apart from a chain of check posts, *chaukis*, provided essential support for all military engagements. The latter also worked as a key element of espionage and other diplomatic relationship. Overland fortification was done on both the banks of the Brahmaputra River. Topography played a key role in the selection of sites for fortification. Additional buffer zone was also created between the war sites and the fortified places. A good selection of local timber and other forest produce supported the field fortification conducted by the army during campaigns. Added to this was the innovative military engineering which helped in the construction of marine forts.[18] The Ahom rulers successfully harnessed the topography to their military strategy.

Several Ahom chronicles had also grasped the essentials of Mughal warfare. It is doubtful whether they tried to integrate this understanding to their military engineering. Innovation in strategy became gradually rare and by the late eighteenth century the Ahom kingdom had to depend on hired mercenaries who also failed to protect the kingdom's territorial integrity from the aggression of the Burmese.

AHOM-MUGHAL WARS: UNDERSTANDING THE POLITICAL ECONOMY OF WARFARE

The Mughal's early interaction with the people of the region living in Bengal's eastern frontier along the river Brahmaputra was on the familiar lines as those followed by the previous Muslim conquerors of this region. However, since the second decade of the seventeenth century, with Emperor Jahangir in control, events acquired a dramatic turn. The next seven decades saw both the Mughal Empire and the Ahom kingdom engage in aggressive war punctuated by years of relative absence of direct confrontation.[19] The long years of military engagement can be broadly divided into four distinct phases: first phase, 1613-39; the second phase, 1639-61; the third phase, 1661-71 and the final phase, 1671-82.

The First Ahom-Mughal War took place in 1615. It was preceded by a couple of years of Mughal attempt to assert its territorial claim in Kuch Bihar and Kamrup. An access to this region was vital from the perspective of trade in various forest produce. Mughal political intervention in the western territories of the Ahom Kingdom also resulted in political dissent. To thwart any aggression, the Ahom Kingdom pursued a policy of extending friendly overtures towards rebel political forces. A war in 1613 led to the annexation of both Kuch Bihar and Kamrup. The annexed territory was integrated into the Mughal revenue system. Increased revenue burden led to peasant dissatisfaction which was suppressed.[20]

The prospect of the western frontier working as buffer zone against the Mughal Empire being lost, the Ahoms got involved in an aggressive political culture. Conflicts of commercial interest led to diplomatic fallout and the first phase of war began in AD 1615. Both sides incurred losses but the Ahoms, mostly due to rethinking of their war strategies, could repulse an early Mughal invasion. For the Mughal Empire, scope for rich trade in elephants, gold, pepper and lignum wood was sure to bring its interests to this part of the country.[21] Also textile production from Mughal India had a readymade market in the Brahmaputra Valley. The loss of Mughal imperial authority though did not result in any territorial gain for the Ahom kingdom, but it had a direct bearing on the contemporary political culture of the region. It led to realignment of anti-Mughal forces with that of the Ahom Kingdom in a renewed thrust. This resulted in the disruption of Mughal commercial and economic interests such as failure to procure wild elephants.

The Ahom-Mughal relations moved into a fresh round of diplomacy during the reign of Shahjahan (1628-58). The western frontier of the Ahom Kingdom was well fortified.[22] Balinarayan, the tributary king of the Ahoms, had fortified Darrang and acted as a buffer against any Mughal aggressiveness. Finally war broke out in 1636. Unlike 1615, this time both sides had to wait for years to see a decisive result coming in. The Mughals won a critical military victory in 1639 which led to the conclusion of a treaty. Forced by strategic compulsion, both sides expressed their keenness to conclude a treaty of peace in February 1639. Through this treaty, the Ahoms formally acknowledged the Mughal control of Kamrup; and the Mughals acknowledged the independent status of the Ahom monarchy.

Though it took another two decades for resumption of any formal war between the two, the Ahom-Mughal relations following the treaty was far from comfortable. Trade and commercial activities were resumed. Yet, despite a treaty and peace overtures, both sides felt humiliated in turn over access to wild elephants in the form of '*Kheda*' operations, trade and commercial intercourse, boundary disputes, extradition of political offenders, and violation of personal liberty and privileges of the subject people. Meanwhile, despite an 'expansive, invincible and wealthy' empire, the Mughal court culture and imperial ambitions underwent rapid changes.[23] After a war of succession which led to Aurangzeb occupying the Mughal throne in 1658, another phase of Mughal imperial expansion started. Within the Ahom kingdom too, after years of succession war amongst the Ahom ruling families, a resolute Jayadhwaaj Simha (1648-63) occupied the throne.[24] By then, the region had become an integral part of Bengal's export economy.[25] And it was in this context that the third phase of aggressive imperial policy took shape in the Mughal north-east under Aurangzeb's stewardship (1658-1707).

Before Aurangzeb could assert his hold and order his nobles to launch a renewed imperial aggression, the Ahoms took full advantage of the apparent political fluidity in the Mughal realm and swiftly occupied Mughal Kamrup in 1659. Realizing the diplomatic fall-out of this loss to the Ahoms, the emperor appointed Mir Jumla, who had acquired vast military and diplomatic experience in the Deccan, as Governor of Bengal in 1660. Mir Jumla was ordered to conquer Assam and to expand the Mughal frontier to Arakan. While Mir Jumla was in no haste to invade the territories beyond the hills of Assam he decided to attack Assam as a matter of restoring 'imperial prestige, and the safety of imperial dominions' apart from the release of Muslim captives of war. Actual war preparations began in 1661 when the Mughal governor marched to Assam at the head of a strong army consisting of cavalry, infantry, artillery and a flotilla of boats. After conquering Kuch Bihar, Mir Jumla rapidly moved towards Ahom-occupied Kamrup in the early days of 1662. He had to not only encounter a new topography, but also could hardly garner any support from the local sources. However, topographical challenges were quickly overcome by the Mughals and within a period of five months both Kamrup and Assam came under Mir Jumla despite the Ahoms taking recourse to defensive guerrilla warfare.[26] As the fall of the Ahom capital was imminent, the Ahom king sought refuge in the distant Naga Hills. The Ahom bureaucratic system also disintegrated but the Ahoms continued with their guerrilla system. Mir Jumla decided to enforce a Mughal military system in both Kamrup and Assam. This went on along with collection of war booties; punishment to political opponents was also meted out. Months of enforcement of military siege alienated the local population. A conciliatory approach to the general population could have shown some positive direction towards reducing the gap between the populace and the Mughal invaders. Further, the Mughal military rule was also thwarted by the region's climate. A torrential rainy season obstructed Mughal siege operations; their supply lines were cut-off leading to re-newal of full-forced guerrilla attacks by the Ahoms. The latter were able to recapture some fortifications and the siege continued till the end of the rainy season without Mir Jumla showing any signs of a peace offer. The end of the rainy season placed the Mughal force at a formidable strength. An ailing Mir Jumla broke into the Ahom nobility and a leading noble offered support in return for his prospect of becoming a ruler of Mughal-occupied Assam. Such tactical gains convinced Mir Jumla to advance further eastward with an intention of final assault on the Ahom king. Rather than an assault and capture of the king, this march resulted in the conclusion of a treaty in January 1663. The treaty was largely an acceptance by the Ahom Kingdom of the Mughal imperial authority but regaining the territorial right in return for payment of annual tribute. After the Mughal imperial authority was forcefully asserted in its eastern-most frontiers, Mir Jumla decided to return only to breathe his last in March 1663 due to poor health.

A couple of years of Mughal rule and increase in trade and commerce and change of guard in the Ahom Kingdom reversed any probability in the status quo of the imperial hegemony. Preceded by diplomatic negotiations, the Ahom kingdom finally went to war in 1667 and Guwahati was recovered from the Mughals. The latter reacted quickly and Aurangzeb deputed Ram Singh in December 1667 as the head of the imperial army. Between 1668 and 1671 several assaults took place. While the Ahoms suffered an almost decisive loss in 1669 in Alaboi, it was followed by another crucial battle where the Ahom general Lachit Barphukan inflicted a huge defeat on the Mughal Army in 1671. The Battle of Saraighat, as it came to be popularly known, was an ambitious confrontation. The Ahoms fully executed their guerrilla tactics and taking advantage of the local ecology made the Mughal Army almost helpless. That the war occupies immense importance in the Assamese historiography can be appreciated from this comment: 'It left an underlying legacy of unflinching bravery and unalloyed patriotism of the Assamese.'[27]

This defeat, however, did not last long. A renewed effort on the part of Aurangzeb began in 1677. This time the neighbouring Bengal became the centre from where the Mughals started their military preparations. A poorly planned defence as well as an inferior military strategy on the part of the Ahoms resulted in a Mughal victory in 1679. A long period of succession battle in the meantime weakened the Ahom monarchical control over Guwahati which saw slow integration with Mughal monetized economy. Hardly the kingdom was in a position to relocate its logistical supports to challenge the Mughal reoccupation of Guwahati. Stability after the succession war came in 1682. Gadadhar Singh (1681-96) or Gadapani, the new king, quickly reorganized the bureaucracy and adopted plans to ensure economic stability to the kingdom. Loss of Guwahati meant loss of strategic access to economy and its recovery became the utmost necessity for the king. On the other hand, the Mughal rule in Kamrup lacked a firm grounding. The Mughals could not offer any resistance to the Ahom aggression from various fronts and they admitted defeat in 1682. While the Ahoms began to fortify and assert their political and social control of regained territories, the Mughals under Aurangzeb pursued diplomatic efforts. Their attention had shifted to Deccan, and, thus, several decades of Ahom-Mughal military hostility came to an end.

Contemporary scholars suggest that these wars were mostly fought on the lines of a national, people's war.[28] Such a claim, however, blurs the strategic dimension of the Ahom military system. Occasional defeat of the Mughals, as that at the Saraighat, is also seen as a rare moment in the Mughal imperial strategy. This has been attributed to Ahom's ability to deploy the guerrilla system of warfare. One modern military historian comments:

> The Ahoms were particularly adept in interdicting the Mughal supply system and succeeded in starving many Mughal garrisons. When retreating under attack the Ahoms, adopted a scorched-earth policy, destroying crops, stores, equipment and dwellings, and moving the local populace from the area abandoned to the Mughal. In doing so the Ahoms evolved a classic system of guerrilla resistance to counter the Mughal superiority in conventional military system.[29]

A long (1613-83) military engagement in the form of Ahom-Mughal confrontation primarily aimed at acquiring commodities for the Mughal Empire was narrated through several mechanisms and came to have an enduring impact on the Assamese historical imagination. How did these years of military engagement capture the imagination of contemporary Assamese scholars or those who were responsible for reporting the wars? Or, how did the strategies of wars reported by later Assamese historians? An understanding of these issues is possible by a close reading of key texts known as the *buranjis*. The following sections examine these issues of remembering and reproducing wars.

BURANJIS: INSTRUMENT OF PRE-COLONIAL HISTORICAL NARRATIVE

Several Ahom *buranjis* provide us with key understanding of the dynamics of war between the Ahoms and the Mughals. Skilful appropriation of various agencies involved in the wars was a hallmark of these descriptions. War ambassadors were cited and directly quoted in them who gave vivid descriptions of actual combat taking place. Often such descriptions were ascribed to certain key figures who were present in the fields. Before we embark on the issues of narration it is important to understand the dynamics of these *buranjis* as an instrument of pre-colonial narrative.

Modern scholars who are accustomed to reading Assamese *buranji* literature would find it difficult to distinguish between pre-colonial *buranji* and one that is available in the printed form. There is no doubt that the pre-colonial practice of recording of various events, with the consent of royal house, was clearly an indication of historical consciousness. Quite often those who actually wrote these *buranjis* were also actual participants in events which came to be recorded. This was one of the principal reasons why the *buranjis* acquired were believed to be authentic in contemporary scholarly debates. These *buranjis* were produced repeatedly, often with alteration. Interpolations occurred during copying mainly due to the mistakes of the copyists. Often, various *buranjis* were destroyed by officers of Ahom monarchy ostensibly for containing malicious information.[30] Such facts of destruction of *buranjis* should not be merely attributed to the personal likes and dislikes of some powerful nobles, but also to the power and value of these chronicles in the political function of the pre-colonial state. The unstable character of the underlying narrative in the *buranjis* meant that facts and associated narratives were liable to change depending on the nature of polity. *Buranjis* also competed with other forms of chronicles which recorded the past.

The established fact is that the *buranji* tradition had close similarity with the South-East Asian tradition of historical chronicles.[31] Lakshminath Bezbaruah, a leading Assamese litterateur, believed that the *buranjis* were also an instrument of creation of public opinion. Writing *buranji* was a way to express dissatisfaction with the contemporary polity. Thus, the task of composing *buranjis* was not simply confined to the official chroniclers but others also equally participated in the production of the pasts into a formal category. We know more clearly how the scholars who were trained in the pre-colonial regime of *buranji* writing worked out a new edition of chronicle. The most vivid example is with reference to the compilation of *Kashinath Tamuli Phukanor Asom Buranji*, an early-nineteenth-century text. The author made clear that he had only added to an earlier addition of *buranji* which in his estimate had missed many crucial dimensions of Ahom polity.[32]

A century later Assamese historians who wrote historical textbooks also merely re-designed and rearranged the contents of the *buranjis* by changing its prose style and expanding its chronology. Padmanath Gohain Baruah who wrote one of the earliest Assamese textbooks indicated that he had 'endeavoured to embody in this little book, entitled *Asomar Buranjee*, as many collection of authenticated historical accounts of Assam as available up to date, in a systematic order and abridged form, easy for comprehension of the readers of tender age and the general reading-public as well'.[33] By early twentieth century, *buranji* came to be equivalent to history and *itihash* both in terms of etymological meaning and formal understanding of the past.

While Suryya Kumar Bhuyan took up the task of studying and editing these *buranjis* for the benefit of those 'who would love to know about Assam's antiquity', it was not too far away from those days when the last generation of Ahom elites were still comfortable with the process of compiling *buranjis*. Bhuyan met a few last surviving members from the previous century who used to write *buranjis* thus exposing him to the world of complexities involved in narrating the past. Bhuyan himself had spelled out his stages of involvement in bringing out an edited version of a *buranji*. Thus, before a reader could read a *buranji* a certain procedure worked as a mediator between the original texts and to be ready for reading finished text. Bhuyan was also aware of the limitations of *buranjis* as instruments (*sajuli*) to recast the past for the historians. He thus despite his complete dependence on the *buranjis*, partially lamented that '*buranjis* recorded only those events which were crucial to the royal polity'.[34] Bhuyan cites seventeenth-century evidence to emphasize his argument. Quoting Siva Singha (1714-44), Bhuyan indicated how the king had actually instructed the Ahom pandit to write only about the chronology of the Ahom kings and their works.[35] Bhuyan, however, also claimed that 'small events, slip of tongue have also been included in the narratives of the *buranjis*' which could play a more important role in the use of *buranjis* as a tool for the construction of the past.[36]

In the twentieth century, the most common reference to the pre-colonial historical works is its identification to literature. A number of Assamese historians who have studied *buranjis* refer them as *Buranji Sahitya,* a literary genre. By doing this, these scholars, however, have never dismissed the objectivity and truth inside these works. In fact, throughout his career, Bhuyan pursued both history and literature without actually making distinction between the two. Why were the *buranjis* characterized as literature? Was it because increasing pressure from the western notions of history made them hesitant to accept the historicity of this genre? Though a majority of European scholars tried to negate the existence of any historical consciousness which became increasingly evident in a number of nineteenth-century writings, those who were engaged in the investigation of historical past of Assam were comfortable with the pre-colonial historical sources of the region.

The presence of certain key elements in the narrative style of *buranjis* makes them depart from other contemporary literary works. One of the key components was the presence of letters in the *buranjis* which were often reproduced verbatim.[37] This gave diplomacy a central position in the social function of *buranjis.* The next important element was the supposed restaging of conversations amongst various actors which had something to do with the central narrative. There is no way that one can actually verify the authenticity of short sentences representing the conversation, but in actuality these conversations along with the letters endowed the *buranjis* with the much needed legitimacy of truth. Bhuyan claimed that the essential strength and ideology of a nationality were hidden in these conversations. Bhuyan carefully reproduced such selected conversations which also carried the conviction of truth in his narrative.[38]

Bhuyan had chosen to retain these essentials as representatives of truth in several of his edited *buranjis.* By adding marginalia to these texts, he rarely took the help of footnote or endnote in these works; he not only essentialized diplomacy as the main theme of the *buranjis* but also brought the readers' attention to the core of the Ahom statecraft. In fact, it was the latter which emerged as the central theme of his numerous works. His *buranjis* placed Ahom diplomacy in opposition to contemporary Mughal politics. Inclusion of numerous letters and transactions between various kingdoms became the hallmark of his edited *buranjis*. He carefully added titles to these edited *buranjis*, giving a unitary character to a number of connected ones. He was equally defensive of his choice to retain the dialogues or diplomatic conversations, more especially in the context of contemporary political situation which certainly had a strong appeal to the cause of the nation. Bhuyan had no doubt about these dialogues signifying the spirit of regional heroes during the time of national crisis.[39] In his own words:

> During the crisis of national issues these conversations of these leaders tell us how the Assamese mind could reach a certain height. They also inform us that the virtues which could help a *Jati* to stabilise and united were all present with the Assamese leaders. The practices of these virtues are the central needs of the present hour as we are now exposed to the intricacies of independent India.[40]

Bhuyan's *buranjis* became the most standard in post-independent Assam. A contemporary reader interested in reading the *buranjis* could easily fall back on one of Bhuyan's edited volumes. And very few would actually have access to the original *buranjis*, as there were only a few printed in the original form.[41] Due to easy style and availability in printed form, Bhuyan's *buranjis* became the most standard compilations and served as equivalent to the pre-colonial text. Bhuyan claims that *buranjis* 'have conserved the feelings, customs and manners and institution of the people of Assam, and couched as they are in a natural and racy prose style, they constitute an unrivalled monument of national literature which few other peoples of India possess'.[42]

His internal criticism of the sources was, however, extremely preliminary and needs attention. It is doubtful to what extent Bhuyan relied on contemporary methods of textual criticism in his reading of *buranjis*.[43] Commenting on Bhuyan's edition, Maheswar Neog, who pioneered the tradition of textual criticism for Assamese texts, argued that Bhuyan was never comfortable with the tradition of textual criticism. Though he claimed that 'however only those facts which could be surely taken to be *decided* (*thawar*) they are only used here (emphasis mine)',[44] his examination of truth essentially came both from his judgemental observation and some primary textual criticism. What was his method of understanding the consistency of text in the *buranjis*? Only in a few cases, did Bhuyan have access to several copies of *buranjis*. That he carefully and systematically examined the *buranjis* can be explained from the following observation, which he made in his study of *Ramsinghor Yudhar Katha*, while writing the biographical work, *Lachit Barphukan*:

> The text contains 28 folios. Pages are found to be arranged in two pattern; the first pattern is from the first page to page number seven while the second order is arranged from page number three to page twenty three. We have only two pages between page number three and seven, even though the inserted pages are not of similar pattern. Most probably the first seven pages were composed initially and at the same time . . . there are some inconsistencies (*maje-maje pathor lorchor ache*) in the text.[45]

How one could overcome these inconstancies? Bhuyan did not provide any significant answer, but he often reproduced different texts or provided his own value judgement. A scholar uncomfortable in textual criticism, however, had used methods of drawing inferences from other *buranjis* to give a complete picture to a *buranji*.[46] Bhuyan was more interested in the internal flow of central narrative in the *buranjis*.[47] A lacuna in the central narrative was overcome by interpolations from other contemporary *buranjis*.

WARFARE AND *BURANJIS*: UNDERSTANDING MILITARY STRATEGIES

Before we discuss the key aspects of *buranjis* and their narration of Ahom-Mughal wars it is pertinent to emphasize that the *buranjis* also described the affairs of Mughal Empire. One of the classic accounts of the Mughal Empire was an Assamese *buranji* titled *Padshah Buranji*.[48] Bhuyan, who edited and published it, thought of its strength in this way:

> its primary importance to Assam can never be questioned. Assam, in those critical days of war and foreign invasion, wanted to know the forebears of Mir Jhumla, Ram Singha and Aurangzeb who were so vitally connected with her own destiny. Assam demanded knowledge of

Moghul strategy and warfare the efficient counteracting of which alone could safeguard her well-being and independence.[49]

What Bhuyan thought of the *buranjis* only overshadowed the underlying elements which are central to medieval warfare. It will not be wrong to suggest that the *buranjis* continuously evoked the passion of territorial integrity and commitment to this space. Evocation of passion and various diplomatic manoeuvres to defeat or overcome any threat to the territorial integrity became the core component of these narratives. Diplomatic letters contained not only aspects of diplomacy but also strategic tactics employed by both the sides to optimize benefits of diplomacy. The letters also spell out the role played by the ambassadors. Several *buranjis* had major disagreements on crucial questions like cause of resumption of hostility or which side was the aggressor, etc., with that of the accounts given by Persian chroniclers.

The Ahom *buranjis* were serving several tasks while narrating the wars: first, they were making an assessment of the Ahom military tactics; it was almost an assessment of the Assamese internal military strength. A single event was reported in several *buranjis* while it was most likely that only an independent account was available for a single event. Their production was exclusive to that of the contemporary Persian chronicles. The very process of production of *buranjis* had led to continuous retelling of the Ahom-Mughal engagement. Most of the time the *buranji* writers were present during the actual war and they reported from the field itself.[50] Edward Gait also argued that unlike the paucity of figures for estimating the total strength of the Mughal army in Assam in the Persian chronicles, several Ahom *buranjis* provide details of the logistics of the Mughal Army.[51] Some strategic defeats were understated by the *buranjis* too.[52]

How sensitive were the *buranjis* to the war tactics of their army? For instance, *Kamrupor Buranji* (hereafter KM) tells '*Ahome Chapi Nadhare, Kakharar Pora Kanda Guli Mare Mathun* (The Ahom do not charge the army, they only fire from across).'[53] The Mughal army was largely identified as *bangal*. War booties were duly reported. That the astrologers played a key role in warfare has been reported in several *buranjis*. Reports from the battlefields recounted various incidences, but mostly they were confined to the war efforts of higher ranks. Thus, KM recounts:

> *Pache Samaste Barua Goiya, Hajoke Beri Garh dilegoi/Bangaleo garh sang nou haotei hasti aag kari tansu sandikeior garhat dharilehi, chay danda mane yudhya hal/pache yudhyat Abdul Islam Nababat kanda lagil, Muhudi Nababor'gha hal, aru hastir kampalat guli lagilat hasti ulati palal/hastir bhange bangalo palal; ghora paril nota/ tane bangale aponar garhat bhanga huiya rahil, achameu bangalak beri garh dilegoi/bangale ulotai yudhya nidile, pache erah noari kakuti kari bat mage, bule, "ami yudhya arilo, tumara dharmapathaloi chai eri diya, amar desholi jao"/tathapi Barphukane nerile, maharajak bhoie/eimote ek mah hal/bangale khaibak napai garhar bhitare sukhai mare.*[54]
>
> (After that all the Barua went to Hajo and fortified it. Before the fortification could be completed the Mughal Army ahead of its elephantry charged the Ahom fortification. Battle ensued but Abdul Islam was hit, Nabab Muhdi was also injured and as the elephants were also hit they fled away. As the elephants had retreated the Mughal Army also fled. Eight horses were captured. The Mughal Army took protection inside their fortification but the Ahom Army laid a siege to their fortification too. The Mughals did not retaliate and pleaded with the Ahoms, 'We had left the field, please allow us to go back to our own place as per the ethics of war.' Barphukan, the Ahom commander refused to agree as he might come under the wrath of his king. Accordingly one month was passed and the Mughal soldiers died as they did not get their supply of ration.)

The *buranjis* also took note of the importance given to war strategies in later court affairs. Thus, one *buranji* recounts how several decades later in the court of another Ahom King Rudra Simha, the Mughal invasion of Assam under Mir Jumla was seriously deliberated upon to drive a point by a leading minister of the king:

> *Swargadevor purbe pulin rajadeve tejasaktir bale rangamati charai karotowa gangat khanda pakhali goishe/tetiya tat achal hen dekhi guwahatit thana kari manaha sima kari thoi goise/Jayadhwaj rajar dinat ene ahil pati bahut achil, tatrapi nam hol, bhaganiya raja/ astra-sastra ahila-pati samasto jadr, swaradevor bandi-betahe sasteton, saye solalehe sole, jay parajay duoi ache.*[55]
>
> (Before this other kings too fought hard with their physical strength and the Ahom Army washed their hands in rivers like Ganga. Since then the river Manah has became the boundary and Guwahati was

> the chief post. During the king Jayadhwaj Simha we had too lots of arms and weapon but the king was still nicknamed as fleeing king. All arms and weapon are non-living and had no sense. The king's servants are only trained and hence it was they who could use arms and weapon. One should know very well the pulse of king's men and also the mind of the enemy. There is both the possibility of victory and defeat.)

It is beyond doubt that wars were planned, and the *buranjis* played an important part in crafting the Ahom war strategies and arrangement was made so that every step was taken in the spirit of warfare as understood by the contemporary experiences. The Ahoms derived their war strategies from two different ecological settings: while its guerrilla ethics was gained from the South-East Asian background and modified in the Assamese context they also learnt the Mughal methods of warfare and war diplomacy. Both these two streams added to their topographical advantage to act as a strong force to thwart the Mughal imperial challenge in this region.

IMPERIAL STRATEGY, PERSIAN CHRONICLES AND *BAHARISTAN-I-GHAIBI*

The Mughal perspective did not go unrepresented though some had partial presence in the Ahom chronicles. Several accounts could be credited with significant portrayal of these wars. Unlike the Turko-Afghan case of lesser numbers of chronicles as regards the north-east India, the Mughal chronicles were highly vocal in telling what happened in Kamrup and Assam. As mentioned earlier, the intensity of Mughal military deployment increased in the seventeenth century and these military engagements were accompanied by several learned scholars who could be relied on by the Mughal state to get a better insight into Kamrup-Assam and its natural resources as well as state institutions. Several Persian accounts could be easily located.[56] Amongst them the *Akbarnama* of Shaikh Abul Fazl opens up the underlying diplomacy of the Mughal north-eastern frontier policy. Another text which has often been credited for offering insight into the Ahom-Mughal wars is *Fathiyyah-i-Ibriyyah*.[57]

Apart from *Fathiyyah-i-Ibriyyah* it is the *Baharistan-i-Ghaibi* (hereafter *BG*), an account left by Mirza Nathan, the general of the Mughal Emperor Jahangir, and also a Persian nobleman, had wider scope of representing aspects of Mughal diplomacy. The book was completed in 1632 and hence left unattended the later diplomatic developments. This work contains a full account of diplomacy and other political questions which came to the forefront in the Mughal eastern frontier. But, unlike other accounts, *BG*'s primary attention was to unfurl Mughal diplomacy and war strategies and give a longer treatment to the affairs of Assam, which makes it singularly important to attempt a closer scrutiny of the Ahom-Mughal military engagement in the light of the narrative strategy of *BG*.[58]

BG's author Ala-ud-din Isfahani, also well known as Mirza Nathan, began his diplomatic career in the time of Emperor Jahangir.[59] His father Ihtimam Khan came to Bengal as *Mir Bahr*, serving as admiral of the Mughal imperial flotilla in 1607 along with Islam Khan Chishti. As part of contemporary Islamic court culture, Mirza Nathan acquired a principal position and acquired the rank of 500 *zat*, 250 *sawar* in 1612. He continued to progress and in 1621 he became an *amir* and he was rechristened with the title of Shitab Khan along with a full robe of honour. Nathan also held a position of high order in Mughal Kamrup during 1612-25. His stay and diplomatic responsibility in Kamrup led him to witness the region's political events, everyday life as well as the Mughal officers' personal rivalries. His campaign in the region also resulted in a series of battles.

The *BG* is an extensively documented source of history of contemporary Mughal eastern India. It may be placed as a single most authoritative account against *Tuzk-i-Jahangiri*, the official memoirs of Jahangir which only briefly mentions a few events in Bengal. Mirza Nathan's account acquires importance as he was witness to the period when the Mughal Empire began a serious re-thinking of its eastern frontier policy as well as an equal challenge from this region in spearheading a campaign for political independence. Thus, the *BG* identifies and describes the regional political and military leaders and warriors who played instrumental roles in the evolution of a Mughal eastern polity. The narrative of *BG* is arranged in four chapters, called *daftars;* the narratives, *dastan,* making a treatment of interrelated but separate political phases involving different governorship. A total *dastan* has been devoted to the affairs of Kamrup and Assam.

Like other manuscripts, *BG*, too, could not escape various phases of the pre-print culture like ownership, readers' criticism, etc., and such social dynamics have been embodied in the manuscript.[60]

Away from the affairs of Bengal, *BG* enters into the complexities of war, diplomacy, Mughal frontier policy in Kamrup and Assam.[61] The region was yet to be in firm grip of the Mughal political system. The region was not yet brought under extensive cultivation, while forest-produce formed a major part of the royal revenue. As mentioned earlier, a serious form of Mughal expedition to this frontier began in CE 1612 and *BG* reflects the significant changes in the frontier policy of the Mughals.

The *BG* carefully describes the strategies of Ahom warfare. While detailing the military strategies of the Ahoms, Mirza Nathan recounts:

> The Rajkhawa, and the Kharghuka (Khargharia Phukan) were to take the command of the fleet consisting of four thousand war-boats of the class of *mand, bachari, kusa* and *kus*, in order to attack the fleet of the Twelve Bhuyans who were loyally supporting the imperialists;—to seize them and not to allow any of them to escape by the river with his fleet.[62]

Mirza's observation was not echoed by Ram Singh who participated in the Battle of Saraighat. The latter emphasized the value of Ahom military engineering:

> Forts have been constructed by the Ahoms on tops of hills, and the outlying plains are also too narrow for the purpose of an open engagement. It is for this reason that the Assamese had proved invincible in the wars against foreigners. The fortifications are intricate and complex, and to each fort there are three passages. The enemy is beyond the reach of our heavy artillery: there is no opportunity for fighting with the reach of our heavy artillery: there is no opportunity for fighting with arrows and guns. Their ministers, commanders and infantry are all to be admired for having constructed such an impregnable wall of defence.[63]

BG also carefully records series of Mughal war strategies which were adopted consequent to impending difficulties advanced by the Ahoms and the Kuch kingdom. An instance of such first hand account is a policy decision which recounts Mughal's assessment of the war fields: 'After inspection it was decided that they should construct two strong forts on either side of the river where its course was comparatively narrow and that they should not proceed any further.'[64] *BG* did not ignore the fact as to what would happen even after this fortification and hence recounted that: 'If in spite of this the enemy would become too bold, then they should not stay at Hajo but should move up to this island.'[65]

Nathan's location within the battlefield as a key person made him privy to various phases of ups and downs as well as other challenges during the war and the preparation before resorting to war. Thus, narrating the failure of his army while he was ill Nathan rebuked even his personal attendants for their inability to form opinion:

> As long as you are my personal assistants you have ample powers to censure and send these foolish and cowardly people back to their posts; of if through their cowardice, they had not courage enough to proceed, you yourselves ought to have striven for the welfare of the Emperor and left me for dead. With these powers in your hands, you ought to have ordered them about. When they could not be successful in the war, they should have fortified Hajo, the seat of the governor, within the night instead of running about and dashing their heads against walls and stones. One of you ought to have gone to Barnagar to Qulij Khan, the lover of pomp, to bring him here whether he wished it or not.[66]

Like the practices of contemporary Assamese *buranjis*, *BG* also reproduced demi-official communications between key officials. These communications were also crucial indicators of the evolving policies of the Mughal state. One such long communication describes the early days of Mirza's career in Kamrup. The letter was written by Mirza to Qulij Khan:[67]

> I desire that you should not lose your fame and prestige only because I am keen about the welfare of the master and the Qibla. The Jagirdarship and the commandership of this territory has been assigned to you by the imperial court. God forbid, if there is a setback, you will also be taken to task. The rebellion of Ibrahim came in a little while ago. He wasted his own money and misappropriated the imperial revenues. We saved the (imperial) territories (in this crisis). It was, therefore, incumbent upon you to come to Hajo, as soon as you heard of this incident. . . .

BG is also a report on the affairs of internal Mughal administration on Mughal eastern frontier in general and, the affairs of Kamrup in particular. Conflicts between two rival bureaucrats often formed the core of the narrative of wars. For *BG*, however, a public gesture showcasing firm friendship between Mirza and Shaykh Khan, the ruler of Kamrup would be good war strategy to demoralize the Ahom king. Nathan also took care to mention the personal safety of Mughal officials.

BG did not hide the fact that rivalry and wars proceeded simultaneously with several layers of secret strategy. 'You will give signal to your *paik* (footmen) to cut off the legs of the horse of the Shaykh. . . '.[68] Despite such intense rivalry with Shaykh Khan, Mirza went ahead with war planning and urged his officials both offensive and defensive strategies. That the frontier enemy and their strength at first strike should not be taken lightly became manifested on several times. How the war scene is reported in *BG*? Nathan's observation was made on a realistic assessment of the battlefield.

> Towards the end of this day, Baldev, the brother of Raja Parikshit, came with a force of eighteen thousand hill-men and attacked the fort under cover of chariots. . . . We defended the fort to the best of our abilities. Many people were killed on both sides. As long as the gunpowder and the lead lasted the matchlock-men did splendid service. Now the enemy has grown bolder and has advanced their *garduns* (chariots) up to the bank of the ditch of the fort and are fighting under their cover. If possible reinforcement comes (to our aid), it will not be possible to defend the fort with this regiment, and we shall all perish with our men.[69]

That, Nathan's experience in his first encounter with this frontier war strategy was far from good could be appreciated from the following lines:

> . . . Every one of the these trenches should be assigned to the different *sirdars* who should take their stand with a strong determination either to attain victory or to die, so that they may be acquitted of the charge that the imperialists failed to conquer the fort of Dhubri and were *wallowing perpetually in mud like buffaloes.* (emphasis added)[70]

The Persian chronicles as exemplified through the example of *BG*, which were primarily aimed at a different audience unlike their Assamese counterparts, were often a defensive mechanism to legitimize their performances in the field. It was rarely that the Mughal imperial authority could verify various claims put forward by their representatives in the war zones, who were also responsible for the production of these accounts. But, and more importantly, these chronicles left behind ample scope as the sole and authoritative texts representing Mughal imperial interests *vis-à-vis* a frontier polity.

REMEMBERING WARFARE: THE AGE OF NATIONALISM

The peoples have been attaining in struggle in different crucial historical moments against foreign invader to keep alive their independent entity. They defended their independence successfully resisting the invasions of the mighty Mughals seventeen times.

United Liberation Front of Assam[71]

Historical research, popular narrative as well as public celebration of war figures had immensely contributed to these hostilities between the Ahom-Mughals being remembered in public memory. However, such remembrance largely began in the second half of the previous century. During the height of the anti-colonial movement aspects of Ahom-Mughal war hardly attracted the attention of public discourse. The Assamese nationalist intelligentsia had no ambiguity towards Assam's political position *vis-à-vis* a larger Indian political idea. Before hero worship began, scholars were not inattentive to the aspects of war and war tactics which had rather a central role in the Ahom-Mughal wars. Hemchadra Goswami, despite his observation on Ahom war strategies, could not escape from lamenting that a 'nation whose war tactics were even appreciated by the enemies should suffer from all these ignominies presently'.[72] Some early attempt was made to place the significance of Ahom-Mughal wars in the Assamese public memory by Assamese nationalist Padmanath Gohain Barua in the early decades of twentieth century. Barua authored a drama on the life of Ahom general Lachit Barphukan whom he considered as worthy of hero worship by the nation.[73] A short biography which was part of Gohain Barua's anthology of Assamese biography argued that contemporary Assamese should learn the values of patriotism, discipline, commitment and loyalty from the example of Lachit Barphukan.[74]

Academic history too is generally imbued with the idea of 'Assam's phenomenal success' against the mighty Mughal or 'war fought by the people as a nation'.[75] What have been missed are the complexities of the task of writing military history. No discussion has drawn our attention to the topographical or ecological setting of the battlefields which played a crucial role in determining Ahom victory and Mughal defeat. That the ecological setting of the battlefield for Saraighat has key role to play, particularly the naval warfare tactics of the Ahoms, has been squarely ignored in entire corpus of post-independent writings. The subject of Ahom-Mughal wars came to occupy the centrestage of Assamese nationalism. An illustrative example of such enduring impact is the substantial literary production of the Battle of Saraighat. Leading Assamese historian Surya Kumar Bhuyan could rightly appreciate the general connection between Assamese nationalistic consciousness and the need for such heroes who matched the aspiration of nationalism. The geographical disjuncture which the region had experienced as a political unity on the eve of Mughal assault became a united geographical block. The united geographical block became identified as Assam. The Ahom rule became the most powerful political culture in the region; several other contending political cultures either accepted Ahom supremacy or their rebellious voice became pale. It was only in the middle of the twentieth century that the Ahom rule came to acquire a new position at par with the Mughal imperial culture in Assamese historiography. Lachit Barphukan was the natural choice as Assam's military hero. In Bhuyan's heroic portrayal, Lachit eventually became an astute military commander who had the skill and tactical superiority to challenge the might of the Mughal Army.

Erection of commemorative stones in various places led to the consolidation of this aspect. Emergence of loosely organized political pressure groups which were christened *Lachit Sena* was derived from this understanding only. Movies made centred on the military career of Lachit Barphukan appeared also in the second half of the twentieth century.[76] Ultra-nationalist political groups professed to derive their ideological inspiration from the life and times of Lachit.[77] All this was possible through the medium of historical narratives which originated in the context of the Ahom-Mughal conflicts. While the narratives were sensitive to the complexities of warfare, nationalist remembrance had blurred those distinctions and placed these wars as mere extensions of nationalist physical strength.

NOTES

1. For brief bibliographical overview of the Ahom *buranji* and Persian records see, J.N. Sarkar, 'The Sources', in H.K. Barpujari (ed.), *Comprehensive History of Assam* (hereafter *CHA*), vol. 2 (Guwahati: Assam Publication Board, hereafter APB, 2004, 2nd edn.), pp. 1-15; Lila Gogoi, *The Buranjis: Historical Literature of Assam* (Guwahati: Omsons Publishers, 1986).
2. The most classic example of such attribution of state use of Ahom-Mughal military engagement was the case of Assam Governor Lieutenant-General S.K. Sinha's project of bringing back the 'heroic' military strategy of Lachit Barphukan who defeated the Mughal Army. During his tenure as governor of Assam Sinha made several public comments of the importance of Lachit Barphukan as an important Indian Army general. Sinha argues, 'Lachit Barphukan was a military leader in the mould of Rana Pratap and Chhatrapati Shivaji. All three fought for the freedom of their region against Mughal imperialism.' See, S.K. Sinha, 'Emulate the spirit and skill of Lachit Barphukan', in http://www.hvk.org/articles.0801/92.html (accessed on 29 November 2008). See also Jayeeta Sharma 'Reading Lachit, Reading Assam: The Heroic "History" of an Indic Periphery', unpublished conference paper presented at the 33rd Annual Conference on South Asia, Wisconsin-Madison, 2004.
3. J.N. Sarkar, 'The Ahom Administration' in *CHA*, vol. 3, p. 64.
4. A number of works have discussed the Mughal military system in detail. See, for instance, Iqtidar Alam Khan, *Gunpowder and Firearms: Warfare in Medieval India* (New Delhi: Oxford University Press, 2004).
5. Richard M. Eaton, *The Rise of Islam and the Bengal Frontier 1204-1760* (New Delhi: Oxford University Press, 1997), p. 189.
6. Gait mentions that when Shekh Qasim, the Bengal governor sent an imperial expedition to Assam with 'ten thousand horse and foot and four hundred large ships' to invade the Ahom kingdom the force was accompanied by Sattrajit son of Dacca zamindar and he was later rewarded. Edward Gait, *A History of Assam* (Guwahati: Lawyers' Book Stall, hereafter LBS, 1984, 1st print 1905), p. 108.
7. This section is largely based on S.K. Bhuyan, *Atan Buragohain and His Times* (Guwahati: LBS, 1957); S.K. Bhuyan, 'The Ahom Military System', unpublished lecture, Pratibha Devi Memorial Lecture Series, 1941; Edward Gait, *A History of Assam*; P. Gogoi, *The Tai and Tai Kingdom: With a Fuller Treatment of the Tai-Ahom Kingdom in the Brahmaputra Valley* (Guwahati: LBS, 1999, 1st print 1968); H.K. Barpujari (ed.), *Comprehensive History of Assam*, vols. 2 & 3, Guwahati, 1994; M.I. Bora, 'Sutora Satikat Asomiyar Ran Bal', in *Assam Sahitya Sabha Patrika*, vol. 3, no. 6 (1951), p. 212.

8. Amalendu Guha, 'From Tribalism to Feudalism: 1600-1750', in Amalendu Guha (ed.), *Medieval and Early Colonial Assam: Society, Polity, Economy* (Kolkata: KP Bagchi, 1993), p. 87.
9. Ibid.
10. J.N. Sarkar, 'The Ahom Administration', in *CHA*, vol. 3 (Guwahati: APB, 2004), pp. 63-83, argues that their presence in the Mughal Army has serious negative impact in the Mughal war strategies.
11. Ibid., *CHA*, vol. 3, p. 66.
12. Amalendu Guha, 'From Tribalism to Feudalism, in *Medieval Economy, Society and Polity*, p. 85.
13. For Mughal superiority in gunpowder see, Iqtidar Alam Khan, *Gunpowder and Firearms.*
14. Written by Sukumar Borkath during the eighteenth century under the guidance of Ahom king Siv Singha and his wife Ambika Devi. Two illustrators Dilbar and Dosai had done the illustrations for the manuscript. See, P.C. Choudhury (ed.), *Hastividyarnava* (Guwahati: APB, 1975).
15. The fact of Mughal Army's heavy reliance on cavalry has been highlighted by Irfan Habib in this way: '. . . their main strength initially lay in their cavalry, or rather mounted archers, and it was in a battle in the open field, and in rapid movements that they remained invincible'. Irfan Habib, *Agrarian System of Mughal India, 1556-1707* (New Delhi: Oxford University Press, rpt., 1999), p. 364.
16. J.N. Sarkar, 'The Ahom Administration', in *CHA*, vol. 3, pp. 78-81.
17. Ibid., pp. 85-6.
18. Details of war technology as displayed through these ramparts and embankments were all embodied in the records of an officer, Chang-Rung-Phukan. See, Bhim Kanta Baruah ed. *Chang Rung Phukanar Buranji* (Dibrugarh: Dibrugarh University, 1992).
19. This section is based on J.N. Sarkar, 'Assam-Mughal Relations', in *CHA*, vol. 2, pp. 148-256; Eaton, *Rise of Islam and the Bengal Frontier*, pp. 186-91; S.N. Bhattacharya, *A History of Mughal North-East Frontier Policy* (Calcutta: Chuckervertty, Chatterjee & Company, 1929); Bhuyan, *Atan Buragohain and His Times.*
20. For details see, Gautam Bhadra, 'Two Frontier Uprisings in Mughal India', in R. Guha (ed.), *Subaltern Studies II, Writings on South Asian History and Society* (New Delhi: Oxford University Press, 1982), pp. 43-59.
21. Jos Gommans argues that the 'royal prerogative' of rights to elephants 'was the main attraction that drew them towards the unhealthy, malaria-infested forest fringes of the Himalayas, Assam, Bengal and Orissa', Jos Gommans, *Mughal Warfare: Indian Frontier and High Roads to Empire 1500-1700* (London, Routledge, 2002), p. 14.
22. John F. Richards, *The Mughal Empire: The New Cambridge History of India* (New Delhi: Cambridge University Press, 1998), p. 136.

23. Ibid., pp. 150-1.
24. J.N. Sarkar, 'Assam-Mughal Relations', in *CHA*, vol. 2, p. 164.
25. Richards, *The Mughal Empire*, p. 165.
26. Bhuyan, *Atan Buragohain and His Times*, pp. 221-35.
27. Sarkar, 'Assam-Mughal Relations', in *CHA*, vol. 2, p. 228.
28. Hiren Gohain, 'Yudhya aru Rajniti: Asom Buranjir Eta Agyat Dish', in *Sahityar Aru Satya*, Guwahati, 1991 (2nd print), p. 247. The term was initially used by Vo Niguyen Giap in his *To Arm The Revolutionary Masses, To Build the People's Army* (Hanoi: Foreign Language Publishing House, 1975).
29. Pradeep P. Barua, *The State at War in South Asia* (Lincoln: University of Nebraska Press, 2005), p. 39.
30. One of the most commonly cited evidence of such mass destruction of *buranjis* for personnel motive was that of Ahom minister Kirti Chandra Barbaruah who supposedly collected all available *buranjis* and then selected those which contained 'misrepresentation' on him and their families.
31. For an idea of such chronicles in the neighbouring Manipur see, S.N.A. Parratt, *The Court Chronicles of the Kings of Manipur: The Cheitharon Kumpapa* (London: Routledge, 2005).
32. 'Introduction' in Kashi Nath Tamuli Phukan (ed.), *Assam Buranji* (1844, rpt., Calcutta: unknown, 1906).
33. Padmnath Gohian Barua, 'Preface', in *Asomar Buranjee* (Guwahati: APB, 2004), p. ii.
34. S.K. Bhuyan, *Lachit Barphukan* (Guwahati: APB, 1989, 1st print, 1971), p. 115.
35. 'This buranji will only contain the names of Swargadeo and their works', ibid., p. 115.
36. Bhuyan, 'Introduction', in *Tunkhungia Buranji* (Guwahati: DHAS, 1990), p. 9.
37. For further discussion on these letters see, Sudhanshushekhar Tunga, *Banglar Baire Bangla Gadya Charchal* (Calcutta: University of Calcutta, 1985).
38. See Bhuyan, Appendix I, *Lachit Barphukan*.
39. Bhuyan, 'Preface', in *Lachit Barphukan*, p. vi.
40. Ibid.
41. The first ever *buranji* which acquired a modern print form was that of Kashi Nath Tamuli Phukan's *Assam Buranji*, published by the American Baptist Missionaries in 1844. In 1922, Hemchandra Goswami published another *buranji*. Since then the number of such reproduction of original *buranjis* remained scanty. See, Kashi Nath Tamuli Phukan (ed.), *Assam Buranji*; Hemchandra Goswami (ed.), *Purani Asom-Buranji* (Guwahati: LBS, 1977, 1st print 1922).
42. S.K. Bhuyan (ed.), *Bulletin*, no. 1 (Guwahati: DHAS, 1932), p. 17.

43. The tradition of textual criticism in Assam in the twentieth century acquired a new dimension only with Maheswar Neog. Neog trained in the contemporary Indian scholarship under the guidance of scholars like Sukhtanker, etc., began a systematic examination of a number of texts whose origin goes back to pre-print days. The early days of print also witnessed some form of textual criticism. The task acquired significance with the beginning of various works of Sankardev getting printed form. For example, linguist Kaliram Medhi brought-out a critical edition of various one-act dramas. The discovery of a number of inscriptions also opened up vast opportunities for the spread of textual tradition. However, the most significant contribution came only from Maheswar Neog who critically edited both inscriptions and Vaishnavite texts. For further discussion on textual tradition in Assam see, Maheswar Neog, *Path Samiksha* (Guwahati: Granthapith, 1998).
44. *'Abasye, jibur kathak nichinta bhabe thawar kariba pari takhe eiyat sanibista kora hoiche'.* Bhuyan, *Lachit Barphukan*, pp. 189-90.
45. Ibid.
46. Maheswar Neog wrote that Bhuyan had successfully dovetailed various *buranjis* into a single narrative which fits into his central question.
47. Neog, *Path Samiksha*, p. 12.
48. S.K. Bhuyan (ed.), *Padshah Buranji* (Guwahati: Kamrup Anusandhan Samiti, 1935). An English translation of this appeared in S.K. Bhuyan (tr. and ed.), *Annals of the Delhi Badshahate* (Guwahati: DHAS, 1947).
49. S.K. Bhuyan (tr. and ed.), 'Introduction', in *Annals of the Delhi Badshahate*, p. 43.
50. Bhuyan, *Lachit Barphukan*, p. 189. Bhuyan had mentioned about one such *buranji* named *Ram Simhar Yudhya Katha* was authored by the participants of the war.
51. Gait, *A History of Assam*, fn., p. 129.
52. Referring to a naval defeat of the Ahom Army in the hand of Mir Jumla, Gait mentions that 'it is not mentioned in the Buranjis, which are usually frank in admitting reverses.' Gait, *A History of Assam*, p. 132.
53. S.K. Bhuyan (ed.), *Kamrupor Buranji* (hereafter *KM*) (Guwahati: DHAS, 1987, 1st edn., 1930), p. 35.
54. Ibid., pp. 36-7.
55. An unnamed *buranji* quoted in S.K. Bhuyan, *Mir Jhumlar Asom Akramon* (Guwahati: LBS, 1956), p. 150.
56. The complexities of Persian chronicles in reference to Assam has been briefly described in J.N. Sarkar, 'The Sources', in *CHA*, vol. 2, pp. 9-15.
57. Also known as *Tarikh-i-mulk-Asham* and authored by Muhammad Wali Ahmad, *Fathiyyah-i-Ibriyyah* graphically portrays the expedition of Mir Jumla to Assam. For an intellectual history see, *CHA*, vol. 2, p. 13, fn. 40.

I have an opportunity to read a press copy of an English translation of *Tarikh-i-mulk-Assam* courtesy Akdas Ali Mir. The work is done by Mazhar Asif of Gauhati University. The present translation is based on a manuscript edition of *Tarikh-e-Asham* in Khuda Bakhsh Oriental Public Library. The translator informs that he has compared this manuscript edition with a printed version in Persian originally published from Aftab Alamtab Press, Calcutta in 1849.

58. I have only referred to English translated version of *BG*, though the accuracy of this translation has been doubted by some. M.I. Bora, *Baharistan-i-ghaibi: A History of the Mughal Wars in Assam, Cooch Behar, Bengal, Bihar and Orissa during the Reigns of Jahangir and Shahjahan by Mirza Nathan* (Guwahati: Department of Historical and Antiquarian Studies (first printed 1936) (hereafter *BG*). The translation was done by M.I. Bora (1899-1944), a distinguished scholar of Persian literature who taught at University of Dhaka. Bora earned his doctoral degree from School of Oriental and African Studies, London, for his work on Amir Hasan, the Persian poet from Delhi. For biographical details of M.I. Bora see, S. Barman (ed.), *Assomiya Jibani Abhidhan* (Guwahati: Banalata, 2008, 1st print 1992), p. 180. A Bengali translation of Bora's English translation was published in 1985. See, Khalekdad Chaudhuri, Mirza Nathan's *Baharistan-i-ghaibi* (Dhaka: Dhaka Academy, 1985). The original Persian copy of *BG* is available in Bibliotheque Nationale, Paris.
59. Richards, *The Mughal Empire*, pp. 107-8.
60. 'Introduction', in *BG*, vol. I, pp. xxi-xxv.
61. Till eighteenth century the present western Assam districts were known as Kamrup while the eastern Assam districts which were mostly under the Ahom rule was known as Assam.
62. *BG*, vol. II, p. 488.
63. Ram Singha to Rashid Khan quoted in *CHA*, vol. 3, p. 248.
64. *BG*, vol. II, p. 481.
65. Ibid.
66. Ibid., p. 482.
67. Nathan reproduced several such demi-official communications. *BG*, vol. II, p. 482.
68. *BG*, vol. II, p. 451.
69. Ibid., p. 452.
70. Ibid., vol. 1, p. 236.
71. This is how United Liberation Front of Assam, a group propagating the cause of the Assam's freedom from the federal structure of India had liked to describe Assam's history of liberation movement in the past. Retrieved from http://www.geocities.com/CapitolHill/Congress/7434/ (accessed on 4 November 2008).
72. The best example of such work is that of Assamese historian Hemchandra

Goswami who while writing on Battle of Saraighat had reminded the readers of the importance of Ahom war strategy. See, Hemchandra Goswami, 'Saraighator Yudhya', in *Usha*, 1st part, no. 8, 1906, pp. 180-3 in L.N. Tamuli (comp. and ed.), *Usha* (Guwahati: Assam Sahitya Sabha, 2005).

73. Preface to the Second Edition, Padmanath Gohain Barua, *Lachit Barphukan* (Assamese), Tezpur, 1915 in Maheswar Neog (introduced and ed.) *Gohain Barua Rachanawali* (Guwahati: APB, 1987).
74. Padmanath Gohain Barua, 'Lachit Barphukan', in *Jibani Sangrah* (1st part), p. 99 (Guwahati: LBS, rpt., 1998).
75. Such scholarship ranges from Marxist to nationalist, for instance Gohain, 'Yudhya aru Rajniti: Asom Buranjir Eta Agyat Dish', in *Sahityar Aru Satya*, or Bhuyan, *Lachit Barphukan*.
76. One of the first such movies centred on the genre of Ahom-Mughal conflicts, titled *Lachit Barphukan*, directed by the Assamese film director Sarveswar Chakravarty was done in the 1960s.
77. The most notable amongst them was an Assamese nationalist student union known as Assam Jatiyatabadi Chattra Sanstha.

CHAPTER 6

Responses to Religion and Politics

Riti-kal Poetry, *c.* 1550-1850

SANDHYA SHARMA

This paper attempts to present a fresh view of some aspects of religion, politics and society in Mughal India as it emerges in the *Riti-kal* poetry. The poetry was composed in Braja-bhasha between sixteenth and eighteenth centuries and it encompassed largely north Indian regions. Rejection of Braja-bhasha poetry in name of vernaculars and recognition to Hindi during the nineteenth century has been seen as an attempt of colonial and British-trained scholars to project a common Hindu past-positioned against the Muslims.[1] In spite of the advocacies for the need to analyse vernaculars for historical purposes, their use as sources of history is still contested on account of several objections.[2] Some recent studies have highlighted the significance of vernacular sources for historians.[3] Poetry in Braja evolved in a certain political and socio-cultural context. I refer here to some *Riti* texts to examine conflicts, harmony or interaction between different social groups in medieval India.

I focus here only on Hindu and Muslim communities following Hinduism and Islam respectively, though I am aware that both Hinduism and Islam are admittedly broad ideologies serving narrow modern politics. Still, Hinduism is used here for Hindu traditions, the genealogies of which are often traced to ancient India. Islam is understood as the religion of the Muslim conquerors who began to settle in India after the Arab conquest of Sind, though followers of Islam had been living even before that. Though the parameters to define a Hindu and a Muslim are also still not clear, I intend to see how Hinduism and Islam, on the one hand, and Hindus and Muslims, on the other, were portrayed in a dominant literary mode known as *Riti* poetry. Since the period, *Riti-kal,* corresponds to the Mughal age, one may also take cognizance of some details regarding religion and politics in terms of the relationship between the empire and the regions.

The issues related to antagonism, harmony or interaction between the communities of believers of Islamic and Hindu traditions have been dealt at length by historians. Some researches highlight syncretism both at the political and social levels and indicate transformation of beliefs and practices since Islam was introduced in India. Many writings on expansion of Islam in the Indian subcontinent uncover different facets of Indian Islam.[4] Most of these works are, however, based on Persian sources. The world-views of religion and religiosity in histories written on the basis of Persian court-chronicles and official correspondence are indeed imperial. Sufi and Bhakti literature provide a better view of religious interactions.

This essay examines a largely ignored literary tradition of pre-modern India which owed its origin to Sanskritik traditions with a view to exploring whether Hindu and Muslim communities were two isolated social groups representing divergent cultural beliefs and practices. The poetry analysed here was different from other sources in terms of its origin, spread and impact and represents lived experiences of various social groups. It would be interesting to examine how this literature perceived religion and provided ideals for religious expressions, besides reflecting a Mughal-regional perspective.

The whole period of *Riti* poetry is very extensive, covering a phase which begins from around CE 1550 and extends beyond the Mughal period down to the late nineteenth century. The definition of *Riti* is interpreted differently by Hindi scholars in the context of the poetry under review. As all major Sanskrit poetics were discussed and delineated by the poets in Braja during the period between sixteenth and nineteenth centuries, the poetry of the period was assigned different names.[5] It came to be known as *Riti, Riti-shringar* or *Alankrit-kal* poetry. It is, however, commonly known as *Riti-kal* poetry with the distinction of *Riti-baddha-kavya* and *Riti-mukta-kavya*. The poets and poetry abiding by the doctrines of *Riti* school of Sanskrit poetics fall in the *Riti-baddha* category known for a particular style. Those who transgressed the *Riti* criteria were called *Riti-mukta* and their poetry suggests a different milieu which enabled the poets to include divergent themes in their compositions. Some narratives from the past were re-presented in Braja dialect and some versified historical poems were also composed. The term *Riti* was invoked by the poets to become great *acharyas* (distinguished scholars), like erstwhile pundits, and secure royal patronage for fame and wealth.[6] In this sense, it represents a process of historical development in which literature became a link between politics and culture.

Students of literature have largely been indifferent to this poetry for many reasons.[7] In their opinion, *Riti* poetry does not reflect any new features that could merit becoming a subject worthy of study. Moreover, literary critics feel that most *Riti* poets were not conversant with Sanskrit poetics, and therefore could not produce good work. The poets remained limited to a stereotyped diction and the literature they produced was stale and clichéd. None of the *Riti* poets could be given credit for a distinctive style. The language of the *Riti* poets has also been criticized for its imperfections and deviations from established grammatical principles. *Riti* poetry has also been condemned for its erotic descriptions. The critics consider it prurient and therefore do not include it in serious literary discussions.

Further, *Riti* poets are commonly dismissed as *darbari kavis* on account of their association with one court or the other. It is contended that the main aim of these poets was to please their patrons by describing them or their courts or by composing poems on the themes and topics suggested by their patrons. Scholars of Hindi literature believe that their patrons were not always aware of the finer points of the accepted poetics and they simply enjoyed the pleasure poetry provided. Some of the verses, however, reveal that kings were capable of critical appreciation as they honoured intellectual and skilled poets. Thakur, a poet of the last decades of the eighteenth century, writes as follows:

> *Thakur so kavi bhavat mohin jo rajsabha me badappan pavai.*
> *Pandit lok pravinan ko joi chitta hai rasau kavitta kahavai.*[8]
>
> (Thakur says that he likes only those poets who get honour in the court assembly. He who enraptures the knowledgeable and intelligent people through his *Rasa* verses.)

While court patronage might have certainly tutored the kind of literature to be created, a closer reading of the biographies reveals that all poets were not associated with courts. Some rulers, Jaswant Singh Rathor, Nripshambhu and Rasnidhi (Raja Prithvi Singh of Datiya) were great poets. Association of Kriparam, Alam, Mubarak and Giridhar with some courts may be negated because all those poets who received patronage identified their patrons at least. Even those who stayed in courts often renounced their affiliations. Padmakar and Bodha may be cited in this context. Mobility of poets from one court to another suggests that they enjoyed discretion and liberty. Variety in themes and veneration of gods of their choice in introductory verses also reflect the independence of poets. Therefore, court patronage should not be the reason to condemn this rich literature as unimportant.

Further, court patronage is significant because regional rulers and elites apart, the Mughal rulers were great patrons of learning and art. The famous poet Keshavdasa was a close associate of Jahangir. Vrind was the teacher of Prince Azam Shah. Kalidas Trivedi, a noted Hindi *Riti* poet, accompanied Aurangzeb to Golconda. Alam was patronized by Prince Muazzam even after he became the emperor in CE 1707. Abdur Rahman Premi lived in the court of Emperor Farrukhsiyar while Surati Mishra and Ghananand illuminated the court of Emperor Muhammad Shah. It is in this milieu that a vernacular language was enriched under the Mughals. The regional patrons and ruling elites, affluent merchants and mercenary commanders also promoted literary activities, though on a lesser-scale compared to the Mughals. For instance, Bahadur Anup Giri Gosain, a noted warlord during the eighteenth century, patronized the great poet Padmakar. The poet also visited the courts of Jagat Singh of Jaipur and of Raja Raghunath Rao of Nagpur.

Poetry thus blossomed in imperial and regional courts, houses of affluent merchants and courtyard of zamindars. These patrons belonged to ruling groups with varying authority and different lineages (not necessarily Kshatriyas). The poets and their audience were also heterogeneous. It was not only Persian that was promoted by the Mughals for different reasons but Braja-bhasha as the language of the masses was also elevated due to imperial patronage. The poets themselves admitted that their primary aim was to create poetry for the masses in a language of their own:

Dev dev bhasha kari nag naga bhashani.
Nara hoi nara bhasha kari Gita gyan praman. . . .
Samajhen bala balakahu varnana panth agadh.
Kavi Priya keshav kari chhamiyo kavi aparadha.[9]

(Gods composed in the language of gods, snakes in the language of snakes. I, being a man, reveal the knowledge of *Gita* in the language of masses. For children to appreciate descriptions of schools of profound thought. Keshav composes *Kavi Priya,* forgive the poet for this fault.)

The impact of poetry may also be seen in its connections with other fine arts of the period. The themes of *Riti-kal* poems were expressed with equal force through other media like music and painting.[10] In the field of music, *dhrupad* occupied the highest place during the reign of Akbar. However, by the end of the seventeenth century, the esoteric lost its popularity with audiences. *Khyal* or *thumri,* songs in the regional languages, and *bhajans* were generally sung. All the Hindustani music compositions in Braja were based on themes constituting the core of *Riti* poetry. Further, the subject matter of paintings during the eighteenth century comprised court and kings, religion and mythology, popular folk themes and ethnological depictions. Some painters borrowed verses from Keshavdasa's *Rasikpriya* as themes for illustrations. They were also influenced by Matiram's classification of heroines, on the basis of which they picturized different types of heroines.

The texture of *Riti-kal* poetry was indubitably informed by Sanskrit. In the initial stages when poets began to produce Braja version of the themes which were earlier written in Sanskrit, they confessed their guilt of violating standard literary conventions. Keshavdasa, one of the earlier exponents, wrote:

Moorh lahen jyon goorh mati amit anant agadh.
Bhasha kari taten kahon chhamiyo budh aparadha[11]

(Even the ignorant, like the intelligent ones, can comprehend the undefined, infinite and deep concepts. I thus compose in bhasha; and ask the learned to forgive my fault.)

Reference to Bharata, the author of the authoritative text *Natya Shastra,* was made in order to secure acceptance of the Braja-bhasha as a literary language. Kriparam, another poet of mid-sixteenth century, tacitly acknowledged Bharata's *Natya Shastra*:

> *Bina prayojan vyartha hai akatha kahai bahu bar.*
> *Tahi pralap kahai sukavi Bharatha granth anusar.*[12]
>
> (To utter something many times without context what is not needed. Good poets call it useless discourse according to the text of Bharata.)

A number of Sanskrit narratives from the past were rendered into Braja dialect. Somnath composed *Madhav Vinod* which was based on Bhavbhuti's *Malti Madhavam* and *Shrimad Bhagvatam* of Krishna Dwaipayan Vyas was translated as *Ras Panchadhyayi. Prabodh-Chandrodaya* was composed as a drama by Krishna Mitra in Sanskrit during the eleventh century. It was rendered in Persian, Braj and Gurmukhi as well during the eighteenth century. As for *Singhasan Battisi*, its translator, Somnath himself admitted in the first verse of his adaptation that he had transmuted the Sanskrit text *Singhasan Dwa Trinsica.* Somnath called his translation *Sujan Vilas.* Newaj wrote *Shakuntala* in the court of Emperor Farrukhsiyar and he confessed that there could be distortions in the story as he wrote whatever he had seen. It implies that the famous Sanskrit play *Abhigyan Shakuntalam* of Kalidasa was dramatized. Brijwasidas, the author of Braja version of *Prabodh-Chandrodaya*, himself admitted that he wrote it for *Nat-Lila* or stage show. Noteworthy is his source which was not original Sanskrit drama but a Persian version of the Sanskrit text. Abdur Rahman Premi composed his *Nakh-Shikh* in the court of Farrukhsiyar. Earlier, Abdur Rahim Khan-i-Khana, who composed various works in Hindi, Sanskrit and a language mixing Hindi, Sanskrit and Persian, wrote *Barvai-Nayika-Bhed* based on the *Shringar Rasa.*

The contents of the texts of poets like Dev, Rahim, Raslin, Bakshi Hansraj, Padmakar, Thakur, Tosh or Surati Mishra, are primarily of local interest. Keshavdasa's *Ratan Bavani*, *Veer Charitra*, *Jahangir Jas Chandrika* and *Vigyan Gita* were composed in the Orchha court. *Rajvilas* of poet Maan was produced in the court of Rana Raj Singh while *Chhatra Prakas* of Gore Lal was addressed to Champat Rai Bundela and his son Chhatrasal. *Sujan Charitra* of Sudan is another historical poem which describes major battles fought by the Jat ruler Suraj Mal.

These narratives describe different aspects of the political and social culture of the locality in relation to the Mughal Empire and other regions.

The need for transmutation was also explained by the poets. They believed that Braja was a simple language and masses had affinity with it. Importantly, both Sanskrit and Persian were treated as difficult languages by the poets. Brajwasidasa, in his Braja version of *Prabodh-Chandrodaya* informs that one Bali Ram rendered the Sanskrit text into Persian and the common people could not understand it. He therefore translated the Persian text into Braja:

Baliram taki kari bhasha yaman kitab.
Sou vidya ati kathinsamujhin parai shtab.
Mitra eik aisi kahi joy eh bhasha hoy.
Saral hoy to sabin ko suni such pavai loy.
Tate yeh bhasha kari kari apni mati anusar.[13]

(Bali Ram translated that text into Persian. That language is very difficult to understand. The language should be easy enough so that everybody can enjoy listening to the text. I translate it into Braja bhasha according to my intellect.)

This language could then be seen as interface between Sanskrit and Persian. As will be discussed later, the expressions of political culture, explanation of poetics, devotional poems and social realities were indeed influenced by the Mughal ways of life. Kumkum Chatterjee has analysed two *Mangalkabya* narratives of the eighteenth century and suggested that the literary tradition of rewriting the Puranas in regional dialect was influenced by the Mughal rule in Bengal.[14] However, the influence was not just unilateral. Abdur Rahim Khan-i-Khana's poetry is exemplary for suggesting acceptance to Sanskritic traditions. Jitendra Bimal Chaudhary cites some Sanskrit verses of Rahim where he qoutes Radha and Ahalya in the context of receiving blessings from Lord Rama and Krishna.[15] Similar expressions in Braja and Persian-Braja by Rahim indicate that the Mughal courtly culture did not treat Braja as language of others.

More importantly, the literary themes which were earlier monopolized by the élites using the highly developed Sanskrit or Persian language now became the subject matter of the relatively inferior groups also through Braja dialect. At the same time, the Mughals, who delved into Persian language for creating their distinct identity, not simply accommodated Braja language but contributed to its promotion. They extended this support at a juncture when Sanskrit poetics were on the verge of decline and this tradition might have disappeared. The Mughal patronage to Jagannath and Akbariya Kalidas, the last among the scholars to write on Sanskrit poetics, or to Rahim was significant for survival of the Sanskritic tradition which became a dominant theme in Braja in a short span of time. It is therefore not feasible to consider Persian as the language of the Mughals and Braja as the language of the non-Muslims.

Gradually, local Hindu rulers began to promote Braja-bhasha and Sanskritic culture.[16] The majority of the poets, generally Brahmins by caste, found shelter in regional and local courts of Awadh and Bundelkhand. It could be suggested here that these regional rulers and local chiefs also attempted to integrate and consolidate their position by mobilizing local support in their favour. For this purpose, they appointed learned Brahmins and reputed poets to their courts who narrated popular legends, Sanskrit dramas and religious themes in local languages. The literature produced a common culture out of a vast and heterogeneous mass of local beliefs, myths and legends and thus strengthened their position. The regions where these poets lived were significant in eighteenth-century politics. It is evident that patronage to *Riti* poetry soon cut across distinctions between Mughal and regional rulers on the one hand, and between regions on the other. It would be worthwhile to see how poets portrayed these rulers. More significant may be their construction of kingship as they discuss universal notions of *rajdharma*, no matter their patron happened to be a Mughal or some regional ruler. The acceptance of the ideals of *rajdharma* in different courts with varying political antecedents also deserves notice.

The identities of these poets are largely obscure. It appears strange that the poets who constructed genealogical accounts of their patrons avoided introducing their own ancestry in most of the cases. Details of their lives are therefore generally based on whatever scanty information is available in their texts. Distinguished poets tutored the aspirants and were treated as gurus. To become a poet of repute, a person had to know the literary traditions. Frequent references to religious, metaphysical, philosophical and literary texts of the earlier period indicate that the poets were well acquainted with ancient texts. Composition of *Riti* poetry also called forth perfection in Sanskrit poetics. Keshavdasa taught poetics to Bihari whose *Bihari-Satsai* became exemplary for the poets of later phase.

Noteworthy is the fact that these gurus as experts of Sanskritic traditions were not always Hindus. Raslin dedicated the following verse in honour of his guru Tufail Muhammad:

> *Des Bidesan ke sab pandit sewat hain sab sishya kahai.*
> *Aayo hai gyan sikhavan ko sur ko guru manus roop banai.*
> *Balak briddha subuddhi jahan lag bolat hain yeh baat sunai.*
> *Gau man mail gahe subh kel tufail muhammad pai.*[17]

> (The intellectuals, both natives and foreigners, serve him and are called his disciples. God of Music has come in human form to impart knowledge. Children, old and wise people from far away tell this. Dirt in heart is cleansed by holding auspicious feet of Tufail Muhammad.)

Interestingly, Tufail Muhammad is being portrayed as god incarnated in human form. The community of his disciples was also heterogeneous. Whosoever the guru, the disciples had different potential to acquire these skills and the poetry they composed was accordingly evaluated.

The poets identified themselves as members of a larger community which they called family of poets (*kavikula*) or society of poets. The poets first acquired poetic skills and then moved to different courts for some position through their connections. The poets were recommended on account of their skills. Kriparam, during the initial phase of *Riti-kal*, guided poets to display their skills at the right time and place:

> *Samay saaj laun baraniye kavikula ki marjadi.*[18]

> (Describe prestige of the lineage of a poet after judging time and place.)

The community of poets included their patrons and their audience. The audience was also capable of evaluation as the poets called them *prabin* or *pandit* which means intelligent. As discussed earlier, the poetry was recited in different circles depending upon the status of the patron. It could be a grand imperial court, regional courts, army camps or a public place in some village. Lala Bhagwan Deen cites one incident in his introduction to *Thakur-Thasak*, that Thakur, during his stay in village Bijawar, was fascinated by the beauty of a goldsmith's wife. He drew her attention by reciting aloud the verses composed in her praise. The lady also responded to the verses. Such episodes indicate that intelligence to understand and appreciate poetry was not the domain of male audience alone and that it could be comprehended by women as well. The literary culture of the period thus eliminated the boundaries not only between different communities but also between gender by providing avenues for interaction.

Yet another interactive feature of *Riti* poetry was reflected in the effective use of metaphor. Metaphorical expressions become profoundly significant when properly interpreted. They demand continuous word-play; it is perhaps for this reason that the *Riti* poets utilized language according to their needs and mixed Awadhi, Braja, Arabic and Persian words whenever they found it appropriate. The language of this literature is thus not an easy register as words are also frequently incorporated with or without variations. The meanings of such words need to be located contextually. The interpretation of the language in *Riti* poetry, whether clearly stated or implied, should be construed on the basis of the intention and tone of the poet and his social and historical presuppositions. Thus, in addition to other factors discussed earlier, a syncretic linguistic culture encouraged creation of *Riti* poetry during the seventeenth and the eighteenth centuries.

Now, it may be interesting to examine some details of the Mughal and regional political culture to see if it encouraged community consciousness in their respective zones of influence. The perceptions of Hindu-Muslim divide were derived largely by drawing references from purposely chosen sources by British historians. Though significant works written on the basis of devotional literature composed in regional dialects during the period suggest existence of composite culture with compatible ideals, historians of Mughal India still review political culture either in terms imperial and/or regional identities.[19] The regions are viewed against the backdrop of a grand Mughal Empire and this approach to writing history extends support to one's understanding of the Mughals and the regional powers as two culturally divided groups. It also leads one to understand that adherents of Hindu and Persian culture were two different groups with varying levels of interaction at different points of time.

The community consciousness is clearly reflected in some historical poems of the period. Keshavdasa's *Ratan Bavani* and *Veer Charitra* were composed when the Mughal Empire was believed to have been on its firm footing under Akbar. *Jahangir Jas Chandrika* by the same poet is dedicated to Emperor Jahangir. *Chhatra Prakas* of Gore Lal describes the political developments in another Bundela court to be established in Panna under Chhatrasal during the reign of Aurangzeb. *Rajvilas* of poet Maan is yet another narrative of Mewar court which describes the political developments during the reign of Rana Raj Singh when the Mughal throne was occupied by Aurangzeb. Shridhar Ojha describes in his *Jungnama* the war of succession between Jahandar Shah and Farrukhsiyar after the death of Mughal Emperor Bahadur Shah (CE 1707-12). *Sujan Charitra* of Sudan contains description of battles fought by Suraj Mal (CE 1743-53), the Jat ruler of Agra-Mathura region. These texts may have deep implications for a historian because they represent two significant phases of medieval Indian history, one that witnessed the climax of Mughal authority and the other when it withered away. It would be interesting to compare the perceptions about communities in both the phases.

Keshavdasa presents Bundela kings as Vaishnavaite rulers who promoted Brahmanical culture by building temples, observing religious rituals and maintaining the *varna* system in which Brahmins occupied the highest position. Ratan Sen is portrayed in *Ratan Bavani* as an obedient son who died fighting with Mughal forces. The poet calls imperial forces as *mlechha* in many verses. Akbar is addressed as Ravana and Ratan Sen is Lord Rama.[20] The words Hindu and Turk have also been used to describe rival groups.

References to religious persecution are however missing in all the texts of Keshavdasa. Bir Singh Deo in *Veer Charitra* aspires for the Orchha throne but Akbar acknowledges Bir Singh's brother Ram Shah. The emperor negotiates for peace with Bir Singh through dominant nobles of his court and offers him *jagir* in Deccan. Bir Singh keeps encroaching upon the imperial territories in his region with a forceful demand for homeland and even crowns himself. Then an agitated emperor seeks the support of Ram Shah and asks him to kill Bir Singh if he cannot be made to accept the terms. Bir Singh also allies with rebel prince Salim who had by then crowned himself at Prayag. At Salim's behest, Bir Singh even planned and executed the murder of Abul Fazl. The emperor, though shattered emotionally by the murder, does not indulge in oppressive acts of religious persecution. The retaliation was expressed in planning armed attacks for political defeat only. In spite of these strained political relations, Keshavdasa avoids metaphors like *mlechha* or *pishacha* for the Mughals.

By contrast, *Chhatra Prakas* and *Rajvilas* refer to Mughal emperors Shah Jahan and Aurangzeb as *asura*, *pishacha*, *yavana* and *mlechha*. Gore Lal explains the religious fanaticism of Aurangzeb as an unfavourable context for the Bundelas:

Aurangsah takhatpati jagyo. Metan Hindu dharma kon lagyo.
Hindu Turak din dvai gaye, tinson bair sada chali aaye.
Lekhyo sur asuran kon jaiso, kehari Karin bakhanyo taiso.[21]

(Aurangzeb, the Emperor wakes up and begins to destroy the Hindu faith. Hindus and Turks preach two different religions and have been hostile to each other forever. They may be described as gods and demons, respectively, they may also be called the lion and elephant.)

Chhatrasal's frustrations guide him to change his course of action. The poet finds a wise preceptor in the person of Shivaji who resisted the Mughals. He consults Shivaji before undertaking the next move, who guides him as follows:

Turkani ki partit na mano. . . .
Ham turkani pai kasi kripani, mari karenge kichak ghani.
Tumahin jai des dal jorau, Turak mari tarwarin torau.[22]

(Do not trust the Turks. . . . I have raised my sword against the Turks, I will kill them and shed much blood. You also return to your region and raise an army, kill the Turks and break your swords.)

Similar references may be cited in the context of Mewar under Rana Raj Singh, who, soon after his accession, attacked the Mughal *jagir*, Malpura. The attack has generally been seen as the tradition of embarking upon a programme of conquest after coronation but the poet explains it as an act of *mlechha* genocide:

Jai Hindu dhani yavaneshahin jitan maran tun hi yu mlechha.
Avatar tuhin il bhar utaran to kar khagga praman kahin.[23]

(Victorious Hindu, you will conquer the king of *yavanas* and you remove the *mlechhas* from the earth. You have incarnated to remove the burden, and there is no match for your sword.)

In another couplet, the princess of a peripheral state declines to marry Aurangzeb on account of his religion. More derogatory adjectives are deployed:

Jarten jhar pawak kund giron, barihaun sur asura na barihaun.
Jin naam malechha jano....[24]

(Prefer falling in the terrible fire, I will marry a god and not a devil. Identify him as *mlechha*, the devil. . . .)

B.D. Chattopadhyaya has explained the use of such vocabulary for representing the conqueror as 'the other'.[25] The otherness in this context may be visible as Champat Rai Bundela and Chhatrasal in Bundelkhand were contesting for power with the Mughals. Rana Raj Singh in Mewar was also trying to settle some political issues with Aurangzeb and the portrayal of the emperor as *mlechha* or *asura* could be viewed as ideological strands involving religious divide. More important is a deeper analysis of these texts for qualifying these notions of otherness of the Mughals.

In *Veer Charitra*, Keshavdasa uses *jalim* as prefix for Akbar. *Jalim* Jalal Shah is outraged when he hears of the alliance between 'Shah Salaim' and Bir Singh.[26] Interestingly, in *Jahangir Jas Chandrika*, Jahangir is introduced as *jalim Jalal suta* (son of cruel Jalal) and also as king of kings.[27] While Akbar was *mlechha* in the context of Ratan Sen and Bir Singh Deo, Jahangir becomes lord of both the religions *duhun din ka swami.*[28] The emperor goes beyond mere tolerance to Hindu religion and protection of cows. He is capable of destroying the evils of Kali Age. If one reads further, Bhagya and Udaya, two Brahmin characters, visit the court of Jahangir. The emperor welcomes them in the following manner:

Mile sahiju uthi tinhain singhasan baithare.
Bibidh bhanti pooja kari kari bahut manuhari.[29]

(The emperor got up and received them, got them seated on throne. Worshipped them in many worldly ways.)

For the poet, the emperor possessed all those mythological attributes and divine features which signified a perfect blending of age old Hindu religious ideals and Islamic beliefs. As a king, he was like Nala, Harish Chandra, Prithu, Bali, Dadhichi, Ambarish, Bhrigupati, Hanumant, and Vikramaditya.

Harmony between the two religions could be a feature when the Mughals and the regional kings were allies. It could also be achieved temporarily when some agreement was concluded between two rival groups. Maan informs that Rana Raj Singh and the combined forces of Rajputs were ready to fight a battle with Mughal Army under Prince Akbar, the son of Aurangzeb. The Rajputs were invited to Ajmer to negotiate for peace and the emperor assures them to enthrone the son of Jaswant Singh. As a result, peace is concluded and differences resolved, at least, for the time being:

Kamdhajja kari rasa rang kari, bhayo mel duhun din bhal.[30]

(The Rajputs amicably sorted out the affairs, and relations between both the religions became cordial.)

Though Shridhar Ojha in *Jungnama* narrates the war of succession between Jahandar Shah and Farrukhsiyar, he concludes his text with appreciation for Farrukhsiyar as the protector of both the faiths:

Shridhar bhanat patshahin kau patshah,
Farrukhsiyar bho panah duhun din ko[31]

(Shridhar says that king of kings Farrukhsiyar has become the protector of both the religions.)

Similar references are available in *Chhatra Prakas* too, where age old rivalries between the two religions disappear as and when balance in political powers is established. Chhatrasal wins the Battle of Loh Garh for Aurangzeb and visits the imperial court in Delhi. Aurangzeb offers him a lucrative *mansab*. Chhatrasal expresses his gratitude as follows:

Ham bagsis yahi kari paavai, Kaam lagai jab aap bulaavai.
Hukam sunat ham haajir hovai, hajrat ke ran kaam sanjovai.[32]

(I accept your benovelence, call me whenever you have some work. I will appear as I hear your order, will serve His Majesty.)

Significantly, Chhatrasal even addressed Aurangzeb as God:

Ham prabhu ke vishvasmaya, bachan bhashi Chhatrasal.[33]
(I am trustworthy of the Lord, Chhatrasal uttered these words.)

Interestingly, ethnic differences and sectarian conflicts within Islam also feature in the narratives under review. The poets have used categories such as Syed, Barha, Khoja, Irani, Turani, Pathan, Afghan, Turk, Mughal, Shaikh, Pir, Balkhi, Arabi and Khurasani to identify certain individuals. These distinctions were also marked by special attributes with which groups were generally known. The word *musalman* is rarely used to identify a non-Hindu person. This particular term in the poetry was applied to denote a larger group. Amongst Hindus, Sikarwar, Gaharwar, Hada, Chauhan, Chandela, Bai, Baghela, and Kachhwaha, Sisodiya, Bundela, Solanki, Jadav, Jagre, Tomar, Khichi, Gujar, Maina, Jat and Ahir were identified as different social groups. The caste structure during *Riti-kal* period was fluid. Occupational and regional identities were replacing the fourfold division of Indian society. Each of these communities had some peculiar traits and the poets used these identities as attributes and not as conflict-ridden camps.

It may further be noted that political alignments cut across community divisions. In *Jungnama*, a number of Hindu chiefs are referred to as supporters of Farrukhsiyar. Many of them have been been mentioned in other historical works as well and it is evident that they rose to eminence after Farrukhsiyar became emperor. Sudan informs that Suraj Mal fought a battle against Asad Khan, the governor of Kol/Aligarh for defending Fateh Ali Khan, a local potentate of the Chandos-Khurja region. He also killed his own kinsman Rao Bahadur in a battle at Ghasira as the emperor sent an order to do so. Suraj Mal further got entangled in an armed conflict with the imperial *Bakhshi* Salabat Khan following a dispute over *jagirs*. In yet another conflict between Imperial Wazir Safdar Jung and Ahmad Khan Bangash in 1749-50, Suraj Mal supported the wazir as the latter succeeded in persuading him.

Suraj Mal was not guided by any religious sentiment and the reason for his support to the wazir was his loyalty to the Mughal throne. In earlier battles also, Suraj Mal is portrayed as a servant of the emperor. Sudan further qualifies in some other context Suraj Mal's loyalty not to any emperor but to the Mughal throne:

Ham chakar hain takhat ke sakti kari na jai.[34]

(We, the servants of the throne, cannot perpetrate atrocities.)

The role of religion in politics thus varied at different intervals depending upon regions and individuals involved. The religious identities, whether Hindu or Muslim, were not static. The transformation in attitudes and behaviour of the rulers and the ruled was taking place at each level of society. The poetry, as noted earlier, was composed for different sections of society and represents change at every level. Contrarily, in the process of adjusting the political relations, the regions and the Mughals both exchanged beliefs and practices. The administration in regional courts was not elaborately defined in any of these narratives but references to some designations and posts indicate Mughal influence. Land being the prime source of income, people made every possible effort to appease the king, who if pleased, might confer *jagirs*.

In *Veer Charitra*, Keshavdasa narrates an incident when Bir Singh Deo and the rebel prince Salim concluded an alliance in Allahabad. When Bir Singh sent the severed head of Abul Fazl, Prince Salim acknowledged Bir Singh Deo, the king of Orchha, against Ram Shah whom Emperor Akbar had already granted *tilak*.

Further, the administrative set up of Vikramaditya's court had also been given an Indo-Persian touch by Somnath in *Sujan Vilas*, the Braja mutation of *Singhasan Battisi*. Interestingly, the officers in the court of Vikramaditya carried Mughal titles:

Ya singhasan pitt ho so Bikram Abikar
Mantri baksi sab thare he sirdar[35]

(Vikramaditya, the unblemished, sits on the throne. Ministers, *bakhshi* and chieftains are standing.)

The *kotwal*, *chubdar*, *faujdar* are some positions which denote the Mughal milieu. The gesture to greet or wish were also Persianized and not surprisingly, in *Sakuntala*, the charioteer of Indra greeted King Dushyanta in Islamic style:

Matali karyo salaam tab poochhan lagyo naresa.[36]

(When Matali bowed to say *salam*, the king enquired the matter.)

Muzaffar Alam has suggested that the Mughals deliberately promoted Persian as the court language and accommodation to

Braja in the imperial court was also a political consideration.[37] In some references, *Riti* poets also expressed language as a marker of identity. Maan, for example writes, while describing an attack by Mewar army on Malwa:

Kaji pakari quran garahi bandh
Bhesh badal ripu bhagat badali bani Turkani[38]

(The *qazis* tie their *Quran* to their necks and run away. The enemy escapes in disguise and they have to speak a non-Turkish language.)

It was not politics alone which promoted a language in some political circles; it was an outcome of complex social and cultural processes. The language and concepts in Kesavdasa's poetry clearly indicate a shift not only in favour of a local dialect but also a bent towards Persian language. Persian expressions had become part of this literary tradition. The following verse reflects a natural expression of the Indo-Persian culture:

Payani pari taslim kari bolyo Birsingh raj
Haun garib tum pragat hi sada garibniwaj
Sada garib niwaj laaj tum hin laghu laami
Binti kariyai kaha mahaprabhu antarjaami[39]

(Falling at the feet [of Prince Salim], King Bir Singh said: I am humble and you are caretaker of poor. As the caretaker of the poor, I request you to uphold my dignity. What should I request, you are the all-knowing Almighty.)

The percepts in this verse clearly indicate that it was not a deliberate borrowing of words but a natural expression. The impressions of Mughal influence were also expressed in descriptions of the cities. Somnath, the court poet of Suraj Mal, while composing *Sujan Vilas*, was perhaps so accustomed to see *havelis* in the Agra-Mathura region that he deviated from the original Sanskrit text in his description of cities. Therefore, Vikramaditya, while visiting different places also visits some city and observes as follows:

Chal nagari me Bikram rajai....
Bade bajar biland haveli....[40]

(King Vikrama went to the city....
There were big markets and huge *havelis*/mansions....)

Also amazing is to note Vikramaditya distributing *dinars*, a medieval currency, as alms to Brahmins and the poor.[41] It is not simply some citations but the context of poetry in general which negates the otherness of Persian language and culture. Newaj frequently used Persian and Arabic words, in pure or distorted forms; vocabulary of Somnath and of Brijwasidas in *Prabodh Chandrodaya Natak* is an index of the changing milieu. It may be significant that Brijwasidasa recreated *Prabodh Chandrodaya Natak* not from the Sanskrit original but from the Persian translation of the original text.

If one moves away from historical poems and narratives, the same trend is apparent in devotional compositions also. In spite of its connection with Sanskritic culture, the poetry is believed to have deviated from the established traditions. Hazari Prasad Dwivedi decisively registers names of eminent *Riti* poets who admittedly borrowed themes from erstwhile Sanskrit texts and added new elements according to their wisdom.[42] It was a shift influenced by Persian culture. The poets used metaphors and similies which clearly indicate Mughal context. Rasnidhi compares the beauty of *nayika* with the *takht* (throne) of the Sultan (Muslim ruler) and the hardness of her breasts with the arrogance of the *zamindar*.[43] Frequent comparisons of breasts with *gumbaj* in place of Lord Shiva's nectar pots express a changing context. In the *Nakh-Shikh* description of Radha, the poet calls her breast *kadim darban* (ancient doorkeepers) of the heart.[44]

Muslims too could express the divinity of Hindu gods. Bodha's *Ishqnama* is an exemplary text wherein one may clearly locate Persian and Sufi themes being applied to Radha and Krishna. Rasnidhi even proposed oneness of divinity for both Hindus and Muslims:

Hindu me kya aur hai Musalman me aur
Sahib sab ka ek hai vyap raha sab thor.[45]

(Is He someone for Hindu and someone else for Muslim.
As Lord of all, He exists everywhere.)

The narrations in praise of the Prophet and Caliph Ali by Raslin and those dedicated to Lord Krishna cannot be distinguished except by names. All were to be worshipped eight times a day. The poet employed the metaphor Bahubali (an epithet of Hanuman) for Ali who churned this worldly ocean to enable his devotees to encompass the Universe (*bhavsindhu*).[46]

The Mughals also learnt and followed Indian beliefs and practices. For Keshavdasa, Prince Salim performed the ritual of conferring kingship on Bir Singh Deo through a Brahmin. Shridhar Ojha equated Farrukhsiyar's presence in the battlefield with the greatness of Lord Indra (*Indra si prabhuta birajat*).[47] Syed Husain Ali, while fighting for Farrukhsiyar, manages the affairs in the manner the divine serpent Shesh beholds the earth.[48] Afrasiyab Khan and many more Muslim commanders in *Jungnama* are compared with Hanuman. One comes across innumerable verses of eulogizing patrons or defining their *rajdharma* wherein the Mughal and Muslim elites were compared with iconic figures of the Hindu pantheon. It is difficult to differentiate if a verse was dedicated to a Hindu or Muslim ruler unless the reader knows the name of the poet and his patron. Circulation of this literature in remotest corners of Mughal India and its popularity in terms of volumes is a proof that society was not divided on religious grounds.

The literary culture of the period thus reflected conflict collaboration and synthesis in different contexts. It would be inaccurate to perceive a uniform or homogeneous relationship between Hindus and Muslims during *Riti-kal*. Despite conflicts and contradictions, it may not, however, be denied that the regions were viewed in relation to the Mughal Empire and the struggle was simply regarding sharing of political power. The Mughals were always acknowledged as the *Shah* or *Padshah* of the vast land of Hind.

The relations between Muslims and non-Muslims as the rulers and the ruled in pre-modern India were never uniform and static. The sentiment which persisted was loyalty to the Mughal throne; allegiance to the emperor and to the throne was always emphasized. The reason was perhaps clear for Shridhar Ojha, the author of *Jungnama*:

Shridhar Shahanshah Faruksiyar nara
Saton dip sarhad Hind ki milayo hai.[49]

(Shridhar says King of kings, Farrukhsiyar, has incorporated seven islands into the boundaries of Hind.)

In the light of the above discussion it may be submitted in conclusion that the *Riti-kal* Hindi literature reveals complex negotiations in the domain of literary and political cultures of medieval India, something which is often confused by religious fundamentalists and other interested parties of modern times.

NOTES

1. Shahid Amin, 'Representing the Musalman: Then and Now, Now and Then', in Shail Mayaram, M.S.S. Pandian and Ajay Skaria (eds.), *Muslims, Dalits, and the Fabrications of History, Subaltern Studies* XII (New Delhi: Permanent Black, 2005), pp. 1-35.
2. For a discussion see, Allison Busch, 'Literary Responses to the Mughal Imperium: The Historical Poems of Kesavdas', *South Asia Research*, vol. 25, no. 1 (May 2005), pp. 31-54. See also, idem, 'The Anxiety of Innovation: The Practice of Literary Science in the Hindi/*Riti* Tradition', in *Comparative Studies of South Asia, Africa and the Middle East*, vol. 24, no. 2 (2004), pp. 45-59. See also, V. Narayana Rao, David Shulman and Sanjay Subrahmanyam, *Textures of Time: Writing History in South India 1600-1800* (New Delhi: Permanent Black, 2001); V. Narayana Rao, David Shulman and Sanjay Subrahmanyam, 'Forum: Texture of Time: A Pragmatic Response', *History and Theory*, vol. 48 (October 2007), pp. 409-27.
3. Sheldon Pollock (ed.), *Literary Cultures in History: Reconstructions from South India* (New Delhi: Oxford University Press, 2004); idem, *Languages of Gods in the World of Men: Sanskrit, Culture and Power in Premodern India* (New Delhi: Permanent Black, 2007). Kumkum Chatterjee, 'The Persianization of *Itihasa*: Performance Narratives and Mughal Political Culture in Eighteenth-Century Bengal', *Journal of Asian Studies*, vol. 67, no. 2 (May 2008), pp. 513-43. Raziuddin Aquil and Partha Chatterjee (eds.), *History in the Vernacular* (New Delhi: Permanent Black, 2008); Ramya Sreenivasan, *Many Lives of a Rajput Queen: Heroic Pasts in India c. 1500-1900* (New Delhi: Permanent Black, 2007).
4. Muzaffar Alam, *The Languages of Political Islam in India: c. 1200-1800* (New Delhi: Permanent Black, 2004); Richard M. Eaton (ed.), *India's Islamic Traditions: 711-1750* (New Delhi: Oxford University Press, 2006); idem, *Rise of Islam on the Bengal Frontier 1204-1760* (rpt., New Delhi: Oxford University Press, 2007).
5. Bhagirath Mishra, *Hindi Kavya Shastra Ka Itihas,* Seth Bhola Ram Saksaria Smarak Granthmala I (Lucknow: Lucknow University, 1948); idem, *Hindi Riti Sahitya* (Bombay: Raj Kamal Prakashan, 1956). See also, Nagendra (ed.), *Hindi Sahitya Ka Itihas* (Delhi: National Publishing House, 1973); Ram Chandra Shukla, *Hindi Sahitya Ka Itihas* (Varanasi: Nagri Pracharini Sabha, 1992).
6. Bhagirath Mishra, *Hindi Kavya Shastra Ka Itihas,* p. 37. See also, Nagendra (ed.), *Hindi Sahitya Ka Itihas,* p. 292.

7. Bhagirath Mishra, *Hindi Riti Sahitya,* pp. 30-5 and see also, Shukla, *Hindi Sahitya Ka Itihas*, pp. 161-7.
8. Thakur, *Thakur-Thasak*, ed. Chandra Shekhar Mishra Shastri (Varanasi: Nagri Pracharini Sabha, 1973), v.13.
9. Keshavdasa, *Keshav Granthavali*, Part III, ed. Vishwanath Prasad Mishra (Allahabad: Hindustani Academy, 1987). See also, *Vigyan Gita*, p. 644; idem, *Kavi Priya*, v. 3 in the same volume.
10. Bonnie C. Wade, *Creativity Within North India's Classical Music Tradition* (Cambridge: Cambridge University Press, 1984), p. 278; O. Goswami, *The Story of Indian Music* (Bombay: Asia Publishing House, 1961), p. 140; W.G. Archer, *Indian Paintings from the Punjab Hills: Paintings of the Sikhs* (London: George Allen and Unwin, 1957); B.N. Goswami, *Paintings at the Sikh Court Based on Twenty Documents* (Wiesbaden: Verlag Steiner, 1975); Chintamani Vyas, *Rasikpriya* (Jhansi: Gita Publishers, 1988); M.S. Randhawa, *Kangra Paintings of the Bihari Satsai* (New Delhi: National Museum, 1966).
11. Keshavdasa, *Vigyan Gita*, p. 644.
12. Kriparam, *Kriparam Granthavali*, ed. Sudhakar Pandey (Varanasi: Nagri Pracharini Sabha, 1971); *Hit Tarangini*, v. 375; See also, Kriparam, *Hit Tarangini*, v. 6 and Bhikharidas, *Bhikharidas Granthavali*, ed. Vishwanath Prasad Mishra (Varanasi: Nagri Pracharini Sabha, 1956), *Shringar Nirnaya*, v. 3.
13. Brijwasidasa, *Prabodh Chandrodaya Natak*, ed. Munshi Newal Kishore (Kashi: Sisakshar Yantralaya, 1875), v.18-20.
14. Chatterjee, 'The Persianization of *Itihasa*'.
15. Jatindra Bimal Chaudhury, *Muslim Patronage to Sanskrit Learning*, pp. 20-1.
16. For development of vernacular dialects during the period under review and of Braja in particular, see Pollock (ed.), *Literary Cultures in History*; Idem, *Languages of Gods in the World of Men*. See also, Busch, 'The Anxiety of Innovation'; S. Masud Hasan Rizvi Adeeb, 'Nawaz and *Shakuntala Natak*', *Nuqush*, Lahore, June 1963.
17. Raslin, *Raslin Granthavali*, *Futkal Kabitta*, v. 22.
18. Kriparam, *Hit Tarangini*, v. 11.
19. The empire and the region are treated in many works by eminent historians. See, for example, Muzaffar Alam and Sanjay Subramanyam (eds.), *The Mughal State: 1526-1707* (New Delhi: Oxford University Press, 1998).
20. Keshavdasa, *Ratan Bavani*, p. 468, v. 17 & p. 470, v. 28.
21. Lal Kavi, *Chhatra Prakas*, ed. Mahendra Pratap Singh (Delhi: Shri Patal Prakashan, 1973). *Chhatra Prakas*, Section 9, p. 73 and for similar sentiment, see also, Section 11, p. 86.
22. Ibid., Section 11, p. 89.
23. Maan, *Rajvilas*, ed. Bhagwandeen (Varanasi: Nagri Pracharini Sabha, 1912), p. 1021.

24. Ibid., p. 107.
25. B.D. Chattopadhya, *Representing the Other: Sanskrit Sources and the Muslim* (New Delhi: Manohar, 1998). See also, Aloka Parashar, *Mlechhas in Early India* (Delhi: Munshiram Manoharlal, 1991) and Cynthia Talbot, 'Inscribing the Other, Inscribing the Self: Hindu-Muslim Identities in Pre-colonial India', *Comparative Studies in Society and History,* vol. 37 (1995), pp. 692-722.
26. Keshavdasa, *Veer Charitra*, p. 511, v. 10.
27. Keshavdasa, *Jahangir Jas Chandrika*, p. 621, v. 32.
28. Ibid., p. 620, v. 31.
29. Ibid., p. 633, vv. 130-1.
30. *Rajvilas,* p. 168, v. 124.
31. Shridhar Ojha, *Jungnama*, ed. Bhagwandeen (Varanasi: Nagri Pracharini Sabha, 1904), p. 65.
32. Lal Kavi, *Chhatra Prakas*, p. 194.
33. Ibid.
34. *Sujan Charitra*, p. 153.
35. Somnath, *Somnath Granthavali,* Part I, ed. Sudhakar Pandey (Varanasi: Nagri Pracharini Sabha, 1972); *Sujan Vilas*, p. 677, v. 3.
36. Newaj, *Shakuntala*, p. 77.
37. Muzaffar Alam, 'The Pursuit of Persian: Language in Mughal Politics', *Modern Asian Studies,* vol. 32, no. 2 (1998), pp. 317-49.
38. *Raj Vilas*, p. 237, v. 8.
39. Keshavdasa, *Veer Charitra*, p. 501, v. 52.
40. Somnath, *Sujan Vilas,* p. 794, v. 16.
41. Ibid., p. 808, v. 73.
42. Hazari Prasad Dwivedi, *Hindi Sahitya Udbhav aur Vikas*, p. 185.
43. Rasnidhi, *Ratan Hazara*, ed. Jagannath Prasad Kayashta (Kashi: Bharat Jeevan Press, 1892), vv. 190 & 114. See also vv. 119, 126 & 142 for similar description.
44. Thakur, *Thakur-Thasak*, p. 11, v. 38.
45. Rasnidhi, *Ratan Hazara*, v. 69.
46. Raslin, *Futkal Kavitta*, vv. 5, 7 and 10.
47. *Jungnama*, p. 15.
48. Ibid., p. 38.
49. Ibid., p. 65.

CHAPTER 7

Indian Subaltern Autobiographies

Two Asian Officers in the Eighteenth-Century Bengal Army

MICHAEL H. FISHER

> No elevation of character can be expected among [Indian] men who in the military line cannot attain to any rank above that of a subedar, where they are as much below a [British] ensign as an ensign is below the commander-in-chief. . . .
>
> SIR THOMAS MUNRO (1767-1827)

ASIANS IN THE EAST INDIA COMPANY'S ARMIES

From their very inception, the East India Company's armies consisted mostly of Indians, serving as soldiers, subaltern officers, and camp-followers. Yet, most writing about these colonial armies has concentrated on the much fewer European officers who commanded them.[1] Joining scholars who have begun to reconstruct the careers and roles of Indians in these armies during the pre-1857 period, this chapter explores the perspectives and lives of two Asian subaltern officers who joined the Bengal Army in the eighteenth century.[2] Through their own representations of their lives, we can better understand the attraction of the Bengal Army to men like themselves and thus how that army emerged from asymmetrical interactions among Europeans, Asians, and their distinct military cultures.

In 1770, Joseph Emin (1726-1809) enlisted as a subaltern officer in the Bengal Army, bringing with him formidable credentials: professional officer's training at the English Royal Military Academy at Woolich, service as a gentleman officer attached to the royal English and Prussian armies during the

Seven Years War in Europe, and eight years of experience in guerrilla-style warfare to liberate Armenia. Nonetheless, because the East India Company excluded non-Europeans from its commissioned officer corps, Emin achieved only a peripheral place as most junior brevet ensign, attached to irregular cavalry (*Turksowars*) in the Bengal Army's First Brigade. After 30 months active service, in 1797 he was transferred to the Third Company of European Invalids and pensioned-off. Emin described his military aspirations first in a long autobiographical letter of 1756 (circulated among the elite of London) and then in his 640-page book (self-published in London in 1792).[3]

In 1769, young Sake [Shaikh] Dean Mahomet (1759-1851) followed his father and elder brother into the world of the Bengal Army. He initially attached himself as a camp-follower to a sepoy regiment, rising over the next 15 years of military campaigns across north India to hold appointments as market-master, then ensign (*jemadar*) and finally lieutenant (*subedar*) in an elite grenadier company of the 30th Native Infantry in the Second Brigade. He eventually resigned, in part due to tensions between the Bengal Army and Indian society. In 1794, a decade after he immigrated to Ireland, he self-published a two-volume book describing his military career, including incidents from the Rohilla War (1774), the First Anglo-Maratha War (1775-82), the Second Anglo-Mysore War (1780-4), and the conflict with Raja Chait Singh of Benares (1781).[4]

These two autobiographical accounts reveal the complexity of the culture, composition, and functions of the Company's armies from an Asian perspective. Emin and Mahomet never served in the same regiment, nor mentioned the other, although their years of service overlapped, they lived in the same cantonments, and they passed each other on their respective marches up and down the Ganges during the early 1770s. Yet, their extensive accounts made similar arguments, explicitly and implicitly, about the conflictual relationship between themselves, the Bengal Army, and the people of India generally. Each explicitly explained how the prestige and apparent power of British military culture initially attracted them, but also how hierarchies based on race marked each interaction within the army, to the detriment of Asians. Both Emin and Mahomet oriented themselves through their self-representations toward European officers rather than toward the Indian sepoys they commanded. Yet, Mahomet in particular showed how the frontier between the Company's armies and the surrounding society proved extremely diffuse and contested: a variety of camp-servants and camp-followers linked the official army personnel to the Indian countryside, which was being conquered and subdued by the Bengal Army which he himself, and tens of thousands of other Indians, had volunteered to serve or serve in. These multifaceted accounts and relationships guard us against anachronistic presuppositions about dichotomies of a single Indian nation resisting or succumbing to European imperialism; they thus contribute to the new military history of India.

DIVERSE ORIGINS OF THE BENGAL ARMY

Over the late eighteenth century, the Bengal Army expanded rapidly in size and power by amalgamating Indian and British military traditions and personnel. Following the decisive Battle of Plassey (June 1757), Indians, mostly drawn from the extant military labour market including soldiers of the defeated Nawab of Bengal, swelled this army by thousands each year. By 1770, as Emin and Mahomet joined it, the Bengal Army comprised 27,277 serving Indian officers and men (in addition to 522 European officers and 2,173 European soldiers).[5] By the time Mahomet resigned (1782), some 1,15,000 Indians were currently serving in the Company's three armies. By 1857, these armies contained 2,28,000 Indian soldiers (in addition to 43,000 Europeans) and had control over a million square miles with another half a million under their indirect military domination. Further, soldiers consisted of only a fraction of the population of a Bengal Army encampment: Indian camp-followers outnumbered soldiers many times over. Thus, large numbers of Indians chose to enter or support the Company's military over the years and their experiences in or around the Company's armies cascaded outward through Indian society.[6] These Asian lives and experiences should not be overshadowed by British written accounts of the Bengal Army.[7]

From the beginning, British authorities sought to homogenize the traditional varieties of Indian soldiers by arming, dressing, and training them uniformly in semi-European patterns.

Nevertheless, colonial armies contained many military traditions, domestic customs, and personal values which reflected the ways Indian soldiers adapted innovations derived from Europe to their own interests. These interactions produced a new military type: the *sepoy*. The Persian term *sipahi* had long meant a cavalryman in India.[8] After the mid-eighteenth century, however, the term shifted to mean an Indian infantryman with some European training and accoutrements, including a European-style military coat and English-manufactured musket, yet with Indian features like a turban and aigrette and a necklace of conch, glass, or wooden beads denoting rank.[9] In his autobiography, Mahomet provided illustrations of the respective uniforms of an Indian officer and a sepoy (Figure 7.1).

FIGURE 7.1: INDIAN OFFICER AND SEPOY, FROM MAHOMET, *TRAVELS*

The key elements that made the Bengal Army distinct from earlier armies in India involved its hardware, but even more its software—its British-influenced military drill, tactics, strategies, and culture.[10] The quality of European weapons was not superior to the best that Indian craftsmen could produce by hand. England's system of mass manufacture meant, however, that large numbers of identical weapons of reasonable quality could be supplied at relatively low cost. The standard sepoy armament included the 'Tower musket' (a musket stamped as tested at the Tower of London) and flints and gunpowder (also generally imported from England, although much of the saltpetre used in the gunpowder originally came from Bihar and Orissa). This meant uniform weaponry and other equipment conducive to routinized patterns of drill, supply, and conduct in battle, thus apparently minimizing individuality and ethnic differences.

Strikingly, neither Emin nor Mahomet particularly noted the weaponry of the Bengal Army. Rather they both extensively lauded the uniform appearance, periodic drill, and practised field manoeuvres of the British and Bengal armies, contrasting them with the motley armies of their allies and enemies. For example, Mahomet described a skirmish in 1772 between his Bengal Army contingent and Indian mountaineers (*Paharis* in Bihar): 'our men, arranged in military order, fired on them; some of the savages fell on the plain, others were wounded; and the greater part of them, after a feeble resistance with their bows, arrows, and swords, giving way to our superior courage and discipline, fled to the mountains for shelter. . . .'[11] Similarly, describing the Battle of Hastenbeck, Germany (26 July 1757), in which he fought, Emin identified the French with Indian undisciplined armies: 'The [French] Enemy begun to advance with their Musick, and Drums, making a very great noise, more like Indians than Europeans . . . [The French] are vastly like black Indians, [both] fire at a great distance and run away.'[12] Thus, for Mahomet and Emin, British military culture distinguished their armies above others in India and also in Europe.

The Bengal Army drilled its sepoys to manoeuvre as a unit. As European military theorists discovered empirically over decades of costly war on that continent, rigorous close-order drill by a professional infantry enabled trained officers to reposition tactical units even while under fire, coordinated with effective field artillery. In India, this meant that the companies of sepoys with European (or European-trained) officers could stand up to—and manoeuvre while under attack by—Mughal-style heavy cavalry, the core of many Indian armies. Further, larger armies of less drilled foot-soldiers under Indian rulers lost to smaller units of more disciplined sepoys. A contemporary of Emin and Mahomet recognized in his Persian language commentary: so long as sepoys 'maintain their formations, which they call "lines", they are like an immovable volcano spewing artillery and rifle [*sic*, musket] fire like unrelenting hail on the enemy, and they are seldom defeated.'[13]

As sepoys became increasingly a factor in warfare from the mid-eighteenth century onwards, some Indian rulers added sepoy battalions to their armies which were undergoing their own 'Military Revolution', belated and incomplete as it may have been.[14] Further, such battalions often proved fatally expensive. The weapons, uniforms, training and salaries of sepoy battalions drained the treasuries of rulers who employed them. Mercenary European officers demanded large salaries (and often, autonomy) to drill and command sepoys. Some Indian rulers rented parts of the Company's sepoy armies, but military dependency on the Company meant gradual loss of control over their treasuries, sources of revenue, and political independence. Ultimately, only the English East India Company could sustain the cost of such sepoy armies, due to: extensive extraction of revenues from the Indian lands it annexed, subsidies from the Indian rulers it subordinated, profits from international trade it controlled, and loans from the English state it lobbied.[15]

Yet, the homogenization of sepoys in the Bengal Army (and elsewhere) had limits. The sepoy's uniformity extended to almost all aspects of his outward appearance, except his face. Mahomet explained: 'The Sepoys are composed of Mahometans and Hindoos, who make no other distinction in their exterior appearance, than that the Hindoos colour each side of the face and forehead with a kind of red paint, produced from the timber of the sandal tree.'[16] Off duty and out of uniform, sepoys cooked and dined according to their own norms, living separately among their family members, often attended by their servants. Their loyalties toward the army tended to be personalistic, directed toward the British officer who commanded them rather than to the Bengal Army or the Company in the abstract. Neither Emin and Mahomet (nor later Indian military autobiographers, like Sita Ram) referred to their regiments by their official numerical designations, but rather by the surnames or nicknames of their European commanding officers.[17]

Further, Britons commanding the Bengal Army recruited and classified Indians in terms of European stereotyped preconceptions about inherent characteristics of each Indian region, caste, and religion. From quite early, the Company preferred to recruit for its Bengal Army men of what came to be known as 'martial communities' from outside of Bengal: it discounted the Bengalis as soldiers. In 1768, for example, British commanders sought to recruit 'the fighting Tribes of the Hindoos and Musselmen, and as many of the latter as can be procured'; they believed a balance of Hindus and Muslims would 'encourage a rivalship of disc[ipline] between them' and thus prevent 'their holding Cabals'.[18] Thus, patterns from the Indian military culture combined with European prejudices shaped the Bengal Army's composition, despite its European-style uniformity of accoutrements and dress.

Throughout this period, negotiations between troops and their commanders continued, despite British policies to professionalize the Bengal Army. The Company sought to reorient sepoys until they saw themselves as individuals bound loyally to the Company's army, or at least to their regiment. Nevertheless, many sepoys continued to regard the Company's army as a temporary job opportunity, to be entered into or left at their pleasure, rather than a career or ideological cause. Sepoys as well as European officers and soldiers resigned, deserted or mutinied *en masse*. For example, the Company complained for decades that whenever a sepoy battalion relocated away from one region, many sepoys who had enlisted in there deserted it, often re-enlisting in the new battalion transferring in, rather than accept relocation to a different region. Emin avoided such a transfer late in his military career, while Mahomet resigned as *subedar* and emigrated.[19] Further, under the pressures of war and finance, the Company recruited and discharged whole units on an ad hoc basis. In particular, since maintaining standing cavalry was especially expensive, the Company hired and then dismissed entire troops of 'irregular' cavalry as needed—like Emin's *Turksowars*, disbanded in 1772.[20] The idea of indestructible 'honour' binding each sepoy to his regiment, which Philip Mason presents as the soul of the Company's Army, was clearly not operative in this period, despite British efforts to instill it.[21]

British personnel formed only a small proportion of the Bengal Army, but they assumed a disproportionate prominence. In its early years, the Company experimented with appointing independent Indian commandants over Indian troops, but this sometimes proved disastrous for the Company.[22] Thereafter, the Company determined to commission only Europeans to command its regular regiments; Catholics and non-Europeans, by regulation, could not hold such commissions except under special dispensation.[23] Mahomet and his father, as *subedars* (the highest rank open to Indians in this period, except for commandant which was being phased out), still took orders from the lowest European commissioned officer. Emin could not rise above a brevet (temporary) ensign, junior to all European officers. Thus, the line separating European officers on one side and Asian subaltern officers and sepoys on the other remained firmly drawn throughout this period.

While Emin and Mahomet admired British military science, concurring that its order and discipline surpassed the traditions of Asia, yet the ordinary European soldiers present in India proved unimpressive. Even their European officers denigrated them. The Bengal Army's Commander-in-Chief wrote in 1768: our European recruits '. . . are exceedingly bad . . . the refuse of our metropolis. . . . [A]t present our European Regiments compared to a Battalion of Sepoys appear like a Regiment of Dwarfs.'[24] Despite difficulties in recruiting and maintaining European soldiers, and the relatively abundant and much less expensive supply of Indian soldiers, the Company and many Indians saw these European infantry regiments (which comprised only about 12-15 per cent of the Company's army) as its moral core. In 1766, the Calcutta government warned: '. . . we cannot avoid being alarmed at the extraordinary disproportion of numbers between your European and Black Infantry . . . their dangerous insolence and turbulent spirit . . . evinced the necessity of keeping the Black troops in awe and subjection.'[25] An explanation in many British minds for the later bloody 1857 'Mutiny' was the inadequate ratio of European to Indian troops in the Bengal Army. Many Britons in the Company believed sepoys would only stand firm in battle if European regiments provided 'stiffening'. Some Indians, including Mahomet and Emin, apparently accepted this notion of European moral superiority as well. Mahomet judged sepoys above ordinary Indian warriors but secondary to European troops: 'The Sepoys, who are in general well disciplined in the use of arms, serve as a strong reinforcement to a much less number of Europeans, and on many occasions, display great firmness and resolution.'[26] Similarly, Emin identified himself as an Asian, below Britons: 'The singularity of his sufferings would, in his opinion, scarce excite curiosity had he been an Englishman; for there are many private soldiers and daring mariners in England, whose excessive hardships and dangerous lives, in dreadful storms at sea, and hazardous battles by land, are an hundred times superior to whatever he has undergone. . . .'[27] The British 'empire of opinion' thus stands evident in these accounts.[28]

Therefore, many British asserted that superior British military culture, embodied most strongly in its European officers and men, empowered the Bengal Army over its rivals and allies. Many Indians who served them accepted this cultural assertion, but also held that British military culture was accessible, albeit to a lesser degree, by Indians. Both Emin and Mahomet attempted to demonstrate to the British through their lives and writings that they themselves had mastered at least some of that British military culture. But neither man received full acceptance by the British officer corps that they served.

JOSEPH EMIN

Emin lived over 35 years in India, but he was by birth a Christian Armenian of Hamadan, Iran. Emin immigrated at 18 to Bengal in 1744, where he joined his family and the other 3,000-4,000 Armenians ensconced there. Emin's father and grandfather were merchants who opposed his military aspirations, but Emin's great-grandfather and namesake had been an inspiring military hero. Emin determined to travel to England in order to learn European military science which he could then deploy in the emancipation of his persecuted people:

> [In Calcutta] I saw the Fort of the Europeans and the Soldiers Exercise, . . . they were dextrous and perfect in all things, then I grieved with

myself, for my [Armenian] Religion and my Country, that we were in Slavery and Ignorance like Jews Vagabonds upon Earth . . . but I understood that the black Armenians in the Mountains were free, and handled Arms from their Childhood, and [although they] are subject to the Turks and Persians, did not want Courage, but they are all Ignorant, and fight only with a wild and natural fierceness, and so they have no order and do nothing but like Robbers, but I resolved I would go to Europe to learn Art Military and other Sciences to assist that Art; and I was sure that if I would go into Armenia like an European Officer, I may be useful at least in some degree to my Country. . . .[29]

In pursuit of this aim, in 1751 Emin worked his passage to England as a sailor. After various adventures, he:

met by chance some Gentlemen who encouraged me, and gave me Books to read and advised me to kiss Colo[nel] Dingley's hands and shew my business to him, he was a brave Soldier, took me by the hand, spoke to his own Serjeant, an Honest Man, to teach me Manual Exercise and gave me Blands Military Discipline[30] and promised to help me to learn Gunnery and Fortification; but . . . when light just began to come to my Eyes he died, and I was like before except that I knew a little of Manuel Exercise and read some of the Roman History. . . . Now I [will be] happier than all Mankind if. . . . I may go through Evolutions with Recruits, and learn Gunnery and Fortification; and if there is a War to go one Year as a Volunteer. . . .[31]

Emin's London patrons fulfilled his wish; the royal Duke of Cumberland enrolled Emin in the Royal Military Academy at Woolich in 1756, providing his fees and a living allowance. Emin studied Euclid's *Elements* and books on military arts of gunnery and fortification.[32] When the Seven Years War erupted against the French, Emin cut short his academic training after only thirteen months, asserting (referring to himself in the third-person): 'he preferred a campaign, where the practice of the art of war was displayed, to living in the dull theory of it; that as he was then thirty-one years of age, the seeing of one campaign might be more useful to him than study at home for five years. . . . The Duke . . . was glad to hear Emin preferred fighting to study.'[33] Emin served as a gentleman officer attached to the English Army under the Duke of Cumberland and the Prussian Army under Frederick the Great, fighting on the continent (1757-8) at the Battle of Hastenbeck and the British raid on St. Malo.

Emin then made two expeditions to Armenia (1759-60, 1761-9).

With modest Russian support and financial subsidies from Lord Northumberland, he fought for Armenia's liberation from the Persian and Turkish empires. Emin uniformly represented himself as empowered above other Asians by his European military training, which to him meant: scientific appraisal of the terrain and disposition of forces, systematic preparation of military equipage, and disciplined detachment in battle. In contrast, Emin denoted Asians (both his enemies and his allies) as bombastic, ill-prepared, and pusillanimous in the face of European-style order and professionalism. As with so many other Armenian liberation struggles, however, his efforts proved bloody but futile.

Emin returned to Calcutta in 1770, to pursue a military career in the Bengal Army, declaring: 'he was young and stout, and could serve the Honourable Company, if they thought him fit. . . .'[34] Yet, he ran up against stronger social and racial barriers in Bengal than those he had overcome in London. Over the decades, the expanding British Empire was changing the rules of social intercourse and political participation, to the detriment of non-Britons, especially in the colonies. Thus, Emin could gain access to the Bengal Army only at the most marginal officer's rank: appointed (27 October 1770) as the most junior brevet ensign (*risaldar*) of irregular cavalry (*Turksowars*) in the First Brigade, but at an officer's pay of Rupees 300 per month (including *batta*).[35] He only received this minimal appointment due to a narrow vote in the Calcutta Council, in which the swing vote in his favour came from a classmate: 'Mr. Eyre [probably Francis Hare], Emin's old acquaintance in London, when they learned the use of the small-sword [together from] Sherlock the fencing master'.[36]

Seeking full officer's rank, Emin appealed to his powerful English patrons, petitioning for legal nationalization as British. Not even the dukes of Cumberland or Northumberland, however, could arrange this from London.[37] Emin's friend and supporter Edmund Burke lamented that 'a man once countenanced by the first people of this kingdom as well as of Germany, should . . . pass his life in misery and contempt in an English settlement. I know many think him an impostor, but I can bear witness to the truth of what he asserted. . . .'[38]

Emin spent two years of undistinguished service with the Bengal Army, mostly in garrison. Compared to his frequent fighting while on the European continent and then in Armenia, Emin found life in the Bengal Army relatively uneventful: 'Emin was ordered to go and join his corps, then at Dinapoor. . . . He staid there doing but very little. . . .' In 1771, Emin 'advanced with part of the army commanded by Sir Robert Barker to the assistance of Sujah Dowlah [of Awadh] at Shahabad, or the Rohillas country. Still nothing was to be seen, nor any real service to be done, in two years and an half; so that he marched down again to Benares, and the rainy season being over, was ordered to return to Calcutta. . . .'[39] When Governor-General Warren Hastings disbanded the Bengal Army's irregular cavalry in 1772, Emin perforce retired at half-pay.

Still seeking advancement for himself and the Armenian cause, Emin took indefinite leave of absence from the Bengal Army and journeyed to support an unsuccessful British expedition at Basra, Iran (March 1775) as volunteer.[40] The British frequently used manpower derived from South Asia for expeditions not only in Iran but also in West Asia, East Africa, and South-East Asia. Eventually, in 1784, Emin resettled in Calcutta, petitioning repeatedly for restoration of his rank and unpaid salary.[41] The severe racial barriers prevalent in colonial Calcutta proved difficult for Emin to overcome. Only when a friend from Europe, General Sloper of the Royal Army, took temporary charge as Commander-in-Chief in Calcutta (July-December 1786) did Emin briefly find a patron. As Emin stated:

> This honourable officer happened to know Emin twenty-six years before during the last war in Germany, and immediately on seeing him, took him by the hand, and protected him in a manner becoming the dignity of a brave soldier. He, in a few weeks time, having procured an order of the Honourable Council for the arrears of Emin's pay, and his rank in the army, posted him in the third company of European invalids. Earl Cornwallis succeeding both to the government and the command of the army, the General went home, and left Emin to shift for himself. . . .[42]

Throughout Emin's career, his greatest supporters were London-based, where racial prejudices tended not to develop as strictly or early as in the colonies.

After Emin had been comfortably posted with the Invalids in Calcutta for a decade, they were transferred up-country. Emin had no desire to leave his home or to interrupt writing his memoirs to follow them. Once again, a friend from England intervened:

fortunately, Colonel [Thomas Deane] Pearse took the command of the garrison in Fort William; and having known Emin at the Royal Academy of Woolwich, condescended to renew an acquaintance of thirty-six years singular kindness, and took him entirely under his patronage. The third company of invalids being ordered to move to Chunagur, Emin wished to remain in Calcutta to finish [writing] his narrative. The colonel obligingly interposed with Earl Cornwallis; and his lordship signified his pleasure, in a general order, that Ensign Emin was not to proceed with the corps, but was to draw regularly, according to his rank, for his pay, batta, and house-rent. This great indulgence he owes to the colonel, for had he not been present to use his interest with the Governor General, Emin could never have finished his Memorial. . . .[43]

Thus, once again, a friend from Emin's days in England as a gentleman officer protected him. When Emin reached 60, he sought and received a monthly pension of Rupees 91 (granted from February 1797).[44] He thereafter lived among the struggling Armenian community in Bengal, dying on 2 August 1809.

Emin's pursuit of access to British military culture and the status of an officer had empowered him in London. His deployment of that training had distinguished him on the European continent and in West Asia. Yet, his race barred him from commissioned rank in the Bengal Army. In many ways, Emin's 1791 book proved his final assertion to a British audience of his military prowess and accomplishments, futile as they proved.

SAKE DEAN MAHOMET

Like Emin, Mahomet inherited traditions of military service from a family that immigrated from Iran to India in the eighteenth century. Mahomet's Shi'ite Muslim family, however, had ties to the ruling Nawabi dynasty of Bengal, whom they served in Patna. Like Emin, Mahomet's father, elder brother, and he himself envisioned opportunities for advancement, prestige, and power through access to British military culture. Like Emin, Mahomet achieved far greater acceptance as a gentleman in Britain than he did in India. Unlike Emin, who returned to India, Mahomet remained an immigrant in Britain and thus never experienced the diminution of his status based on the stricter racial distinctions prevalent among the British in the colonies.

As the mainly Muslim-ruled states of north India declined politically over the eighteenth century, many Muslim service elite—like Mahomet's family—attached themselves to the rapidly expanding English East India Company. Muslims served in the Company's armies far in excess of their minority proportion of the general population: Muslims consistently provided nearly half of Indian subaltern officers, about two-fifths of Indian petty officers, and about one-third of sepoys over the period of Mahomet's career.[45] This disproportion resulted from both the supply of willing Muslims and also the Bengal Army's recruitment policy, as we have seen.

Following Plassey, the Nawab of Bengal served British masters. In Bihar, where Mahomet's family lived, this meant Deputy-Governor Raja Shitab Rai collected land revenue under British supervision, with the Bengal Army as enforcer. Mahomet's father apparently commanded as *subedar* one of the ten companies in the 31st Battalion of Pargana [revenue collection] Sepoys under Captain Thomas Goddard.[46] During the 1769 famine, a refractory landholder, resisting revenue collection, killed Mahomet's father. In recompense, the Company appointed Mahomet's elder brother in his place. Mahomet and his widowed mother lived in precarious gentility on income from the family's small landholding and the occasional charity of their distant relative, the Nawab of Bengal.[47]

Mahomet determined to gain access to the prestige and power of British military culture so evident in Patna. He recalled how, at age 11, he became fascinated with the colourful uniforms and confident bearing of the Company's British officers:

> My mother's house was not far from the Raja's palace; and the number of [British] Officers passing by our door in their way thither, attracted my notice, and excited the ambition I already had of entering on a military life. With this notion, I . . . seized the happy opportunity, and followed them directly to the palace [gaining] . . . admittance, on account of the respect the guards paid my father's family. The Gentlemen . . . take tea and coffee, and frequently amuse themselves by forming a party to dance; when they find themselves warm, they retire to the palace yard, where . . . on the ground is spread a beautiful carpet; the

Raja sits in the centre; the European Gentlemen on each side. . . . Dancing girls are now introduced . . . while the servants of the Raja are employed in letting off the fire-works, displaying, in the most astonishing variety, the forms of birds, beasts, and other animals . . . the Gentlemen sit down to an elegant supper, prepared with the utmost skill, by an Officer of the Raja, whose sole employ is to provide the most delicious viands on such an occasion: ice-cream, fowl of all kinds, and the finest fruit in the world. . . . The Raja was very happy with his convivial friends; and though his religion forbids him to touch many things handled by persons of a different profession, yet he accepted a little fruit from them. . . .[48]

The contrasts of the famine prevalent in the region with this lavish feast and of the highest ranking Indian official, Shitab Rai, as obsequious host of, and yet dependent on, British officers made the world of the Bengal Army most attractive to Mahomet.

Few Indian rulers offered such promising career prospects. By 1769, the Nawab of Bengal, pensioner of the Company, was downsizing his army. The Company limited the size of the army of Nawab of Awadh, Shuja al-Daula, by treaty, less than a third of whom, 10,000 sepoys, could be trained in the 'European model'.[49] Additionally, Mahomet excoriated Shuja al-Daula as a 'brutal ravisher' driven by 'licentious desires'.[50] Thus, for Mahomet, a military career in the Company's service seemed especially attractive while service to an Indian ruler appeared most discouraging.

Seeking a British patron, Mahomet caught the eye of a teenage Anglo-Irish cadet in the 3rd European Regiment in the Third Brigade, Godfrey Evan Baker.

I followed him without any restraint. . . . Nothing could exceed my ambition of leading a soldier's life: the notion of carrying arms, and living in a camp, could not be easily removed. . . . [Finally, Baker] in a very friendly manner, asked me how I would like living with the Europeans: this unexpected encouragement, as it flattered my hopes beyond expression, occasioned a very sudden reply: I therefore told him with eager joy, how happy he could make me, by taking me with him. He seemed very much pleased with me, and assuring me of his future kindness, hoped I would merit it.[51]

Despite his mother's pleas not to desert her, Mahomet joined Baker, remaining with him for 15 years until Baker's death.

A variety of formal and informal camp-servants and camp-followers enveloped the European and Indian officers and soldiers in a brigade. While Baker served as quarter-master of the Third Regiment (1770-82), he commanded the regiment's 700 camp-servants plus additional camp-followers, whose complex hierarchy Mahomet delineated:

[they were] composed of the lowest order of the people residing in the country, and forming many distinct tribes, according to their various occupations. We had a certain number of these men appointed to attend the garrison, which was usually augmented on a march, and distinguished under . . . various appellations. . . . They set out with us, a day before the main body of the army, accompanied by several classes of tradesmen, such as shoe-makers, carpenters, smiths, sail-makers, and others capable of supplying the camp; and were ranged into four departments, in order to perform the laborious business of the expedition without confusion . . . : the employment of the Lascars, who wore mostly a blue jacket, turban, sash, and trousers, was to pitch and strike the tents and marquees; load and unload the elephants, camels, bullocks, waggons &c. The Cooleys were divided into two distinct bodies for different purposes; to carry burthens, and to open and clear the roads through the country, for the free passage of the army and baggage: The Besties were appointed to supply the men and cattle with water: and the Charwalleys,[52] who are the meanest class of all, were employed to clean the apartments, and do other servile offices.[53]

In addition, individual soldiers and officers retained a variety of personal servants and camp-followers, according to their rank and purse. Although Mahomet himself dressed and drilled in imitation of the regimental style, he nevertheless remained attached to the Bengal Army for 12 years only as a member of Baker's entourage, sleeping in an unused palanquin in Baker's store-tent. Over Baker's career, his entourage grew significantly. A captain might have 40 servants and attendants, a lieutenant-colonel over 100.[54] The Indian mistresses or families of soldiers or officers, both European and Indian, often accompanied the army even in the field but stood outside of the formal authority of the British commander. A contemporary wrote: 'The Camp followers are a very independent set of people; and only remain with the army to which they attach themselves as long as it suits their convenience.'[55]

A vast number of Indians found it convenient. The ratio of

servants to soldiers varied but generally averaged about 5 per soldier, far more for officers: some 30,000-35,000 per brigade. For example, Goddard's Bengal Army detachment to Bombay in 1778 contained only 103 European soldiers (only 0.2 per cent of the men with him) and 6,624 Indian soldiers (16 per cent) but they were attended by 19,779 official camp-servants (47 per cent) and some 12,000 camp-followers (28 per cent).[56] Markets attached to each encampment extended less visible but extensive supply networks into the countryside, affecting the price of food, fuel, and cattle for miles around.[57] Provisioning, moving, and defending this huge concourse of people presented continual logistical problems of immense proportions.[58]

Mahomet recounted several instances where camp-attendants drew his brigade into conflicts with surrounding villagers. In 1772, his Third Brigade marched through hills separating Bihar from Bengal. As the brigade's 'market people' foraged from the countryside, they clashed with the hills-people living there. The brigade's rear guard rushed to the scene, killing many local villagers and capturing 30 of them. Subsequently, the hill-people retaliated:

> Next morning, as our hotteewallies ['elephant-keepers'], grass cutters, and bazar people, went to the mountains about their usual business of procuring provender for the elephants, grass for the horses, and fuel for the camp; a gang of those licentious savages, rushed with violence on them, inhumanly butchered seven or eight of our people, and carried off three elephants, and as many camels, with several horses and bullocks. Such of our hotteewallies, &c. as were fortunate enough to escape with their lives from those unfeeling barbarians . . . related the story of their sufferings to the Commanding Officer [Lieutenant-Colonel Hugh Grant], who . . . instantly [ordered] the pursuit of the lawless aggressors, some of whom, they luckily found ploughing in a field, to which they were directed by two of the men whom Providence rescued from their cruelty; and observed numbers flocking from the hills to their assistance. . . . Our gallant soldiers, swift as the lightning's flash, pursued, overtook, and made two hundred of them prisoners, who were . . . severely punished for their crimes; some having their ears and noses cut off, and others hung in gibbets. . . .[59]

Mahomet clearly regarded the Bengal Army's mass torture of these hill-people (with no attempt to prove individual culpability) as just punishment. Later, Mahomet himself served as market-master, extracting provisions, occasionally with violence, from the countryside for a detachment under Baker's command, yet he eventually questioned such depredations.[60]

After a dozen years serving Baker, Mahomet achieved the subaltern officer's rank. In January 1781, Baker obtained the command of a sepoy battalion in Major William Roberts' 30th Native Infantry Regiment in the Second Brigade, then at Kanpur. Baker used his influence to have Mahomet appointed *jemadar* in an elite grenadier company under him.[61]

In recounting his battle-career against Indian opponents, Mahomet sometimes, but not always, concurred with prevailing British assessments. Like many contemporary British writers, Mahomet regarded the Marathas as unworthy opponents. He reported his battalion 'scoured the neighbouring country [around Kalpi], in order to disperse [Marathas], those disturbers of the public tranquillity who, after some slight skirmishes, entirely fled, overawed by the terror of our arms'.[62] The Company then appropriated Kalpi's land-revenues.

Mahomet, however, disagreed with most British participants in Governor-General Hastings' battles with Raja Chait Singh of Benaras (August-September 1781). Mahomet strikingly portrayed Hastings as violating law and order and esteemed Chait Singh's 'philanthropy . . . humility and sufferings'.[63] In contrast, most European witnesses demonized Chait Singh as a traitorous murderer of European officers and their sepoys.[64] Although Mahomet's company led the attack on Chait Singh's fort at Patita, he modestly highlighted Baker's exploits rather than his own.[65]

Mahomet concluded his military career after suppressing popular resistance in the Benaras countryside. Once, Mahomet (now a *subedar* under Baker's command) 'disperse[d] the unruly natives who assembled in a hostile manner within a fort . . . leaving a number of their dead behind them'. Such suppression of Indian peasants, however, apparently pained Mahomet. He lamented: 'The refractory [peasantry] were awed into submission by the terror of our arms; yet humanity must lament the loss of those whom wasting war had suddenly swept away'. He followed this account with elegiac poetry about war's tragic devastation.[66]

Subsequently, local peasants charged Baker with extorting money from them.[67] Hastings recalled Baker in disgrace (July

1782); although this charge remained unproven, Baker resigned his commission.[68] Mahomet also resigned, at the age of twenty-three.[69] They left India together (January 1784), settling in Cork, Ireland, where both soon married. Mahomet published his account of the Bengal Army early in 1794, explaining himself and Indian culture to the British among whom he lived the rest of his life. While the Bengal Army elevated Mahomet to a subaltern officer's rank, its prevalent racial distinctions located him below all European officers. Further, the depredations that the Bengal Army imposed on some Indians clearly taxed Mahomet's sense of justice. Nevertheless, his Bengal Army service proved a credential that enhanced his later career as a gentleman surgeon in England, where he died (24 February 1851).

ASIANS AND THE BENGAL ARMY

Our analysis of the autobiographical writings and careers of Emin and Mahomet reveals the internal complexity of the Bengal Army during its formative period. These two subaltern officers, like many Asians, sought to use British military culture for their own purposes. As Emin demonstrated, even before Plassey, some Asian men sought access for themselves and their people to the power and prestige that mastery of British military science promised. Indeed, in England, Emin found British elites recognized his military aspirations as worthy of their support, even of their emulation. Mahomet described how, compared to service in the pay of a subordinated north Indian ruler, the Bengal Army appeared the most attractive career available. Both men achieved the subaltern officer's rank but the Bengal Army's racial rules limited their careers within it and ultimately served British goals, not their own.

Europeans commanded but they could not fully control their Indian soldiers. The Bengal Army (like other European-commanded colonial armies in Asia and Africa) embodied an asymmetrically mixed variety of ethnicities and orientations. The Company armed the sepoys with British weapons, drilled them in European-style discipline, and dressed them in partially European-style uniforms. Its formal hierarchy of rank largely reinforced distinctions of race, and relegated all women to peripheral roles. The Company thus altered the appearance of sepoys and, to some extent, their on-duty behaviour. Yet, this reshaped but could not eradicate their personal and cultural identities.

During the late eighteenth century, the Company recruited men from the extant military labour market, initially on a relatively casual basis; soldiers entered their service from other armies (and vice versa) fairly easily. Their heterogeneous military encampments contained a variety of camp-servants and camp-followers, far outnumbering the soldiers. These encampments extended indirectly and diffusely into the countryside, often generating tensions and social and economic dislocations. The colonial armies which emerged thus represented new forms, and new patterns of military deportment, produced out of unequal negotiations among diverse European and Asian traditions, and ultimately distinct from any army found in either tradition. These conflicting interactions among diverse groups produced a contact zone.[70]

This model of the colonial army as a contact zone problematizes dichotomous notions of a 'bureaucratic-rational' army of Europeans overmastering bands of indigenous non-White warriors. Ness and Stahl portray European colonial armies in Asia as:

> bureaucratically arranged . . . substituting *rules* administered by technologically qualified officials for the *personal decisions* of an ascriptively qualified elite. Thus, the military superiority displayed by European troops against superior numbers of brave and individually skillful native [Asian] horsemen was the supremacy of the bureaucrat-technician over the hero. . . . One might even see the history of [colonial] warfare as a continuous replacement of heroes with bureaucrat-technicians.[71]

This argument both understates the Asian component and overstates the 'rational-bureaucratic' character of colonial armies, particularly in their early stages. We should rather regard the colonial army as emerging out of interactions—unequal as they may have been—betweeen Asians and Europeans, all participants drawing their own traditions and values into the process, using their positions to pursue their personal interests and values, and being altered by the experience. The extensive autobiographical descriptions by Emin and Mahomet of the composition of the Bengal Army, its cultural meanings to Asians, and its relationships with Asian society thus reveal processes that contribute to India's military history from the perspective of these subaltern officers.

NOTES

1. Studies of the Bengal Army during this period include: Premansu Kumar Bandyopadhyay, *Tulsi Leaves and the Ganges Water* (Calcutta: K.P. Bagchi, 2003); T.A. Heathcote, *The Military in British India: The Development of British Land Forces in South Asia* (Manchester: Manchester University Press, 1995); G.J. Bryant, 'Military Imperative in Early British Expansion', *Indo-British Review*, vol. 21, no. 2 (1995); Douglas M. Peers, *Between Mars and Mammon: Colonial Armies and the Garrison State in Early Nineteenth-century India* (London/New York: I.B. Tauris, 1995); Kaushik Roy and Sabyasachi Dasgupta, 'Discipline and Disobedience in the Bengal and Madras Armies: 1807-56', in Kaushik Roy (ed.), *War and Society in Colonial India: 1807-1945* (New Delhi: Oxford University Press, 2006), pp. 55-81; Kaushik Roy, 'The Armed Expansion of the English East India Company: 1740s-1849', in Daniel P. Marston and Chandar S. Sundaram (eds.), *Military History of India and South Asia: From the East India Company to the Nuclear Era* (Westport, Conn : Praeger Security International, 2007), pp. 1-15.
2. Studies of sepoys during this period include: Seema Alavi, *The Sepoys and the Company: Tradition and Transition in Northern India, 1770-1830* (New Delhi: Oxford University Press, 1995); Pradeep P. Barua, *Gentlemen of the Raj: The Indian Army Officer Corps, 1817-1949* (Westport, Conn.: Praeger, 2003); Jeffrey Greenhunt, 'Sahib and Sepoy: An Inquiry into the Relationship between the British Officers and Native Soldiers', *Military Affairs*, vol. 48, no. 1 (1984), pp. 15-18; Dirk H.A. Kolff, *Naukar, Rajput & Sepoy: The Ethnohistory of Military Labour Market in Hindustan, 1450-1850* (Cambridge: Cambridge University Press, 1990); David Omissi, *Sepoy and the Raj* (London: Macmillan, 1994); Channa Wickremesekera, *'Best Black Troops in the World': British Perceptions and the Making of the Sepoy, 1746-1805* (New Delhi: Manohar, 2002). For the Indian women who had relations with British officers see: Durba Ghosh, *Sex and the Family in Colonial India: The Making of Empire* (Cambridge: Cambridge University Press, 2006).
3. Joseph Emin, *Life and Adventures of Joseph Emin* (London: The Author, 1792); 2nd edn., ed. A. Apcar (Calcutta: Asiatic Society of Bengal, 1918).
4. Dean Mahomet, *Travels of Dean Mahomet* (Cork: The Author, 1794); rpt., ed. Michael H. Fisher (Berkeley: University of California Press, 1997). For a biography, see Michael H. Fisher, *First Indian Author* (New Delhi: Oxford University Press, 1996).

5. 'General Return of the Troops under the Command of the Presidency of Fort William', 31 July 1770, National Archives of India [hereinafter NAI], New Delhi. See also Bengal Public Consultation, 16 December 1769: Statement of the Army, India Office Library, British Library [hereinafter IOL], whose figures roughly accords with From Court of Directors [hereinafter CoD], 16 March 1768 in NAI, *Fort William-India House Correspondence*, 21 vols. (New Delhi: NAI, 1949-85), vol. 5, pp. 99-100. The figures in 'Return of the Company's Troops in India, in the Eighth Report of the Committee of Secrecy', however, gives a far less rapid rise in the number of sepoys. I have accepted the consensus of the reports from India rather than this latter compilation from London.
6. See Seema Alavi, 'The Company Army and Rural Society', *Modern Asian Studies*, vol. 27, no. 1 (1993), pp. 147-78.
7. One central debate was over British use of existing Indian traditions *versus* retraining Indians in European military patterns: the 'Orientalist' *versus* the 'Anglicist' school.
8. Henry Yule and A.S. Burnell, *Hobson-Jobson* (New Delhi: Munshiram Mahoharlal, rpt., 1968), q.v. 'Sepoy'.
9. Thomas Williamson, *East Indian Vade Mecum*, 2 vols. (London: Black, Parry, and Kingsbury, 1810), vol. 1, p. 426.
10. There is much debate over the significance of any technological advantage European military science may have had over indigenous Asian armies. The Calcutta Council believed at the time that European small arms, artillery, and other weapons were superior and had to be kept under their monopolistic control. Letter to CoD, 3 September 1766, in J. Long, *Selections from Unpublished Records of Government* (Calcutta: Superintendent of Government Printing, 1869), vol. 1, p. 427 For somewhat differing scholarly assessments see Bruce P. Lenman, 'Weapons of War in Eighteenth-Century India', *Journal of the Society for Army Historical Research*, vol. 36 (1968), pp. 33-43; Gayl D. Ness and William Stahl, 'Western Imperialist Armies in Asia', *Comparative Studies in Society and History,* vol. 19 (1977), pp. 2-29; Wickremesekera, '*Best Black Troops in the World'.*
11. Mahomet, Letter IX.
12. Emin (ed. Apcar), pp. 78-81.
13. Mir Abdul-Latif Khan Shustari, *Tuhfat al-Alam va Zayl al-Tuhfah*, tr. Juan R.I. Cole, 'Invisible Occidentalism', *Iranian Studies*, vol. 25, nos. 3-4 (1992), pp. 3-16.
14. Wickremesekera argues the crucial centralized command structure of the European military system 'was almost completely neglected' even by innovative Indian rulers. Wickremesekera, *'Best Black Troops in the World',* p. 71.
15. C.A. Bayly, *Indian Society and the Making of the British Empire*

(Cambridge: Cambridge University Press, 1988); Fisher, *Indirect Rule* (New Delhi: Oxford University Press, 1991); Bruce P. Lenman, 'Transition to European Military Ascendancy', in John Lynn (ed.), *Tools of War* (Bloomington: University of Indiana, 1990); Douglas M. Peers, 'War and Public Finance', *International History Review*, vol. 11, no. 4 (November 1989), pp. 628-47; Kaushik Roy, 'Rockets Under Haidar Ali and Tipu Sultan', *Indian Journal of History of Science*, vol. 40, no. 4 (2005), pp. 635-50 and 'Military Revolution in Mysore?', *Contemporary India*, vol. 3, no. 3 (2007), pp. 19-37.

16. Mahomet, Letter XVI.
17. Sita Ram Pandey, *From Sepoy to Subedar*, ed. and tr. James Norgate (Lahore: W. Ball, 1873).
18. From CoD 16 March 1768, in *Fort William*, vol. 5, p. 100; General Department 29 April 1782, Minutes of Council 22 April 1782; General Orders of Commander-in-Chief 11 May 1782, NAI.
19. E.g., Bengal Secret and Military Consultation 18 August 1769, 6 August 1781, IOL; From CoD 11 April 1781, in *Fort William*, vol. 8, p. 295.
20. E.g., Major Fletcher to Futteh Aly Cawn, Persian Department No. 46 (1765), Long, *Selections*, vol. 1, p. 415; From CoD to Fort William 25 March 1772, in *Fort William*, vol. 6, p. 159; Provincial Commander in-Chief 10 June 1782, Bengal Public Consultation 9 August 1782, IOL. The Company also required its Indian allies, including Chait Singh, to supply cavalry contingents.
21. Philip Mason, *Matter of Honour* (New York: Holt, Rinehart, Winston, 1974). See also Henry Dodwell, *Sepoy Recruitment in the Old Madras Army* (Calcutta: Superintendent Government Printing, 1922), pp. 29-30.
22. See S.C. Hill, 'The Old Sepoy Officer', *English Historical Review* (April-July 1913), pp. 260-91, 496-514 and *Yusuf Khan, The Rebel Commandant* (London: Longmans, Green, 1914).
23. French officers and men of mixed ancestry faced similar barriers to regular careers in the Bengal Army. See Rosie Llewlyn-Jones, *A Very Ingenious Man: Claude Martin in Early Colonial India* (New Delhi: Oxford University Press, 1992) and Antoine-Louis Henri Polier, *A European Experience of the Mughal Orient*, tr. Muzaffar Alam and Seema Alavi (New Delhi: Oxford University Press, 2001).
24. Letter from Richard Smith, 2 November 1768, Bengal Secret and Military Consultation, 17 November 1768, IOL.
25. Letter to CoD, 5 December 1766 in Long, *Selections*, p. 467.
26. Mahomet, Letter XVI.
27. Emin (1792), p. 3.
28. Douglas M. Peers, 'Habitual Nobility of Being', *Modern Asian Studies*, vol. 25, no. 3 (1991), pp. 545-69.
29. Emin to Northumberland, 1756, in Emin, *Life and Adventures*, p. 101.

30. Humphrey Bland, *Treatise of Military Discipline* (London: S. Buckley, 1727).
31. Emin to Northumberland, 1756, in Emin, *Life and Adventures*, pp. 101-2.
32. Northumberland to Emin, 1756, reproduced in Emin (ed. Apcar), pp. 58-60.
33. Emin (ed. Apcar), p. 69.
34. Ibid., p. 431.
35. *Batta* was a supplementary allowance. 'General Return of the Troops under the Command of the Presidency of Fort William 1770-78'; List of the Bengal Army, NAI. V.P.C. Hodson, *List of the Officers of the Bengal Army 1758-1834*, 4 vols. (London: Constable and Phillimore, 1927-47), vol. 2, p. 137. Emin (ed. Apcar), pp. 439, 483.
36. Emin (ed. Apcar), p. 432.
37. Northumberland to Emin, 17 May 1771, Emin (ed. Apcar), pp. 440-1.
38. Burke to John Stewart, 30 October 1772 in Edmund Burke, *Correspondence of Edmund Burke*, ed. Thomas W. Copeland, 10 vols. (Cambridge: Cambridge University Press, 1958-78), vol. 2, pp. 359-60.
39. Emin (ed. Apcar), p. 339.
40. Ibid., pp. 441-55.
41. Emin's Application for Arrears of Pay, Calcutta, 14 April 1785, and Emin's Petition, Calcutta, 30 March 1786, Emin (ed. Apcar), pp. 480-3.
42. Emin (1792), pp. 636-7.
43. Ibid., pp. 337-8. See also Thomas Deane Pearse, 'A Memoir of Colonel Thomas Deane Pearse of the Bengal Artillery', *Bengal Past and Present*, vols. 2-6 (1908-11).
44. Bengal Army List, February 1797, p. 54; Pensioner Artillery, Ensign Joseph Emin in Emin (ed. Apcar), p. 479.
45. Later Rajputs and Brahmins from the Awadh area rose as a proportion of the Bengal Army. I calculated the above figures for sepoy battalions from 'Infantry Native Officers and Sepoys Examined', Bengal Military Consultations 1778-1784, IOL. A similar study of the Madras Army of the 1760s-1860s shows Muslim were well over half of *subedars* and *jemadars*, but only about one third of non-warrant officers and sepoys. Dodwell, *Sepoy Recruitment*.
46. Rumbold to Council, 22 September 1769; Bengal Secret and Military Consultations 19 October 1769, IOL. Arthur Broome, *History of the Rise and Progress of the Bengal Army*, 3 vols. (Calcutta: W. Thacker, 1850), vol. 1, pp. 618-19.
47. Mahomet, Letter II.
48. Ibid.
49. C.U. Aitchison, *A Collection of Treaties*, 14 vols. (Calcutta: Foreign Office Press, 1909), vol. 1, pp. 92-3.
50. Mahomet, Letter XXI.

51. Ibid., Letter II.
52. Here and in Letter XVIII, Mahomet classed *charwalley* among the lowest categories yet in Letter XVIII, he spelled it *cherwallees* and glosses it 'gold-finders'. This may be a typographical error for *charawaha*, 'grass-finder, fodder-cutter, or herdsman'. A less likely possibility is that he meant *char*, 'scout or spy'.
53. Mahomet, Letter V.
54. Broome, *History*, vol. 1, pp. 552-4; Innes Munro, *Narrative of Military Operations against the French, Dutch, and Hyder Ally Cawn, 1780-84* (London: The Author, 1789), p. 186.
55. James Forbes, *Oriental Memoirs*, 2 vols., 2nd edn. (London: Richard Bentley, 1834), vol. 1, p. 410.
56. James Rennell, *Marches of the British Army in . . . India*, 2nd edn. (London: The Author, 1792), 99 n; Raymond Callahan, *East India Company and Army Reform, 1783-1798* (Cambridge: Harvard University Press, 1972), p. 9.
57. This problem is discussed in Select Committee to CoD, 9 May 1770, in *Fort William*, vol. 6, pp. 203-4.
58. Arthur Wellesley (later Duke of Wellington) maintained that his experience of organizing the logistics of his campaigns in south and west India (1799-1804) prepared him for his successful contest with Napoleon in the Iberian Peninsula.
59. Mahomet, Letter IX.
60. Ibid., Letter XXXI.
61. This regiment was raised in 1778 (as the 37th Regiment), renumbered in 1781(as the 30th) and in 1784 (as the 33rd), and disbanded in 1785.
62. Mahomet, Letter XXXI.
63. Ibid., Letter XXXIII.
64. E.g. William Hodges, *Travels in India* (London: The Author, 1793), pp. 48-57 and Warren Hastings, *Narrative of the Insurrection* (Calcutta: Governor General, 1782). The English Parliament, however, concurred with Mahomet and made Hastings' treatment of Chait Singh a major accusation in his impeachment and seven year trial before the House of Lords. See E.A. Bond (ed.), *Speeches of the Managers*, 4 vols. (London: George E. Eyre and William Spottiswoode, 1859); Nicholas B. Dirks, *Scandal of Empire* (Cambridge: Belnap, 2006).
65. Mahomet, Letters XXXI-XXXIII; Hastings, *Narrative*, pp. 180-4.
66. Mahomet, Letter XXXIV.
67. Persian Correspondence, Translations of Issues, 1781-85, 26, pp. 1-18, No. 38, NAI; Warren Hastings, *Memoirs* (ed.), G.R. Gleig, 3 vols. (London: Richard Bentley, 1841), vol. 2, pp. 584-7; Hastings letter, 15 July 1782, Addl. 29,115, British Library.
68. Mahomet, Letter 7; Hastings, *Memoirs*, vol. 2, pp. 587-8.

69. Mahomet, Letter XXXV.
70. Pratt identifies contact zones as 'social spaces where disparate cultures meet, clash, and grapple with each other, often in highly asymmetrical relations of domination and subordination.' Mary Louise Pratt, *Imperial Eyes* (London: Routledge, 1992), p. 4.
71. Ness and Stahl, 'Western Imperialist', pp. 26-7.

CHAPTER 8

Strategies Under Stress

Army Management and Environment in Late Pre-Colonial Bahawalpur

RICHARD B. BARNETT

In 1831, on a mission to scout the commercial possibilities of Indus navigation for the East India Company, Lieutenant-Colonel Alexander Burns made the following note concerning the state of Bahawalpur. The land, he said, is mostly

> . . . a barren waste of Land hills which encroach upon the Rivers, but in their vicinity the tract is rich and fertile, and watered like the other banks of the Indus by the periodical swell. . . . Its ruler wielded little power, he continued, and enjoyed annual revenues of only ten lakhs, or one million rupees, excluding income from lands leased from Ranjit Singh on the other side of the Indus; . . . yet Bahadur Khan maintains some State and has about 2,000 regular Troops such as they are, with a train of Artillery to second the efforts of his Feudatories in the field, and his forces collected would exceed 20,000 Men. . . .[1]

This observation, coming seven years before Bahawalpur's military autonomy was eroded by a 'protective' British treaty in 1838, neatly illustrates the several purposes of this paper. Burns refers first of all to the unique territorial and environmental features of this western Indian frontier state; features that, as we shall see, played an important role in its military and political survival. Secondly, he portrays the economic base of the realm as limited, fragmented and threatened by neighbouring powers. Finally, he somewhat dismissively assesses the nawab's army, a force that was not only small, but also, in his view, indifferently organized, dispersed, and overwhelmingly feudal in structure—by which he probably meant segmentary and patrimonial rather than centralized and bureaucratic. Not only could it never pose a threat to British arms, but in the official imagination, its very existence after seven generations of independent rule in this turbulent part of the subcontinent seemed, if not a miracle, at least a curious accident.

I plan to show how this regional regime, with all these perceived limitations, nonetheless exploited its geography and environment to survive, I will also assess the role of its military, in both management and tactics, in the state's survival. In the process, I hope to trace the ways in which limited economic, political and military resources were brought to bear, often against great odds and formidable foes, during the period 1730 to 1840. These foes included the Afghan rulers of Kabul, the Kalhoras of Sind, and the Sikhs in Lahore, as well as the more modest Rajput powers in Bikaner and Jaisalmer (see Figs. 8.1 and 8.2).

Figuring prominently in the narrative are the identity and legitimacy of the ruling nawabs, their occasional and selective reliance on the *makhdums* (managers) of major Sufi shrines, and their close study of the strengths, weaknesses, and beliefs of the changing roster of enemies. Equally crucial to the survival of this state were its careful investment in appropriate weapons technology in the relative absence of European adventurers, and—most importantly—their keen appreciation of the Indus riverine ecosystem and its immense flanking scrubland to the south-east, known both then and now as Cholistan.

First, a few words by way of introducing the context, since eighteenth-century Bahawalpur—and its proper pronunciation (the second 'a' is long)—is yet relatively unknown.[2] Bahawalpur is located along the left, or south-east, banks of the Sutlej, Chenab, and Indus rivers, between Multan on the north-west and Rajputana on the south-east. It was a state constructed from a scattered network of riverine market towns and Sufi pilgrimage centres, in what had been largely a desert. It first put down distinctive agrarian, commercial, and political foundations in the 1730s. Its growing population ingeniously exploited a riverine ecology that had been undeveloped for thirty-five centuries, expanding into the *rohi* (desert) and attracting tens of thousands of new settlers from Sind, Punjab, Multan, and Rajputana. At its greatest extent in the 1830s, Bahawalpur was the size of modern Austria, with a population of some 3,50,000.[3]

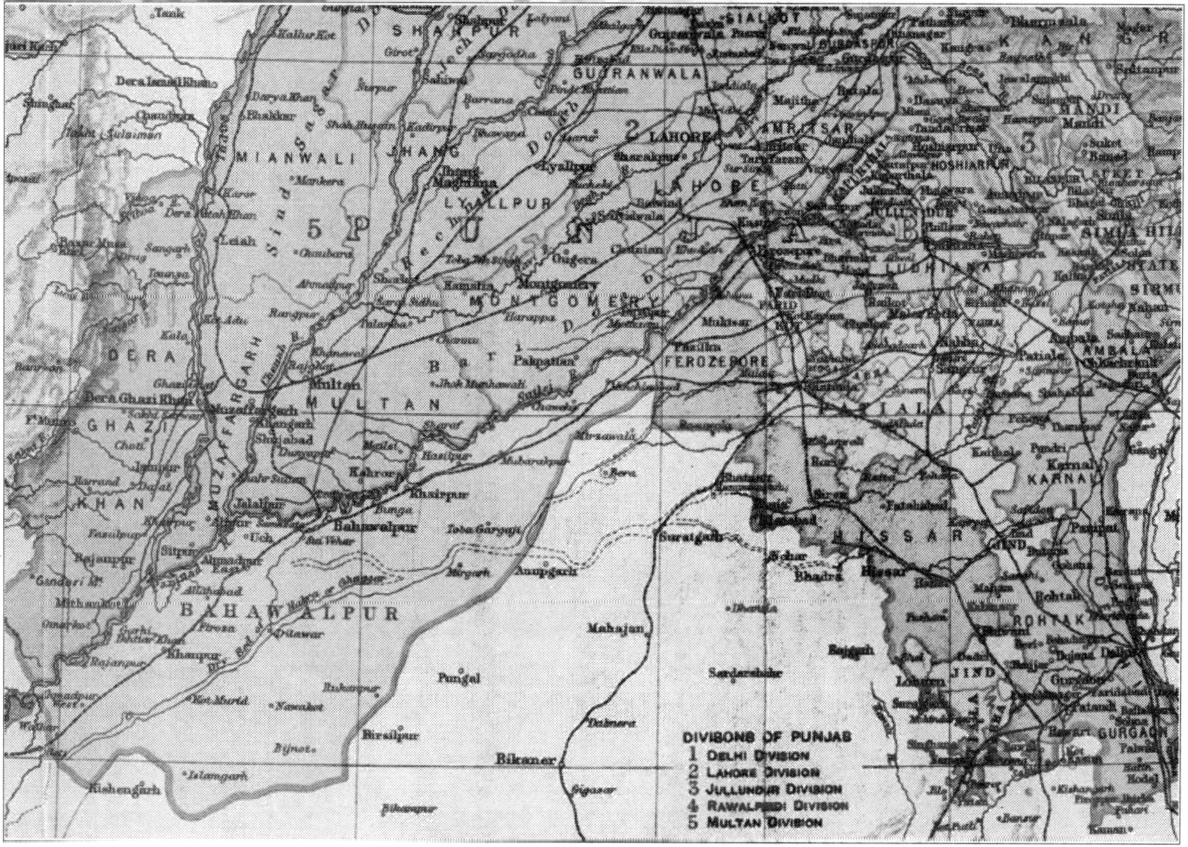

FIGURE 8.1: MAP OF SOUTHERN PUNJAB

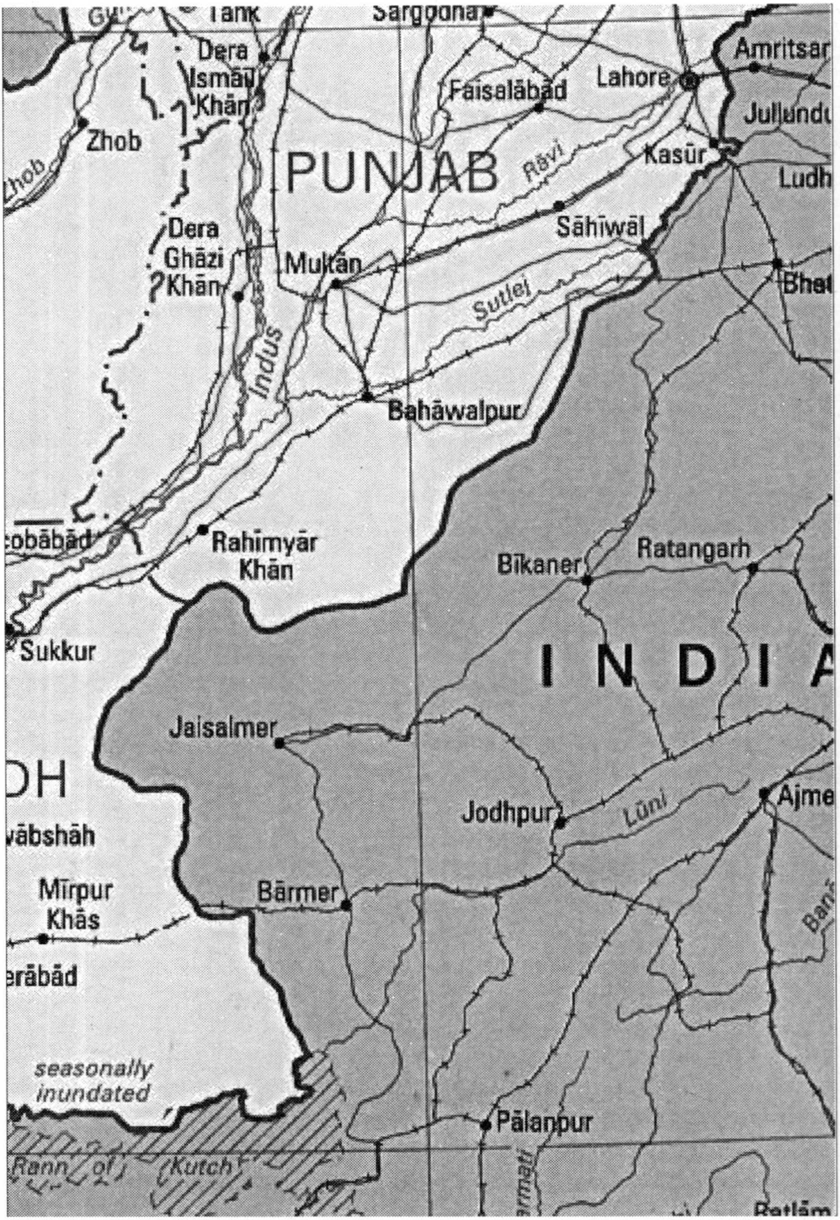

FIGURE 8.2: MAP OF MODERN BAHAWALPUR

Its ruling elite traced its ancestry to one of the Prophet's most famous uncles, Abbas, and thus styled itself as Abbasi. It came to rule a population that had accepted Islamicate values for over a millennium, intermarried largely with indigenous Jat families, and for seven generations prudently avoided or overcame the military adventurisms of the Durranis, Sikhs, Multanis, Rajputs, and British. Incorporating Rajputs, Baluchis, Multanis, Sindhis, Pathans, Gosains, Punjabis and Cholistanis, this society quickly recognized the enormous potential of irrigation, and developed simple, appropriate technology to turn the desert into a garden well before British technical supervision was admitted into the realm in the 1860s. It fostered and encouraged the many Hindu and Muslim trading partnerships working the Panjnad sector of the Silk Route to Central Asia, as well as the overland trade along the Indus system, and became an important manufacturing and transhipment depot for caravans connecting Calcutta with the distant Aral Sea region. As a result, no less than one-third of its state income came from customs duties. Local Sufi orders (powerful since the early Delhi Sultanate) grew in importance, such as the Bukhari and Gilani *silsilas* or lineages of Uchch Sharif, and so tested their clout that they later had to be checked by the nawab's regular army. Further defining the region's identity was a popular literature in a distinct language, Saraiki, common also to Multan, with much of its common vocabulary from Sindhi and Punjabi, developing a poetic genre during the century that celebrated these geopolitical, cultural, and religious configurations.[4]

All these factors enabled Bahawalpur to survive as a distinct socio-political entity—although a protected and monitored one after 1838—until after Independence. Though it was not a self-sufficient society, its prosperity, resilience and autonomy carry implications for continuity and growth in post-Mughal pre-colonial India. By the time the Raj arrived to make it into a princely state, so much of its modern agrarian and commercial infrastructure had already been laid down that British advisors and experts would exert only a relatively minor influence on its social, political, and economic institutions.

From a military and strategic point of view, the terrain that became Bahawalpur was mostly desert, at least since the end of the Indus Civilization (2350-1750 BCE), when a major riverine complex watering what is now the Thar Desert either changed course or dried up. This complex has been called variously the Mihran, Hakra, Wahindah, Sind Sagar, or Ghaggar; several theories compete to explain its extent, course, origin, and disappearance.[5] Dozens of protohistoric Harappan sites lie along these channels, which are exposed clay, baked into such hardpan that the hooves of a galloping horse produce a loud ringing sound.[6]

Beyond the immediate vicinity of the Sutlej, Chenab, and Indus rivers, which formed its most frequent north-western boundary, Bahawalpur was almost entirely barren during the Mughal period. Imperial revenue documents labeled it, rather dismissively, *berun Panjnad* (Outer Panjnad), beyond the citied area of the riverine confluences south-west of Multan, and by implication a useless tract of unpopulated desert. Attached administratively at first to *Suba* Multan, it was shifted to *Sarkar* Sirhind of Delhi Province, the demotion apparently indicating its insignificant value as a source of revenue.[7]

The limited rural population of this area in 1700 was mainly Jat, living on animal husbandry rather than farming. The main contemporary authority on irrigation in this region, whose family had served the state as engineers for generations, wrote from what was probably urban chauvinism that 'people used to live more on the theft of cattle than on cultivation'.[8] Such a pastoral-nomadic mode of existence was well suited to regional climatic conditions, since there is a mean annual rainfall of less than 12 cm between the Makran coast of Pakistan and northern Multan.[9]

This pastoral-nomadic way of life was altered dramatically in the first half of the eighteenth century. A large clan of warrior chieftains known as Daudputra—sons of Da'ud, the lineage founder—whose political history dates back to eighth-century Sind, and who styled themselves Abbasi (since they were putatively descended from Abbas, the Prophet's uncle), established themselves in Shikarpur in upper Sind. The rivalry of their Sindhi kinsmen, the Kalhora *amirs*, became more threatening in the declining years of the Mughal Empire, despite the fact that one Daudputra supposedly had enough power to have boasted extravagantly of a *mansab* of 5,000, obviously derived from revenues outside Bahawalpur, in Akbar's reign.[10]

Seeking to improve their fortunes, they accepted an invitation from the Gilani and Bukhari *makhdums* of Uchch Sharif, Sufi saints whose *khanqahs* (hospices) date back to the thirteenth-century Mongol invasions of Khurasan, and settled near them just east of the confluence of the Indus and the Chenab rivers.[11] From this new and strategic location, Amir Sadiq Muhammad Khan (ruled 1723-46) managed not only to fend off the Kalhoras of Sind, but to conquer in 1733 the desert fortress of Derawar or Derawal from the ruler of Jaisalmer, Rawal Akhi Singh (thus its name, Dera Rawal—the 'Abode of Rawal'). This fortress was soon to play a major role in the success of this nascent regional power.

The *amir* also took special pains to gain favour with Nadir Shah during the Perso-Afghan invasion of 1739, although he sensibly realized that the Shah would remain a potential adversary. It must be noted that the treaty between Nadir Shah and the Mughal ruler Muhammad Shah that concluded the 1739 invasion clearly stipulated that most of Multan was to be ceded to Kabul, but that Bahawalpur was to remain under Sadiq's control.[12] After several successes and reversals, the entire clan settled in the strip of territory south-east of the Sutlej-Chenab-Indus riverine sequence. They also held smaller areas across the rivers from time to time, either directly or on lease. Soon after, the construction of an extensive inundation canal network was begun where none had existed. The only remnant of previous interest in such a project was a small *wah*, or canal, near Khairpur, dug hurriedly in Aurangzeb's time, that had become clogged with silt and refuse, but the Daudputras had renewed and extended it by 1753. Reclamation of this scrubland was encouraged by the state through revenue holidays for up to five years after first ground-breaking. Hundreds of Abbasid clan members eagerly accepted their leader's assignments of such newly wet agrarian leases, and the patronage ties that came with them, ties that deepened existing kinship and clientage identities into fierce military loyalty.

New towns were founded, surrounded by irrigated fields, and populated first by the ruling elite, and then by immigrants from beyond the rivers to the north-west and the desert to the south-east. Wells were sunk to obtain fresh water from beneath the Hakra depression, and forts, such as the one at Dingarh, were built over them to serve as refuges from invasions. Some lesser forts also became way-stations on caravan routes across the Thar Desert. The annual snowmelt from the Punjab's rivers became the lifeblood of this new state, which captured it in a growing network of canals, held it, and made ample water available for both *kharif* (autumn) and *rabi* (spring) harvests.[13]

This unique society, beyond the fringes of the old Mughal regime—thus largely unaffected by its decline—also remained outside the Afghan confederacy, by means to be discussed below. It was able to not only dodge the snares of the Sikh powers, but to avoid, by collaboration and conciliation, political absorption into British India. Thus Bahawalpur, on an admittedly small scale, is an unmistakable instance of political and economic continuity amidst the dislocation usually associated with the eighteenth century. There indeed were, in Bahawalpur as elsewhere, succession struggles, poisonings, diplomatic manipulations, boundary conflicts, insurrections, and many challenges to the nawab's authority. Moreover, the realm endured fairly frequent, wanton depredations at the hands of Ahmad Shah Abdali, Taimur Shah, and the Sikhs; the temporary look of some of its towns is the result of their having been sacked and burned from time to time during the century. Most of its cities, such as Ahmadpur Sharqia, had no fortifications whatsoever.[14] There was an informal capital, centrally located on the Sutlej River, which was always targeted by Bahawalpur's enemies. Even today, the old defensive wall around Bahawalpur city remains in place, encompassing its division into four quarters similar to those of a pie or a pizza, with reinforced, shuttered gates facing the four points of the compass. The other capital, or headquarters, was the fort in the desert, at Derawar (see Fig. 8.3).

With the foregoing paragraphs as context, let us examine the military transactions of this sector of the Indus Valley from 1730 to 1840, the period of its clearest, if admittedly contested, autonomy. As we do, it is important to keep in mind two inescapable features of Bahawalpur's military history: first, its enemies did not stay enemies for long, but became its friends and allies, and vice versa, repeatedly, for reasons that both Kautilya and Shakespeare could explicate; second, this realm never fought the East India Company, and—most notably—never hired European freebooters to command troops or organize artillery. It thus is a case-study of a century of utterly indigenous

FIGURE 8.3: FORT OF DERAWAR

methods of resource discovery, definition, investment and allocation, as well as decision-making.[15]

Overall, Bahawalpur's military strategy was based largely on its geography. Its landscape contained a series of three strips of sharply contrasting ecosystems, all parallel to the rivers. Within 30 km, or a day's march, from the rivers, growing in width and density during the century due to the expansion of inundation canal networks, was a cultivated riverine agrarian subregion, which contained all of the realm's cities and towns. Bordering this was a narrow scrubland strip, consisting of small trees, shrubs, nomadic encampments, and failed hamlet experiments. Beyond these two zones lay Cholistan and the westernmost beginnings of the Thar Desert. Amidst this arid waste, on an artificial mound near the long-dry bed of the prehistoric Hakra River, was a fortress, the core of which was probably also prehistoric, that became the focal point of the state's success.[16]

Derawar Fort, this main strategically defensible point in the realm, is a large brick fortress built atop two sweet-water wells, and surrounded by desert on all sides.[17] It was built on a clay mesa 20 m high and 1200 by 900 m in area. Not an imposing structure, its strength lies almost entirely in its location—60 miles in a straight line south from Bahawalpur city, with neither fixed habitation nor source of water within 25 km in any direction. A besieging army must therefore either carry its own supplies of food and water, or invest heavily in digging wells that must be at least 20 m deep.[18] The fort has dozens of tunnels, clearly designed for use both in the hot season, and to resist an entrenched attacking force.[19] Derawar was made sufficiently comfortable over the decades, including the construction of a late-Mughal-style marble mosque, and rulers used the fort as a centre of administration, spending roughly half of the century ensconced in it. The investment in the supply and conveyance of food, clothing, military stores, and luxuries must have been considerable (see Fig. 8.4).

The Abbasids first conquered the fort in 1733, on the pretext that the ruler of Jaisalmer, who had occupied and extended it for generations, had raided and plundered Bahawalpur's then limited territory. Not then possessing any artillery, the Daudputra army dug a mine under one of the ramparts, the ensuing explosion allowing a general assault through the breach.[20]

FIGURE 8.4: MOSQUE AT DERAWAR

Interestingly, this was the last time such a tactic was used at Derawar, since the occupants now knew how to guard against its further use by an enemy. Thirteen years later, the Afghans under Sardar Tahmasp, carrying orders from the post-Safavid Emperor Nadir Shah, invaded Bahawalpur. Together with the rulers of Dera Ghazi Khan and Multan, they overwhelmed all resistance until they besieged Derawar Fort, which held out until the fort commander, in the nawab's absence, was tricked into visiting the Afghan camp and made prisoner. Fleeing into the desert, the surviving Daudputra elite and their followers were hotly pursued by Tahmasp. Seeing themselves cornered, outnumbered, and threatened with annihilation, they first put their womenfolk to death, to save their honour in Rajput fashion, and then desperately attacked the Afghans, routing the royal troops in a remarkable turnabout. Tahmasp's retreat was through the same unfamiliar desert that by now was home to the Abbasids, and numerous Afghans of all ranks died of thirst as well as their wounds on their way to Sind, where but a few of Tahmasp's officers eventually turned up. This show of valour, which may be considerably buffed up in the Persian chronicler's sponsored prose, seems to have impressed Nadir Shah, who ordered Tahmasp to invite the Daudputras to settle in Ghazni and serve him. The offer was refused, and hostilities resumed in northern Sind, leading to the near-death of Tahmasp (both his ears were hacked off in the fighting), and the death of the nawab, whose son fought on with redoubled vengeance mere days after the funeral, causing the once-feared Afghan general to flee for his life back across the Indus.[21]

These early confrontations cost the Daudputras dearly in blood, energy, agrarian disruption, and revenues, but during them they seemed to have established a reputation and tradition of pugnacity and bravery, of fighting desperately, and of not yielding even when facing much more numerous and better-armed combatants. In the remaining decades of their rule, the nawabs of Bahawalpur readily rented portions of their growing military to their neighbours, and seemed to be both feared and in demand, not on account of any new fighting methods or even greater discipline, but because they were able to recover from military adversity, recruit more relatives and clients to fill gaps in the ranks, and put upon spirited combat.

In 1752, when Ahmad Shah Durrani had succeeded Nadir Shah in Kabul, his governor of Multan wished to annex an increasingly prosperous Bahawalpur, and ordered the *nazim* of Dera Ghazi Khan to help in the conquest. The latter, however, happened to be a friend and ally of Nawab Mubarak Khan Abbasi, and warned him to prepare, which he did and crushed the Multanis just after they crossed the Indus at Khairpur.[22]

The nawabs seemed to have no trouble militarily handling their Rajput neighbours to the south-east and early Sikh attacks from the north. Jai Singh of Bikaner sent his entire army of 10,000 horse and foot-soldiers to stop Bahawalpur from building the forts of Anupgarh and Sardargarh near their common frontier in 1760, but the Daudputras repulsed it in an apparently uneven battle. First contact with the growing power of the Sikhs came in 1766, when Hari Singh, Ganda Singh, and Jhanda Singh marched southwards to test the nawab's forces, only to be fought to a standstill near the famous shrine town of Pakpattan, which then became their mutual frontier by written treaty.[23] A much greater Sikh force, however, upwards of 1,00,000 under Ganda Singh, in spite of being a signatory to the treaty, attacked Multan and then Bahawalpur in 1771, when the nawab's heir-apparent was sent to command an army to repel them. After a series of pitched battles that took the lives of several Daudputra chiefs, the nawab sent reinforcements, which turned the tide against the Sikhs. Majja Singh, a feared Sikh general, was killed by a musket ball in this engagement.[24]

The accounts of this fighting are frustratingly vague. We look mostly in vain for tactics, battle plans, acts of individual bravery, or details of gunpowder technology, and are compelled to search for hints about Bahawalpur's military success that might lurk in non-military accounts. It is not enough to rehearse the tradition that the Abbasids were excellent hunters, and thus presumably marksmen with the matchlock. Further, there is no evidence that Bahawalpur made decisive use of swivel cannon mounted on camels, even though we know such cannon existed. The reason for this is that these battles were not won by volley firing artillery fire or musketeers, but by swordsmen on foot, on camelback, and on horseback, who would, after one shot, ride and run through their enemies' limited artillery barrages to engage in hand-to-hand combat, not wanting to pause and reload and thus lose mobility and initiative. We are tempted to visualize a very messy, chaotic battlefield in which coordinated command structures were less important than what we might call the common reliance on a Daudputra ethos, that over time rewarded fighting valour with greater access to irrigated land. There was no question of the state running out of potential resources, given the continuous investment in new canal networks in the fallow season, and given the ongoing population increase from natural causes as well as from immigration.

Bahawalpur in fact came, during the second half of the century, to be considered widely as a refuge, attracting elite immigrants, especially from Sikh territories, including Multan, between 1772 and 1780. The Sikhs, notorious for ethnic cleansing, arbitrary expulsions, exploiting mercantile houses, razing public buildings to recycle brick and tile, and persecution of old-regime service gentry families, caused large numbers to flee Punjab. Both the Khorasan monarchy and Mughal remnant in the Delhi kingdom were also receding in the 1770s, causing thousands of families to seek their fortunes in places like Bhopal, Hyderabad, Lucknow, and Bahawalpur.

One notable sidelight on creative battlefield tactics emerged in 1780, when a coalition of the weakened ruler of Kabul, Taimur Shah, plus Muzaffar Khan of Shuja'abad, and the Nawab of Bahawalpur, Bahawal Khan II, joined to besiege the Sikhs in Multan. The besiegers had sufficient force to stop a Sikh relief column sent from Lahore, which then attacked Shuja'abad 40 km south of Multan, as a diversion, drawing away much of the besieging force for a pitched battle. A strong dust storm blew in, however, blinding both armies, during which the Afghans captured a Sikh drummer, whom they forced to sound the call for the Sikhs to assemble. Arranging his troops in two lines, Muzaffar Khan caught Sikh soldiers by the dozens as they ran through the howling wind toward the hapless drummer, and put them to the sword, so that many hundreds of Sikhs unknowingly sacrificed themselves. When the dust cleared, the Sikhs realized their losses, and not only retreated to Lahore but soon surrendered the fort of Multan, which again came under the control of the Afghans until Ranjit Singh reconquered it in 1818.[25]

In 1779, the nawab obtained formal recognition, several titles, and a robe of honour from the Mughal Emperor Shah Alam—a formality no doubt, but one that reveals a sensibility concerning outside legitimation.[26] It is also noteworthy, however, that the same nawab later saw fit to strike coins, in the new Bahawalpur mint, in the name of the Afghan king in 1801.[27] These acts reveal a regime at once flexible, pragmatic, and perforce aware of multiple inexpensive survival strategies.

It was during Bahawal Khan II's, reign, 1772-1809, that the state had its greatest economic successes, but also its most severe military challenges. Its revenues increased to Rs. 3,400,000 (3,40,000 pounds sterling); other Rajput forts were annexed; much territory was leased successfully from Multan, Dera Ghazi Khan, and the Sikhs; and trading networks flourished under a regimen of comparatively low transit duties. In the 1880s, however, exasperated largely because the nawab had neglected (perhaps deliberately) prompt payment of claimed tribute, the Durranis launched several full-scale invasions of Bahawalpur, sacked its cities, burned its public and commercial buildings, and demolished all stone structures in the cultivated area. The cultivators, traders, and artisans were encouraged and assisted to flee into the desert by Bahawalpuri officials. The first Afghan appearance before Derawar Fort was turned away with a payment of Rs. 60,000, whence they turned toward Sind.[28]

The following year, when Taimur Shah himself led the full Afghan army across the Indus, Bahawalpur's entire elite had to abandon Derawar, after a three-day bombardment by siege artillery, which nonetheless made no breach in its thick brick walls. The nawab and his court, even though the Afghans were suffering from lack of water, realized the hopelessness of their situation and fled to relative safety in Jaisalmer and Bikaner, the courts and forts of their erstwhile enemies 300 km to the south-east, who welcomed and sheltered them. For his personal safety, however, Bahawal Khan lived a nomadic existence under canvas for several tense weeks. This second invasion was ended by the nawab agreeing to turn over his own son as a hostage for good behaviour. The ending of hostilities being agreed to in person, when the arrears of tribute, sweetened by lavish gifts, were turned over to the Shah.[29]

Once again, however, Bahawalpur quickly recovered its former status. Taimur Shah, having garrisoned Derawar with Multanis and installed Daudputra prisoners-of-war in Dera Ghazi

Khan, hastily crossed back over the Indus to respond to an insurrection in Balkh. The nawab then employed a remarkable (and largely non-violent) stratagem to regain the fort at Derawar: informed that the families of the Multani troops occupying Derawar were housed in Sitpur, on the right bank of the Sutlej, he collected 300 boats from the ferry at Uchch Sharif, brought his forces to surprise the guard at Sitpur, and dragged these Multani women and children, with constant abuse and deliberately offensive disrespect, across the desert, lining them up in the heat under the walls of the fort. The Multani chiefs inside, sensible that their honour had been thus stained, abandoned the fort on the guarantee that they and their families would be safely escorted back to Dera Ghazi Khan, which they were.[30] Meanwhile, Taimur Shah had released the nawab's hostage son, which allowed the nawab to attack and defeat the nawab of Multan, lay siege to Dera Ghazi Khan and thus obtain release of Daudputra prisoners, and restore to Bahawalpur control all of the leased territories on the north-west side of the rivers. All this was accomplished before Taimur Shah could reach Peshawar.[31]

There followed several years of peace during which the nawab, utilizing local expertise, developed a factory in Bahawalpur for the casting of cannon and muskets; their court historian boasts, 'work in iron at that place carried to a perfection which was unknown either at Lahore or Multan. The rifle barrels made there surpass anything of the kind made elsewhere in India'.[32]

Internal troubles continued, one of the most severe coming from a refractory holy man with an army, the incredibly wealthy and influential *makhdum* of Uchch Gilani, Hamid Muhammad Ganj Bakhsh, who was widely known to be mentally unbalanced, often to the point that he would chase his own courtiers around the room wildly waving a drawn sword. The nawab tolerated this and other more rebellious behaviour for over a decade, and then responded to open treason in 1806 by attacking Uchch Gilani, destroying its defensive wall, plundering the *makhdum*'s treasury and belongings, and exiling him to Sind.[33]

The nawab's army readily assisted in Multan's defense against Ranjit Singh's first siege in 1807, which was unsuccessful. Four years later, Bahawalpur was again at war with Multan, which had supported a coup attempt against the nawab. In this conflict we do find that the large artillery arm that had been built up by

Bahawal Khan II, amounting to '115 pieces of ordnance of various caliber',[34] was decisive, meeting an admittedly rash and ill-advised charge of dismounted Afghan swordsmen with a withering fire.[35]

It remains to deal with Bahawalpur's relations with the British; these were not initiated until 1809, shortly before Nawab Bahawal Khan II's death from an unspecified digestive illness. That year, Elphinstone's mission to Khorasan was lavishly received as it passed through Bahawalpur, the nawab's court having been fully appraised of the success of British arms elsewhere in India. The nawab heard strident criticism from his courtiers for this hospitality, but had the foresight to cooperate with what by then was clearly the power destined to achieve paramountcy in South Asia. The contrast between Bahawalpur's welcome and the mission's reception at Peshawar, where they were almost attacked by disgruntled Pathans, was not lost on the British, who regarded the Bahawalpur nawabs as highly cultured, worldly-wise friends and allies, and rewarded them accordingly over the decades starting in the 1830s, with ceded territories and inclusion in several military expeditions against common enemies.[36]

British interest in Bahawalpur accelerated during the 1830s, because of its strategic location on the Indian frontier, and also because adjacent to its territories flowed what the East India Company fancied would be a major commercial highway: the Indus. Accordingly, European visitors arrived in Bahawalpur to discover its potential as a market and as an ally against likely enemies to the west and north. One such visitor has provided our first quantified assessment of the nawab's military establishment as of 1837.[37] The infantry under the nawab's direct command numbered 2,000, divided equally between a Hindu general and an English freebooter named McPherson, both being paid five rupees a day, three in cash, two in grain. Added to 760 reliable irregulars under one Muslim and two Hindu commanders, this constituted the nawab's uniformed standing army. The artillery arm amounted to twenty-two serviceable field pieces, four serviceable garrison guns, and twenty-five dismounted cannons—all of various irregular calibers, and served by 147 *golandazes*, 60 of whom served another British freebooter named Crawford, whose pay was a mere rupee per day. The irregular levies scattered in the countryside—Burns' 'feudatories'—

came to a total of 1,920 more men, under commanders of various ethnicities. One of Leech's more interesting observations is that, although there were about 12,000 Daudputras in the realm, only 3,000 of them were employed in the military.[38]

Even though the regime's military may have dwindled slightly in the early years of British interest and protection, formalized initially in 1838, these figures portray an exceptionally modest military force, the command structure of which had moreover passed out of Daudputra hands and into those of late-pre-colonial military entrepreneurs. The state's investment in its army depicts a defensive, economizing, flexible, pragmatic military institution, forged in the experience of the preceding century of warfare, compromise, and geopolitical experimentation. In the context of Bahawalpur's environment and history-mindedness, the regime could either repel or evade intruders with a standing force of less than one-half of 1 per cent of its population. This does not present us with the image of a society preoccupied with fighting, or a frontier state armed to the teeth to defend itself.

In conclusion, some tentative generalizations could be suggested about military management in this strictly indigenous Indian frontier state, a realm revealing that the commercial and agrarian, and perhaps therefore also military, configurations of the late pre-colonial period are still full of surprises. This society developed utterly new resources in the midst of a desert, well away from European advice, technological modelling or interference, and well before Karachi flourished as a port city. Just as one is hard pressed to find the basic enabling conditions for such a flourishing new economy, so also do we gape in amazement at its army's resistance and survivability. Its geopolitical and environmental situations may have contributed to its growth and survival, but it was invaded, plundered, and sacked repeatedly, only to recover and thumb its Abbasid nose at its rivals.

This is the major theme of political and military survival in late pre-colonial western India: utilize the environment as a military resource, and recognize that it is better to live, even ignominiously, to fight another day than to sacrifice a limited army in the face of overwhelmingly powerful outside aggression. Resources other than brute strength and demographic vigour could be brought into play. At times of crisis, especially when clearly outnumbered, the Abbasids and their variously-sized mini-army of not more than 2,500 regulars and some 12,000 provincial levies, sometimes together but often in dispersed segments, would not always stay and fight. When overwhelming force intruded, they would trudge out to their several desert fortresses, or beyond them, to wait out the storm, washing down their curried turnips and *naan* with sweet water from secret wells, while relying on the ability of a willing cultivator population in the newly-irrigated agrarian countryside to survive depredation, and then raise enough surplus wealth during the coming harvests to keep the limited needs of the regime satisfied. Retreat in such circumstances is not cowardice, but pragmatic tactical action, and was occasionally just enough to buy time to turn the tables, in the long run, on much more mighty adversaries.

NOTES

1. Alexander Burns, 'Memorandum on the Indus and the Punjab Rivers, with remarks on the people', 1831, Dalhousie Muniments, GD45/5/80, fols. 104-109, Scottish Record Office, Edinburgh.
2. Professional historians have overlooked this area and its implications for the eighteenth century, and none outside Pakistan is working on even its nineteenth or twentieth centuries. The region does, however, have an ardent amateur historian, to whom I am grateful for advice and commentary. See Nurul Zaman Ahmad Auj, *Cholistan, Land & People* (Multan: Caravan Book Center, 1991); *Ancient Bahawalpur* (Multan: Caravan Book Center, 1987); and (with Munawwar Ali Khan), *Select Bibliography on Bahawalpur* (Bahawalpur: Islamia University, 1984). See also his anthology, which contains articles in Urdu, Saraiki, and English: *Bahawalpur ka Sadiq Dost* (Bahawalpur: Urdu Academy, 1992). For background, see also my 'The Greening of Bahawalpur: Ecological Pragmatism and State Formation in Pre-British Western India, 1730-1870', *Indo-British Review*, vol. 15, no. 2 (December 1988), pp. 5-15, reprinted in Nurul Zaman Ahmad Auj (ed.), *Bahawalpur ka Sadiq Dost* (Bahawalpur: Urdu Academy, 1992); also my 'Natural Resources and Water Conservation in 18th-century States', in Nazir Ahmad and Asloob Ahmed Ansari (eds.), *Fakhruddin Ali Ahmad Memorial Volume* (New Delhi: Ghalib Institute, 1994), pp. 179-96.
3. Estimating pre-census populations is an occupational hazard, but based on travellers' estimates of populations within the realm's cities and towns, as well as upon the size of its military, this figure seems reasonable. In 1951, after three decades of colonial and official Pakistani settlement of

Punjabi *abadis* in Bahawalpur, its population was 5,27,942, about the current size of Aligarh, UP, or three times the number of American football fans attending the Super Bowl. *1981 District Census Report* (Lahore: Government of Pakistan, 1981), p. 5.

4. For the extent and variety of traded goods, artisanal production, and cash crops, see my 'The Greening of Bahawalpur'. See also Christopher Shackle, *The Saraiki Language of Central Pakistan* (London: SOAS, 1976); *Styles and Themes in the Saraiki Mystical Poetry of Sind* (Multan: Bazm-e Saqafat, n.d. [1976]); and *From Wuch to Southern Lahnda: A Century of Saraiki Studies in English* (Multan: Bazm-e Saqafat, 1984).
5. The most detailed and pedantic account is Henry George Raverty, *The Mihran of Sind and Its Tributaries* (London, 1870; rpt. edn., Lahore: Sang-e Meel, 1979). See also Government of Punjab, *Gazetteer of Bahawalpur State* (Lahore: Civil & Military Press, 1908), text by Malik Muhammad Din, and J.W. Barns, cited above. A sample of Raverty: '. . . there is little of the vast, sloping alluvial tract of Sind, below the parallel of Uchch, and extending from Birsilpur of Jaisal-mir [*sic*] to Shadad-pur [*sic*] of Upper Sind, a space of four geographical degrees in breadth, that the Hakra or Wahindah and the Sindhu, Ab-i-Sind, or Indus, have not, at different epochs, within about the last 1500 years, flowed over; for the whole is literally seamed with their channels of a lesser or greater age, and in all and every direction' (*Mihran*, p. 361). These channels are still visible from commercial airliners on daytime routes between Delhi and the Persian Gulf.
6. The intrepid Ian Stephens, driving a Land Rover, chased deer and cheetahs along this packed clay depression in the 1950s; see his 'Bahawalpur State', *Geographical Magazine* (November 1954), pp. 328-38.
7. Irfan Habib, *An Atlas of the Mughal Empire* (New Delhi: Oxford University Press, 1982), plates 4A and 4B, plus notes, pp. 9-10. Plate 4A shows only five settlements within 15 km along the 475-km length of territory that became Bahawalpur State, and only two, known for their wells, farther away than 15 km.
8. Radhika Lal Mehta, *Note on the History of Bahawalpur State Canals* (Bahawalpur: Irrigation Department, 1932), p. 3.
9. *Gazetteer*, p. 21; J.W. Barns, p. 391.
10. *Gazetteer*, p. 48.
11. The early history of the Daudputra *Amirs*, including their putative lineage, can be found in the following: Shaikh Muhammad Azam, *Jawahar-i Abbasiyya* (1830), roughly translated from Persian by R. Maclagan in 'Fragments of the History of Multan, the Derajat and Bahawalpur (from Persian MSS)', *Journal of the Asiatic Society of Bengal*, vol. 17, no. 2 (November 1848), pp. 559-72; anonymous Urdu history ending in 1811, India Office Library and Records, U. 25; Mirza

Ashraf Gurgani, *Sadiq ut-Tawarikh*, roughly translated by Nazir Ali Shah in *Sadiqnamah* (Lahore: Maktaba Jadeed, 1959); Saiyad Murad Shah, untitled Urdu history of Bahawalpur, vol. 1, *c*. 1845, India Office Library and Records, U. 177; H.G. Raverty, *Notes on Afghanistan and Baluchistan* (London, 1888; rpt. edn., Peshawar, 1976), pp. 614, 622, 662-74; Daulat Ram, *Mir'at-i Daulat-i Abbasiyya*, an 1800 Persian history of Bahawalpur, and Shaikh Muhammad Azam, *Jawahir'i Abbasiyya*, an 1830 Persian court history of Bahawal Khan II (r. 1772-1809), both translated by Pir Ibrahim Khan and edited by Shahamat Ali as *The History of Bahawalpur, with Notices of the Adjacent Countries of Sindh, Afghanistan, Multan, and the West of India* (London: James Madden, 1848); and Masud Khan Shahab Dehlvi, *Bahawalpur ki Siyasi Tarikh* (Bahawalpur: Maktaba al-ham, 1977).

12. Raverty, *Mihran*, p. 320n, which translates the original Persian language of the treaty. Part of the line dividing Durrani annexations from the Mughal lands ran along the long-dry Hakra depression, which was still a landmark after more than 3,000 years.

13. It is important to note the special collaborative, politically successful, and mutually beneficial nature of canal building. By mid-century, what the British were later to call 'canal communities' (and, incidentally, mislabel as 'companies', implying ritual equality and legal incorporation) were established by apportioning shareholders of interest in water, labour and revenue rights. This institution provided a widely recognized framework for recruitment, population settlement, political patronage, the cultivation of cash crops such as indigo—much in demand in the Durrani Empire to the north-west, where it could not be grown—and the resulting prosperity of the entire region. The implications of this shareholding institution are neatly drawn out in David Gilmartin, 'Labor, Investment and Water: Indus Valley Inundation Canals in the 18th and 19th Centuries', paper presented to the annual meeting of the Association for Asian Studies, San Francisco, March 1988, pp. 6-11. The dimensions of this pre-colonial irrigation system, in its mature phase after a century of expansion, emerge from a British engineer's report, dated 1871, five years after the first official British presence in Bahawalpur. Forty-five canals of various sizes tapped the Sutlej, the Chenab, and the Indus rivers, and totaled 2,176 km of engineering achievement. Another 4,800 km of cultivators' ducts branched out from these canals. Virtually all such channels, large and small, predated the arrival of British supervision. J.W. Barns, 'Notes', p. 395. The entire system carried, at peak flow during the snowmelt, 20,000 cubic feet (566 m^3) per second, or enough water to irrigate, at the rate of 20 to 50 acres (8.1 to 20.2 hectares) per cusec (ft^3/sec.), between 400,000 and a million acres (161,878 to 404,694 hectares) of land.

14. Major William Hough, *Narrative of the March of the Army of the Indus*

in the Expeditions of Afghanistan, 1838-39 (London: W.H. Allen, 1841), p. 12.

15. Original sources that describe war strategies, the strength of armies, battles, and detailed military technology in Bahawalpur proper are relatively scant. My main sources are Daulat Ram, *Mir'at-i Daulat-i Abbasiyya*, an 1800 Persian history of Bahawalpur, and Shaikh Muhammad Azam, *Jawahir'i Abbasiyya*, an 1830 Persian court history of Bahawal Khan II (r. 1772-1809), both translated by Pir Ibrahim Khan and edited by Shahamat Ali as *The History of Bahawalpur, with Notices of the Adjacent Countries of Sindh, Afghanistan, Multan, and the West of India* (London: James Madden, 1848). Since Shahamat Ali puts their translations back to back, it is easy to differentiate them, and I cite them hereinafter as Daulat Ram and M. Azam, respectively. Daulat Ram was official court historian to Nawab Bahawal Khan II, and M. Azam was the same nawab's ambassador to the court of the Sindhi *Amirs* of Khairpur. They can thus be relied upon to provide a contemporary, if perhaps biased, version of things military and political.
16. Sir Aurel Stein thought Derawar to be the only settlement in the Indus Valley to have been occupied 'since time immemorial', since it is so strategically situated. It contains Harappan pottery shards by the ton. 'A Survey of Ancient Sites along the "Lost" Sarasvati River', *The Geographical Journal*, vol. 19, no. 3 (March 1942), pp. 181-2, quoted in Ahmad Auj, *Cholistan*, p. 108. See also Rafique Mughal, 'New Archaeological Evidence from Bahawalpur', typescript, 1984.
17. Burns, 1831 'Memorandum'.
18. Mirza Shah Hussein Arghun, the ruler of Sind, marched on Derawar in 1525, and had to bring supplies for a month so that his troops could dig 100 wells around the fort before beginning the siege. He was fighting the ruler of Multan, Sultan Hussein Langah, who then held Derawar. H.T. Lambrick, *Sind: A General Introduction* (Hyderabad: Sindhi Adabi Board, 3rd edn., 1986, original edn. 1964).
19. In 1866, however, Cherry Minchin, the British agent, excavated Derawar looking for buried treasure, having Gurkha troops do the job 'in a most indiscreet manner', ruining most subsequent archaeological efforts. Ahmad Auj, *Cholistan*, p. 118.
20. Daulat Ram, pp. 23-5.
21. Ibid., pp. 31-4.
22. Ashiq Muhammad Khan Durrani, *Multan Under the Afghans (1752-1818)* (Multan: Bazm-i Saqafat, 1981), pp. 49ff.
23. Daulat Ram, pp. 48-52.
24. Ibid., p. 55.
25. Makhdum Syed Muhammad Yusuf Gardezi, *Tazkirat ul-Multan* (Persian, 1861), cited in Durrani, pp. 84-7.
26. Daulat Ram, pp. 64-5.

27. Ibid., p. 113.
28. Daulat Ram, pp. 76-9.
29. M. Azam, *Jawahar-i Abbasiyya*, pp. 190-2.
30. *Tawarikh-i Abbasiyya*, tr. Lt. R. Maclagan as 'Fragments of the History of Mooltan, the Derajat, and Buhawwulpoor, from Persian MSS', *Journal of the Asiatic Society of Bengal*, vol. 17, no. 2 (November 1848), pp. 569-70.
31. M. Azam, pp. 192-3.
32. Ibid., p. 193.
33. Daulat Ram, pp. 130-45; Ghulam Sarwar, *A Descriptive Catalogue of the Oriental Manuscripts in the Durgah Library of Sharif Gilani, Bahawalpur State* (Bahawalpur: Urdu Academy, 1961), pp. vi, ff.
34. Daulat Ram, p. 148.
35. Ibid., p. 166.
36. Ibid., pp. 143-6.
37. Lt. R. Leech, Bombay Engineers, 'Report on the Sindhian, Khelat and Daoodputr Armies, with a Collection of Routes', British Library, Oriental and India Office Collections, Official Publications, Monographs (Political), V/27/270/7 (Calcutta: Bengal Military Orphanage Press, 1939), No. 11. Leech seems to have overcome considerable secrecy and official silence on the military strength of a potential ally, but his report's validity probably rests on the nawab's presumed interest in a fair portrayal of his forces, since the British could not then demand to use more than he actually had against a common enemy.
38. Leech, 'Report on the Sindhian, Khelat and Daoodputr Armies, with a Collection of Routes', pp. 81-2.

CHAPTER 9

Science and Secularization of War

Transition in Siege Warfare in South Asia from Medieval to Modern Times

KAUSHIK ROY

In 1700, the population of Europe was 120 million. In the sixteenth century, the population of England was 4 million, that of Spain was 8 million and France's manpower stood at 16 million. Towards the end of the sixteenth century, the population of the Ottoman Empire was about 35 million. It is to be noted that the population of Bengal *suba* of the Mughal Empire was greater than the population of Elizabethan England. The population of late Mughal India was about 150 million and that of China was higher than that of India. While the Mughal Empire (1526-1857), at its height (1707) controlled a territory of 3.2 million sq km, the Ottoman Empire covered 2.5 million sq km.[1] Even as late as 1750, India produced 200,000 tons of iron, which is about the same as produced by Europe (except Russia).[2] Despite superior economic and manpower resources, the mighty empires of Asia collapsed under the onslaught of the West Europeans in the early modern era.

One of the factors which propelled the West European states to the stage of world history was their superior way of making warfare both in the land and sea. Land warfare included battles, sieges and pacification campaigns. In this essay, our object is to analyse siege warfare practised by the British in particular and the Europeans in general. We will try to understand how the West Europeans evolved a superior way for conducting siege warfare. Answering this question requires tackling the dynamic and often contradictory relationships between warfare and the collective mentality of the societies that spawned different types of military establishments. Hence, in addition to military technology, strategy and tactics, we have to tackle cultural generalities in order to understand the interrelationships between warfare, religion and science. This essay attempts to trace continuities and changes from a *longue duree* perspective, from the Late Middle Age to the early modern era.

With the onset of the Renaissance, West Europe experienced what could be categorized as 'secularization of the mind'. The Enlightenment Age witnessed the application of reason to the existing problems. Collective consciousness encouraged a questioning of established precepts and practices and an interest in new ideas. The focus was on reforms which meant change for improvement. Instead of religious orthodoxies, rational bureaucratic approach became the leitmotif of the collective consciousness. Rather than black magic and divine interventions, greater application of science and technology in day-to-day affair became the norm. Like business and politics, the dynamics of warfare was also shaped by the marginalization of the church and greater intervention of mathematics, engineering and instrumental rationality. In this essay, we will make a case study of siege warfare conducted by the British East India Company (hereafter EIC) in South Asia during the eighteenth century and the first half of the nineteenth century, to show the rising importance of science at the cost of religion in war making. Siege warfare means the development of techniques and technologies associated with the objective of capturing and destroying forts and development of fortress architecture in response to the above-mentioned threat.

This article is divided into three sections. The first section elucidates the rise of science-oriented fortress technology and siege techniques in West Europe. It is to be noted that the British culture of siege craft was an integral part of the culture of scientific siege warfare which emerged in West Europe in the post-Renaissance era. The next section narrates the nature of siege warfare in pre-colonial South Asia and contrasts it with the Western culture of siege warfare. We will also compare and contrast the nature of siege warfare in South Asia with the culture of siege craft of the other non-European powers (especially the Ottomans) and also Manchu China (a great agrarian bureaucratic empire like the Mughal Empire) in order to get an idea about the uniqueness (if any) of the Indian scenario. The third section describes in detail the import of and implementation of scientific siege warfare in South Asia by the EIC till the first half of the nineteenth century.

THEORY AND PRACTICE OF SIEGE WARFARE IN WEST EUROPE DURING THE EARLY MODERN ERA

Warfare during the high Middle Age was dominated by the knights whose reigning ideology was chivalry. In the mental climate of the feudal age, all secular activities were given a religious meaning. The task awarded to the chivalrous knights was to protect and defend the followers and kingdom of Christ and to wage just war against the enemies of the religion. The Crusades were considered as just wars of the Christian knights of the Middle Age. Since just warfare represented the fulfilment of a religious and moral duty on part of the chivalrous knights fighting on behalf of the church, there was a strong inclination to conduct warfare according to fixed rules and maintain a code of conduct even during combat. The knights were bound to serve their overlords (kings) who were in turn entrusted with the role of governing the temporal domain of Christ.[3]

The Western theoreticians of the post-feudal era attempted to replace divine intervention in human affair with a sort of instrumental rationality. Niccolao Machiavelli (1469-1527), a theoretician-cum-politician of the Florentine Republic, in his writings emphasized that man is not entirely in the hands of Fortuna. When people and states become strong and powerful, then they cease to become helpless toys in the hands of Fortuna. The only way for the states to counter Fortuna is to apply reason and to expand and conquer.[4]

Justus Lipsius (1547-1606), a neo-Stoic philosopher and an admirer of Machiavelli, had a direct influence on Maurice of Nassau (1567-1625), the military commander of the Dutch Republic, who during the seventeenth century raised a firearms-equipped, disciplined army. Lipsius was a professor at the University of Leiden and taught Maurice of Nassau for a while.[5] Lipsius argued that war is not merely an act of uncontrolled violence but orderly application of force directed by a competent and legitimate authority in the interest of the state. A military officer unlike, a chivalrous knight, in Lipsius' eyes, does not fight for individual glory, but considers himself as a professional serving the community. Both Machiavelli and Lipsius emphasized the necessity of drill and collective training for turning out effective and disciplined soldiers.[6]

The Military School of Enlightenment which emerged in the 1600s argued that the conduct of warfare was susceptible to reason. The proponents of this school attempted to identify the universal principles underlying human behaviour and tried to make the chaotic phenomenon of warfare more comprehensible to the practitioners of organized violence. They argued that Machiavelli's notion of principles of war is susceptible to scientific analysis, identifying laws and mathematical equations to guide the conduct of campaigns. The military thinkers of the Enlightenment School used natural sciences as a model for their enquiries into the nature and conduct of war.[7] Mathematical neo-rationalism of Rene Descartes, the *espirit geometrique* detected and recorded by Pascal with the attendant mechanical philosophy influenced the French military establishment of Louis XIV. The army was considered as a machine where every cog performed its own specialized function.[8]

The crucial link between scientific theorization and military practice was provided by the print media. The culture of print in early modern Europe created a dynamic relationship between applied science and military practice. Military tracts and books aided original thinking of ideas and their diffusion. Leonardo da Vinci (1452-1519) produced copious sketches of various lethal machines like rapid-fire catapults, breech-loading guns, tanks, and so on.[9] Biringuccio's *De la pirotechnia* (1540) discussed the metallurgy of cannon. The theory of exterior ballistics was worked out by the Italian mathematician Niccolo Tartaglia and Galileo (1564-1642). In the 1530s, Tartaglia worked out the relation between the angle of fire and the range of the projectile. He calculated that the angle for maximum range was 45 degrees and it resulted in the widespread use of artillerist's square or quadrant. Galileo worked out that the trajectory of the projectile is parabolic due to resistance offered by air.[10] The period between 1660 and 1760 witnessed the linkage of Newtonian science with military engineering. In the first half of the eighteenth century, Benjamin Robins invented new instruments which discovered and quantified the air resistance to high-speed projectiles. Leonard Euler solved the equations of subsonic ballistic motion in 1753 and summarized some of his results in published tables. All these theoretical advances increased the predictive power of ballistics and transformed gunnery from a craft to a science which could be taught. Outside West Europe, the first printed book on military affairs was published in Russia in 1647. This manual had sketches and emphasized training.[11]

The rulers of West Europe, unlike the Indian monarchs, were aware of the importance of new learning and opened institutions where such learning could be carried out and disseminated among the officer corps. In 1662, King Charles II opened the Royal Society of London and in 1666, the French minister Colbert opened the *Academie Royale des sciences.* In both these academies, several experiments related with ballistics, recoil and properties of gunpowder were undertaken for the army and navy. Colbert also urged the *Academie* to initiate cartographic surveys so that the commanders could get an accurate topographic map of the country where they would operate the troops under them.[12] The Enlightenment Age witnessed 'geometrization of space'. It means mapping sea and land space because of the intellectual process which transformed actual space into mathematical abstraction.[13] In 1744, an artillery school was opened at Naples and an engineering academy in 1754. In 1764, these two institutions were amalgamated into the *Reale Academie Militarie,* where ballistics, experimental physics and chemistry were taught to the officer cadets.[14]

The practitioners of science not only wrote military tracts and taught in the universities but also participated in warfare directly. Tartaglia and the Dutch Simon Stevin were famous fort builders. Even Galileo taught fortifications at the University of Padua. The founding father of the French school of fortification was the engineer Errard de Bar-le-Duc who in 1594 published *Fortification reduicte en art.*[15] For siege warfare and military technology, Maurice depended on his chief tutor in mathematics named Stevin. Stevin became the chief engineer of the Dutch Army and conducted many sieges and also established the corps of military engineers.[16]

Even generals started writing scientific tracts connected with warfare. Raimondo Montecuccoli (1609-80), the Field-Marshal of the Austro-Habsburg Army, wrote a compendium titled *Dell'arte militare* which discussed mathematics, logistics and fortifications.[17] Montecuccoli believed that knowledge of arithmetic and trigonometry was essential for conducting war.[18] He was a rationalist trying to discover by empirical inquiry the permanently operating principles while formulating a theory of warfare. Religion did not always oppose scientific thinking. Montecuccoli was both a scientist and a devout Catholic. His approach was both scientific and religious. The humanism in his theory was partly derived from rationalism and Christianity. Besides dealing with the mechanical aspects of warfare, he was also concerned with moral, psychological, social and economic considerations.[19] Henry Lloyd (1729-83), a British mercenary officer, attempted to develop a universal theory of warfare from the study of history. His aim was to derive scientific principles that governed war and existed in nature like Newton's laws of gravity and physics. In 1799, a Prussian military officer named Adam Heinrich Dietrich von Bulow (1757-1807) came out with a geometrical model of warfare. According to Bulow's theory, the success of a military campaign depended on the attacker's advance in relation to the width of his base of supplies. Finally, Antoine Henri Jomini (1779-1869) used the concept of lines of operations as used by Bulow and Lloyd. For Bulow and Lloyd, the lines of operations were the routes linking the armies to their supply depots and magazines. Jomini broadened the concept of lines of operations to include the army's potential routes of retreat and its communication links with the allied forces in addition to the supply lines.[20]

Even though religion was marginalized, its influence was not completely absent. Maurice influenced by his Calvinist upbringing and neoclassical teachings, regarded military command as a public trust with authority derived not from noble birth but from a commission awarded by the state. This notion combined with the concept of unconditional obedience within an established hierarchy of ranks as inherent in Calvinism, generated the groundwork for the foundation of a modern command structure. As regards some of the demands of warfare, religion and science were not always contradictory to each other. In 1621, Gustavus Adolphus, the Swedish monarch, introduced a strict military code backed up by the army chaplains who emphasized daily prayers and other moral sanctions for controlling the soldiery.[21]

The rise of science in warfare also heralded the induction of a new social group into the military community. During the seventeenth century, in France, the bourgeoisie joined the technical and engineering branches of the army.[22] M.D. Feld asserts that the rise of scientific warfare was partly due to the emergence of 'rational' bourgeoisie and the resulting political decentralization. Maurice of Nassau and his cousin William Louis of Nassau (1560-1620), who first created the rational military organization, were the products of Dutch military establishment which in turn was characterized by civilian control. Civilian control over the military was one of the crucial characteristics of modernity. The Dutch Republic was dominated by the merchant class.[23]

Let us look at the evolution of fortress architecture in West Europe. As regards siege warfare, Machiavelli in *The Art of War* (1521) speaks through Fabrizio:

> Towns and fortresses, you must know, may be strong either by nature or by art. Those surrounded by rivers or morasses . . . or situated upon a rock or steep hill . . . are strong by nature; those situated upon hills that are not difficult of ascent, are deemed weak since the invention of mines and artillery. Hence, those building fortresses in these times often chose a flat site and make it strong by art. For this purpose, their first care is to fortify their walls with angles, bastions, casemates, half-moons, and ravelins, so that no enemy can approach them without being taken in both front and flank. If the walls are built very high, they will be too much exposed to artillery; if they are built very low, they may be easily scaled.[24]

Thus, we see that Machiavelli was well aware of the revolution in fortress architecture which West Europe experienced from the Age of Renaissance onwards. As regards the use of siege artillery, Machiavelli notes:

> The heavy artillery used for the town's defense should be planted on the inside of the wall supporting the ditch. . . . If the enemy attempts an escalade, the height of the first wall protects you. If he batters you with artillery, he must first beat down that wall; but once it is beaten down—since a wall always fall towards the side from which it is battered and since its ruins have no ditch in which to be buried—the outside must naturally add to the depth of the ditch behind the enemy; so, he cannot easily advance any further because he is stopped there not only by those ruins but by both ditch . . . and the artillery planted on the other side of the ditch. The only expedient the enemy has left

upon such occasions is to fill up the ditch; this is a very difficult matter for him because of the great width and depth of the ditch, the danger of approaching it from the bastions and other fortifications with which it is flanked, and the labour of climbing over the ruins with the burden of fascines upon the backs of his men.[25]

Machiavelli does not mention the trebuchet because the cannon had replaced it in northern Europe by the middle of the fifteenth century. The bronze cannons were cast whole during the Renaissance period. This technique was borrowed from the methods used to cast the great bells of West Europe's cathedrals. The Renaissance period also witnessed specialization of the functions of the guns. While the big cannons and the culverins were used to blast away the ramparts and towers of the forts, the smaller artillery pieces and the handguns of the infantry were used to keep the defenders busy and to harass them and prevent them from undertaking repair work in an orderly manner. And the mortars were used to rain death and destruction inside the fortified cities.[26] *The Art of War* was translated into English in 1560 under the reign of Queen Elizabeth I.[27]

Clifford J. Rogers argues that West Europe from the Late Middle Age onwards experienced a series of Military Revolutions. The period between each Military Revolution was characterized by gradual evolution in weapons and warfare. Each Military Revolution after a period generated its own counter-revolution in the form of another Military Revolution. The threat-response mechanism explains the series of Military Revolutions. The Artillery Revolution occurred between the 1420s and the 1440s. The increasing lethality of siege artillery generated radical changes in fortress architecture. This resulted in the rise of *trace italienne* which Rogers categorizes as an Artillery-Fortress Revolution.[28] Though the concept of Military Revolution is challenged by a group of scholars, it seems that despite limitations, the Military Revolution model could be used as a heuristic device to explain the rise of West *versus* the 'rest' in the early modern age.

In 1494, Charles VIII, the King of France invaded Italy. His siege train comprised cannons with bronze barrels, each about eight feet long and which discharged wrought iron balls.[29] By the mid-fourteenth century, the Chinese had come up with cast iron guns and solid metal round shots.[30] The production of cast iron ordnance became an important industry in Elizabethan England.[31] The French easily battered down the high-walled medieval fortifications of Italy. In response, the Italians introduced a new outline (trace) in the shape of a polygon with sharply angled bastions projecting from each angle. The trace of the fort resembled a star and the star-shaped forts were designed to resist cannonballs and maximize the defensive fire from their own guns. This is known as *trace italienne* as the design of such fortress architecture first emerged in Italy and then spread to West Europe. This style was also known as *alla moderna*.[32] Such a fort consisted of three main divisions: a thick low rampart with parapet, a broad ditch and an outer rampart known as the *glacis* which sloped gently down to the level of the surrounding countryside.[33] The masonry rampart was progressively introduced in the sixteenth century and it was sharply scarped at the base. The angled out base helped to resist artillery fire and made it difficult to place scaling ladders by the assailants. The strength of the rampart depended on the large mass of earth supported by internal buttresses known in Italian as *contraforti*.[34]

The Siege of Pisa in 1500 demonstrated the ability of the sloping rampart of earth to absorb cannonballs. While medieval square and round towers provided flanking positions from which to fire down on the attackers before the main walls, they left 'dead zones' at the base of such towers, where the attacking force could take shelter from the defending fire. The arrowhead design of the artillery towers, i.e. bastions themselves allowed gunfire from neighbouring bastions to sweep the ditches as well as the ground in front of the walls before the faces of threatened bastions, thus eliminating the 'dead zones'. The attacker laying siege to such a fort faced an effective crossfire. The siege of Padua in 1509 showed the power of enfilade fire in the ditch against infantry assault by the besieging force.[35] With the passage of time, the architecture of the forts became more elaborate. Detached outworks (like ravelins, which were flankless pointed artillery platforms, counterguards and demi-lunes hornworks) protected the forts.[36] Towards the end of the fifteenth century, octagonal bastions replaced the cylindrical gun towers of the medieval fortifications. During the mid-sixteenth century, pointed bastions around the outer circuit of the fort became common. In 1630, these pointed bastions were modified and were known as *orrechioni* (big ears, somewhat curved in shape) which concealed the *traditore* (traitor) batteries in the flanks.[37] As the *trace italienne* spread across France and Germany, large round gun towers and elaborate earthworks which characterized medieval fortifications became obsolete.[38] However, even within West Europe, some variations occurred. Alessandro Farnese, the Imperial Governor of the Low Countries towards the end of the sixteenth century argued that modern ramparts of required height and thickness could be obtained by building them with rammed earth without the brickwork *camiciatura* (the outer skin which protected the earthwork from weather). This became the favoured technique in the Low Countries.[39]

Blaise de Pagan (1604-65) was a siege warfare theorist. Henry Guerlac asserts that the famed French military engineer of Louis XIV named Sebastien Le Pestre de Vauban's (1633-1707) first system was the adoption of Pagan's style. Pagan argued that the lethality of cannons was increasing both for offence and defence. To counter it, the bastions were most important part of the fort. The positions and shape of the bastions are determined by the geometric rules he formulated in respect to the terrain outside the fort. Vauban's system involved the sappers digging a trench which moved slowly towards the fort. After this had progressed to some distance, a deep trench paralleling the point of future attack was flung out at right angles to the trench of approach. This was the first parallel. From it, the trench of approach moved forward again, zigzagging as it approached the fort. After it had gone for some distance, a second parallel was constructed.[40] We will see in Section III that Vauban's parallels were put to use with great effect by the EIC while conducting sieges in the Indian subcontinent. Vauban built 34 forts and conducted more than 50 sieges. In addition, he wrote extensively on siege warfare. A taste of his writings comes from the following passage:

> Always attack at the weakest points, and never at the strongest. . . . Open the trench only when the lines are well advanced. . . . Always make three big lines parallel to the rallying areas. . . . Linked attacks are preferable to others. Use the sap as soon as the trench becomes dangerous. . . . Never attack along narrow enclosed places or across marshes; even less along causeways when you can do so over dry, open ground. . . . Make sure that the *batteries plongeantes* [firing from a superior position] known as 'ricochets' are always situated on the

enfilades and the outside of the pieces being attacked. . . . Stray from the rules as little as possible in any case.[41]

Vauban invented ricochet fire. It involved reducing the propelling charge of the solid shots so that the ball after striking the target would rebound in various directions and thus would be a peril to the defending garrison and their animals. Ricochet firing was used at the siege of Philipsbourg.[42]

PRE-COLONIAL SIEGE WARFARE IN SOUTH ASIA

The premier Muslim powers of Asia in the pre-modern era were the Mughals of India and the Ottoman Empire. The dominant interpretation is that Mughal warfare was a sort of theatre war characterized by treachery and intrigues backed by force rather than decisive set-piece battles and sieges. Several historians argue that due to the political culture of *fitna* (which is somewhat similar to the Hindu concept of *bheda*), military loyalty was always for sale. The objective of Mughal warfare was to incorporate the enemy by displaying minimum violence.[43] As far as the Ottoman military was concerned, the general view is that they were falling behind the Europeans in military science and technology from at least the sixteenth century. Thomas F. Arnold claims that from the last third of the sixteenth century, a cordon of rampart- and bastion-defended fortifications blocked the Ottoman expansion westward. The Ottomans depended on imprecisely directed artillery fire and human wave assaults.[44] During the first half of the sixteenth century, the Ottomans hired Christian gunners.[45] The failed Ottoman siege of Corfu in 1537 showed that a fortress built according to the lessons of Pisa and Padua and defended by a small garrison could not be easily taken by a large besieging force.[46]

Our main sources for Mughal warfare are the chronological narratives known as *namas* named after the various reigning emperors written by the court chroniclers. Each *nama* (*Akbar Nama*, *Shah Jahan Nama*, etc.) was divided into several chapters and each chapter represents a particular year in the reign of the respective emperor. Probably, the writers of the *namas* utilized the reports generated by the news writers who were posted at various parts of the empire. These chroniclers aimed to glorify the rule of the various emperors whom they were serving. One advantage is that they provide a lot of details as regards the political and military affairs. However, none of these chroniclers were military officers. These chronicles were political and military narratives and not pure military tracts which had appeared in China from the era of Sun Tzu onwards and in West Europe from the time of Classical Greece.

Adam Schull (1592-1666), the first incumbent of the Imperial Board of Astronomy in China with a Chinese colleague in 1643 wrote two books on gunnery. After Schull, Ferdinand Verbiest succeeded to his post. Verbiest wrote a treatise on artillery and ballistics in 1681, where he noted the importance of the uniformity of cannonballs and on the critical difference a cannon's angle of elevation could make to its accuracy. If the gunners knew the exact distance between the target and the gun, and the weight of the cannonball, they could accurately hit their targets. In mid-eighteenth century, the Copernican theory reached China. Towards the end of the eighteenth century, at least some reforming Chinese scholars of the Manchu Qing dynasty (1644-1911) criticized the Confucian tradition for preferring metaphysics to mathematics.[47] We do not find any scholarly group either in the Mughal Empire or in its successor states criticizing the ulama and their over-reliance on the Koran or the Hindu pundits for focusing on Vedic metaphysics.

Peter A. Lorge asserts that South Asia experienced a Military Revolution in the sixteenth century. One aspect of the Military Revolution was the extension of the outer curtain wall of the fort in order to encompass a larger area to keep the fort outside the range of mortar fire.[48] Jos J.L. Gommans claims that rather than the sixteenth century, between CE 1000 and 1200, South Asia experienced a Cavalry Revolution due to the intrusion of mounted Turks equipped with composite bows. Gommans asserts that since in medieval and late medieval India, most of the forts were constructed on inaccessible hill tops and inside forests, the *trace italienne* sort of thing was superfluous to the requirements of the fort builders.[49] Gommans has a point. Kautilya's *Arthashastra*, composed between 300 BCE-CE 300, gives some space to forts. Kautilya mentions that *giridurga* (hill fort) and *vanadurga* (forest fort) are most important for a ruler.[50] The later Hindu works like *Manusamhita* and *Kamandaka Nitisara* repeat Kautilya's suggestions on fortifications. And in medieval India, the Hindu rajas constructed forts on hilltops.

The Mughals maintained a siege train for capturing forts. The siege train maintained *beldars* and *tabardars* (pioneers and sappers).[51] The Achilles heel of the Mughal cannon manufacture was the absence of powerful bellows to construct a single large furnace with adequate capacity. Zahir-ud-Din Muhammad Babur's (1483-1530) Ottoman engineers used to cast the stone chamber separately from the powder chamber. The net result was exacerbating the problem of inconsistent metal in the manufacture of guns.[52] The two Dutch historians, Gommans and Dirk Kolff write that pre-British India failed to manufacture cast iron guns and in the long run, this hampered the mass production of standardized guns. This was probably because the blast furnace and the finery with water powered hammer were introduced in West Europe during the fifteenth century, but remained unknown in India. In addition, the gun carriages of the Indian powers remained pathetic.[53] However, the Mughal ordnance department was not static. During the seventeenth century, the Mughals attempted to strengthen the wrought iron barrels with the addition of cast bronze casings around the barrels. Mortars were used by Emperor Akbar in 1570 during the siege of Ranthambhor. However, even under Emperor Aurangzeb (1627-1707, emperor from 1658), the weakness of the Mughal guns was their slow rate of fire. A Mughal cannon fired four to five times a day. Iqtidar Alam Khan asserts that the later Mughals failed to copy West European cast iron cannons. During the seventeenth century, the Mughals bought shells from the EIC at Surat.[54] The West European travellers observed that during the seventeenth century, the rulers of India, Malaysia and Siam possessed several artillery pieces but lacked a proper doctrine and adequate training for the gunners in order to use the guns effectively.[55]

Let us analyse some of the siege operations undertaken by the Mughals. In October 1666, the Mughal Army appeared within 5 *kos* (1 *kos* =1.5 to 2 miles) of Bijapur, which was a large fortified place with an enclosure measuring more than 10 km.[56] Generally, the walls of the Chinese fortified cities often exceeded 10 miles in circumference.[57] The citadel of Bijapur was constructed between 1514 and 1544. The thickness of the wall of Bijapur varies between 9 to 10 m and the height is about 10 m. There are crenellations on the city walls; the crenels are in the shape of regular notches pierced by loopholes. The merlons are pierced by a single loophole on the inner face. Another modification was construction of barbicans for defending the gateways. The barbican is an outwork which took the form of two walls that extended out which in turn forced the assailants to enter a narrow bent or semi-circular corridor where they were fired from both sides. The southern gate of the citadel had been repaired and remodelled several times between 1514 and 1542. It consists of a barbican rectangular in shape and provided with guardrooms. The main entrance is flanked by two huge towers, which lead to a semi-circular inner courtyard lined up in the face of the curved wall with many recesses.[58] A modern French expert on South Asian fortifications, Jean Deloche, asserts: 'The rectangular plan of the Hindus is progressively abandoned in the Deccan.... Most of the towers are either polygonal or semicircular.'[59] At Bijapur, several towers are polygonal in the citadel and all the enormous *burj* in the large town enclosure are semi-circular. *Burj* means an isolated tower or flanking tower or a cavalier. On the south-east wall of Bijapur, the Firangi Burj, built in 1576 probably by a Portuguese, rises about 9 m above the curtain walls. This tower is hollow, lined with guardrooms and in the front of each embrasure, there are masonry blocks for cannons. To the west is Sherja Burj, a large circular platform built in 1658, and to the south is Landa Qassab built in 1609. On the north-west part of the enclosure is the Haidar Burj built in 1583. It is circular in structure and rises to a height of about 24 m. A narrow staircase ascends from the southern side to the top where two platforms with recoil wall are present. Two iron guns are still mounted on them.[60]

As regards the ordnance used by the garrison in the Bijapur Fort we have some evidence. The largest bronze cannon in Bijapur known as Malik Maidan is at Sherja Burj and placed on large wooden logs. It was cast by a Turkish engineer named Muhammad Bin Hasan Rumi. This cannon is 426 cm in length and the bore diameter is 71.2 cm. Its estimated weight is 55 tons.[61] Not only is this cannon extremely heavy but also basically immobile and hence not manoeuvrable. Similarly, the Ottomans during the late eighteenth century, for defence of the Dardanelles, deployed huge guns made of brass without trunnions and carriages and laid on hollowed pieces of wood and their breaches were secured by large stones to prevent their recoil. These guns continued to use stone shots even in the first decade of the nineteenth century.[62]

In the words of Saqi Mustad Khan, the author of *Ma'asir-i-Alamgiri* which was completed in 1710, Adil Khan, the ruler of Bijapur, 'after strengthening the fort of Bijapur, cut the banks of his tanks, filled up the surrounding wells with briars, razed to the ground homesteads outside the fort, stood a siege, and appointed his army to repel the imperial forces. As the Raja [Jai Singh, the Mughal *mansabdar*] . . . had not brought with himself siege-materials, he halted for some days, and then marched away'.[63] The Mughal Army returned in 1685. It made trenches in front of the fort.[64] The zig-zag trenches and covered passages were known as *sabats*.[65] These trenches were made in a random manner and were not cut in accordance with the scientific plan of Vauban. Saqi Mustad Khan notes: 'The powder magazine of the army of Muhammad Azam Shah [a Mughal prince] caught fire; nearly 500 *bahalias* (hill climbing infantry) and musketeers were killed'.[66] Besides the handguns-equipped infantry, the Mughals also maintained light infantry for escalading the hill forts. The garrison of the Bijapur fort launched repeated attacks to destroy the Mughal trenches.[67] As regards the continuation of siege operation on 4 July 1686, the *Ma'asir-i-Alamgiri* tells us: 'the Emperor ordered the trenches to be advanced, the towers to be overthrown by cannonade, the moat to be filled up'.[68] The garrison opposed the besieging army with musket fire, cannon shots and rockets. Just opposite the *kangurah* (turret) of the fort, the Mughals raised a battery.[69] However, the Mughal artillery failed to demolish Landa Qassab.[70] Finally, on 12 September 1686, the fort was captured.[71]

In December 1686, the Mughal Army advanced towards Golkunda fort which was held by Abul Hasan, the ruler of Hyderabad. The Golkunda fort is situated on a hill and two *kos* from Hyderabad.[72] It was fortified with two lines of defence. The inner rampart, about 5 km in circumference, protected the palace and the garrison located on the Golkunda hill. The outer rampart protected the Golkunda city which was about 11 km long. At regular intervals, the outer rampart had *burjs* equipped with iron and bronze cannons. The iron cannons lacked trunnions and had rings.[73] The Musa Burj is semi-circular in shape and consists of three storeys built of solid blocks of granite cemented and at times bound with iron clamps. The height of the lowest storey from the bottom of the moat was 18 m and this structure was rebuilt in 1666, to resist mining. To the west of Fateh Darwaza is a small square platform for mounting cannon. This structure, known as cavalier, is provided with a low recoil wall. The Bala Hisar is shielded by a powerful outwork, horseshoe shaped, and defended from within from a platform raised to the height of its battlement accessible through two flight of steps. The gateway is closed by a two leaved door and is provided with a strong guardroom on either side. On the main enclosure, the Moti Darwaza to the north-east is equipped with a semi-circular crenellated barbican which is approached through a staircase.[74]

As far as the chroniclers are concerned, causation of events for them unlike the Enlightenment theorists was not rational but divine. Saqi Mustad Khan writes: 'Qalich Khan [a Mughal officer] galloped up to the fort and wanted to enter it immediately. But God had willed it otherwise.'[75] Secular writing on warfare was yet to appear in the contemporary Indian cultural milieu. On 28 January 1687, the Mughals launched an assault but it was turned back due to the firing of the *zamburaks* (same as *shutarnals*) by the besieged.[76] Iqtidar Alam Khan asserts that the *zamburaks* were introduced in India from West Asia during the beginning of the seventeenth century. And the *zamburaks* were equivalent to cast iron field guns of West Europe.[77] It seems that the *zamburaks* were Asian equivalent of the gallopers guns (later horse artillery) of the West European military establishments.

The *Ma'asir-i-Alamgiri* continues:

> On . . . 7 February 1687 orders were issued for digging trenches . . . the imperial army under the leadership of Saf Shikan Khan . . . carried the trenches to the foot of the ditch in the space of one month. . . . Heavy guns were mounted opposite the fort, the pillars of which were demolished by the fire of their guns. . . . Saf Shikan Khan, having constructed a lofty gun-platform raised it up to the height of the turret of the fort and mounted guns on it. . . . At midnight owing to the neglect and self-will of the chiefs, the enemy fell upon the raised battery, spoiled the gun, bound and carried off . . . a party that had fallen into their hands.[78]

The Mughals resorted to mining the walls. The garrison also used *huqqa* (a sort of grenade) bombs against the besiegers. From the twelfth century, the Chinese also used such devices. The Chinese *huoqiu* (fire balls) were containers with low nitrate gunpowder.[79] Ahsan Jan Qaisar writes that the West Europeans aided the Mughals in manufacturing mortars and grenades.[80] Aurangzeb, who was personally inspecting the siege, decided that a fort of wood and mud should be built around the Golkunda fort, which was soon completed.[81] In medieval Japan also, the besieging force while taking a fort constructed another type of fort known as 'facing fort', which was used as a base for launching attacks against the garrison.[82] After a siege of eight months and a few days, the Golkunda fort was captured not by firepower of the besieging army but by treachery. Sarandaz Khan, an officer of the fort, opened the gates in the midnight of 21 September 1687 and allowed the Mughal soldiers to enter.[83] Treachery was not unique to pre-colonial India as the British officers of the colonial period and some modern historians believed. In 1596, the fortress of Erlau belonging to the Habsburg Empire fell to the Ottomans due to the treachery of the mercenary garrison.[84] Treachery and betrayals by the garrison and their commanders were quite common in medieval Japanese siege warfare.[85]

In October 1690, Aurangzeb's *mansabdar* Zulfiqar Ali Khan with 26,000 soldiers (including 10,000 cavalry and 8,000 musketeers), 1,000 *shutarnals*, eight heavy cannons and 70 field pieces (between 1 to 4-pounders) besieged the Maratha fort of Gingee. This place was 150 km from Madras. The powder and iron shots were supplied by the EIC at Madras and about 100 European gunners were employed by the Mughals.[86]

The use of European guns and gunners was also common in China. The Kangxi Emperor (1662-1722) used Dutch cannon for capturing the Russian fort of Albazin in 1685.[87]

Muhammad Hashim Khafi Khan in *Muntakhabul Lubab* describes Gingee: 'The fortress of Gingee occupies several adjacent hills, on each of which stands a fort bearing a distinct name. Two of these hills are very high, and the forts were well furnished with artillery, provisions and all necessary stores.'[88] Actually, the fort complex of Gingee comprises a triangle formed by three hills: Krishnagiri, Rajgiri and Chandradurg, which were enclosed by an outer wall. Of these three hills, Rajgiri is the highest (i.e. about 600 feet) and on its top is the citadel. The citadel is surrounded on three sides by walls 20-5 feet high and on the fourth side is a narrow steep ravine. The access to the citadel was from the north by way of a timber drawbridge over the ravine which is 24 feet wide and 60 feet deep.[89] Khafi Khan, the Mughal chronicler, describes the siege operation during 1694 in the following words:

> It was impossible to invest all the forts . . . and every exertion was made for digging mines and erecting batteries. . . . The garrison also did their best to put the place in order, and make a stout defence. From time to time they fired a gun or two. The zamindars far and near of the country round, and the Maratha forces, surrounded the royal army on all sides, and showed great audacity in cutting off supplies. Sometimes they burst unexpectedly into an entrenchment, doing great damage to the works, and causing great confusion in the besieging force. . . . The siege had gone on for a long time, and many men fell. . . . Intelligence now came of the approach of Santa, and the enemy's forces so closed round the royal army and shut up the roads, that for some days there were no communications whatever between the army and His Majesty.[90]

Overall, we see that by eighteenth century, Manchu China, Mughal India and the Ottoman Empire were suffering from a technological lag *vis-à-vis* the West and at times had to borrow Western military technologies and technicians. Probably, China, threatened from the north by continuous raids of mobile light nomadic cavalry found heavy guns not that useful. Hence, instead of stressing gunpowder technology and static forts, China's strategic managers had to look for other military options.[91]

In India, the steppe nomadic ethos of the Mughal aristocracy functioned as a brake as regards vigorous adoption of gunpowder technology. If artillery was made the 'God of War' within the Mughal military establishment, naturally, the *mansabdars* excelling in cavalry combat would be sidelined. And they could not be accused of committing *hara-kiri.* Unlike the West European armies, the late Mughal Army did not witness the entry of the bourgeoisie in the engineering and artillery department. Whether a bourgeois class in pre-British India existed or not, is a question for the economic historians to answer. Hypothetically speaking if Aurangzeb attempted to demobilize the *mansabdars* and fill up the vacant slots in the army with *ahadi* musketeers (most of them were Hindus from Bihar and Karnatak) and *firangi* gunners, then the emperor would have faced a rebellion from the Mughal aristocracy.

In 1730, the ulama with mass support opposed the Ottoman Sultan's Westernization programme. This backlash was known as Patrona Halil rebellion. Jeremy Black writes that the Russsian Orthodox Church was in a weaker position to challenge the Petrine reforms of Westernization.[92] Probably, this has to do with the separation of Church and State in West Europe. However, in Islam there is no separation of religion and politics. Of course, experts could argue against such an assertion. Kolff claims that due to the overwhelming presence of dharma in the Hindu political culture till the advent of the British, there was no difference between the secular public domain of the Kshatriyas and the religious realm dominated by the Brahmins.[93]

One can speculate that the influence of religion in the mind of the common soldiers and the officers of the Mughal Army also obstructed the emergence of 'rationality' of the Western kind. Simon Digby shows Mughal soldiers fighting Aurangzeb's war in Deccan maintained close affiliations with the Naqshbandi Sufis. The Sheikh Baba Palangposh was a travelling *pir* who attended to the spiritual and supernatural requirements of the Mughal military personnel. While campaigning against the Marathas, the Mughal soldiers made offerings to Baba Palangposh in order to ensure their safety in the battlefields. The communal angle was not totally absent. Baba Palangposh depicted war against the Marathas as war against the unbelievers. Such a depiction naturally raised the motivational zeal of the Muslim military personnel. The babas were famous for their *karamat* (miracles) and revelations.[94] One example will suffice:

> Mir Shibab al-din at that time had the rank [*mansab*] of/commander of/400. With a contingent of imperial troops and a body of companions of his father he had been appointed by the emperor to reduce one of the fortresses of Deccan. He was worried about the length of this operation, which was as yet uncompleted. That night he saw in a dream that a man with the form of Baba Palangposh appeared and said: 'Why are you worried?' Mir Shibab al-din told him about the state of affairs, and Baba Palangposh took his hand in his own and brought him with him some steps in the direction of the fortress and he said: 'This is the road to the gate of the fortress'.[95]

The ulama denigrated the so-called visions of the Sufis. Nevertheless, many junior and mid-level officers in the artillery departments were *murids* of various babas and some of them occasionally gave up their military careers and became *faqirs*. Digby notes that the influence of the Naqsbandi *silsila* was most noted among the military adventurers from Transoxiana who joined the Mughal military. Those commanders who were disciples of the babas after gaining success in the field graciously donated money, horses as well as funds for expansion of the existing mosques as well as construction of new mosques.[96]

From the time of Babur to Aurangzeb, one notices a shift. From depending on Ottoman gunners under Babur, the Mughals under Aurangzeb started to depend on the *firangis*. This shift was probably related to the military decline of the Islamic world *vis-à-vis* the West, a theme which is partly discussed in the Introduction of this volume. M. Athar Ali notes that the breakdown of the Mughal, Safavid and the Uzbeg empires was due to a cultural failure of the Islamic world. The cultural blockage prevented the Muslim polities from harnessing science and technology for economic purpose which first resulted in economic impoverishment and then military failures.[97] What exactly within Islam obstructed the march of science is not spelled out. Again, the Ottoman Empire faced greater military pressure from the European powers compared to the Uzbegs, Safavids and the Mughals, and despite being Islamic in spirit survived till the end of the First World War. And all the non-Islamic cultures (Confucian ethos of China, not to mention Africa and the Maya and Aztecs) failed to stop the march of the West towards global preponderance.

There is a danger in arguing that due to its extreme religiosity, Islam is averse to scientific progress. Even Hindu military thought was not faring much better in late pre-colonial India. This was probably because of the dominance of dharma in the collective consciousness of the Hindu rulers. Even Mahadji Sindia, one of the chiefs of the Maratha Confederacy who consistently followed the policy of Westernizing his army, employed armed *sadhus* in his force.[98] The Maratha cannon making was quite backward during the first half of the eighteenth century. To give an example, the Bhavani Shankar cannon in Jhansi fort was manufactured in 1725. Its length is 502 cm and the weight is 5 tons. The main barrel was manufactured by hooping two layers of iron rings over 15 longitudinally placed iron staves. About 125 iron rings were used in the construction of the cannon.[99] But the field artillery was modernized due to the utilization of the mercenary French officers by Mahadji Sindia from late eighteenth century onwards.[100]

THE EIC's CONDUCT OF SIEGE WARFARE IN SOUTH ASIA

Contrary to the contemporary general expectations, religious intermediaries were unable to save the Mughal Empire. Three important polities rose on the ashes of the Mughals: Mysore under Haidar Ali and Tipu Sultan, the Maratha Confederacy and the Khalsa kingdom in Punjab. They failed to survive the onslaught of the EIC. A group of historians like G.J. Bryant, Gommans and Lorge argue that the British initiated a Military Revolution in South Asia between 1750 and 1850.[101] In this section, we will analyse some of the significant sieges undertaken by the EIC and try to flesh out the scientific elements inherent in the British conduct of siege warfare. In 1775, the EIC opened a regimental school in the Bengal Presidency where the Indian officers (*subadars* and *jemadars*) and the gunners were taught elementary aspects of gunnery.[102] In 1776, the directors of the EIC sent a specialist tactician named Lieutenant Primrose Thompson (who carried Guibert's work with him) in an attempt to sharpen up the combat effectiveness of the EIC's armies.[103] Jacques De Guibert (1743-90) is famous for his *Essai generale de tactique* (1770). Perhaps the last of the Enlightenment theorists, Guibert writes:

> I say that the science of modern war, compared with that of the ancients, is vaster and more difficult. . . . Our firearms are superior to the missile weapons of the ancients. The science of artillery is superior to their ballistics, our fortifications to theirs: fortified places are now besieged and defended with more art. Such is the progress of the moderns. Such is the effect of mathematical enlightenment spread through the science of war. . . . Artillery and fortifications would become increasingly enlightened. In each century, they would follow the advances of mathematics, which are their foundation.[104]

Continuous innovations characterized British siege operations in India. For example, shrapnel shell was a spherical hollow shell filled with bullets and bursting charges was first used by the British in 1804.[105] These shells were used with devastating effect during the siege of Multan (1848-9).

SIEGE OF SERINGAPATNAM: 7 APRIL-4 MAY 1799

In 1792, Lord Cornwallis laid siege to Seringapatnam, the capital of Tipu's Mysore. By the end of February, the British commanders planned to open a crossfire with two breaching batteries and one enfilading battery. However, the failure of logistics forced Cornwallis to retreat from Seringapatnam to Bangalore. An additional factor was Cornwallis lacked 24-, 18- and 12-pounder guns, a deficiency which was met during the 1799 siege operation. By February 1799, the EIC amassed the following load of shots and shells that they planned to use against the Seringapatnam fort: 5,989 barrels of powder, 860 barrels of musket ammunition, 4,800 barrels of 24-pounder shot, 36,400 barrels of 18-pounder shot, 10,400 barrels of 12-pounder shot, 3,600 barrels of 6-pounder shot, 1,200 barrels of 3-pounder shot, 1,000 barrels of 8-inch shells, 4,000 barrels of 5/2-inch shells and 400 barrels of 4/2-inch shells. The iron guns carried by the ordnance stores were as follows: four 24-pounders, thirty 18-pounders, eight 12-pounders. In addition, the following brass guns were also present: four 18-pounders, eight 12-pounders, thirty-four 6-pounders, two 8-inch howitzers and four 5/2-inch howitzers. Thus, there were 52 cannons and howitzers of brass plus four galloper 6-pounders attached with the artillery. The grand total of iron and brass guns was 98 pieces.[106]

By early March 1799, the combined forces of the EIC and the Nizam numbering 37,000 soldiers marched towards Mysore. About 21,800 soldiers and 287 ordnance pieces were deployed by Tipu for defending Seringapatnam.[107] Seringapatnam stands on an island in the Kaveri River. The island is 3.5 miles in length and 1.5 miles in breadth across the centre, which is its broadest part. The fortress covered 2,000 square yards. The eastern and western side was covered with double walls and each wall was covered by a ditch. In the centre of the fortress and on the southern rampart were strong cavaliers. Tipu started strengthening the fort from 1792 onwards. To the north-east angle of the fort, courtesy French mercenary officers, a European-style bastion was added. Just before 1799, a second interior rampart covered by a deep ditch was erected along the northern face of the fort. Several sluices were constructed for admitting and retaining river water in the ditches. From the north-east angle of the fort, the river bank was scarped and covered by a parapet.[108]

On 7 April 1799, the engineer's park was established on the south side of Sultanpetta Tope (grove of trees). A working party was employed for making a battery for two 12-pounders during the night. For starting the siege, the engineer's park was supplied with gabions and fascines. The wood was acquired by cutting down the Sultanpetta Tope and other *topes* in the rear. The ruinous state of the inner wall favoured the breaching of the south-west angle of the fort. So, on 13 April, it was decided to attack the south-west face of the fort.[109] As regards operation on that day, Alexander Allan Bart who had participated in the campaign writes:

> Our troops during the night established themselves at this post, which was the ruins of a redoubt and village, within 960 yards of the west end of the fort. A breastwork was thrown up on the top of the ruins; and a battery for 6 18-pounders, was constructed on the right, to enfilade the enemy's entrenchments on the south side of the river, which were seen in reverse; and also to scour the ground between them and the advanced posts of the Grand Army. . . . A battery for 2 6-pounders was begun close to the Cauvery, to protect the left of our advanced posts and to drive the enemy from the bed of the river, from which they kept up a teasing fire of musketry.[110]

While the heavier 18-pounder guns were used for disabling the fort, the lighter 6-pounders were used in an anti-personnel role in order to protect the EIC's trenches and advanced batteries from Mysore's troops.

On 20 April, the Bombay battery opened, enfilading the south-west face of the fort, taking in reverse the entrenchments on the south bank of the river and scoured the ground between the fort and the advanced post of the EIC's army. Then, two 12-pounders were placed near the tombs in front of the Sultanpetta Tope and opened a cross fire upon the entrenchments. A swell in the ground covered the 12-pounders from the guns on the south side of the fort. Credit is due to the engineers for positioning the guns and constructing a battery which took advantage of the terrain in order to mask it from the direct fire of the hostile artillery. The garrison harassed by the enfilading fire from the Bombay battery discontinued their repair work on the south face and their fire also slackened. The six-gun battery near the mill was opened in the early morning of 22 April. The fire was directed against the Flag Staff Cavalier, the work at the west end of the fort, the round towers of the south-west face and to enfilade the north rampart. All the guns of the garrison in those portions of the fort were silenced by sunset. It was a typical case of counter-battery bombardment. After silencing the guns in the fort, the above-mentioned battery engaged the parapets, cavalier and the west end of the fort. Since a detachment of the garrison was harassing the outposts of the Bombay battery, a breastwork for two 6-pounders was thrown upon the left of the parallel, in front of McDonald's Nulla. The guns were opened at one in the night. During the night, two embrasures were added to the six-gun battery near the mill. During the night of 25 April, a battery for four guns was constructed in the front and to the right of the mill, in order to silence the guns of the besiegers at the round towers and at the south-west angle of the fort. A ruined village on the left was fortified and the entrenchment which connected the battery was strengthened.[111]

By 27 April, the chief engineer started constructing the breaching battery within 400 yards of the fort. On 28 April, the two 12-pounders in front of Shawe's post fired all over the town of Seringapatnam and the west end of the fort was shattered. On 30 April, the breaching battery started firing and by sunset the *fausse-braye* (the platform behind the parapet of the ramparts) wall was breached. On 2 May, 35 guns and mortars opened up and by sunset the breach was widened. It was decided that another day's battering would make the breach large enough to launch infantry assault. The garrison during the night of 3 May repaired the breach with stone and earth and was busily employed in palisading a high mound of earth on the right of Flag Staff Cavalier and behind the breach.[112]

Scaling ladders were lodged in the advanced approaches. The storming party comprised 2,494 Europeans and 1,882 Indians. The right attack column headed by General Baird moved along the rampart of the south face. The left attack column met opposition from the garrison posted behind the traverses on the rampart of the north face. The left column was galled by musketry from a high bank of earth (separated by a deep wet ditch and which formed the inner rampart). Lieutenant Ingram with a party gained the cavalier behind the breach and drove away Tipu's troops. Tipu died fighting near the breach. Of the 4,376 EIC troops involved in the assault, 408 were either killed or wounded.[113]

Mir Hussain Ali Khan Kirmani while writing a history of Tipu Sultan in Persian, like the Mughal authors, attempted to describe victory and defeat in warfare through divine causation rather than due to any scientific reasoning which characterized the works of Enlightenment theorists. Kirmani while describing the siege of Seringapatnam in 1799 writes: 'Fortune, however, was adverse to giving aid or success to the Sultan's troops, and they lost or neglected the proper modes of prosecuting the war successfully'.[114] Fortuna which Machiavelli took pains to discard maintains an overwhelming presence in the work of Kirmani. In some of the passages, Kirmani implies that human beings are pygmies in the hand of God who has predetermined the fate of warfare. Kirmani writes: 'Although from the battle of that day, it appeared evident how the war would end, still, the faithful troops of the Sultan performed many worthy and gallant actions, and fought with the artillery of the enemy hand to hand, shoulder to shoulder'.[115] It did not appear foolish to Kirmani that a frontal charge towards enemy artillery is sure to lead to defeat. At times, even though defeat is predetermined, the soldiers of Islam appear as sacrifice for the cosmic drama chalked out by God in heaven. The concept of predetermination in Kirmani's work is somewhat similar to Hindu fatalism, a byproduct of *karma* theory, which is partially discussed in the Introduction. The holy war angle is also not completely absent from the chronicle. Kirmani notes: 'When the Ghazis of the Faith saw they had no choice but to light up the flames of war, they every day well armed and appointed threw themselves on the troops of the enemy, as the moth flies at the lamp, and is destroyed by it'.[116]

SIEGE OF BHARATPUR: 28 DECEMBER 1804-24 FEBRUARY 1805, 11 DECEMBER 1825-18 JANUARY 1826

The walls of Chinese fortifications were built of tamped earth usually thicker than its height. During the thirteenth century, brick facing was added to the walls. These walls were completely fireproof and highly resistant to battering. The sieges were generally decided by starvation or escalade. Lorge, a modern military historian of China, claims that even twentieth-century explosive shells had difficulty in blasting such walls.[117] In 1513, the Italian city Lucca thickened the medieval walls with earth-filled ramparts for protection against the impact of cannon balls.[118] In India, the same technique was followed by the Jats for protecting the Bharatpur fort (in present-day Rajasthan), which proved to be a hard nut to crack for Gerald Lake's (Commander-in-Chief of British-India) army during the Second Anglo-Maratha War (1803-5).

On 28 December 1804, Lake reached the vicinity of Bharatpur whose *raja* had joined Jaswant Rao Holkar, then fighting the EIC. The town stands in a plain and had a perimeter of about 5 miles and was surrounded by a great mound of mud which in turn was protected by a wet ditch 8 feet deep. The mud wall of the fort was between 50 to 64 feet thick.[119] The garrison was 50,000 strong and Lake had 7,800 soldiers. Later, Lake received some reinforcements and the total force deployed against Bharatpur numbered 12,100. Lake had two 24-pounders (with limited ammunition), six 18-pounders and eight 5.5-inch and 8-inch mortars. However, there were only three engineer-officers and three pioneer companies.[120]

On 5 January 1805, construction of a battery started about 700 yards from the Anah Gate. On 8 January, a breach in the curtain about 350 yards north of the gate was made. The British officers viewed the breach with telescopes and pronounced it practicable for launching an infantry assault. However, the infantry assault launched on the night of 9 January was hurled back by the garrison because by that time, the garrison had stockaded and repaired the breach. On 16 January, a second breach was made about 150 yards south of the Anah Gate. The infantry assault was launched on 20 January and it was also beaten back. The assault infantry used portable bridges for crossing the ditch but the bridges were found to be shorter. Hence, the stormers were massacred on the counterscarp. Another factor behind the failure of the infantry assault was that lack of adequate artillery and ammunition for the guns prevented Lake to bring down continuous harassing fire on the garrison in order to keep it away from repairing the breach before the infantry assault was launched.[121]

The ammunition situation for the British somewhat improved on 28 January, when Lake received a convoy which brought in eight thousand 18-pounder shots.[122] On 4 February, a parallel was opened. On 11 February, another breach was made but the trenches to conduct the stormers from the battery which was 430 yards away from the breach was not completed. By 20 February, when the trenches were completed and the assault was made, it failed because by that time, the breach was strongly retrenched. On 21 February, the fourth and the last assault was made and it was also turned back by the garrison. On 24 February, Lake's army withdrew from Bharatpur. The four infantry assaults cost Lake 374 man and left 2,263 wounded. Lake lost about 3,100 men (i.e. 25 per cent of the force engaged) killed and wounded before Bharatpur.[123]

James Young, Captain of the Bengal Horse Artillery, was in Lake's army. In his journal, under the entry dated 26 March 1805, he noted:

> I have taken some pains to collect from the intelligent friends, I have in the artillery & engineer corps—what has been the real cause of our want of success in our different attempts against Bharatpur. . . . On the 21 January, [actually 20 January] the great breadth & depth of the uninjured ditch, was the obstacle. . . . But the true & grand cause, in a greater of less degree of all these misfortunes—has been the want of a sufficient ordnance establishment—I mean of an adequate field engineers establishment of European & Native artificers & pioneers as well as of a sufficient siege train & artillery officers & men. Wet ditches been unusual—I may almost say unknown. . . . I hesitate not to say that Bharatpur required far more guns & men to besiege it—than almost any European fortress—the curtains and the bastions though small were twice as high—planted more closely—the circumference of the place so vast that to enfilade the curtains of faces (The 1st grand rule of besieging) was impossible.[124]

After the siege of 1805, the fortifications of Bharatpur were strengthened. Additions had been made to the enceinte and one bastion known as Fateh Burj was added to the previous 34 bastions. In total, there were 135 ordnance pieces in the fort. The garrison comprised 25,000 newly raised Jat and Pathan soldiers when the second siege was undertaken by Lord Combermere (the Commander-in-Chief of British-India) in 1825. The EIC's army which assembled at Agra in November 1825 for undertaking the siege had 154 guns.[125] During the first siege, British operation was hampered by the fact that the engineers lacked adequate knowledge of the terrain which had a negative effect on proper dispositions of the guns. Hence, Combermere and his engineers after besieging Bharatpur on 11 December spent nine days in reconnoitering every part of the fortress. While Lake had made his approaches towards the south-west portion of the fort, Combermere decided to attack the north-east angle of the fort. This was because the ditch at that place was almost dry and shallow.[126]

On 23 December, Combermere sent two columns to seize the village of Kadam Kandi and Baldeo Singh's garden. These two places provided good cover to the working parties who were constructing the first parallel. The garrison tried to attack the working parties but failed to depress their guns sufficiently for accurate shooting. Meanwhile, fire from the besieging troops' mortars caused great damage to life and property within the city. Next day, the besiegers widened the parallel to a breadth of 10 feet and carried out an approach in advance of it by means of a flying sap. They also started working on a breaching battery of eleven 24-pounder guns. On 27 December, the second parallel was completed at a distance of 250 yards from the ditch. It was armed with two batteries: one for two 12-pounders and another for twelve 24-pounders. The following day, the approaches were brought to within 40 yards of the ditch. On 3 January 1826, the third parallel was extended and next day, vigorous mining was undertaken. On 9 January, the engineers blew up a scarp gallery which was occupied by the garrison.[127]

Meanwhile, Combermere had trained the infantry in the use of ladders made of bamboo, and hand grenades. At 4.30 in the morning of 18 January 1826, the three columns as well as the fourth reserve columns entered the trenches. After 8, three mines (one at the breach, another at the counterscarp and the third at the north-east bastion) were exploded. The columns rushed forward. Within the city, close quarter combat broke out between the Jats and Afghans equipped with sword and shields and British infantry with their bayonets. Though the city was gained, the citadel still held out. Soon it surrendered under the threat of bombardment. Darjan Sal, the ruler of Bharatpur was captured. Combermere's force lost 1,050 men, wounded, missing or killed, and the casualties of the garrison numbered to 4,000.[128]

Siege of Multan: 31 March 1848-22 January 1849

The rebellion of Diwan Mulraj at Multan in March 1848 resulted in the beginning of the Second Anglo-Sikh War. The EIC's response was indeed slow. On 18 August, the Ravi Column proceeded to Seetul Ki Mari, 3 miles east of the fort, where it was joined next day by the Sutlej Column. The disembarkation of the siege train occurred on 4 September.[129] At that time, General Whish had 32 siege guns and 61 light guns. He had under him two horse artillery troops, four foot artillery companies, five sapper companies, three cavalry regiments, two British infantry regiments and four sepoy regiments. Herbert Edwards had under him 13,400 Indian infantry and 5,000 cavalry. They were mostly soldiers from Bahawalpur and Pathan levies. Sher Singh had with him 900 infantry and 3,400 cavalry. All of Sher Singh's troops were Sikhs. For an estimate of Mulraj's force see Table 9.2. It was planned by the British officers to construct a trench to a point called Ram Teerut and to establish batteries there. By 6 September, the mortar batteries started raining death and destruction within the town of Multan. It was an example of harassing operation to prevent the garrison from commencing repair work as well as to prevent them from launching any sallies against the besieging force. Construction of trenches (first parallel, Vaubanian style) started on 7 September. The first parallel was opened at a distance of 1 mile from the city. The engineering operations were under the supervision of Major Napier (later Lord Napier of Magdala), who was the chief engineer. The soldiers of Bahawalpur and the Pathan levies refused to construct trenches and battery. Constructing fieldwork was considered an essential part of soldiering duties even by German infantry during Second World War. However, the martial ethos of the traditional Indian soldiery prevented them from taking up the spade. On 10 September, the trench connecting the first parallel (which was opened about 1,600 yards from the enceinte attacked) with the advanced picquet was widened and a battery of four 18-pounders was made and on their right four 5.5-inch mortars were placed.[130] Even during the second half of the seventeenth century, the Ottomans continued to place their siege guns behind the first parallel on natural or artificial hills. They failed to plant their siege artillery on the approaches due to the difficulty of bringing cannons across the maze of ditches and saps.[131] On 14 September, Sher Singh deserted to Mulraj and took position beneath the walls of the fort.[132] On 9 October, Sher Singh marched towards west Punjab to join his father Chattar Singh who was in open rebellion against the *durbar* dominated by the EIC.[133] Whish decided to wait for further reinforcements. Thus, ended the first siege.

On 30 November, Colonel Cheape arrived to take control of the engineering operation. It marked the beginning of the second siege. He proposed that the main attack should be directed at the southern bastion known as the Khuni Burj. This was approved by Whish. Meanwhile, the artillery at the disposal of the besieging force went up to 67 siege pieces and 30 field guns. A site about 120 yards from the Khuni Burj was selected for establishing the breaching battery.[134] On 21 December 1848, the Bengal Sappers and Miners brought with them 12,000 gabions and 8,000 fascines.[135] On 29 December two mortar batteries opened at the citadel at 500 yards. On 30 December, the breaching battery of 18-pounders started blasting away at the Khuni Burj. The garrison's large magazine on the south face of the fort was blown up by mortar fire.[136] On 2 January 1849, the breaches in the wall were found practicable for launching infantry assault. The EIC's infantry was able to capture the city but Mulraj with 4,000 men still held the citadel. Meanwhile, saps or regular trenches of approaches (which were dug 5 feet deep and the earth was thrown on the reverse side of the trench to give further protection to the EIC's soldiers inside the trench from the garrison's bombardment and musketry) were advanced from the north of the fort.[137] On 7 January, a battery of seven 18-pounders was completed and a battery of three 10-inch howitzers was also finished. Next day, work commenced for the construction of six 24-pounder and six 18-pounder guns.[138] On 8 January, the engineers were sapping up to the foot of the glacis on the north-east angle of the fort. On 22 January, Mulraj surrendered unconditionally.[139]

The first siege of Bharatpur proved to be more costly for the EIC compared to the two sieges of Multan. The total casualties suffered by the EIC's force (excluding the forces under Herbert Edwards and other chiefs allied to the British) were 1,192 (210 killed and 910 wounded).[140]

The second siege was successful unlike the first one because during the second siege, unlike the first one, there was no Sikh field army hovering around the fort to distract the besiegers from concentrating fully on the siege operation. It is to be noted that after Sher Singh's departure, Whish had to keep an eye on his force besides conducting the siege operation. After the departure of Sher Singh's army for west Punjab, there was no Sikh field army to distract the British from conducting the siege of Multan. Further, the second siege was successful because of more intense firing by the besiegers which is evident from greater expenditure of shots and shells as shown in Table 9.1.

TABLE 9.1: EXPENDITURE OF SHOT AND SHELL DURING THE SIEGE OF MULTAN: 1848-9

Bengal Division			
Nature of Ammunition	First Siege	Second Siege	Total
24-pounder round shots		4,386	4,386
18-pounder round shots	400	5,011	5,411
18-pounder shrapnel shells	150	4	154
18-pounder case shells		314	314
10-inch common shells		3,450	3,450
10-inch case shots		1	1
8-inch common shells	496	7,189	7,685
5.5-inch common shells	160	2,918	3,078
5.5-inch light balls		50	50
68-pounder shrapnel shells	100	20	120
8-inch case shots	8	38	46
8-inch carcasses		102	102
5.5-inch carcasses		30	30
Powder expended: ordnance = 85,331 pounds; musketry = 20,530 pounds			
Bombay Division			
18-pounder round shots		3,751	3,751
18-pounder case shots		206	206
8-inch shrapnel shells		160	160
5.5-inch and 24-pounder shrapnel shells		552	552
42/5 or 12-pounder shrapnel shells		290	290
9-pounder shrapnel shells		106	106
10-inch common shells		474	474
8-inch common shells		6,075	6,075
5.5-inch common shells		1,876	1,876
42/5-inch carcasses		10	10
8-inch case shots		52	52
Hand grenades		680	680
Ammunition (shots and shells) used by the brass field guns		2,582	2,582
powder expended = 56,900 pounds			

Source: Major Siddons, 'The Siege of Multan: 1848-9', *Professional Papers of the Corps of Royal Engineers*, vol. 1 (1849-50), Appendices M&N, p. 459, College of Military Engineering, Pune.

TABLE 9.2: MULRAJ'S FORCE ON 13 OCTOBER 1848

Description of Troops	Outside the City	Inside the Fort
Ghura Foot Regiment	500	
Rohilla Regiment	500	500
Hurdos Singh's Regiment	600	
Dedar Singh's Infantry	1,000	
Etein Troops		6,000
Akalis	300	
Infantry sent by Sher Singh	150	
Recruits	300	
Horse and Foot under the following chiefs: Narain Singh, Mulah Singh, Lal Singh and Bal Sodhia	3,000	
Total	6,050	6,500
Grand Total = 12,550 horse and foot with 59 guns and 5 mortars		

Source: Major Siddons, 'The Siege of Multan: 1848-9', *Professional Papers of the Corps of Royal Engineers*, vol. 1 (1849-50), Appendix B, p. 447, College of Military Engineering, Pune.

As regards the impact of artillery, Major Siddons, a Bengal Army engineer, noted:

> The walls are mostly of mud, or brick and mud; and it so happened that the part selected for the breach was very defective—a mere facing over the old wall. In this the 24-pounder shot brought down large masses; but where the wall was sound the shot buried themselves, whereas the shell penetrated and then acted as small mines. Against a mud fort, an howitzer must therefore be considered far preferable to a gun, though of course the latter would be more effective against a well-built stone wall. The inconvenience to howitzers is the difficulty of preserving the cheeks of the embrasures. The iron howitzer might, perhaps with advantage be lengthened.[141]

The problem with thick mud walls which bedeviled Lake at Bharatpur was finally solved by Siddons during the siege of Multan.

The EIC unlike the Mughals did not take several months for capturing the forts of their opponents even though some of the forts like Seringapatnam were modernized in accordance with West European principles. Except the first siege of Seringapatnam and the first siege of Bharatpur, the EIC's siege operations moved with clockwork precision. Lake's siege arsenal was quite small when compared with the EIC's sieges of Seringapatnam and

Multan. The secret of British victory was in their conduct of siege warfare in accordance with scientific principles. Application of massive firepower in an efficient way was a characteristic of the British sieges. From the above analysis it is clear that the concepts of enfilading fire, crossfire, etc., were new techniques introduced in the Indian subcontinent from West Europe by the British. Roughly, the siege operation had three phases: in phase 1, the besieging army took position and in accordance with a scientific plan started building zig-zag trenches gradually advancing towards the fort. In phase 2, the advancing trenches were protected by gun batteries which engaged in harassing operation against the besieged. The harassing operation involved anti-personnel bombardment of the enemy troops and counter-bombardment of the garrison's guns within the fort. The objectives of harassing fire were to prevent the garrison from undertaking any repairs and from launching any attacks against the advancing positions, batteries and trenches of the besieging force. In phase 3, the breaching battery blasted a portion of the fort's wall (especially the curtain wall) and an infantry assault with covering fire provided by mobile artillery was launched for capturing the fort. Breaching was effected by the heavy guns (18 and 24-pounders) sited at a distance of about 400 yards from the wall and the common shells of the howitzers were used for dispersing the debris.[142]

CONCLUSION

This essay raises more questions than it purports to answer. The realm of history of ideas is a messy field because a historian can only speculate rather than get hard evidence about the impact factor of particular ideas on the material things of a particular period. Superficially, this essay seems to be an account of the triumphal march of the Western amalgam of science and warfare over atavistic feudal east dominated by religiosity. Whether the rise of the West against the 'rest' was inevitable or not, is an issue which needs to be tackled elsewhere. The objective of this essay is more limited. By making the case study of siege warfare conducted by a European power in India, this essay aims to argue that rather than mere technological hardware, collective mentalities of the societies played an important role. The collective mentality of a society shapes how a particular piece of technology should be utilized and what further innovations could be done on that particular piece. And mentality for us means ideologies also which includes religion and science. Interestingly, if we use warfare as a foil, we see that religion and science did not always oppose each other but at times at least for the West Europeans also created a synergy. Hence, it is time to break out of the bipolar contradictory paradigm of religion and science.

Back in India, the Mughal military establishment was not geared for theatrical warfare. True, the Mughal Army was not organized on rigid scientific lines as that of Maurice of Nassau and Gustavus Adolphus but the Mughal siege train was quite sophisticated. The Mughals had assault infantry and capabilities for constructing trenches and batteries. Nevertheless, the Mughals were unaware of the importance of cartography and systematic construction of trenches in accordance with scientific principles. Gunpowder played an important role in Mughal warfare. The general idea that Mughal military mainly comprised rampaging heavy cavaliers equipped with lances and bows is more the creation of the court artists (who eulogized the aristocratic cavaliers and were patronized by the latter group) and modern historians, who after analysing the revenue documents give greater importance to the mounted warriors who were granted *jagirs* by the emperor. Again, the evolution of fortifications was not static in pre-British India. For instance, cavaliers with recoil wall were a response of the Indian fort makers to the rising threat of heavy artillery for taking the forts. One could argue that the fire-resistant qualities of thick mud walls of the Chinese and the Indian fortifications, unlike the tall, thin vulnerable walls of the medieval West European castles, rather than Confucian and Islamic ideologies prevented any further development of siege cannons in China and India unlike in West Europe.

However, from the eighteenth century, the indigenous powers within India, like the Ming and Ottoman empires, tried to incorporate wholesale Western military technologies through the medium of mercenary European military specialists. Copycat mechanism rather than internal innovations characterized the Asian military establishments. This was partially because of lack of emergence of Western rationality and scientific mentality as the Asian intellectual milieu remained embedded in 'medieval religiosity'. The twin concepts of dharma and *fitna* instead of rational consciousness and the idea of progress operated as a negative integer. Academic institutions for teaching scientific military thought and quasi-scientific military tracts emphasizing rules of war and a sense of progress, remained a Western monopoly. The mechanistic collective discipline, i.e. drill—an aspect of culture of early modern West Europe—was absent in India where the soldiers considered themselves as individual warriors rather than cogs in the wheel of a vast machine, i.e. the army. To sum up, rather than any great difference in military hardware, the West Europeans had an edge as regards the theory to use the military hardware properly. Here, scientific methodology emphasizing constant experimentation and innovations had a great role to play. Taking a global approach, the West European development seemed to be abnormal, while the rest of the world was evolving in the normal manner, and the unique Western system was able to overcome most of the non-Western civilizations.

NOTES

1. John S. Nolan, 'The Militarization of the Elizabethan State', in Paul E.J. Hammer (ed.), *Warfare in Early Modern Europe: 1450-1660* (Aldershot, Hampshire: Ashgate, 2007), p. 403; M. Athar Ali, 'The Passing of the Empire: The Mughal Case', in Ali, *Mughal India: Studies in Polity, Ideas, Society, and Culture* (New Delhi: Oxford University Press, 2006), p. 339; Gabor Agoston, 'Ottoman Warfare in Europe: 1453-1826', in Jeremy Black (ed.), *European Warfare: 1453-1815* (Houndmills, Basingstoke: Macmillan, 1999), pp. 123, 130.
2. Stephen Peter Rosen, 'Military Effectiveness: Why Society Matters', *International Security*, vol. 19, no. 4 (Spring 1995), p. 22.
3. Felix Gilbert, 'Machiavelli: The Renaissance of the Art of War', in Peter Paret (ed.), *Makers of Modern Strategy from Machiavelli to the Nuclear Age* (1986, rpt., Oxford: Oxford University Press, 1990), pp. 12-13.
4. Ibid., p. 24.
5. M.D. Feld, 'Milddle-Class Society and the Rise of Military Professionalism', in Hammer (ed.), *Warfare in Early Modern Europe*, p. 253.
6. Gunther E. Rothenberg, 'Maurice of Nassau, Gustavus Adolphus, Raimondo Montecuccoli, and the "Military Revolution" of the Seventeenth Century', in Paret (ed.), *Makers of Modern Strategy from Machiavelli to the Nuclear Age*, pp. 34-5.

7. Nikolas Gardner, 'Military Thought from Machiavelli to Liddell Hart', in Matthew Hughes and William J. Philpott (eds.), *Modern Military History* (Houndmills, Basingstoke: Macmillan Palgrave, 2006), pp. 63-4, 68-9.
8. Henry Guerlac, 'Vauban: The Impact of Science on War', in Paret (ed.), *Makers of Modern Strategy from Machiavelli to the Nuclear Age*, pp. 67-8.
9. Matthew Hughes, 'Technology, Science and War', in Hughes and Philpott (eds.), *Modern Military History*, p. 231.
10. Guerlac, 'Vauban: The Impact of Science on War', in Paret (ed.), *Makers of Modern Strategy from Machiavelli to the Nuclear Age*, pp. 70-1.
11. Jeremy Black, 'Introduction', in Black (ed.), *European Warfare*, pp. 20-1.
12. Guerlac, 'Vauban: The Impact of Science on War', in Paret (ed.), *Makers of Modern Strategy from Machiavelli to the Nuclear Age*, p. 71.
13. Laurent Henninger, 'Military Revolutions and Military History', in Hughes and Philpott (eds.), *Modern Military History*, p. 22.
14. Black, 'Introduction', in Black (ed.), *European Warfare*, p. 21.
15. Guerlac, 'Vauban: The Impact of Science on War', in Paret (ed.), *Makers of Modern Strategy from Machiavelli to the Nuclear Age*, pp. 69-70.
16. Rothenberg, 'Maurice of Nassau, Gustavus Adolphus, Raimondo Montecuccoli, and the "Military Revolution" of the Seventeenth Century', in Paret (ed.), *Makers of Modern Strategy from Machiavelli to the Nuclear Age*, p. 37.
17. Ibid., pp. 55-9.
18. Gardner, 'Military Thought from Machiavelli to Liddell Hart', in Hughes and Philpott (eds.), *Modern Military History*, p. 64.
19. Rothenberg, 'Maurice of Nassau, Gustavus Adolphus, Raimondo Montecuccoli, and the "Military Revolution" of the Seventeenth Century', in Paret (ed.), *Makers of Modern Strategy from Machiavelli to the Nuclear Age*, pp. 62-3.
20. Gardner, 'Military Thought from Machiavelli to Liddell Hart', in Hughes and Philpott (eds.), *Modern Military History*, pp. 64-6.
21. Rothenberg, 'Maurice of Nassau, Gustavus Adolphus, Raimondo Montecuccoli, and the "Military Revolution" of the Seventeenth Century', in Paret (ed.), *Makers of Modern Strategy from Machiavelli to the Nuclear Age*, pp. 42, 49.
22. Guerlac, 'Vauban: The Impact of Science on War', in Paret (ed.), *Makers of Modern Strategy from Machiavelli to the Nuclear Age*, p. 65.
23. Feld, 'Middle-Class Society and the Rise of Military Professionalism', in Hammer (ed.), *Warfare in Early Modern Europe*, pp. 237-52.
24. Niccolo Machiavelli, *The Art of War*, A Revised Edition of the Ellis Farneworth Translation with an Introduction by Neal Wood (1965, rpt., New York: Da Capo Press, 1990), Book 7, p. 183.
25. Machiavelli, *The Art of War*, Book 7, p. 184.

26. Thomas Arnold, *The Renaissance at War* (London: Cassell, 2001), pp. 25-6, 49.
27. Machiavelli, *The Art of War*, Note on the Text, NW, pp. lxxxiv-lxxxvii.
28. Clifford J. Rogers, 'The Military Revolutions of the Hundred Years War', in Rogers (ed.), *The Military Revolution Debate: Readings on the Military Transformation of Early Modern Europe* (Boulder/San Francisco/Oxford: Westview, 1995), pp. 55-93.
29. Christopher Duffy, *Siege Warfare: The Fortress in the Early Modern World, 1494-1660* (1979, rpt., London/New York: Routledge, 1997), p. 8.
30. Peter A. Lorge, *The Asian Military Revolution: From Gunpowder to the Bomb* (Cambridge: Cambridge University Press, 2008), p. 70.
31. Nolan, 'The Militarization of the Elizabethan State', in Hammer (ed.), *Warfare in Early Modern Europe*, p. 287.
32. Paul E.J. Hammer, 'Introduction', in Hammer (ed.), *Warfare in Early Modern Europe*, p. xiii.
33. Guerlac, 'Vauban: The Impact of Science on War', in Paret (ed.), *Makers of Modern Strategy from Machiavelli to the Nuclear Age*, p. 69.
34. Simon Pepper, 'Sword and Spade: Military Construction in Renaissance Italy', in Hammer (ed.), *Warfare in Early Modern Europe*, pp. 117-18.
35. John A. Lynn, 'The *Trace Italienne* and the Growth of Armies: The French Case', and John F. Guilmartin, Jr., 'The Military Revolution: Origins and First Test Abroad', in Rogers (ed.), *Military Revolution Debate*, pp. 172, 174, 307.
36. Pepper, 'Sword and Spade: Military Construction in Renaissance Italy', in Hammer (ed.), *Warfare in Early Modern Europe*, p. 109; Thomas F. Arnold, 'Fortifications and the Military Revolution: The Gonzaga Experience, 1530-1630', in Rogers (ed.), *Military Revolution Debate*, p. 214.
37. Pepper, Ibid., pp. 112-13.
38. Hammer, 'Introduction', in Hammer (ed.), *Warfare in Early Modern Europe*, p. xxii.
39. Pepper, 'Sword and Spade: Military Construction in Renaissance Italy', in Hammer (ed.), *Warfare in Early Modern Europe*, p. 111.
40. Guerlac, 'Vauban: The Impact of Science on War', in Paret (ed.), *Makers of Modern Strategy from Machiavelli to the Nuclear Age*, pp. 70, 79-80.
41. Gerard Chaliand (ed.), *The Art of War in World History from Antiquity to the Nuclear Age* (Berkeley/Los Angeles/London: University of California Press, 1994), pp. 560-2.
42. Guerlac, 'Vauban: The Impact of Science on War', in Paret (ed.), *Makers of Modern Strategy from Machiavelli to the Nuclear Age*, p. 78.
43. William Irvine, the historian of British-India, introduced this interpretation and the Dutch historian Jos J.L. Gommans accepts it. Irvine, *The Army*

of the Indian Moghuls: Its Organization and Administration (1903, rpt., Delhi: D.K. Publishers, 1994); Gommans, *Mughal Warfare: Indian Frontiers and the High Roads to Empire, 1500-1700* (London/New York: Routledge, 2002); Gommans, 'Warhorse and Gunpowder in India: *c.* 1000-1850', in Jeremy Black (ed.), *War in the Early Modern World: 1450-1815* (1999, rpt., London/New York: Routledge, 2004), pp. 108-9; Andre Wink, 'Sovereignty and Universal Dominion in South Asia', in Jos J.L. Gommans and Dirk H.A. Kolff (eds.), *Warfare and Weaponry in South Asia: 1000-1800 AD* (New Delhi: Oxford University Press, 2001), pp. 99-130.

44. Thomas F. Arnold, 'War in Sixteenth-Century Europe: Revolution and Renaissance', in Black (ed.), *European Warfare*, pp. 31, 33.
45. Duffy, *Siege Warfare*, p. 192.
46. Guilmartin , Jr., 'The Military Revolution: Origins and First Tests', in Rogers (ed.), *Military Revolution Debate*, p. 307.
47. Joanna Waley-Cohen, 'China and Western Technology in the Late Eighteenth Century', *American Historical Review*, vol. 98, no. 5 (December 1993), pp. 1531-2, 1535.
48. Lorge, *Asian Military Revolution*, pp. 114, 120.
49. Gommans, 'Warhorse and Gunpowder in India', in Black (ed.), *War in the Early Modern World*, pp. 109-12, 114.
50. *The Kautilya Arthasastra*, Part II, An English translation with Critical and Explanatory Notes (1963, rpt., Delhi: Motilal Banarsidass, 1992), Book 2, Chapter 3, Section 21, pp. 61-2.
51. *Maasir-i-Alamgiri* of Saqi Mustad Khan, tr. into English and annotated by Jadunath Sarkar (1947, rpt., Calcutta: Asiatic Society, 1990), p. 58.
52. Lorge, *Asian Military Revolution*, p. 121.
53. Jos J.L. Gommans and Dirk H.A. Kolff, 'Introduction: Warfare and Weaponry in South Asia, 1000-1800 AD', in Gommans and Kolff (eds.), *Warfare and Weaponry in South Asia*, pp. 34-5.
54. Iqtidar Alam Khan, *Gunpowder and Firearms: Warfare in Medieval India* (New Delhi: Oxford University Press, 2004), pp. 95, 97, 107, 110, 112-13.
55. C.R. Boxer, 'Asian Potentates and European Artillery in the 16th-18th Centuries: A Footnote to Gibson-Hill', *Journal of the Malaysian Branch of the Royal Asiatic Society*, vol. 38, no. 208 (July 1966), pp. 162-5.
56. Jean Deloche, *Studies on Fortification in India* (Pondicherry: French Institute of Pondicherry, 2007), p. 77.
57. Lorge, *Asian Military Revolution*, p. 32.
58. Deloche, *Studies on Fortification in India*, pp. 85, 90, 109, 111, 124-5.
59. Ibid., p. 94.
60. Ibid., pp. 85, 94, 101, 109.
61. R. Balasubramaniam, 'A Catalogue of Massive Forge-Welded Cannon in India: Part I', *Journal of Ordnance Society*, vol. 17 (2005), p. 77.

62. Duffy, *Siege Warfare*, p. 214.
63. *Maasir-i-Alamgiri*, p. 39.
64. Ibid., p. 161.
65. Gommans and Kolff (eds.), 'Introduction', in Gommans and Kolff (eds.), *Warfare and Weaponry in South Asia*, p. 36.
66. *Maasir-i-Alamgiri*, p. 161. [ ] bracket is mine, ( ) is that of the editor.
67. Ibid., p. 162.
68. Ibid., p. 169.
69. Ibid., p. 170.
70. Deloche, *Studies on Fortification in India*, p. 101.
71. *Maasir-i-Alamgiri*, p. 171.
72. Ibid., pp. 174-5, 183.
73. Balasubramaniam, 'A Catalogue of Massive Forge-Welded Cannon in India: Part I', p. 81.
74. Deloche, *Studies on Fortification in India*, pp. 101, 104, 110.
75. *Maasir-i-Alamgiri*, p. 176.
76. Ibid., p. 176.
77. Iqtidar Alam Khan, 'Gunpowder and Empire: Indian Case', *Social Scientist*, vol. 33, nos. 3-4 (March-April 2005), p. 58.
78. *Maasir-i-Alamgiri*, p. 177.
79. Lorge, *Asian Military Revolution*, p. 40.
80. Ahsan Jan Qaisar, *The Indian Response to European Technology and Culture, AD 1498-1707* (1982, rpt., New Delhi: Oxford University Press, 1998), p. 55.
81. *Maasir-i-Alamgiri*, p. 180.
82. Paul Varley, 'Warfare in Japan: 1467-1600', in Black (ed.), *War in the Early Modern World*, p. 64.
83. *Maasir-i-Alamgiri*, pp. 182-3.
84. Duffy, *Siege Warfare*, p. 202.
85. Varley, 'Warfare in Japan', in Black (ed.), *War in the Early Modern World*, p. 66.
86. Lorge, *Asian Military Revolution*, p. 144; Amrit Verma, *Forts of India* (1985, rpt., New Delhi: Publications Division, Govt. of India, 2003), p. 93.
87. Lorge, *Asian Military Revolution*, p. 166.
88. *The History of India as Told by its Own Historians, The Muslim Period, The Posthumous Papers of the late H.M. Elliot*, edited and continued by John Dowson (1867-77, rpt., New Delhi: D.K. Publishers, 2001), vol. 7, Muhammad Hashim Khafi Khan, *Muntakhabul Lubab*, p. 348.
89. Verma, *Forts of India*, pp. 93-4.
90. *The History of India as Told by its Own Historians*, vol. 7, Khan, *Muntakhabul Lubab*, pp. 348-9.
91. This argument is well developed in Kenneth Chase, *Firearms: A Global History to 1700* (Cambridge: Cambridge University Press, 2003).

92. Jeremy Black, *War and the World: Military Power and the Fate of Continents, 1450-2000* (1998, rpt., New Haven/London: Yale, 2000), p. 107.
93. Dirk H.A. Kolff, 'A Millennium of Stateless Indian History?', in Rajat Datta (ed.), *Rethinking A Millennium: Perspectives on Indian History from the Eighth to the Eighteenth Century: Essays for Harbans Mukhia* (Delhi: Aakar Books, 2008), pp. 51-67.
94. *Sufis and Soldiers in Awrangzeb's Deccan: Malfuzat-i Naqshbandiyya*, tr. from the Persian with an Introduction by Simon Digby (New Delhi: Oxford University Press, 2001), pp. 3-4, 13, 48, 71.
95. Ibid., p. 70.
96. Ibid., pp. 22-3, 29, 33, 65-6, 73, 77.
97. Ali, 'Passing of the Empire', in Ali, *Mughal India*, pp. 342-3.
98. W.G. Orr, 'Armed Religious Ascetics in Northern India', in Gommans and Kolff (eds.), *Warfare and Weaponry in South Asia*, p. 193.
99. Balasubramaniam, 'A Catalogue of Massive Forge-Welded Cannon in India: Part I', p. 78.
100. Kaushik Roy, 'Firepower-Centric Warfare in India and the Military Modernization of the Marathas: 1740-1818', *Indian Journal of History of Science*, vol. 40, no. 4 (2005), pp. 597-634.
101. Lorge, *Asian Military Revolution*, p. 114; G.J. Bryant, 'Asymmetric Warfare: The British Experience in Eighteenth-Century India', *Journal of Military History*, vol. 68 (April 2004), pp. 431-69; Gommans, 'Warhorse and Gunpowder in India', in Black (ed.), *War in the Early Modern World*, p. 119.
102. *Memoir of the Services of the Bengal Artillery from the formation of the Corps to the Present Time with Some Accounts of its Internal Organization*, by Captain E. Buckle, ed. J.W. Kaye (London: W.H. Allen, 1852), p. 49.
103. Bryant, 'Asymmetric Warfare: The British Experience in Eighteenth-Century India', p. 441.
104. Chaliand (ed.), *Art of War in World History*, pp. 625-6.
105. Black, *War and the World*, p. 162.
106. Alexander Allan Bart, *An Account of the Campaign in Mysore (1799)*, ed. N.K. Sinha (Calcutta: University of Calcutta, n.d.), pp. 25, 110; Major Dirom, *A Narrative of the Campaign in India Which Terminated the War with Tippoo Sultan in 1792* (1793, rpt., New Delhi: Asian Educational Services, 1997), p. 219.
107. *The History of Hyder Shah alias Hyder Ali Khan Bahadur and of His Son Tipu Sultan,* by MMDLT, General in the Army of the Mogul Empire, revised and corrected by Prince Gholam Mohammed (1855, rpt., Delhi: Cosmo, 1976), pp. 299, 310-11.
108. *History of Tipu Sultan Being a Continuation of the Neshani Hyduri,* Mir Hussain Ali Khan Kirmani, tr. from Persian by Col. W. Miles (1864,

rpt., New Delhi: Asian Educational Services, 1997), 'Seringapatnam: The Capital of Tipu, by G.B. Malleson', pp. 138-9.

109. Bart, *An Account of the Campaign in Mysore (1799)*, pp. 59-60, 62.
110. Ibid., pp. 62-3.
111. Ibid., pp. 64-6, 68.
112. Ibid., pp. 70-2.
113. Ibid., pp. 73-6; *The History of Hyder Shah alias Hyder Ali Khan Bahadur and of his Son Tipu Sultan*, p. 308.
114. *History of Tipu Sultan Being a Continuation of the Neshani Hyduri*, p. 124.
115. Ibid., p. 122.
116. Ibid., p. 124.
117. Lorge, *Asian Military Revolution*, pp. 29, 43.
118. Pepper, 'Sword and Spade: Military Construction in Renaissance Italy', in Hammer (ed.). *Warfare in Early Modern Europe*, p. 111.
119. Verma, *Forts of India*, p. 98.
120. Major H. Helsham Jones, 'The Campaigns of Lord Lake Against the Marathas, 1804-6', *Professional Papers of the Corps of Royal Engineers* (henceforth *PPCRE*), vol. 8 (1882), pp. 102-3, 123 (College of Military Engineering [hereafter CME], Pune).
121. Jones, 'The Campaigns of Lord Lake against the Marathas, 1804-6', p. 103; Col. G.B. Malleson, *The Decisive Battles of India from 1746 to 1849 Inclusive* (1883, rpt., Jaipur: Aavishkar Publishers, 1986), p. 323.
122. *Memoir of the Services of the Bengal Artillery*, pp. 277-8.
123. Jones, 'The Campaigns of Lord Lake Against the Marathas, 1804-6', pp. 103-5, 123.
124. *The Second Maratha Campaign, 1804-1805, Diary of James Young*, ed. D.D. Khanna (New Delhi: Allied, 1990), pp. 161-3.
125. Malleson, *Decisive Battles of India*, pp. 325-6; Verma, *Forts of India*, p. 100.
126. Malleson, *Decisive Battles of India*, p. 326.
127. Ibid., pp. 326-9.
128. Ibid., pp. 332-6; Verma, *Forts of India*, p. 100.
129. Charles Gough and Arthur D. Innes, *The Sikhs and the Sikh Wars: The Rise, Conquest and Annexation of the Punjab State* (1897, rpt., Delhi: Gian Publishing House, 1986), p. 181.
130. Major Siddons, 'The Siege of Multan: 1848-9', *PPCRE*, vol. 1 (1849-50) pp. 426, 428, CME; Alan J. Guy, R.N.W. Thomas and Gerard J. DeGRoot (eds.), *Military Miscellany I, Manuscripts from the Seven Years War The First and Second Sikh Wars and the First World War* (Stroud, Gloucestershire: Sutton Publishing for Army Records Society, 1997), Daniel George Robinson to His Father, 10 October 1848, p. 175.
131. Duffy, *Siege Warfare*, p. 213.

132. Gough and Innes, *The Sikhs and the Sikh Wars*, pp. 182-4; *Memoir of the Services of the Bengal Artillery*, p. 524.
133. Gough and Innes, *The Sikhs and the Sikh Wars*, p. 185.
134. Ibid., pp. 200-1.
135. Siddons, 'The Siege of Multan: 1848-9', p. 429.
136. *Memoir of the Services of the Bengal Artillery*, p. 550; *The Punjab Papers: Selections from the Private Papers of Lord Auckland, Lord Ellenborough, Viscount Hardings, and the Marquis of Dalhousie, 1836-49 on the Sikhs*, ed. and annotated with an Introduction by Bikrama Jit Hasrat (Hoshiarpur: V.V. Research Institute, 1970), p. 254.
137. Gough and Innes, *The Sikhs and the Sikh Wars*, p. 202; Siddons, 'The Siege of Multan: 1848-9', p. 437.
138. *Memoir of the Services of the Bengal Artillery*, p. 552.
139. Gough and Innes, *The Sikhs and the Sikh Wars*, p. 203.
140. Siddons, 'The Siege of Multan: 1848-9', p. 453.
141. *Memoir of the Services of the Bengal Artillery*, pp. 553-4.
142. B.P. Hughes, 'Siege Artillery in the 19th Century', *Journal of the Society for Army Historical Research*, vol. LX, no. 243 (Autumn 1982), pp. 129, 133-4.

CHAPTER 10

'The Nation Within'

British India at War, 1939-1947

C.A. BAYLY*

In a recent article, David Reynolds has shown how the term, 'the Second World War' came into existence in 1941 and 1942. He suggests that the use of this phrase has tended to obscure the manner in which a series of major regional conflicts, with varied origins, flowed together into a catastrophic maelstrom between 1939 and 1945.[1] To the Japanese, the 'Great East Asian War' stretched from 1933 to 1945. General Mutaguchi, one of the most notorious of the Japanese commanders, certainly saw it in this light. Mutaguchi played a major part in the Marco Polo Bridge incident of 1937, which began the great conflict with China. He made his last throw in the perilous Japanese offensive against India in March-June 1944, which culminated in the battles of Imphal and Kohima. Mutaguchi pressed relentlessly for this campaign, hoping that a great victory here would atone for his leading the nation into the long and bloody Chinese conflict.[2] From an Indian, Burmese or Malayan point of view, however, Japan's Great East Asian War precipitated what we might call a 'Great South Asian War', which lasted from 1941 to 1955 and beyond. This war comprised the Japanese conquest of South-East Asia in 1942, the subsequent British reconquest of 1944-5, the Indo-Pakistan War of 1948-9, the Burmese civil wars of 1946-53 and the Communist insurrection in Malaya. All these conflicts,

*Reproduced by permission from *Proceedings of the British Academy 125, 2003 Lectures*. The author wishes to thank the following who have contributed ideas or critiques during the writing of this paper: Tim Harper, B.R. Tomlinson, Benjamin Zachariah, Shruti Kapila, Rajnarayan Chandravarkar, Jayeeta Sharma, Peter Robb.

along with the contemporary intercommunal massacres across the region, were bound together in tight chains of causation.

The pivotal event in the 'Great South Asian War' was the reconquest of Burma by William Slim's Fourteenth Army, a largely Indian force, between July and August 1945.[3] On the high passes of Assam and north Burma, the Fourteenth Army inflicted on the Japanese the greatest land defeat in their modern history, with more than 1,00,000 casualties. The 'forgotten army' ensured, by a narrow margin, that the British would retain a degree of initiative in their dealings with South and South-East Asian nationalisms. It secured the partial continuation of British power in the East from 1945 to 1965, especially in the critical tin and rubber economy of Malaya. Along with D-Day, it made possible Britain's escape from complete eclipse by US power and resources, even though as Robinson and Louis argued, the British Empire hereafter became an 'Anglo-American' empire.[4] Most significantly, the British reconquest of Burma determined the future of a series of regional conflicts which were to govern the history of South and South-East Asia over the next two generations. It destroyed the Indian National Army, which had fought on the Japanese side, so ensuring the emergence of Nehru's socialist and non-aligned India. It swung the balance towards Aung San's Burmese Independence Army and against the Communists. Broadly, too, the great 1944-5 offensive militarized and mobilized India, contributing to the tensions which exploded during 1947-9 in Partition, communal massacre and post-colonial warfare.

In this essay, I intend to explore India's response to the Second World War from 1942 to 1945. Over these years, a deeply unpopular alien government managed to mobilize more than three million men for active warfare and at least another ten million men and women for war-related service and labour which many of them viewed with ambivalence. It considerably extended, even if it did not systematically 'develop' the infrastructure of a poor country which had been battered by years of depression and official neglect. In the midst of a major famine, when as a senior financial official said, 'you cannot tighten the belt of a skeleton',[5] it supported a huge range of hospital support staff and civilian experts. Most remarkable, this etiolated colonial state secured the temporary, ambiguous and partial cooperation of a sufficient number of India's farmer-soldiers, merchants, industrialists and middle-class professionals to defeat Asia's most formidable military power. This was a power that had proclaimed 'Asia for the Asians!' and had been a model for Indian nationalists since 1905. If the British Government of India was, as Gandhi famously said, a 'failing bank' issuing post-dated cheques, its credit seemed surprisingly robust. I consider that this story throws light not only on a critical phase of Indian history, but on the nature of colonial hegemony, on ideologies of cooperation and resistance and on the control of labour in colonized societies more broadly.

To appreciate India's partial, geographically limited and yet profound transformation, we must understand that the colonial system was on the point of almost complete dissolution as late as July 1942. Senior officials conceded that had the Japanese been able to put two divisions into south India that year, they could have conquered the whole of the peninsula within a few weeks. British and Indian troops were struggling back from Burma through Arakan and Assam, demoralized and disordered. Huge numbers of wounded soldiers were left without adequate medical facilities in foetid camps around Gauhati in Assam. British prestige had suffered a near knockout blow as perhaps 1,40,000 refugees struggled through the mud and high passes back to India.[6] Of these, at the lowest reckoning, perhaps 50,000 perished of malnutrition and disease and the figure may have approached 1,00,000. Despite official denials, the evacuation policy was contradictory, incompetently executed and riddled with assumptions about race, nutrition and fitness. The 'Quit India' crowds that raged through the eastern Indian towns in the summer of 1942 had every reason to think that the Raj was at an end.[7] With their own eyes people had seen the lines of demoralized and wounded soldiers and heard from Indian and Burmese refugees of the headlong flight of the white rulers.

The initial riposte, too, was largely a failure, as contemporary unofficial accounts and later memoirs attest. The British attempt to build up again in Arakan and Assam in late 1942 and in 1943 was a dismal failure.[8] David Atkins, a major with a transport corps taking supplies up to the Assam bridgehead at Dimapur, told a sorry story. The authorities insisted that the units stopped overnight in malarious camping grounds with the result that 90 per cent of Atkins's own men developed malaria.[9] The willing drivers, many from Madras, were too weak and malnourished to manoeuvre the heavy Canadian Chevrolet trucks with the result that dozens toppled over crevasses into roadside ravines killing their drivers. In early 1943, India's Eastern Command launched an attack against the Japanese in Arakan. This was another failure. The Japanese were equipped with fast speedboats and well dug-in. British command and logistics were weak. Several Indian units, mainly Sikhs, mutinied and threw down their arms as they were outflanked by the Japanese once again. A local Muslim official observed colourfully that, on the appearance of the Japanese, the lethargic British and Indian troops 'began to run as no deer had ever run when chased by a tiger'.[10] When the *Statesman* of Calcutta, a British-run but Indian-staffed newspaper, queried the competence of the military command, it was ordered to desist and its journalists harassed.[11] An American officer with a penchant for history later wrote that his countrymen were appalled by the inefficiency and unreadiness of the Government of India. This he likened to an amalgam of 'Austro-Hungary and the [French] Third Republic' in their last days.[12] Indian Eastern Command had little up to date experience beyond punitive expeditions against Naga tribesmen. The governments of Bengal and Assam were regarded as the most ineffective, corrupt and demoralized in the subcontinent.

Civilian India was, indeed, hardly more robust. The plains of eastern India were still sullen following the suppression of the Quit India Movement of August-September 1942 and a further outbreak of internal disorder might well have been disastrous. One Indian officer who had joined up in Europe out of anti-fascist sympathies refused to take part in the suppression of Indian political demonstrations.[13] Senior officers wanted him court-martialed and shot. But so general was the sympathy among Indian troops that Indian officers persuaded their British superiors simply to dismiss him from the service. Rumours of defections to the Indian National Army in Singapore soon began to reach units in India, compounding the collapse in morale. Even more devastating was the loss of faith in the competence of the British government following the Bengal famine of 1943. Up to three million people perished that year and deaths from subsequent diseases and malnutrition continued into 1944.[14] The loss of Burma rice to the Japanese was a major cause of the famine. But ill-considered policies of destroying civilian transport to 'deny' it to the enemy drove the hunger deeper. As starving women and children gathered outside the gates of military camps in eastern India, Indian and British soldiers began to share their food with the destitute.[15] The morale of the army crumbled further. These events convinced large parts of the civilian population that British rule was on the point of destroying them altogether. Subhas Chandra Bose, commander of the INA, now based in Burma, played his most effective propaganda card when he offered to supply Bengal with rice on behalf of the Government of Free India. It is not surprising that on several occasions in 1943 and early 1944, the Imperial General Staff considered the complete abandonment of India as a base for operations against the Japanese and the transfer of the whole Allied war effort to northern Australia.[16]

How then was this demoralized army and disintegrating polity able to deliver within two years a massive and effective counter-blow? Of course, there are other examples of precarious and unpopular regimes galvanizing their populations for supreme effort. The Russian and Austro-Hungarian offensives of 1916 or the Ottoman attacks on the British in the Arab provinces in the same year are cases in point. To some degree, the Soviet fight-back from its Siberian hinterland in late 1942-3 provides a parallel. Yet these were cases where embattled authorities could still count on patriotism and a deep hatred of the enemy. Here I want to consider three interrelated issues. These are: the moral rearmament of the Indian Army and its civilian and transport services; the mass mobilization of civilian labour and the propaganda offensive of the British government which secured the partial allegiance or at least acquiescence of part of the population. I then want to turn to the aspirations of Indians themselves during these years. First, however, it is important to take into account the British use of force which, as in the case of Stalin, was of some consequence in holding the line. Antony Beevor, in particular, has shown vividly how, patriotic feeling notwithstanding, terror had to be widely applied to both military and civilian personnel in order to ensure the success of the Stalingrad campaign.[17]

Corporal punishment and violent crowd control with steel-tipped *lathis* were everyday features of colonial India. Landlords, tea plantation owners and factory owners commonly used rattan canes to discipline their subordinates. A young British lawyer arriving in India in 1942 was surprised to find that his superiors quite unselfconsciously tapped or struck Indians with a cane.[18] In 1942 and 1943 the level of physical violence used by the British against Indians increased dramatically. Martial law was invoked frequently. British expatriate opinion was hostile to Indians, seeing them as virtual collaborators with the Japanese, stories of whose atrocities were filtering back to India. The systematic campaign of Congress radicals against lines of communication essential to the war effort in August and September 1942 bore out these fears. The CID noted that there had been strenuous attempts to sabotage the telegraph and railway lines in south-eastern India.[19] These were critical communications with Ceylon, which was believed to be under imminent danger of a sea-borne assault from the Japanese.[20]

The authorities themselves encouraged a violent response against Indian demonstrators whom they classed with potential saboteurs. Lord Linlithgow, the Viceroy, gave orders that suspected saboteurs seen moving along lines of communication should be machine-gunned from the air.[21] An official in London minuted that this was an 'exhilarating development'. Churchill stoked up hatred of the Congress and returned to his youthful populist rhetoric in describing it as an organ of 'big-business', in league with the enemy. Even the Secretary of State himself, Leo Amery, stolid in the face of disturbances and famine, famously described Churchill's 'Nazi-like' attitude to Indians. Local officials took their lead from above. However cruel were Japanese atrocities against civilians throughout South-East Asia, British 'pacifications' in Bengal and Bihar in 1942-3 were acts of considerable violence.[22] The perpetrators were not brought to book, as were the Japanese. One British officer who torched villages and shot and beat their inhabitants in 1942 retired to a peaceful life as rector in a Cambridgeshire village. An official in Bihar had peaceful Indian demonstrators routinely flogged. He believed that he had prevented the spread of Congress demonstrations to the all-important coal fields in the southern part of the province.[23] Responding to hundreds of incidents like this, Amery was obliged to make a statement in Parliament confirming that flogging in India involved only the use of a heavy bamboo cane rather than a 'cat-o'-nine tails'. Military sedition was repaid yet more ruthlessly. There is some retrospective evidence to suggest that the first batches of INA prisoners captured by the British were taken to the Lahore Fort where they were interrogated and summarily executed. Ajit Rudra, one of the most important of the senior Indian officers, certainly believed these rumours. According to him, it was only after he and fellow officers had warned their commanders that Indians would not stand for this, that INA prisoners were routinely imprisoned for later trial.[24]

The repression was extremely successful in the short run. About 66,000 people were detained or convicted and about a quarter, including most Congress leaders, were still in jail in 1944. Up to 2,500 demonstrations had been shot at.[25] The army and the Indian police had not wavered in their allegiance, as they were to do in 1945-6. Resistance had been driven into the Bihar hinterland and distant north Bengal villages where it merged with persistent agrarian conflict. Bose's Indian supporters, formerly grouped in the Forward Bloc, were in prison or under house arrest. All this was strategically most important because it ensured that fewer troops needed for the eastern front would be diverted to internal duties in aid of the civil power. Over the next few months, the unfolding of famine in eastern India also muted or aborted political activity. Many Congress leaders believed at the time, and many Indians still believe, that the famine was a deliberate act of policy.

The violent suppression of dissidence, however, does not explain the most important part of the story, the capacity of India Base to regenerate and deliver a formidable counter-punch to the Japanese over the following two years. Repression might have aborted a popular political movement, but it could not in itself have motivated a wide range of elites and ordinary people to engage in vigorous war work across India. In order to explain the moral rearmament of the Raj, the first thing to note is that the Government of India sustained what amounted to a significant military intervention, if not quite a military coup, in the second half of 1943. British rule, *in extremis*, was returned in part to its origins as a military despotism.[26] This transformation anticipated the military nature of the imperial establishment in late-colonialism: Malaya under Templer, Cyprus, Aden and the suppression of Mau Mau in East Africa come to mind.[27] The issue in the imperial history literature is often still posed in terms of an antithesis between British civil government and the militarism of the French counter-revolutionary drive in Indo-China, Madagascar and North Africa. But this is an exaggeration. In India in 1943, Wavell, former commander-in-chief of the Indian Army, replaced a civilian viceroy and immediately military voices became more powerful at all levels of government. The authorities sent their most trusted Indian soldier, Rudra, to Bengal as a prelude to taking over the management of famine and food supply. Rudra's report was not encouraging. He told of a British district collector who tried to avoid meeting him to discuss relief in a starving district.[28] Army lorries carrying the slogan 'food for the people' in Bengali toured the outlying towns where up to a quarter of the population had already perished.

Wavell fired no magic bullet. Famine deaths continued into 1944 and 1945. The famished population could now not digest food, even when they obtained it. Many died of disease. Nevertheless, contemporary Indian testimony makes it clear that the army's higher profile and Wavell's personal visit to Calcutta, something that Linlithgow never considered, raised civilian morale appreciably. Senior British Bengal civil servants had long been regarded as weedy and incompetent, even by their own officials, such as Arthur Dash. The corruption of the ministers of the Bengal government brought contempt on it. Now American military engineers quietly took over control of sections of the eastern railway network and began to reconstruct the Calcutta port. A sudden surge of infrastructure development began to redress decades of neglect. Military pioneer labour was drafted into coal fields and iron foundries.[29]

Another development contributed to this quiet military coup in the later months of 1943. This was the creation of South-East Asia Command and the consolidation of India Command as a body for logistical support. The new Supreme Allied Commander South-East Asia, Lord Louis Mountbatten, appeared in India with a mixed reputation. Alan Brooke, Chief of the Imperial General Staff, found him an irritant on the western front, citing bizarre schemes of his such as building aircraft carriers out of ice floes. On the other hand, Mountbatten appreciated earlier than most British soldiers or politicians the importance of self-presentation and propaganda.[30] Even though he later moved off from Delhi to Kandy in Ceylon, his ideas were very influential in both SEAC and India Command. The All-India Radio adopted more aggressive and focused propaganda methods, recruiting South-East Asian language specialists from among Malay and Burmese refugees in Delhi. The SEAC and the Government of India held regular and detailed press-conferences. Mountbatten himself personally selected the editor of the *Evening Standard*, Frank Owen, to run two new newspapers for the forces.[31] This switch of emphasis in the late empire to propaganda and publicity has been noted in other contexts. John Lonsdale has written of similar though later developments in East Africa and T.N. Harper in Malaya.[32]

Field-Marshal Claude Auchinleck, who took over India Command in mid-1943, was also a man of mixed reputation. A senior Indian Army officer with a sure political touch, he had been at the forefront of efforts to promote Indian officers (VCOs) and to give them similar responsibilities as their British confreres. As a result of the events of the North African campaign, Churchill and Alan Brooke became dissatisfied with Auchinleck's offensive capabilities and he was placed in a command whose function was apparently little more than to provide logistical support. Yet coordinating the efforts of British and Indian officers, training, supply and logistics, Auchinleck created a consensus for victory that complemented the coercion employed elsewhere. The Commander-in-Chief's new and highly political role was vital in neutralizing even hostile opinion. He moved around India by air, visiting princely states and recruiting zones which were essential for the continued supply of men.[33] He met the Imam of the Delhi Jama Masjid and other Muslim leaders on a regular basis. After their release from prison, he brought senior Congress leaders, including Gandhi, to his house in central Delhi for talks. Auchinleck increased the intensity of propaganda efforts in the villages and secured improved pay and perquisites for the armed forces. He also expanded what were called 'josh groups' for the troops. These were battalion- or unit-level discussion groups, modelled on the practice in Gurkha regiments, which ranged over issues of morale, conditions and politics.[34] The idea was that British and Indian soldiers would talk to other Indian soldiers and confirm to each other the possibility of defeating the Japanese. The army was to be purged of the worst forms of racial segregation, at least on the war fronts, and Indian soldiers would be empowered as thinking individuals who were capable of taking the initiative without a lead from British officers. This policy worked so effectively that Indian troops were being drafted in to strengthen weak British units before 1945. This was the opposite of the philosophy and practice that had prevailed throughout the history of the British Indian Army. There was, of course, a political price to pay. India Command forbade its commanding officers or the leaders of josh groups to denounce Gandhi and Nehru. They realized that even if they disapproved of the Congress's stance on the war, most Hindu and Sikh troops, and even many Muslims, now regarded these men as national leaders.[35] The Indian Army had become a national army during the war, even if it remained politically neutral and wanted merely 'to get on with the job', as its survivors today insist in interviews.

Propaganda, re-equipment and moral rearmament would have been of little use had not the authorities been able to mobilize a military and civilian labour corps up to 15 million strong. It is possible to show how this was done from the very detailed reports on recruitment and basic training which were produced by the authorities throughout the war. These leave little doubt that there was at times serious anti-British sentiment and economic distress even in the heartlands of 'Punjabi Mussulman' and Sikh recruitment in the Punjab and North-West Frontier Province. A substantial number of that epitome of 'martial races', the Pathans, had been influenced by the pro-Congress Red Shirt movement led by Abdul Ghaffar Khan. Some historians and anthropologists, such as Mukulika Banerjee, appear to explain the wartime surge in recruitment by arguing that notables and village leaders used force to procure unwilling recruits and suppress opposition.[36] There were doubtless examples of magnates who were too keen to fill their quotas and magnate groups, such as the Tiwana clan of the Punjab, certainly exercised favouritism, patronage and occasional coercion in the villages to keep recruitment flowing. Another, more sophisticated argument concentrates on what has been called the 'discursive loop' of the martial race theory.[37] The British were in constant dialogue with headmen and family heads in districts such as Rawalpindi, or the Nepal valleys, where more than 40 per cent of the fighting-age male cohort fought in the war. Boys were brought up to believe that family and personal honour depended on a military career. Returning from service, they would reiterate this belief, preparing the next generation for recruitment.

The vast mass of documentation available suggests that the argument of forced conscription explains a relatively limited part of the enlistment. The percentage incidence of desertion was, at less than 5 per cent, very low and remained so during the war. Decisions to send men into the forces were made in general not by big magnates, but by small peasant farmers with a tradition of military service.[38] Family honour was significant to the extent that the aim of service was to increase joint landholdings and to gain a better reputation and better marriage partners for the wider family group. But short- and medium-term economic influences were also critical. When the worst of the economic crisis of 1943 had passed, recruiting officers expressed the worry that the supply of good quality recruits was now drying up. Men could do very well from high agricultural prices and buy land without sending sons into the army or serving themselves. Soldiers complained in 1944 that poor pay and perquisites were even lowering their clout on the marriage market. As pay and expenses were ratcheted up again towards the end of that year recruitment also picked up.

Family honour and income may have been central to the recruitment decisions of peasant farmers, but letters and comments indicate that men were also thinking for themselves. The allure of learning new skills was increasingly important. As late as 1940, the Indian Army was very badly equipped. Most units had not even seen a Bren gun. Budgetary miserliness combined with an atavistic British reluctance to provide Indian soldiers with modern tools and weapons. The pressure of the Japanese war changed this. By 1943 armoured troop carriers and tanks were visiting Punjab villages.[39] Recruits were quickly taught to drive and trained in radio and signals procedures. The very recruitment drive itself exposed villages to new international influences. Recruitment vans were provided with gung-ho Hollywood films dubbed into Punjabi, Urdu and Gurkhali. The 'village uplift' enthusiast, Frank Brayne, helped popularize games amongst the troops.[40] The British tried hard to interest village women in this new expertise. They felt that women would influence their male relatives to join up. The exposure of soldiers and their relatives in the villages to propaganda, military technology and news of the war fronts brought about a significant change in the mentalities of ordinary people in the major recruiting areas. This was by no means completely erased by the problems of demobilization and the horrors of the Partition massacres. Many people were exposed to modern technology and communications for the first time. Others had their mental horizons irrevocably changed by wartime encounters. One villager recounted in a letter that he had met an Italian prisoner of war in Burma. The Punjabi was ashamed to hear that there was a school in every Italian village. He went home determined to build a school in his own village.

The recruitment of civilian labour during the later war years was of even greater significance in forcing social change. R.S. Chandavarkar, in particular, has argued that the control of labour was essential to the practice and rhetoric of British imperialism in India.[41] Now a vast new network of roads had to be punched into Burma from India and China. In addition, the 'backward linkages' in the transport and supply system across the whole subcontinent needed to be strengthened. Several million people were directly recruited into pioneer or civilian labour corps. But millions of others were indirectly touched by developments in the communication system and more intensive use of ports, coal mines and steel-works. India began for the first time to make body parts for tanks, aircraft and jeeps, creating a demand for semi-skilled as well as unskilled labour.[42] In order to satisfy this demand, the Indian Empire entrenched yet more deeply on existing reservoirs of labour power. At the same time, demand broadened to include large numbers of people, especially from 'tribal' and low-caste groups who had not previously appeared on the pan-Indian labour market. This provided a background for the political and social mobilization of low-caste marginal people, including women, in the post-Independence period. It is striking that the 'untouchable' leader B.R. Ambedkar, who became Member for Labour of the Viceroy's Executive Council, was put in charge of war mobilization. In the Naga and Lushai hills of the east, citizen armies were recruited from tribal people which raised complex issues of control for both colonial and independent regimes.[43] Colonial rule had depended in large part on the 'demobilization' of society into disconnected fragments.

Once the state began to develop economy and society, it was impossible to maintain control. Almost by definition, the state began to take the form of a national state.

The British Indian Empire did not really possess a society of white settlers or *colons* similar to the French in Indo-China and Algeria who could be called on to provide indigenous labour during an imperial crisis. There was one exception to this: the Assam tea industry, which was one of the few slick, capitalist operations in the subcontinent. By the 1930s, most Assam tea plantation labour was drawn from marginal and tribal peoples far to the south in the Chota Nagpur area or in the Orissa hills.[44] The conditions of the coolies had improved somewhat in the early years of the century. Even British observers, however, compared the exploitation of this labour to the old American cotton plantations. Tea labourers, including women who were famed for dexterity with their hands, were effectively purchased from their families and headmen. They were subjected to quasi-military discipline and segregated off from the local Assamese. Being illiterate, non-caste people in the main and wholly without political representation, they proved an endlessly malleable and cheap labour reserve. In 1942 and 1943, it was Assam tea workers along with low-caste coal workers from Bihar to the south who were drafted into military and civil public works schemes.[45] Up to 300,000 of these workers were employed in pioneer labour corps at any one time. They often suffered intensely from malnutrition, malaria and exhaustion. In order to boost the supply from the central hills and the south, intensive campaigns of recruitment were instituted. Key figures in these campaigns were retired Indian soldiers who had served during the First World War and local Christian missionaries, especially the Baptists, who were among the few Europeans who could speak the tribal languages.[46]

There were other examples of the 'super-exploitation' of labour pools which went back far into the history of the Raj. For instance, the princely states were called on to supply pioneer labour corps as well as troops. Puddukottai in the far south, which had been in alliance with the British since as early as 1744, was nearly denuded of male labour. Following their great rebellion of 1855-6, the Santal people had been moulded into a labour force for road building and estate work across south-east

Bengal. In June 1943, the great Damodar Dam burst and threatened to cut India's only major rail-link from the west to Calcutta. At this critical juncture, the Santals provided 1,00,000 workers, men, women and children, for the rebuilding programme.[47]

As in the case of the army, a relatively small number of small territories within the subcontinent had provided the vast bulk of its non-local civilian labour. But by 1942, as in the army, labour recruitment was expanding into wholly new areas. The roads and railways needed to carry nearly twice as much freight in 1943 as they had done in 1939. In addition, Indian labour was pathetically malnourished and weak. A Canadian team calculated that an Indian male labourer could expend only 30 per cent of the effort of a British male and only 25 per cent of a Canadian. Poverty and malnutrition, however, held the key to recruitment, too.[48] The Bengal famine and poverty throughout much of the subcontinent threw thousands more people onto the labour market. War and increased communications pushed recruitment into hitherto isolated areas of Nagaland, the Kachin, Shan and Lushai Hills and the whole range of the Himalayan fringe. Hundreds of thousands of young women were enlisted in labour and service gangs. Bengali accounts indicate the existence of a vast sex trade to service both the labourers and the soldiers in base areas. British India had no such wartime institution as the Japanese 'comfort woman'. It did not need to have one, because poverty and free enterprise brought about the same result.

This is another area where the concentration on Partition and its riots has fragmented the history of India. The Indian social history of the poor has scarcely ventured beyond 1942. Labour historians generally treat wars as exceptions. Yet the harsh experience of labour during the war, in pioneer corps, in munitions factories, or even in local military levies on the frontiers, was critical in stimulating popular politics and the ideology of rights after Independence. The 1950s and 1960s generation of Indian anthropologists, such as F.G. Bailey, recorded rapid social changes among low-caste and tribal groups.[49] The 'economic frontier' expanded. People became aware of Indian nationalism, socialism, democracy and the concept of individual rights. Old hierarchies of chiefs and headmen were undermined, as even poor people developed new skills and aspirations. Such a 'democratisation through practice' was as important as the effect of overt ideologies of social liberation propounded by politicians like the 'untouchable' leader B.R. Ambedkar. These changes can, in many cases, be attributed quite specifically to the effects of the Second World War.

The middle years of the war also saw rapid expansion of the technical professions in India. It may be that at the level of ideology the India of Jawaharlal Nehru looked to socialist planning. In terms of the practical application of science to resource mobilization and people's experience of the modern, it was the war which provided the breakthrough. Before 1939, for instance, most Indians had regarded the nursing profession as a low-grade occupation, fit mainly for Eurasians, Christians or Hindu orphans and widows of the low castes. Despite nationalist ambivalence about support for the war effort, nursing became a patriotic duty for many middle-class Indian women after 1939. The number of trained nurses in India had already doubled between 1939 and 1943.[50] Universities initiated degree courses in nursing, while the supply of pharmacists and medical scientists increased greatly.[51] The ideal of a democratic and equal citizenry, which was enshrined in Nehru's independent India, was spread through war work and wartime social service as well as through Congress demonstrations and self-education among nationalist detainees in British prisons.

This sudden step change in the development of expertise took place across the board, though it was very unbalanced. For instance, a new food canning industry took off in response to the need to provide clean food for soldiers on the front. The production of bottled beer trebled. New cigarette factories sprang up. The expansion of munition plants greatly increased the supply of chemists and people with a wide range of metallurgical skills. Just as the Indian Army's war effort became a national effort more than it was an imperial effort in 1942-5, so too Indian business began to play an active and autonomous role over these years. British commercial operations and many older industries stagnated. Instead, it were the Tatas, Birlas and other commercial operations that both benefited from the war and became more and more important in planning its successful prosecution.[52] Commercial acumen and fear both came into play. People were well aware of the destruction that Japanese bombers had wreaked on the infrastructure of Hong Kong, Malaya and Burma. Even more frightening was the British 'scorched earth' campaign. This had setback Burma's economic development by a generation and its effects had been bitterly tasted in eastern Bengal. If Indians were generally excluded from the political management of the war, this was not true of its financial and commercial management in Calcutta, London and even Washington where the voices of Indian business were well represented. India's post-war planning regime took shape in 1944 and 1945 and Indian business made it clear to the government that this was to be a national regime within, at the very least, a Commonwealth Dominion.

This returns us finally to the issue of political obligation. The Raj's war was fought in the midst of repression and poverty. Yet it could not have been fought without some degree of political acquiescence and even assent on the part of the subject people, however circumscribed. There were relatively few natural 'loyalists'. Eurasians, people of mixed race, did, however, play this role and it was a vital one. They flooded into the technical services and armed forces, despite continued British disdain for them.[53] The Anglo-Indians, as they called themselves, were a critical element in colonial India, consistently underestimated by historians. On a small scale, they provide a parallel with patriotic nationalism in the British dominions. A second constituency was the old elites. Indian conservatives, of course, saw the writing on the wall and many, from the rulers of the princely states to ordinary zamindars (landholders), believed that the Raj would help them secure a better position for themselves, if they remained loyal and active through the war years. Neither the British abandonment of the princes nor the Indian National Congress's assault on the landowning system in 1950-1 could have been foreseen in 1943 or 1944. At this date Indian politics still possessed a secular, liberal and right wing, anti-Communist and anti-populist ruling group, composed of lower-level aristocracy, urban landowners and old bureaucratic and military families. That whole range of political opinion was pushed to the margins after 1947. But its fate was not inevitable. Its equivalent survived, after all, and remained cautiously aligned with the British in both Malaya and in the Pakistani Punjab. It is sometimes forgotten that British officers continued to serve in the Pakistan Army until 1951.

Again, as in post-war Malaya, intercommunal antipathies gave support for the war effort an edge in some parts of the subcontinent. Several conservative *mullahs* in the Punjab and North-West Frontier came to the point of declaring jihad against the Japanese for their supposed ill-treatment of Muslims in South-East Asia.[54] Other Muslims expressed hostility to the Indian National Army and restive Forward Bloc politicians in Bengal, whom they pretended to regard as Hindu communalists. As in Malaya, where conservative Chinese supported the Raj, the British also garnered support from the other end of the political spectrum, the Hindu right. Though it is now a matter of acute controversy in India, V.D. Savarkar and other leaders of the Hindu Mahasabha gave support, albeit conditional and ambiguous, to the war effort. Savarkar called on Hindus to enlist in regular and irregular forces in order to make Hindutva a 'nation in arms'.[55] He almost directly paralleled the position taken by Jinnah and the Muslim League. Equally, at the local level, Hindu right organizations were active in refugee and famine relief in 1942 and 1943, in air raid precautions and in associations for the support of Indian soldiers. The right saw the opportunity of the imprisonment of Congress leaders as a chance to colonize the attenuated wartime public sphere. Indian Communists and Socialists did the same.[56] By 1942 with the Stalingrad battle at its height, Moscow was beginning to whip Indian Communists into line. Their leaders were told that solidarity with the Soviet Union took precedence over the anti-colonial struggle, at least in the short and medium term. Public attitudes in Bengal, revealed in newspapers and censored letters, suggest that many left-leaning middle-class people had already come to that conclusion. The tacit alliance with the Japanese counselled by Bose's Forward Bloc made them uneasy when Communist and Guomindang supporters were engaged in a death struggle with the Axis in China. When Thein Pe, the Burmese Communist, appeared in Simla, urging Indians to support the Allies, it had little effect on Congress supporters, sullen and hostile after the Quit India repression.[57] But many Communists and, most significantly, labour union leaders, quietly made their peace with the British authorities.

These ideological fractures within India at war proved important for the future. Even after Independence, the left was to remain split in complex ways between internationalists looking to Communist China, as Bose and his followers had looked to Japan, and Communist nationalists who were never able to transform regional into national power. To some extent, the Hindu right was also hamstrung by its wartime accommodation with the British. Nehru's Fabian socialism narrowly came through as the winner, not perhaps because it represented the 'natural ideology' of the Indian national movement, but in large part because of the polarization and fragmentation brought about by war.

Yet there was something more, beyond conservatism, communalism and strategic political calculation, more even than widespread ideological distaste for the Axis powers among upper middle-class people. There was something, too, beyond formal ideological positions. The Raj survived to deliver its terminal counter-punch because of a phenomenon which is best called quotidian political obligation. This was not the same as loyalism. The British always exaggerated the degree to which even their most conservative Indian subjects felt loyalty to the Crown or the British connection. Instead, Indians felt a need to keep their polity and its segments functioning. For Indian officers to break their oath, or Indian members of the Civil Service to resign or go to jail with the Congressmen, would have required them to rupture the whole set of relationships, and not most importantly relations with the British, which made social life possible. There was little enthusiasm and no love for the Raj itself, but the idea of government and society itself had to be protected. Social chaos or Japanese invasion would have led to incalculable consequences, not least in intercommunal and intercaste conflicts.

This explains the decision of Indian ICS, police and subordinate services personnel to hold the line in 1942. Privately, they argued bitterly with their British superiors and colleagues against the repression being put in train. This becomes very clear from the 1943 volume of *Towards Freedom*, contemporary documents edited by Partha Sarathi Gupta.[58] Coercion alone could not have kept money flowing into the war funds nor voluntary workers signing up far behind the lines. Ordinary people expected independence and wished to approach it with a functioning polity. A future Mau Mau general fighting in the King's East

African Rifles was told by an Indian friend: 'We Indians are fighting for others in this war, but in return we have received a promise of independence when it ends.'[59] Others, though, felt it their duty to support what they saw as India's national armies in the field. In the Punjab alone, 45,000 people worked in Air Raid Precautions and 3,000 carried out other types of voluntary war work. The pledge that they signed contained the following words: 'Because I am proud to be a citizen of India, I solemnly pledge myself to stamp out defeatism and to stamp out alarmist rumours, to face and defy every peril threatening India's national security and to work day by day in certain hope of victory'.[60] This type of feeling spoke not of loyalism, but of a constrained nationalism. Attitudes such as this prevailed among middling and poor people, too. Deference and hope that the authorities would ultimately deliver something kept food riots at bay during 1943 and 1944.

It is important to stress that this national feeling by no means excluded a favourable attitude towards Subhas Chandra Bose and the Indian National Army. People's views of the INA were often ambivalent. But outside some parts of the Punjab and the North-West, even the British were forced to admit that the majority understood the motives of the INA soldiers, even if they felt, along with Gandhi and Nehru, that they were 'misguided patriots'. The ground-swell of opposition to putting them on trial was very great. Even conservative Indian lawyers believed that the British sovereignty had lapsed *de facto* in Malaya and Burma. A free Indian government was therefore quite legitimate and directly comparable, for instance, with de Gaulle's Free French government. Again, this 'national feeling' was highly plastic. It was still not clear in 1944 and 1945 what type of a nation would emerge at the moment of independence, which most people, British and Indian, now believed to be very close. War work was not yet rigidly divided on communal lines. Many Indian Army regiments were mixed, including Hindus, Muslims and Sikhs, and 'josh' groups were often equally heterogeneous. An irrevocable bifurcation of the Indian state into an Indian and a Pakistan element could not have been foreseen before the elections of the spring of 1946. But all these emotions and ideologies also coexisted with a strong desire to finish the war and to keep civil society functioning. Even many of the Congressmen languishing in jail tacitly accepted the need to avoid chaos. This is why the wave of industrial unrest in late 1945 and 1946 did not really presage an Indian revolution.

Here then, in the army 'getting on with its job', the civil services placing their obligation to society above their political feelings and in the patience and hope of ordinary people was the 'nation within'. As post-colonial historiography becomes more distant from the colonial period, the nature of political obligation at that time becomes more and more difficult to re-imagine. Neo-imperial historians still argue that colonized people often saw themselves as beneficiaries of imperial rule. Nationalist historians invoke repression, 'divide and rule', or the notion of elite hegemony to explain the striking persistence of colonial government. All these positions over-privilege formal politics and the salience of abstract and activist ideology. Instead, the approach adopted by Gabriel Almond and the political scientists of the 1960s and 1970s still retain some theoretical relevance.[61] The 'day-to-day' has its own ideologies. In segmented polities, day-to-day patterns of practice and interpersonal obligation within institutions may have been as important as, if not more important than, formal discourses of religion or nationalism, let alone loyalty to a distant Crown. In attenuated civil societies, bureaucrats and local leaders feared the rise of what sociologists such as James Scott called 'amoral familism' amidst the struggle for scarce resources. Scott's study of Malaysia during the early years of its independence showed that political obligation of its civil servants rested on fear of conflict and breakdown as much on their loyalty to the emerging polity.[62] India during the Second World War was a polity posed on the edge of dissolution, yet still sensing a future beyond hardship and the suppression of civil liberties. The minds of many Indians were balanced between fear that the present would dissolve into a Hobbesian chaos and aspiration for that future.

NOTES

1. David Reynold, 'The Origins of the Two "World Wars": Historical Discourse and International Politics', *Journal of Contemporary History*, vol. 38, no. 1 (2003), pp. 29-44.

2. The classic history of the Burma campaign, notable for its use of Japanese sources is Louis Allen, *Burma: The Longest War 1941–45* (London: Dent, 1984).
3. Sir William Slim, *Defeat into Victory* (London: Cassell, 1956).
4. Ronald Robinson and Wm. Roger Louis, 'The Imperialism of Decolonisation', *Journal of Imperial and Commonwealth History*, vol. 22, no. 3 (1994), pp. 462-511.
5. Statement of Financial Adviser, Military Finance, at Army Commanders' Conference, 9 July 1943, India Intelligence Summary, 23 July 1943, Oriental and India Office Collections, British Library (hereafter OIOC), L/WS/1/1433.
6. Hugh Tinker, 'The Indian Exodus from Burma 1942', *Journal of South-East Asian Studies*, vol. 6, no. 1 (March 1975), pp. 1-22.
7. Indivar Kamtekar, 'The Shiver of 1942', *Studies in History*, NS, vol. 18, no. 1 (2002), pp. 81-102.
8. Allen, *Burma*, pp. 91-149.
9. David Atkins, *The Reluctant Major* (Pulborough: The Toat Press, 1982), esp. pp. 55-66.
10. Zainuddin, Assistant Liaison Officer, Kyautaw Area, 'Confidential Account of My Experiences Prior to and During the Re-occupation of the Kyautaw Area by the British', Imperial War Museum, Irwin Papers.
11. Ian Stephens to Vyvyan Edwards, 18 April 1943, Stephens Papers, Box 20 and 'Genl. Irwin's Conference', Stephens Papers, Box 1, Centre of South Asian Studies, Cambridge (hereafter, CSAS).
12. The letter is undated but is from early 1944. Wavell responded to it in a private letter to Amery, 9 May 1944, OIOC, L/P and O/4/24.
13. D.K. Palit, *Major-General A.A. Rudra: His Services in Three Armies and Two World Wars* (Delhi: Reliance, 1997), p. 252.
14. One of the best short sustained analyses of the roots of the famine is to be found in the papers of L.G. Pinnell, Superintendent of Civil Supplies, especially 'Tabular History Statement' and 'Note to Famine Commission', OIOC, Mss Eur D 911/7; cf. Paul Greenough, *Prosperity and Misery in Modern Bengal: The Famine of 1943-1944* (Oxford: Oxford University Press, 1982).
15. Intelligence Report, 1 September, 1943, OIOC, L/WS/1/1433; Barnes Diary, 22 March 1944, CSAS, W.S. Barnes Papers.
16. Chiefs of Staff Committee, 3 April 1944, 'Maintenance of India as a Base', Public Record Office (hereafter PRO), WO/106/3836.
17. Antony Beevor, *Stalingrad* (London: Viking, 1998).
18. Personal communication from the late Dr Richard Gooderson.
19. The best narrative of the Quit India Movement is to be found in 'India Intelligence Summaries', August-October 1942, OIOC, L/WS/1/1433.
20. India Intelligence Summaries, 16 October 1942, OIOC, L/WS/1/1433.

21. Note on Viceroy to Secretary of State, 15 August 1942, 'Disturbances in India, 1942', PRO, WO 106/3721.
22. Vinita Damodaran, *Broken Promises: Popular Protest, Indian Nationalism and the Congress Party in Bihar 1935–46* (New Delhi: Oxford University Press, 1992); G. Pandey (ed.), *The Indian Nation in 1942* (Calcutta: K.P. Bagchi, 1988).
23. Memoir of Lawrence Walter Russell, p. 3, OIOC, Mss Eur D 1041.
24. D.K. Palit, *Rudra*, pp. 252, 256-7.
25. J.M. Brown, *Gandhi: Prisoner of Hope* (New Haven: Yale University Press, 1989), pp. 337-44.
26. The most useful discussion of the colonial state in the twentieth century remains B.R.Tomlinson, *The Political Economy of the Raj 1914-47: The Economics of Decolonization in India* (London: Macmillan, 1979).
27. See for Malaya, T.N. Harper, *The End of Empire and the Making of Malaya* (Cambridge: Cambridge University Press, 1999); A.J. Stockwell (ed.), *Malaya*, part 2, *The Communist Insurrection 1948-53: British Documents on the End of Empire* (London: Institute of Commonwealth Studies, 1995), Introduction; for East Africa, D.A. Low and Alison Smith (eds.), *History of East Africa*, 3 (Oxford: Clarendon Press, 1976).
28. Palit, *Rudra*, p. 269.
29. In 1943 an Anglo-American steel mission visited India to coordinate development. These moves can be traced in WO files in the PRO and Abraham Papers, Centre of South Asian Studies, Cambridge, which contains 'India Base Progress Reports', reports on railway operations, which were militarized, etc.
30. Philip Ziegler, *Mountbatten: The Official Biography* (pb. edn., London: Phoenix, 2001), pp. 220-30.
31. Mountbatten to Frank Owen, 1 October 1943. Southampton University Library, Mountbatten Papers MB/C189.
32. E.g., J.M. Lonsdale with Bruce J.Berman, *Unhappy Valley*, 2 vols. (London: Currey, 1991); T.N. Harper, *End of Empire and Making of Malaya*.
33. Alexander Greenwood, *Field-Marshal Auchinleck* (Brockerscliffe, Durham: Pentland Press, *c.* 1981), p. 243, passim and John Connell, *Auchinleck: A Biography of Field-Marshal Sir Claude Auchinleck* (London: Cassell, 1959), esp. pp. 745-88.
34. Major-General J. Cawthorn's note on anti-Japanese and anti-JIF propaganda, 10 November 1943 OIOC, L/WS/1/1576.
35. SEAC intelligence summary, 5 May 1944, OIOC, L/WS/1/1433.
36. Mukulika Bannerjee, *The Pathan Unarmed* (London: Currey, 2000).
37. I am grateful to Dr Jeevan Singh Deol for the application of this phrase.
38. Appendix C to SEAC intelligence summary, 21 July 1944, political activities and the Army, OIOC, L/WS/1/1433.

39. F. Yeats-Brown, *Martial India* (London: Eyre and Spottiswoode, 1945), p. 26.
40. 'Pir Kaudi and Babbadi', Brayne Papers, OIOC, Mass Eur F 152/79.
41. Rajnarayan S. Chandavarkar, *Imperial Power and Popular Politics: Class, Resistance and the State in India* (Cambridge: Cambridge University Press, 1998).
42. Geoffrey Tyson, *India Arms for Victory* (Allahabad: Kitabistan, 1943), pp. 35 ff. Propaganda documents such as this should be viewed with skepticism, but not dismissed completely.
43. For a good example of this see the papers of A.G. McCall, OIOC, Mss Eur, E 361, which concern the Lushai Total Defence Scheme, modelled on the citizen militias of Scandinavia.
44. The whole issue of labour for the tea estates can be followed in the Indian Tea Asscciation Papers, OIOC, Mss Eur F 174.
45. For the role of the Indian Tea Association, see *Statesman*, 8 April 1942.
46. 'The War Effort in Orissa, 1941', CSAS, Ansorge Papers. In the hills above Cuttack Revd. E.M. Evans, Baptist Missionary and G. Udaygiri who had commanded a labour force in Mesopotamia were key figures recruiting for the Auxiliary Pioneer Company.
47. Margaret Stravridi Memoir, OIOC, Mss Eur., C 808, p. 6.
48. 'Nutritional Survey of Indian Troops', Appendix A, 12 November 1943, PRO, WO 203/269.
49. F.G. Bailey, *Caste and the Economic Frontier* (Manchester: Manchester University Press, 1962).
50. 'Trained Nurses Association of India, Annual Report, 1942-3', Diana Hartly Papers, Royal Commonwealth Society Collection, University Library, Cambridge.
51. T.K. Adranvala, 'Developments in Nursing 1947-57', in *Trained Nurses Association of India 50th Anniversary Volume 1908-58* (Delhi, 1958), pp. 326-8, copy in Diana Hartly Papers.
52. Medha M. Kudaisya, *The Life and Times of G.D. Birla* (New Delhi: Oxford University Press, 2003), pp. 197-226.
53. The crucial role of Anglo-Indians in the later British Raj is in grave need of study. Some preliminary material for the Second World War is available in a file on Anglo-Indians prepared for the Information Department of the Government of India, especially a pamphlet by Frank R. Anthony, MLA, *Will Britain Tarnish Her Honour?* (New Delhi, 1947), OIOC, L/1/1/627.
54. For example, Badshah Gul, spiritual leader of the Mohmand tribal area, described the Japanese as enemies of Islam and stated that all Muslims' duty was to fight, *Statesman* (Calcutta), 9 April 1942.
55. *Amrita Bazaar Patrika*, 11 April 1942.
56. For example, Swami Sahajanand of the Kisan Sabha (Peasants

Association) and member of the Forward Bloc was released from jail; he declared Hitler and Tojo were much worse than Churchill, *Statesman* (Calcutta), 26 March 1942.
57. Thein Pe, 'Wartime Traveller', in R.H. Taylor, *Marxism and Resistance in Burma 1942-5* (Athens, Ohio: Ohio University Press, 1984), p. 135.
58. Partha Sarathi Gupta (ed.), *Towards Freedom: Documents on the Movement for Independence in India, 1943-1944,* Part I (Delhi: Oxford University Press, 1997).
59. Warahiu Itote, *Mau Mau General* (Nairobi, 1967), cited J. Ayo Langley, *Ideologies of Liberation in Black Africa, 1856-1970* (London: Collings, 1979), p. 413.
60. 'War Effort of the Punjab'. DHP 30.5.46, Tiwana Papers, Southampton University Library, Ms 210/10.
61. Gabriel A. Almond and James S. Coleman (eds.), *The Politics of Developing Societies* (Princeton: Princeton University Press, 1960); Gabriel A. Almond and Sidney Verba. *The Civic Culture: Political Attitudes and Democracy in Five Nations* (rev. edn., London: Sage, 1989).
62. James C. Scott, *Political Ideology in Malaysia: Reality and the Beliefs of an Elite* (New Haven: Yale University Press, 1968).

Select Bibliography

Agoston, Gabor, 'Ottoman Warfare in Europe: 1453-1826', in Jeremy Black (ed.), *European Warfare: 1453-1815* (Houndmills, Basingstoke: Macmillan, 1999).

———, *Guns for the Sultan: Military Power and the Weapons Industry in the Ottoman Empire* (Cambridge: Cambridge University Press, 2005).

Ahmad, Aziz, *Studies in Islamic Culture in Indian Environment* (Oxford: Clarendon Press, 1964).

Ahmad, K.M., 'Inscriptions of Raichur in the Hyderabad Museum', *Epigraphia Indo-Moslemica* (1939-40).

Aitchison, C.U., *A Collection of Treaties*, 14 vols. (Calcutta: Foreign Office Press, 1909).

Alam, Muzaffar, 'The Pursuit of Persian: Language in Mughal Politics', *Modern Asian Studies*, vol. 32, no. 2 (1998).

———, *The Languages of Political Islam India, circa 1200-1800* (New Delhi: Permanent Black, 2004).

Alavi, Seema, 'The Company Army and Rural Society', *Modern Asian Studies*, vol. 27, no. 1 (1993).

———, *The Sepoys and the Company: Tradition and Transition in Northern India, 1770-1830* (New Delhi: Oxford University Press, 1995).

——— (ed.), *The Eighteenth Century in India* (New Delhi: Oxford University Press, 2007).

Ali, M. Athar, *Mughal India: Studies in Polity, Ideas, Society, and Culture* (New Delhi: Oxford University Press, 2006).

Allen, Louis, *Burma: The Longest War 1941-45* (London: J.M. Dent, 1984).

Allen, Nick, 'Just War in the *Mahabharata*', in Richard Sorabji and David Rodin (eds.), *The Ethics of War: Shared Problems in Different Traditions* (London: Ashgate, 2006).

Amin, Shahid, 'On Retelling the Muslim Conquest of North India', in Partha Chatterjee and Anjan Ghosh (eds), *History and the Present* (New Delhi: Permanent Black, 2002).

Anthony, Frank R., *Will Britain Tarnish Her Honour?* (Delhi, 1947), L/1/1/627, Oriental and India Office Collection, British Library.

Appleby, R. Scott, *The Ambivalence of the Sacred: Religion, Violence, and Reconciliation* (Lanham, Boulder: Rowman & Littlefield Publishers, 2000).

Aquil, Raziuddin, 'Conversion in Chishti Sufi Literature (13th-14th Centuries)', *Indian Historical Review*, vol. 24, nos. 1-2 (1997-8).

———, 'From *Dar-ul-Harb* to *Dar-ul-Islam*? Chishti Sufi Accounts and the Emergence of Islam in the Delhi Sultanate', in Satish Saberwal and Mushirul Hasan (eds.), *Assertive Religious Identities: India and Europe* (New Delhi: Manohar, 2006).

———, *Sufism, Culture and Politics: Afghans and Islam in Medieval North India* (New Delhi: Oxford University Press, 2007).

———, 'The Study of Islam and Indian History at the Darul Musannefin, Azamgarh', in Raziuddin Aquil and Partha Chatterjee (eds.), *History in the Vernacular* (New Delhi/Ranikhet: Permanent Black, 2008).

———, *In the Name of Allah* (New Delhi: Penguin-Viking, 2009).

——— (ed.), *Sufism and Society in Medieval India*, Debates in Indian History and Society Series (New Delhi: Oxford University Press, 2010).

Archer, W.G., *Indian Paintings from the Punjab Hills: Paintings of the Sikhs* (London: George Allen and Unwin, 1957).

Arnold, Thomas F., 'Fortifications and the Military Revolution: The Gonzaga Experience, 1530-1630', in Clifford J. Rogers (ed.), *The Military Revolution Debate: Readings on the Military Transformation of Early Modern Europe* (Boulder/San Francisco/Oxford: Westview, 1995).

———, 'War in Sixteenth-Century Europe: Revolution and Renaissance', in Jeremy Black (ed.), *European Warfare: 1453-1815* (Houndmills, Basingstoke: Macmillan, 1999).

———, *The Renaissance at War* (London: Cassell, 2001).

Asghar, Ali, *Jawahir-i-Faridi* (Lahore: Victoria Press, 1884).

Asher, Catherine B., 'Excavating Communalism: Kachhwaha Rajadharma and Mughal Sovereignty', in Rajat Datta (ed.), *Rethinking a Millennium: Perspectives on Indian History from the Eighth to the Eighteenth Century, Essays for Harbans Mukhia* (New Delhi: Aakar Books, 2008).

———, and Cynthia Talbot, *India Before Europe* (Cambridge: Cambridge University Press, 2006).

Assam Buranji, ed. Kashi Nath Tamuli Phukan (1844, rpt., Calcutta: Unknown, 1906).

Assamiya Jibani Abhidhan, ed. S. Barman (1992, rpt., Guwahati: Banatala, 2008).

Aubin, Jean, 'Un Voyage de Goa à Ormuz en 1520', *Modern Asian Studies*, vol. 22, no. 3 (1988).

Auj, Nurul Zaman Ahmad, *Cholistan, Land & People* (Multan: Caravan Book Center, 1991).

Avalos, Hector, 'Rethinking Religious Violence: Fighting over Nothing', in R. Joseph Hoffmann (ed.), *The Just War and Jihad: Violence in Judaism, Christianity, & Islam* (New York: Prometheus Books, 2006).

Ayalon, David, *Islam and the Abode of War: Military Slaves and Islamic Adversaries* (Aldershot, Hampshire: Variorum, Ashgate, 1994).

Babur, Zahiruddin Muhammad, *Baburnama*, tr. A.S. Beveridge (Delhi: Munshiram Manoharlal, 1998).

Balasubramaniam, R., 'A Catalogue of Massive Forge-Welded Cannon in India: Part I', *Journal of Ordnance Society*, vol. 17 (2005).

Bandyopadhyay, Premansu Kumar, *Tulsi Leaves and the Ganges Water* (Calcutta: K.P. Bagchi, 2003).

Barani, Ziya-ud-Din, *Tarikh-i-Firuz Shahi*, Ms. 6376, fols. 23b-24a, Oriental and India Office Collection, British Library, London.

———, *Fatawa-i-Jahandari*, ed. Afsar Salim Khan (Lahore: Research Society of Pakistan, 1972).

Barkawi, Tarak, 'Peoples, Homelands, and Wars? Ethnicity, the Military, and Battle among British Imperial Forces in the War against Japan', *Comparative Studies in Society and History*, vol. 46, no. 1 (2004).

———, 'Culture and Combat in the Colonies: The Indian Army in the Second World War', *Journal of Contemporary History*, vol. 41, no. 2 (2006).

Barnett, Richard B., 'The Greening of Bahawalpur: Ecological Pragmatism and State Formation in pre-British Western India, 1730-1870', *Indo-British Review*, vol. 15, no. 2 (December 1988).

———, 'Natural Resources and Water Conservation in 18th-century States', in Nazir Ahmad and Asloob Ahmed Ansari (eds.), *Fakhruddin Ali Ahmad Memorial Volume* (Delhi: Ghalib Institute, 1994).

Bart, Alexander Allan, *An Account of the Campaign in Mysore (1799)*, ed. N.K. Sinha (Calcutta: University of Calcutta, n.d.).

Barua, Pradeep P., *Gentlemen of the Raj: The Indian Army Officer Corps, 1817-1949* (Westport, Conn.: Praeger, 2003).

———, *The State at War in South Asia* (Lincoln: University of Nebraska Press, 2005).

Bayly, C.A., *Indian Society and the Making of the British Empire* (Cambridge: Cambridge University Press, 1988).

Beyerchen, Alan, 'Clausewitz and the Non-Linear Nature of Warfare: Systems of Organized Complexity', in Hew Strachan and Andreas Herberg-Rothe (eds.), *Clausewitz in the Twenty-First Century* (Oxford: Oxford University Press, 2007).

Bhadra, Gautam, 'Two Frontier Uprisings in Mughal India', in Ranajit Guha (ed.), *Subaltern Studies II: Writings on South Asian History and Society* (New Delhi: Oxford University Press, 1982).

Bhattacharya, Neeladri, 'Predicament of Secular Histories', *Public Culture*, vol. 20, no. 1 (2008).

Bhattacharya, S.N., *A History of Mughal North-East Frontier Policy* (Calcutta: Chukrevertty, Chatterjee and Company, 1929).

Bhuyan, S.K., *Mir Jumlar Asom Akraman* (Guwahati: LBS, 1956).

———, *Atan Buragohain and His Times* (Guwahati: Lawyers' Book Stall, 1957).

———, *Lachit Barphukan* (1971, rpt., Guwahati: APB, 1989).

Black, Jeremy, *War and the World: Military Power and the Fate of Continents, 1450-2000* (New Haven: Yale University Press, 1998).

Bora, M.I., 'Sutora Satikat Asomiyar Ran Bal', in *Assam Sahitya Sabha Patrika*, vol. 3, no. 6 (1951).

Boxer, C.R., 'Asian Potentates and European Artillery in the 16th-18th Centuries: A Footnote to Gibson-Hill', *Journal of the Malaysian Branch of the Royal Asiatic Society*, vol. 38, no. 208 (July 1966).

Brekke, Torkel, 'The Ethics of War and the Concept of War in India and Europe', *Numen*, vol. 52 (2005).

Broome, Arthur, *History of the Rise and Progress of the Bengal Army*, 3 vols. (Calcutta: W. Thacker, 1850).

Brown, J., *Gandhi: Prisoner of Hope* (New Haven: Yale University Press, 1989).

Brown, Katherine Butler, 'Did Aurangzeb Ban Music? Questions for the Historiography of his Reign', *Modern Asian Studies*, vol. 41, no. 1 (2007).

Brown, L. Carl, *Religion and State: The Muslim Approach to Politics* (New York: Columbia University Press, 2000).

Bryant, G.J., 'Military Imperative in Early British Expansion', *Indo-British Review*, vol. 21, no. 2 (1995).

———, 'Asymmetric Warfare: The British Experience in Eighteenth-Century India', *Journal of Military History*, vol. 68 (April 2004).

Burke, Edmund, *Correspondence of Edmund Burke*, ed. Thomas W. Copeland, 10 vols. (Cambridge: Cambridge University Press, 1958-78).

Burns, Alexander, 'Memorandum on the Indus and the Punjab Rivers, with Remarks on the People', 1831, GD45/5/80, fols. 104-109, Scottish Record Office, Edinburgh.

Busch, Allison, 'The Anxiety of Innovation: The Practice of Literary Science in the Hindi/*Riti* Tradition', in *Comparative Studies of South Asia, Africa and the Middle East*, vol. 24, no. 2 (2004).

———, 'Literary Responses to the Mughal Imperium: The Historical Poems of Kesavdas', *South Asia Research*, vol. 25, no. 1 (May 2005).

Chakravarti, Ranabir, 'Visiting Faraway Ports: India's Trade in the Western Indian Ocean, *ca.* 800-1500 CE', in Rajat Datta (ed.), *Rethinking a Millennium: Perspectives on Indian History from the Eighth to the Eighteenth Century, Essays for Harbans Mukhia* (New Delhi: Aakar Books, 2008).

Chaliand, Gerard (ed.), *The Art of War in World History from Antiquity to the Nuclear Age* (Berkeley/Los Angeles/London: University of California Press, 1994).

Chandavarkar, Rajnarayan S., *Imperial Power and Popular Politics: Class, Resistance and the State in India* (Cambridge: Cambridge University Press, 1998).

Chang Rung Phukanar Buranji, ed. Bhim Kanta Baruah (Dibrugarh: Dibrugarh University, 1992).

Chase, Kenneth, *Firearms: A Global History to 1700* (Cambridge: Cambridge University Press, 2003).

Chatterjee, Indrani and Richard M. Eaton (eds.), *Slavery and South Asian History* (Bloomington: Indiana University Press, 2006).

Chatterjee, Kumkum, 'The Persianization of Itihasa: Performance Narratives and Mughal Political Culture in Eighteenth-Century Bengal', *Journal of Asian Studies*, vol. 67, no. 2 (May 2008).

Chatterjee, Partha, 'Introduction: History and the Present', in Chatterjee and Anjan Ghosh (eds.), *History and the Present* (New Delhi: Permanent Black, 2002).

———, *The Politics of the Governed: Considerations on Political Society in Most of the World* (New York: Columbia University Press, 2004).

Chattopadhya, B.D., *Representing the Other: Sanskrit Sources and the Muslim* (New Delhi: Manohar, 1998).

———, 'Anachronism of Political Imagination', in David N. Lorenzen (ed.), *Religious Movements in South Asia: 600-1800* (2004, rpt., New Delhi: Oxford University Press, 2006).

Chaudhuri, Khalekdad, *Mirza Nathan's Baharistan-i-ghaibi* (Dhaka: Dhaka Academy, 1985).

Chaudhury, Jatindra Bimal, *Muslim Patronage to Sanskrit Learning* (Calcutta: Prachyavani, 1954).

Complete Plays of Bhasa, text with English translation & notes by K.P.A. Menon, vol. 1 (Delhi: Nag Publishers, 2003).

Cruz, Maria Augusta Lima, 'Exiles and Renegades in Early Sixteenth Century Portuguese India', *Indian Economic and Social History Review*, vol. 23, no. 3 (1986).

———, 'Notes on Portuguese Relations with Vijayanagara, 1500-1565', *Santa Barbara Portuguese Studies*, vol. 2 (1995).

Dale, Stephen F., 'Steppe Humanism: Autobiographical Writings of Zahir al-Din Muhammad Babur, 1483-1530', *International Journal of Middle East Studies*, vol. 22 (1990).

———, 'The Poetry and Autobiography of the Babur-nama', *Journal of Asian Studies*, vol. 55, no. 2 (August 1996).

Dehlvi, Masud Khan Shahab, *Bahawalpur ki Siyasi Tarikh* (Bahawalpur: Maktaba al-ham, 1977).

Deloche, Jean, *Studies on Fortification in India* (Pondicherry: French Institute of Pondicherry, 2007).

Digby, Simon, 'The Problem of Military Ascendancy of the Delhi Sultanate', in Jos J.L. Gommans and Dirk H.A. Kolff (eds.), *Warfare and Weaponry in South Asia: 1000-1800 AD* (New Delhi: Oxford University Press, 2001).

———, *Sufis and Soldiers in Awrangzeb's Deccan: Malfuzat-i Naqshbandiyya,* tr. from the Persian with an Introduction (New Delhi: Oxford University Press, 2001).

Dodwell, Henry, *Sepoy Recruitment in the Old Madras Army* (Calcutta: Superintendent Government Printing, 1922).

Duffy, Christopher, *Siege Warfare: The Fortress in the Early Modern World, 1494-1660* (1979, rpt., London/New York: Routledge, 1997).

Dughlat, Mirza Muhammad Haidar, *A History of the Moghuls of Central Asia being the Tarikh-i Rashidi of Mirza Muhammad Haidar, Dughlat*, tr. N. Elias and E. Denison Ross (London/New York: Curzon Press, 1895).

Dumézil, Georges, *Aspects de la fonction guerrière chez les Indo-Européens* (Paris: Presses Universitaires de France, 1956).

———, *L'idéologie tripartie des Indo-Européens* (Bruxelles: Latomus, 1958).

Durrani, Ashiq Muhammad Khan, *Multan under the Afghans (1752-1818)* (Multan: Bazm-i Saqafat, 1981).

Dwivedi, Hazari Prasad, *Hindi Sahitya Udbhav aur Vikas*, 6th edn. (Delhi: Raj Kamal Prakashan, 1990).

Eaton, Richard, *The Rise of Islam and the Bengal Frontier* (New Delhi: Oxford University Press, 1994).

———, *Essays on Islam and Indian History* (New Delhi: Oxford University Press, 2002).

———, 'From Kalyana to Talikota: Culture, Politics, and War in the Deccan, 1542-1565', in Rajat Datta (ed.), *Rethinking a Millennium: Perspectives on Indian History from the Eighth to the Eighteenth Century, Essays for Harbans Mukhia* (New Delhi: Aakar Books, 2008).

———, '"Kiss my Foot", Said the King: Firearms, Diplomacy, and the Battle for Raichur, 1520', *Modern Asian Studies*, vol. 43, no. 1 (2009).

Ellens, J. Harold, 'The Obscenity of War and the Imperative of Lesser Evil', in R. Joseph Hoffmann (ed.), *The Just War and Jihad: Violence in Judaism, Christianity, & Islam* (New York: Prometheus Books, 2006).

Eltis, David, *The Military Revolution in Sixteenth-century Europe* (London/New York: I.B. Tauris, 1995).

Emaneau, Murray B., 'The Composite Bow in India', in *Proceedings of the American Philosophical Society*, vol. 97, no. 1 (February 1953).

Emin, Joseph, *Life and Adventures of Joseph Emin* (1792, rpt., Calcutta: Asiatic Society of Bengal, 1918).

Erskine, William Esq., *A History of India under the Two First Sovereigns of the House of Taimur: Baber and Humayun*, vol. I (London: Longman, Brown, Green and Longmans, 1854).

Farishta, Muhammad Qasim, *Tarikh-i-Farishta*, Urdu translation by Abdul Hai Khwaja, vol. 1 (Deoband: Maktaba Millat, 1983).

Farrokh, Kaveh and Angus McBride, *Sassanian Elite Cavalry, AD 224-642* (Oxford: Osprey Publishing, 2005).

Fawa'id-ul-Fu'ad, Conversations of Shaikh Nizam-ud-Din Auliya, compiled by Amir Hasan Sijzi. Persian text with an Urdu translation by Khwaja Hasan Sani Nizami (Delhi: Urdu Academy, 1990).

Feld, M.D., 'Mildle-Class Society and the Rise of Military Professionalism', in Paul E.J. Hammer (ed.), *Warfare in Early Modern Europe: 1450-1660* (Aldershot, Hampshire: Ashgate, 2007).

Fitzgerald, James L., *The Mahabharata. 11. The Book of the Women. 12. The Book of Peace* (Chicago: University of Chicago Press, 2004).

Foltz, Richard C., *Mughal India and Central Asia* (Oxford/Karachi: Oxford University Press, 1998).

Forbes, James *Oriental Memoirs*, 2 vols. (n.d., rpt., London: Richard Bentley, 1834).

Gait, Edward, *A History of Assam* (1905, rpt., Guwahati: LBS, 1984).

Gardner, Nikolas, 'Military Thought from Machiavelli to Liddell Hart', in Matthew Hughes and William J. Philpott (eds.), *Modern Military History* (Houndmills, Basingstoke: Macmillan Palgrave, 2006).

Gerow, Edwin, 'Bhasa's *Urubhanga* and Indian Poetics', *Journal of the American Oriental Society*, vol. 105, no. 3 (1985).

———, '*Urubhanga*: The Breaking of the Thighs', in Arvind Sharma (ed.), *Essays on the Mahabharata* (1991, rpt., New Delhi: Motilal Banarsidass, 2007).

Ghosh, Durba, *Sex and the Family in Colonial India: The Making of Empire* (Cambridge: Cambridge University Press, 2006).

Gilbert, Felix, 'Machiavelli: The Renaissance of the Art of War', in Peter Paret (ed.), *Makers of Modern Strategy from Machiavelli to the Nuclear Age* (1986, rpt., Oxford: Oxford University Press, 1990).

Gleave, Robert, 'Crimes against God and Violent Punishment in *al-Fatawa al-Alamgiriyya*', in John R. Hinnells and Richard King (eds.), *Religion and Violence in South Asia* (London/New York: Routledge, 2007).

Gogoi, Lila, *The Buranjis: Historical Literature of Assam* (Guwahati: Omsons Publishers, 1986).

Gogoi, P., *The Tai and Tai Kingdom: With a Fuller Treatment of the Tai-Ahom Kingdom in the Brahmaputra Valley* (1968, rpt., Guwahati: LBS, 1999).

Gohain Barua Rachanwali, ed. and introduced by Maheswar Neog (Guwahati: APB, 1987).

Gommans, Jos, 'The Silent Frontier of South Asia, *c.* AD 1100-1800', *Journal of World History*, vol. 9, no. 1 (1998).

———, *Mughal Warfare: Indian Frontiers and High Roads to Empire, 1500-1700* (London/New York: Routledge, 2002).

———, 'Warhorse and Gunpowder in India: *c.* 1000-1850', in Jeremy Black (ed.), *War in the Early Modern World: 1450-1815* (1999, rpt., London/New York: Routledge, 2004).

———, 'Warhorse and Post-Nomadic Empire in Asia, *c.* 1000-1800' *Journal of Global History*, vol. 2 (2007).

Gordon, Stewart N., 'Symbolic and Structural Constraints on the Adoption of European-Style Military Technologies in the Eighteenth Century', in Richard B. Barnett (ed.), *Rethinking Early Modern India* (New Delhi: Manohar, 2002).

Goswami, O., *The Story of Indian Music* (Bombay: Asia Publishing House, 1961).

Gottschalk, Peter, 'A Categorical Difference: Communal identity in British Epistemologies', in John R. Hinnells and Richard King (eds.), *Religion and Violence in South Asia* (London/New York: Routledge, 2007).

Gough, Charles and Arthur D. Innes, *The Sikhs and the Sikh Wars: The Rise, Conquest and Annexation of the Punjab State* (1897, rpt., New Delhi: Gian Publishing House, 1986).

Green, Nile, *Islam and the Army in Colonial India: Sepoy Religion in the Service of Empire* (Cambridge: Cambridge University Press, 2009).

Greenhut, Jeffrey, 'Sahib and Sepoy: An Inquiry into the Relationship between the British Officers and Native Soldiers', *Military Affairs*, vol. 48, no. 1 (1984).

Grousset, Rene, *The Empire of the Steppes: A History of Central Asia*, tr. N. Walford (New Jersey: Rutgers University Press, 1988).

Guerlac, Henry, 'Vauban: The Impact of Science on War', in Peter Paret (ed.), *Makers of Modern Strategy from Machiavelli to the Nuclear Age* (1986, rpt., Oxford: Oxford University Press, 1990).

Guha, Amalendu (ed.), *Medieval and Early Colonial Assam: Society, Polity, Economy* (Kolkata: K.P. Bagchi, 1993).

Guilmartin Jr., John F., 'The Military Revolution: Origins and First Test Abroad', in Clifford J. Rogers (ed.), *The Military Revolution Debate: Readings on the Military Transformation of Early Modern Europe* (Boulder/San Francisco/Oxford: Westview, 1995).

Gulbadan Begum, *History of Humayun: Humayun-nama*, tr. A.S. Beveridge (New Delhi: Oriental Reprint, 1983).

Gupta, Partha Sarathi (ed.), *Towards Freedom: Documents on the Movement for Independence in India, 1943-1944,* Part I (New Delhi: Oxford University Press, 1997).

Habib, Irfan, *An Atlas of the Mughal Empire* (New Delhi: Oxford University Press, 1982)

———, 'Formation of the Sultanate Ruling Class of the Thirteenth Century', in idem, ed., *Medieval India I, Researches in the History of India, 1200-1750* (n.d., rpt., New Delhi: Oxford University Press, 2002).

Habib, Mohammad and K.A. Nizami (eds.), *A Comprehensive History of India, Volume V, Part One, The Delhi Sultanate* (1970, rpt., Delhi: Peoples Publishing House, 1992).

Haidar, Mansura, *Medieval Central Asia: Polity, Economy and Military Organisation, Fourteenth to Sixteenth Centuries* (New Delhi: Manohar, 2004).

Haig, T.W., 'The History of the Nizam Shahi Kings of Ahmadnagar', *Indian Antiquary*, vol. 49 (1920).

Haldon, John F., *Warfare, State and Society in the Byzantine World, 565-1204* (New York: Routledge, 1999).

Hall, Bert S., *Weapons and Warfare in Renaissance Europe: Gunpowder, Technology, and Tactics* (Baltimore, 1997).

Hannoum, Abdelmajid, 'Translation and the Colonial Imaginary: Ibn Khaldun Orientalist', *History and Theory*, vol. 42 (February 2003).

Hanson, Victor Davis, *Carnage and Culture: Landmark Battles in the Rise of Western Power* (New York/London: Doubleday, 2001).

Harari, Yuval Noah, 'The Concept of "Decisive Battles" in World History', *Journal of World History*, vol. 18, no. 3 (2007).

Hardy, Peter, 'Pre-Modern Concepts of Time in Indo-Muslim Historical Writing', in Iqtidar Husain Siddiqui (ed.), *Medieval India: Essays in Intellectual Thought and Culture*, vol. 1 (New Delhi: Manohar, 2003).

Hasan, Mohibbul, *Babur: Founder of the Mughal Empire in India* (New Delhi: Manohar, 1985).

Hastings, Warren, *Memoirs*, ed. by G.R. Gleig, 3 vols. (London: Richard Bentley, 1841).

Heathcote, T.A., *The Military in British India: The Development of British Land Forces in South Asia* (Manchester: Manchester University Press, 1995).

Hellie, Richard, 'Warfare, Changing Military Technology, and the Evolution of Muscovite Society', in John A. Lynn (ed.), *Tools of War: Instruments, Ideas, and Institutions of Warfare, 1445-1871* (Urbana/Chicago: University of Illinois Press, 1990).

Henninger, Laurent, 'Military Revolutions and Military History', in Matthew Hughes and William J. Philpott (eds.), *Modern Military History* (Houndmills, Basingstoke: Macmillan Palgrave, 2006).

Hill, S.C., 'The Old Sepoy Officer', *English Historical Review* (April-July 1913).

———, *Yusuf Khan, The Rebel Commandant* (London: Longmans, Green, 1914).

History of Tipu Sultan being a Continuation of the Neshani Hyduri, Mir Hussain Ali Khan Kirmani, tr. from Persian by Col. W. Miles (1864, rpt., New Delhi: Asian Educational Services, 1997).

Hodson, V.P.C., *List of the Officers of the Bengal Army 1758-1834*, 4 vols. (London: Constable and Phillimore, 1927-47).

Hough, Major William, *Narrative of the March of the Army of the Indus in the Expeditions of Afghanistan, 1838-39* (London: W.H. Allen, 1841).

Hughes, B.P., 'Siege Artillery in the 19th Century', *Journal of the Society for Army Historical Research*, vol. LX, no. 243 (Autumn 1982).

Hughes, Matthew, 'Technology, Science and War', in Matthew Hughes and William J. Philpott (eds.), *Modern Military History* (Houndmills, Basingstoke: Macmillan Palgrave, 2006).

Husain, Agha Mahdi, *Tughluq Dynasty* (Delhi: S. Chand, 1976).

Husain, Yusuf, *Two Studies in Early Mughal History* (Simla: IIAS, 1976).

Irvine, William, *The Army of the Indian Moghuls: Its Organization and Administration* (1903, rpt., Delhi: D.K. Publishers, 1994).

Islam, Riazul, *Indo-Persian Relations: A Study of the Political and Diplomatic Relations between the Mughal Empire and Iran* (Teheran: Iranian Culture Foundation, 1970).

Jackson, Peter, *The Delhi Sultanate: A Political and Military History* (Cambridge: Cambridge University Press, 1999).

Jalal, Ayesha, *Partisans of Allah: Jihad in South Asia* (New Delhi: Permanent Black, 2008).

Jamali, Shaikh, *Siyar-ul-Arifin,* Ms., IO Islamic 1313, fols. 56b-57a, Oriental and India Office Collection, British Library, London.

Jones, Major H. Helsham, 'The Campaigns of Lord Lake Against the Marathas, 1804-6', *Professional Papers of the Corps of Royal Engineers,* vol. 8 (1882).

Joshi, P.M., 'The Raichur Doab in Deccan History: Re-interpretation of a Struggle', *Journal of Indian History,* vol. 36 (1958).

Juergensmeyer, Mark, *Terror in the Mind of God: The Global Rise of Religious Violence* (Berkeley/Los Angeles: University of California Press, 2000).

Kadiri, A.A., 'Bahmani Inscriptions from Raichur District', *Epigraphia Indica, Arabic and Persian Supplement* (1962).

Kamrupor Buranji, ed. S.K. Bhuyan (1930, rpt., Guwahati: DHAS, 1987).

Kamtekar, Indivar, 'The Shiver of 1942', *Studies in History,* NS, vol. 18, no. 1 (2002).

Kaviraj, Sudipta, 'The Imaginary Institutions of India', in Partha Chatterjee and Gyanendra Pandey (eds.), *Subaltern Studies, VIII: Writings on South Asian History* (New Delhi: Oxford University Press, 1992).

Kelsay, John, 'Al-Shaybani and the Islamic Law of War', *Journal of Military Ethics,* vol. 2, no. 1 (2003).

Khalidi, Tarif, ed. and tr., *The Muslim Jesus: Sayings and Stories in Islamic Literature,* Convergences: Inventories of the Present Series (Cambridge and London: Harvard University Press, 2001).

Khan, Iqtidar Alam, 'Early Use of Cannon and Musket in India: AD 1442-1526', *Journal of the Economic and Social History of the Orient,* vol. 24, no. 2 (May 1981).

———, *Gunpowder and Firearms: Warfare in Medieval India* (New Delhi: Oxford University Press, 2004).

———, 'Gunpowder and Empire: Indian Case', *Social Scientist,* vol. 33, nos. 3-4 (March-April 2005).

Khwurd, Amir, *Siyar-ul-Auliya* (Islamabad: Markaz Tahqiqat-i-Farsi Iran wa Pakistan, 1978).

King, Richard, 'The Association of "religion" with Violence: Reflections on a Modern Trope', in John R. Hinnells and Richard King (eds.), *Religion and Violence in South Asia* (London/New York: Routledge, 2007).

Knecht, Heidi, *Projectile Technology* (New York: Springer, 1997).

Kolff, Dirk H.A., *Naukar, Rajput & Sepoy: The Ethnohistory of Military Labour Market in Hindustan, 1450-1850* (Cambridge: Cambridge University Press, 1990).

———, 'A Warlord's Fresh Attempt at Empire' in M. Alam and S. Subrahmanyam (eds.), *The Mughal State, 1526-1750* (New Delhi: Oxford University Press, 2001).

———, 'A Millennium of Stateless Indian History?', in Rajat Datta (ed.), *Rethinking A Millennium: Perspectives on Indian History from the Eighth to the Eighteenth Century, Essays for Harbans Mukhia* (New Delhi: Aakar Books, 2008).

Kumar, Sunil, 'When Slaves were Nobles: The Shamsi *Bandagan* in the Early Delhi Sultanate', *Studies in History*, vol. 10 (1994).

———, *The Emergence of the Delhi Sultanate, 1192-1286* (New Delhi: Permanent Black, 2007).

Lal, K.S., *Theory and Practice of Muslim State in India* (New Delhi: Aditya Prakashan, 1999).

Lambrick, H.T., *Sind: A General Introduction* (1964, rpt., Hyderabad: Sindhi Adabi Board, 1986).

Lane-Poole, Stanley, *Babar* (n.d., rpt., New Delhi: Low Price Publications, 1990).

Latham, J.D., 'The Mamluk Horse-Archers', *Bulletin of the School of Oriental and African Studies*, vol. 32, no. 2 (1969).

Leech, Lt. R., Bombay Engineers, 'Report on the Sindhian, Khelat and Daoodputr Armies, with a collection of routes' (Calcutta: Bengal Military Orphanage Press, 1939), British Library, Oriental and India Office Collections, Official Publications, Monographs (Political), V/27/270/7.

Lenman, Bruce P., 'Weapons of War in Eighteenth-Century India', *Journal of the Society for Army Historical Research*, vol. 36 (1968).

———, 'Transition to European Military Ascendancy', in John A. Lynn (ed.), *Tools of War: Instruments, Ideas, and Institutions of Warfare, 1445-1871* (Urbana/Chicago: University of Illinois Press, 1990).

Llewlyn-Jones, Rosie, *A Very Ingenious Man, Claude Martin in Early Colonial India* (New Delhi: Oxford University Press, 1992).

Long, J., *Selections from Unpublished Records of Government* (Calcutta: Superintendent of Government Printing, 1869), vol. 1.

Lorge, Peter A., *The Asian Military Revolution: From Gunpowder to the Bomb* (Cambridge: Cambridge University Press, 2008).

Lynn, John A., 'The *Trace Italienne* and the Growth of Armies: The French Case', in Clifford J. Rogers (ed.), *The Military Revolution Debate: Readings on the Military Transformation of Early Modern Europe* (Boulder/San Francisco/Oxford: Westview, 1995).

Maasir-i-Alamgiri of Saqi Mustad Khan, tr. into English and annotated by Jadunath Sarkar (1947, rpt., Calcutta: Asiatic Society, 1990).

Macdowall, Simon, Howard Gerrard, *Adrianople AD 378: The Goths Crush Rome's Legions* (Oxford: Osprey Publishing, 2001).

Machiavelli, Niccolo, *The Art of War*, A Revised Edition of the Ellis Farneworth Translation with an Introduction by Neal Wood (1965, rpt., New York: Da Capo Press, 1990).

Madan, T.N. (ed.), *Muslim Communities of South Asia: Culture, Society and Power* (New Delhi, Manohar, 2001).

Mahabharata Book Two, The Great Hall, tr. Paul Wilmot (New York: NYU Press, 2006).

Mahabharata Book Seven, Dronaparvan, vol. I, ed. and tr. Vaughan Pilikian (New York: NYU Press, 2006).

Mahabharata, Book Nine, Shalya, vol. 1, tr. Justin Meiland (New York: NYU Press, 2005).

Mahabharata Book Nine, Shalya, vol. 2, tr. Justin Meiland (New York: NYU Press, 2007).

Mahomet, Dean, *Travels of Dean Mahomet* (1794, rpt. and ed. Michael H. Fisher, Berkeley: University of California Press, 1997).

Malhotra, Yog Raj, *Babur's Nobility and Administration in Hindustan* (Jalandhar: ABS Publications, 1996).

Malleson, Col. G.B., *The Decisive Battles of India from 1746 to 1849 Inclusive* (1883, rpt., Jaipur: Aavishkar Publishers, 1986).

Mamdani, Mahmood, *Good Muslim, Bad Muslim: Islam, the USA, and the Global War Against Terror* (New Delhi: Permanent Black, 2004).

Manz, Beatrice Forbes, *The Rise and Rule of Tamerlane* (1989, rpt., Cambridge: Cambridge University Press, 1999).

Mapel, David R., 'Realism and the Ethics of War and Peace', in Terry Nardin (ed.), *The Ethics of War and Peace: Religious and Secular Perspectives* (Princeton/New Jersey: Princeton University Press, 1996).

McGrath, Kevin, *The Sanskrit Hero: Karna in Epic Mahabharata* (Leiden: Brill, 2006).

Mehendale, M.A., *Reflections on the Mahabharata War* (Shimla: IIAS, 1995).

Mehta, Radhika Lal, *Note on the History of Bahawalpur State Canals* (Bahawalpur: Irrigation Department, 1932).

Memoir of the Services of the Bengal Artillery from the Formation of the Corps to the Present Time with Some Accounts of its Internal Organization, by Captain E. Buckle, ed. J.W. Kaye (London: W.H. Allen, 1852).

Memoirs of Zehir-ed-din Muhammed Baber, Emperor of Hindustan, tr. John Leyden and William Erskine (London: Longman, Rees, Orme, Brown and Green, 1826).

Minhaj-ud-din Abu-'Umar-i-'Usman [Minhaj-us-Siraj], Maulana, *Tabaqat-i-Nasiri, A General History of the Muhammadan Dynasties of Asia, Including Hindustan*, translated from original Persian manuscripts by

Major H.G. Raverty, 2 vols. (n.d., rpt., Delhi: Oriental Books Reprint Corporation, 1970), vol. 1.

Morgan, David, *The Mongols* (Oxford/New York: Blackwell Publishing, 1986).

Munro, Innes, *Narrative of Military Operations against the French, Dutch, and Hyder Ally Cawn, 1780-84* (London: The Author, 1789).

Murphy, Rhodes, *Ottoman Warfare: 1500-1700* (New York: Routledge, 1999).

Ness, Gayl D. and William Stahl, 'Western Imperialist Armies in Asia', *Comparative Studies in Society and History,* vol. 19 (1977).

Nicholson, Helen, *Medieval Warfare: Theory and Practice of War in Europe, 300-1500* (Hampshire/New York: Palgrave Macmillan, 2004).

——— and Helen and David Nicolle, *God's Warriors: Knights, Templar, Saracens and the Battle of Jerusalem* (Oxford: Osprey Publishing, 2006).

Nolan, John S., 'The Militarization of the Elizabethan State', in Paul E.J. Hammer (ed.), *Warfare in Early Modern Europe: 1450-1660* (Aldershot, Hampshire: Ashgate, 2007).

'Nutritional Survey of Indian Troops', Appendix A, 12 November 1943, PRO, WO 203/269.

Orr, W.G., 'Armed Religious Ascetics in Northern India', in Jos J.L. Gommans and Dirk H.A. Kolff (eds.), *Warfare and Weaponry in South Asia: 1000-1800* AD (New Delhi: Oxford University Press, 2001).

Padshah Buranji, ed. S.K. Bhuyan (Guwahati: Kamrup Anushandhan Samiti, 1935).

Pandey, Sita Ram, *From Sepoy to Subedar*, ed. and tr. James Norgate (Lahore: W. Ball, 1873).

Pant, G.N., *Mughal Weapons in the Baburnama* (New Delhi: Agam Kala Prakashan, 1989).

Parashar, Aloka, *Mlechhas in Early India* (New Delhi: Munshiram Manoharlal, 1991).

Parker, Geoffrey, 'The 'Military Revolution', 1560-1660—A Myth?', *Journal of Modern History*, vol. 48, no. 2 (June 1976).

———, *The Military Revolution: Military Innovations and the Rise of the West, 1500-1800* (Cambridge: Cambridge University Press, 1988).

———, 'Introduction', in Geoffrey Parker (ed.), *The Cambridge Illustrated History of Warfare: The Triumph of the West* (Cambridge: Cambridge University Press, 1995).

Patterson, W.F., 'The Archers of Islam', *Journal of the Economic and Social History of the Orient*, vol. 9, nos. 1/2 (November 1966).

Patton, Laurie L., 'Telling Stories about Harm: An Overview of Early Indian Narratives', in John R. Hinnells and Richard King (eds.), *Religion and Violence in South Asia* (London/New York: Routledge, 2007).

Paul, Michael C., 'The Military Revolution in Russia, 1550-1682', *Journal of Military History*, vol. 68, no. 1 (2004).

Pearse, Thomas Deane, 'A Memoir of Colonel Thomas Deane Pearse of the Bengal Artillery', *Bengal Past and Present*, vols. 2-6 (1908-11).

Peers, Douglas M., 'War and Public Finance', *International History Review*, vol. 11, no. 4 (November 1989).

———, *Between Mars and Mammon: Colonial Armies and the Garrison State in Early Nineteenth-century India* (London/New York: I.B. Tauris, 1995).

Pepper, Simon, 'Sword and Spade: Military Construction in Renaissance Italy', in Paul E.J. Hammer (ed.), *Warfare in Early Modern Europe: 1450-1660* (Aldershot, Hampshire: Ashgate, 2007).

Polier, Antoine-Louis Henri, *A European Experience of the Mughal Orient*, tr. by Muzaffar Alam and Seema Alavi (New Delhi: Oxford University Press, 2001).

Pollock, Sheldon, *Literary Cultures in History: Reconstructions from South India* (New Delhi: Oxford University Press, 2004).

———, '*Ramayana* and Political Imagination in India', in David N. Lorenzen (ed.), *Religious Movements in South Asia: 600-1800* (2004, rpt., New Delhi: Oxford University Press, 2006).

———, *Languages of Gods in the World of Men: Sanskrit, Culture and Power in Premodern India* (New Delhi: Permanent Black, 2007).

Pratt, Mary Louise, *Imperial Eyes* (London: Routledge, 1992).

Qaisar, A.J., *Indian Response to European Technology and Culture* (AD *1497-1707*) (New Delhi: Oxford University Press, 1982).

Randhawa, M.S., *Kangra Paintings of the Bihari Satsai* (New Delhi: National Museum, 1966).

Rao, V. Narayana, David Shulman and Sanjay Subrahmanyam, *Textures of Time: Writing History in South India 1600- 1800* (New York: Other Press, 2003).

Rao, V. Narayana, David Shulman and Sanjay Subrahmanyam, 'Forum: Texture of Time: A Pragmatic Response', *History and Theory*, vol. 48 (October 2007).

Raverty, Henry George, *The Mihran of Sind and Its Tributaries* (London, 1870; rpt. edn., Lahore: Sang-e Meel, 1979).

Rennell, James, *Marches of the British Army in . . . India* (n.d., rpt., London: The Author, 1792).

Reynold, David, 'The Origins of the Two "World Wars"; Historical Discourse and International Politics', *Journal of Contemporary History*, vol. 38, no. 1 (2003).

Robinson, Ronald and Wm. Roger Louis, 'The Imperialism of De-colonisation', *Journal of Imperial and Commonwealth History,* vol. 22, no. 3 (1994).

Rogers, Clifford J., 'The Military Revolutions of the Hundred Years War', in

Rogers (ed.), *The Military Revolution Debate: Readings on the Military Transformation of Early Modern Europe* (Boulder/San Francisco/ Oxford: Westview, 1995).

Rosen, Stephen Peter, 'Military Effectiveness: Why Society Matters', *International Security*, vol. 19, no. 4 (Spring 1995).

Rothenberg, Gunther E., 'Maurice of Nassau, Gustavus Adolphus, Raimondo Montecuccoli, and the "Military Revolution" of the Seventeenth Century', in Peter Paret (ed.), *Makers of Modern Strategy from Machiavelli to the Nuclear Age* (1986, rpt., Oxford: Oxford University Press, 1990).

Roy, Kaushik, 'The Historiography of the Colonial Indian Army', *Studies in History*, NS, vol. 12, no. 2 (1996).

———, 'Mars in Indian History', *Studies in History*, NS, vol. 16, no. 2 (2000).

———, *From Hydaspes to Kargil: A History of Warfare in India from 326 BC to AD 1999* (New Delhi: Manohar, 2004).

———, *India's Historic Battles: From Alexander the Great to Kargil* (New Delhi: Permanent Black, 2004).

———, 'Military Revolution in Mysore?', *Contemporary India*, vol. 3, no. 3 (2004).

———, 'Military Synthesis in South Asia: Armies, Warfare, and Indian Society, *c.* 1740-1849', *Journal of Military History*, vol. 69, no. 3 (2005).

———, 'Rockets under Haidar Ali and Tipu Sultan', *Indian Journal of History of Science*, vol. 40, no. 4 (2005).

———, 'Firepower-Centric Warfare in India and the Military Modernization of the Marathas: 1740-1818', *Indian Journal of History of Science*, vol. 40, no. 4 (2005).

———, 'Introduction: Armies, Warfare, and Society in Colonial India', in Roy (ed.), *War and Society in Colonial India* (New Delhi: Oxford University Press, 2006).

———, 'The Armed Expansion of the English East India Company: 1740s-1849', in Daniel P. Marston and Chandar S. Sundaram (eds.), *Military History of India and South Asia: From the East India Company to the Nuclear Era* (Westport, Conn.: Praeger Security International, 2007).

———, 'Just and Unjust War in Hindu Philosophy', *Journal of Military Ethics*, vol. 6, Issue 3 (2007).

———, 'The Theories of War', in Jyoti Bhusan Dasgupta (ed.), *Science, Technology, Imperialism and War*, vol. 15, Part 1, in D.P. Chattopadhyaya (General Editor), *History of Science, Philosophy and Culture in Indian Civilization* (New Delhi: Longman Pearson, 2007).

———, *Brown Warriors of the Raj: Recruitment and the Mechanics of Command in the Sepoy Army, 1859-1913* (New Delhi: Manohar, 2008).

———, and Sabyasachi Dasgupta, 'Discipline and Disobedience in the

Bengal and Madras Armies: 1807-56', in Kaushik Roy (ed.), *War and Society in Colonial India: 1807-1945* (New Delhi: Oxford University Press, 2006).

Rubiés, Joan-Pau, *Travel and Ethnology in the Renaissance: South India through European Eyes, 1250-1625* (Cambridge: Cambridge University Press, 2000).

Saberwal, Satish, *Spirals of Contention: Why India was Partitioned in 1947* (London/New York/New Delhi: Routledge, 2008).

Sarda, Har Bilas, *Maharana Sanga, The Hindupat: The Last Great Leader of the Rajput Race* (rpt., Delhi: Kumar Brothers, 1970).

Sarkar, Jadunath, *Military History of India* (1960, rpt., New Delhi: Orient Longmans, 1970).

Sarkar, Jagadish Narayan, *The Life of Mir Jumla: The General of Aurangzeb*, (Calcutta: Thacker, Spink and Co., 1951).

———, 'A Phase in Mughal-Assam Relations: Raja Ram Singh's Futile Expedition (1668-71)', *Journal of the Asiatic Society of Bengal*, vol. 29, no. 1 (1987).

Sarwar, Maulwi Ghulam, *Khazinat-ul-Asfiya*, vol. I (Kanpur: Newal Kishore, n.d.).

SEAC intelligence summary, 5 May 1944, L/WS/1/1433, Oriental and India Office Collection, British Library, London.

Shackle, Christopher, *The Saraiki Language of Central Pakistan* (London: SOAS, 1976).

Shukla, Ram Chandra, *Hindi Sahitya Ka Itihas* (Varanasi: Nagri Pracharini Sabha, 1992).

Siddiqui, Iqtidar Husain 'Social Mobility in the Delhi Sultanate', in Irfan Habib (ed.), *Medieval India I, Researches in the History of India, 1200-1750*, (n.d., rpt., New Delhi: Oxford University Press, 2002).

———, 'Learning and Intellectual Thought in the Sultanate of Delhi during the Lodi Period', in Siddiqui (ed.), *Medieval India: Essays in Intellectual Thought and Culture*, vol. 1 (New Delhi: Manohar, 2003).

Siddons, Major, 'The Siege of Multan: 1848-9', *Professional Papers of the Corps of Royal Engineers*, vol. 1 (1849-50).

Sinor, Denis, 'The Inner Asian Warriors', *Journal of the American Oriental Society*, vol. 101, no. 2 (April-June 1981).

Smail, R.C., *Crusading Warfare: 1097-1193* (Cambridge: Cambridge University Press, 1972).

Smith, J. Russell, 'Grassland and Farmland in the Cyclical Development of Eurasian History', *Annals of the Association of American Geographers*, vol. 33, no. 3 (September 1943).

Sreenivasan, Ramya, *Many Lives of a Rajput Queen: Heroic Pasts in India c.1500- 1900* (New Delhi: Permanent Black, 2007).

Srivastava, Ashirbadi Lal, *The Mughul Empire: 1526-1803 AD* (Agra: Shiva Lal Agarwal & Co., 1969).

Stephens, Ian, 'Bahawalpur State', *Geographical Magazine* (November 1954).

Strachan, Hew, 'War and Strategy', in John Andreas Olsen (ed.), *On New Wars*, Oslo Files (Oslo: Norwegian Institute for Defence Studies, 2007).

———, *Clausewitz's On War* (New York: Atlantic Monthly Press, 2007).

Stravridi, Margaret, Memoir, Mss Eur., C 808, Oriental and India Office Collection, British Library, London.

Streusand, Douglas, *The Formation of the Mughal Empire* (Delhi: Oxford University Press, 1989).

Subrahmanyam, Sanjay, 'The *Kagemusha* Effect: The Portuguese, Firearms and the State in Early Modern South India', in *Moyen Orient & Ocean Indien*, vol. 4 (1987).

———, *The Political Economy of Commerce: Southern India, 1500-1650* (Cambridge: Cambridge University Press, 1990).

Talbot, Cynthia, 'Inscribing the other, Inscribing the Self: Hindu-Muslim Identities in Pre-colonial India', *Comparative Studies in Society and History*, vol. 37 (1995).

Thapar, Romila, 'Imagined Religious Communities? Ancient History and the Modern Search for a Hindu Identity', *Modern Asian Studies*, vol. 23, no. 2 (1989).

———, *History and Beyond: Interpreting Early India* (New Delhi: Oxford University Press, 2008).

The Baburnama: Memoirs of Babur, Prince and Emperor, tr., ed. and annotated by Wheeler M. Thackston (New York/Oxford: Oxford University Press, 1996).

The History of Hyder Shah alias Hyder Ali Khan Bahadur and of his Son Tipu Sultan, by MMDLT, General in the Army of the Mogul Empire, revised and corrected by Prince Gholam Mohammed (1855, rpt., New Delhi: Cosmo, 1976).

The History of India as Told by its own Historians, The Muslim Period, The Posthumous Papers of the late H.M. Elliot, ed. and continued by John Dowson (1867-77, rpt., New Delhi: D.K. Publishers, 2001), vol. 7.

The Kautilya Arthashastra, Part II, An English Translation with Critical and Explanatory Notes, by R.P. Kangle (1972, rpt., Delhi: Motilal Banarsidass, 1992).

The Sauptikaparvan of the Mahabharata, tr. W.J. Johnson (Oxford: Oxford University Press, 1998).

The Second Maratha Campaign, 1804-1805, Diary of James Young, ed. D.D. Khanna (Delhi: Allied, 1990).

The Travels of Ludovico di Varthema, tr. John Winter Jones (1863, rpt., New York, n.d.).

Tinker, Hugh, 'The Indian Exodus from Burma 1942', *Journal of South-East Asian Studies*, vol. 6, no. 1 (March 1975).

Tomlinson, B.R., *The Political Economy of the Raj 1914-47: The Economics of Decolonization in India* (London: Macmillan, 1979).

Tripathi, R.P., 'The Turko-Mongol Theory of Kingship', in M. Alam and S. Subrahmanyam (eds.), *The Mughal State, 1526-1750* (New Delhi: Oxford University Press, 2001).

Trivedi, Madhu, 'Images of Women from the Fourteenth to the Sixteenth Century: A Study of Sufi *Premakhyans*', in Rajat Datta (ed.), *Rethinking a Millennium: Perspectives on Indian History from the Eighth to the Eighteenth Century, Essays for Harbans Mukhia* (New Delhi: Aakar, 2008).

Veer, Peter Van Der, *Imperial Encounters: Religion and Modernity in India and Britain* (2001, rpt., New Delhi: Permanent Black, 2006).

Venkatachalam, V., *Bhasa* (Delhi: Sahitya Publishing, 1986).

Verma, Amrit, *Forts of India* (1985, rpt., New Delhi: Publications Division, Govt. of India, 2003).

Vyas, Chintamani, *Rasikpriya* (Jhansi: Gita Publishers, 1988).

Wade, Bonnie C., *Creativity within North India's Classical Music Tradition* (Cambridge: Cambridge University Press, 1984).

Waley-Cohen, Joanna, 'China and Western Technology in the Late Eighteenth Century', *American Historical Review*, vol. 98, no. 5 (December 1993).

Wickremesekera, Channa, '*Best Black Troops in the World': British Perceptions and the Making of the Sepoy, 1746-1805* (New Delhi: Manohar, 2002).

Williamson, Thomas, *East Indian Vade Mecum*, 2 vols. (London: Black, Parry, and Kingsbury, 1810).

Wink, Andre, *Al-Hind, The Making of the Indo-Islamic World, Volume 2: The Slave Kings and the Islamic Conquest, 11th-13th centuries* (Leiden: E.J. Brill, 1997).

———, 'Sovereignty and Universal Dominion in South Asia', in Jos J.L. Gommans and Dirk H.A. Kolff (eds.), *Warfare and Weaponry in South Asia: 1000-1800 AD* (New Delhi: Oxford University Press, 2001).

Winternitz, Maurice, *History of Indian Literature*, volume III, tr. Subhadra Jha (1922, rpt., New Delhi: Motilal Banarsidass, 1985).

Yadava, B.N.S., 'Chivalry and Warfare', in Jos J.L. Gommans and Dirk H.A. Kolff (eds.), *Warfare and Weaponry in South Asia: 1000-1800* (New Delhi: Oxford University Press, 2001).

Yong, Tan Tai, 'Mobilisation, Militarisation and "Mal-Contentment": Punjab and the Second World War', *South Asia: Journal of South Asian Studies*, NS, vol. 25, no. 2 (August 2002).

Index